TEXT READING PROGRAM

If it were not for these enlightening Text commentaries, we would still be floundering in an intellectual soup. The soup was mighty tasty, but was difficult to get our teeth into without these brilliant observations, comparisons, and analogies. We know this is a vast body of work that has been given us and we are grateful from the bottom of our hearts.
—SYLVIA AND CAP LYONS

A very powerful tool to keep me on track, reading and absorbing just a few pages each day. This process has been an invaluable source of inner peace during this past year.
—CONNIE PORTER

Robert Perry and Greg Mackie are experts at making the sometimes challenging Text not just understandable, but rich with meaning and poignancy. This is a priceless gift to anyone who wants to fully understand the awesome teachings of *A Course in Miracles*. I can think of no better form of support than this!
—JULIA SIMPSON

The Text commentaries offer insights I could not have had alone, because of the deep understanding Robert and Greg have.
—DIETRUN BUCHMAN

An amazing journey into the genius and magnitude of this material. Don't miss this opportunity.
—SHARON EDWARDS

Robert and Greg's insights illuminate Text principles like never before.
—LORETTA M. SIANI, PH.D

I have studied the Text and read it through at least once a year for the last 19 years. I thought I knew it pretty well. However this year has been a real eye-opener. Many of those little question marks I made in the margins have been erased. I shall be forever grateful for this year of Text study.
—WENDY FINNERTY

After 20 years with the Course, I now understand it on a much different level.
—ULLA WALLIN

Robert and Greg's intelligence, insight, and wit, create a fun climate of spiritual scholarship that helps make the Text more intelligible and alive. They're extraordinarily gifted.
—AMY ELLISON

The clear and down-to-earth commentary has helped me connect with the Text as never before.
—NANCY NEVITT

Robert and Greg have a tremendous comprehension of the Course and provide down-to-earth explanations. I know of no better way to learn the message of the Text than this program.
—JAN WORLEY

Translates the beautiful poetry of the Course's Text into everyday common language, making the valuable meaning of each sentence easily understood.
—KATHERINE LATORRACA

Previously, I had never succeeded in completely reading the Text. Participating was the best thing that I did for myself this year.
—DAVID COLWELL

There is nothing else in my years of studying the Course that has helped me so much!
—GEORGE PORTER

I can honestly say I'll finally complete the reading of the entire Text—and I've been at this for 20 years!
—BARBARA OLSON

Robert and Greg's insights helped me understand and assimilate the Course's otherwise complex and difficult passages. I will do this again next year, and the next, and the next. This program is amazing.
—JO CHANDLER

Your program has been a revelation.
—DON DE LENE

I would like to say that this year has been too amazing to actually put into words.
—KATHY CHOMITZ

Having studied the Course faithfully for 28 years, I never imagined the insights and miracles I would receive from these commentaries on the Text!
—MIRKALICE GORE

I can truly say that this program has made an incredible difference to my life. I wholeheartedly recommend it.
—DAVID FLEMING

Nothing less than totally inspiring.
—REV. JERRY CUSIMANO

THE ILLUMINATED TEXT

Commentaries for Deepening Your Connection with
A Course in Miracles

Robert Perry & Greg Mackie

VOLUME 2

Published by Circle Publishing
A division of the Circle of Atonement
P.O. Box 4238 * West Sedona, AZ 86340
(928) 282-0790 * www.circleofa.org
circleoffice@circleofa.org

Cover design by Thunder Mountain Design and Communications
Design & layout by Phillips Associates UK Ltd
Printed in the USA

ISBN 978-1-886602-33-5

Library of Congress Cataloging-in-Publication Data

Perry, Robert, 1960-
 The illuminated text : commentaries for deepening your connection with A course in miracles / Robert Perry & Greg Mackie.
    p. cm.
 Includes bibliographical references.
 Summary: "Provides in-depth analysis of the Text of A Course in Miracles"--
Provided by publisher.
 ISBN 978-1-886602-33-5
 1. Course in Miracles. 2. Spiritual life. I. Mackie, Greg, 1963- II. Title.
 BP605.C68P455 2010
 299'.93--dc22

                                    2009039354

CONTENTS

Commentaries on Chapter 7: THE GIFTS OF THE KINGDOM

Commentaries on Chapter 8: THE JOURNEY BACK

Commentaries on Chapter 9: THE ACCEPTANCE OF THE ATONEMENT

FOREWORD

The Text is the foundation of *A Course in Miracles*. Doing the Course is simply a process of learning and internalizing its thought system, and the Text is where that thought system is laid out. It is an unparalleled spiritual tour de force. Careful study of it will change your outlook in ways that perhaps nothing else can.

Many students, however, find the Text to be very hard going. Many do not finish it, and even those who make it through, perhaps repeatedly, wish they had a deeper grasp of what they were reading.

For this reason, in 2006, the Circle of Atonement offered the Text Reading Program. This was a year-long tour through the Text of *A Course in Miracles* with commentary on each paragraph, written by myself and Greg Mackie, both teachers for the Circle. Before each weekday, we would send out to all the participants via e-mail the reading for that day. This would usually consist of a single section from the Text, accompanied by our commentary as well as practical exercises.

We often supplemented these sections with material from the Urtext, the original typescript of the Course. Our experience was that, especially in the early chapters of the Text, material from the Urtext that was eventually edited out was very helpful and clarifying. So when we felt it was useful, we included this Urtext material in brackets, and let it inform our commentary. We also indicated where a word had been emphasized in the Urtext, as this too often added clarity.

Note: In this volume, words that were originally emphasized in the Urtext are <u>underlined</u>. So when you see an underlined word here, know that that word was emphasized in the Urtext, but that emphasis was not included in the eventual published Course, which included fewer emphasized words. Again, we did this because quite often that emphasis from the Urtext would add clarity.

The reason we developed this program has a bit of history to it. In 2000, we offered a local program in Sedona that included a daily Text class, using a schedule that took us through the entire Text in a year of weekday readings. (On the sixth and seventh days, we rested!) Our friend, student, and colleague John Perry attended that program. When it ended, he began guiding people through the Text using the same schedule, only doing so online. He sent out the Text material for a given day and interspersed it with his own clarifying comments. In fall 2005 he felt guided to suggest we do something similar. Our guidance told us to go ahead, and so that's what we did. Without John's suggestion, however, it is safe to say we never would have done this.

2006, the year of the program, was an intense one. I would write commentaries for three weeks. Then I got a breather for a week while Greg wrote the commentaries. And then the schedule started over. Each day we wrote the commentary that needed to go out the next day. In addition, we led a weekly phone class for participants, in which we summarized the previous week's sections. (The recordings are still available to students who sign up for the online version of the Text Reading Program.)

The response to our program far exceeded our expectations. We have included a few edited comments at the front of the book, but if you want to read the unadulterated student reactions, straight from the various horses' mouths, then go to www.circlepublishing.org and click on the link for the Text Reading Program. During the year of the program, and actually ever since, we have had consistent requests that we put this material into published form.

So here it is, presented in book form as a multi-volume set. We hope you find these commentaries illuminating, and that they do indeed deepen your understanding of the spiritual masterpiece, *A Course in Miracles*.

ROBERT PERRY
SEPTEMBER 2009
SEDONA, ARIZONA

Commentaries on Chapter 5

HEALING AND
WHOLENESS

Introduction
Commentary by Robert Perry

1. To heal is to make happy. I have told you to think how many opportunities you have had to gladden yourself, and how many you have refused. This is [Ur: exactly] the same as telling you that you have refused to heal yourself. The light that belongs to [Ur: in] you is the light of joy. Radiance is not associated with sorrow. [Ur: Depression is often contagious, but although it may affect those who come in contact with it, they do not yield to its influence wholeheartedly. But] Joy calls forth an integrated willingness to share it, and promotes the mind's natural impulse to <u>respond as one</u>. Those who attempt to heal without being wholly joyous themselves call forth [from those they attempt to heal] different kinds of responses at the same time, and thus deprive others of the joy of responding whole-heartedly.

We may wonder how on earth we heal someone else. Yet healing is very simple—all it amounts to is making someone happy. This implies that sickness is merely unhappiness. It is a depression of our spirits, not a malfunction of our body.

In each and every moment we have an opportunity to accept joy. When we refuse these opportunities (and we refuse so many!), we are also refusing to heal ourselves. We could instead accept the inner light. In doing so, we automatically accept joy, for the inner light is "the light of joy." What else could it be? Radiance and depression do not exactly go together. "Radiance is not associated with sorrow."

Application: Repeat the following words positively and with joy:

The light that belongs in me is the light of joy.
My inner radiance is contagious.
It shines away all sorrow.

What we accept into ourselves also affects everyone we meet. If we refuse joy, our depression will be contagious. If, however, we are filled with the inner light, our *joy* will be contagious. Then, we will heal. And whereas people will take in our depression begrudgingly, they will take in our joy *wholeheartedly*, for everything in them wants to feel joy.

> 2.   To be whole-hearted you <u>must</u> be happy. If fear and love cannot coexist, and if it is impossible to be wholly fearful and remain alive, the only possible whole state <u>is</u> that of love. There is no difference between love and joy. Therefore, the only possible whole state <u>is</u> the wholly joyous. To heal or to make joyous is therefore the same as to integrate and to <u>make one</u>. That is why it makes no difference <u>to</u> what part or <u>by</u> what part of the Sonship the healing is offered. Every part benefits, and benefits equally.

The first four sentences are a great example of Course logic. The first and fourth sentences state the conclusion. The intervening sentences are the argument, which go something like this:

> *Fear and love cannot coexist. A whole state cannot include both,*
>   *only one.*
> *A state of nothing but fear is impossible. It would kill you.*
> *The only whole state is one of love.*
> *Love and joy are the same thing.*
> *Therefore, the only wholehearted state is one of joy.*

Jesus has established that the mind can only be wholehearted about joy. Joy makes all the parts of the mind respond as one. In the exact same way, joy makes all parts of the *one Mind* respond as one. Thus, when you offer joy-based healing, everything in the other person's mind comes together in saying *yes* to that healing. And at the same time, everything in the one Mind—the Sonship—comes together in saying yes to that healing. Everyone gains in joy, and does so equally.

> 3.   <u>You</u> are being blessed by every beneficent thought of any of your brothers anywhere. You should want to bless them in return, out of gratitude. You need not know them individually, or they you. The light is so strong that it radiates throughout the Sonship and returns thanks to the Father for radiating <u>His</u> joy upon it. Only God's [Ur: own] holy children are worthy channels of His beautiful joy, because only they

4

are beautiful enough to hold it by sharing it. It is impossible for a child of God to love his neighbor <u>except</u> as himself. That is why the healer's prayer is:

Let me know this brother as I know myself.

The first line is staggering. Think of this happening right now. All over the world, people are having holy instants, holy encounters, and miracles. Wherever this is happening, their joy is radiating throughout the Sonship and reaching you. Waves of joy from all over the world, then, are converging on you, right now. Without those waves, perhaps you wouldn't have had that "aha" this morning, or that miracle yesterday, or that bit of guidance the day before. Take a moment and silently say to all these people, "Thank you."

The line beginning "Only God's holy children" is such a beautiful line—real poetry. I found myself reading it over and over. Why don't you do the same?

The final lines say that you heal someone by loving her. You heal someone by *knowing* her, in the Course sense of knowing the true essence of her being via direct union with it. Yet you cannot know her without knowing yourself. If you reject yourself, you push away your patient as well.

Application: Choose someone who needs healing and say the healer's prayer, realizing that you are praying to know, via direct union, the true essence of this person's being and your own. Trust that if you contact this knowing, healing will take place.

I. The Invitation to the Holy Spirit
Commentary by Robert Perry

1.   Healing is a [Ur: an act of] thought by which two minds perceive their oneness and become glad. This gladness calls to every part of the Sonship to rejoice with them, and lets [Ur: let] God go out into them and through them. Only the healed mind can experience revelation with lasting effect, because revelation is an experience of pure joy. If you do not choose to be wholly joyous, your mind cannot have what it does not choose to be. Remember that spirit [Ur: the Soul] knows no difference between *having* and *being*.

When you give healing through truly knowing this sister, she will know you, too. The two of you will recognize each other and briefly wake up to your oneness. The joy you experience will then trigger the exact scenario we just saw: It will radiate throughout the Sonship, blessing each and every Son.

Why is it that someone can experience revelation (the mystical experience) and remain unchanged? Because revelation is an experience of pure joy, and if your normal mindset is one that rejects joy, that will cause the afterglow of your revelation to dim and disappear quickly.

The higher mind thinks according to the laws spirit [Ur: which the Soul] obeys, and therefore honors only the laws of God. To spirit [Ur: To Him,] getting is meaningless and giving is all. Having everything, spirit [Ur: the Soul] holds everything by giving it, and thus creates as the Father created. [Ur: If you think about it, you will see that,] While this kind of thinking is totally alien to having things, even to the lower mind it is quite comprehensible in connection with ideas. If you share a physical possession, you do divide its ownership. If you share an idea, however, you do not lessen it. All of it is still yours although all of it has been given away. Further, if the one to whom you give it accepts it as his, he reinforces it in your mind and thus increases it. If you can accept the concept that the world is one of ideas, the whole belief in the false association the ego makes between giving and losing is gone.

2.   Let us start our process of reawakening with just a few simple concepts:

6

> Thoughts <u>increase</u> by being given away.
> The more who <u>believe</u> in them the <u>stronger</u> they become.
> <u>Everything</u> is an idea.
> How, then, can giving and losing be associated? [Ur: How, then, is it possible that giving and losing can be meaningfully associated?]

This is a seminal discussion in the Course. It is referenced many times later on and forms a real backbone of the Course's thought system. Let me briefly summarize it.

If you give away a physical thing, let's say a chunk of money, it is no longer yours. For this obvious reason, we think giving means losing.

Ideas, however, have this amazing quality, such that if you give away an idea, you still have it. It is still there in your mind. And if the other person decides that he believes in the idea, he reinforces it in your mind. Instead of losing it, it has grown stronger inside you. Who hasn't experienced this?

Now comes the really extreme part: That chunk of money is really an *idea*. Everything physical is. As you give it away, the idea behind your gift will not leave your mind. It will actually grow stronger. Perhaps you can see where this is heading. Lesson 187 makes it clear:

> Perhaps the form in which the thought seems to appear is changed in giving. Yet it must return to him who gives. Nor can the form it takes be less acceptable. It must be more. (W-pI.187.2:5-8)

You can't even lose the forms you give, because the thought behind them will remain in your mind, and show up as a new form, one that is even *more* acceptable to you.

Writing exercise: Do you have a story in which you gave something away, only to have its essence come back to you in some new form? If so, you may want to write it down, either as a purely personal exercise, to make this principle more real to you, or as something to share with others, to make the principle come alive for them.

> 3.   This is the invitation to the Holy Spirit. I have said already that I can reach up and bring the Holy Spirit down to you, but I can bring Him to you only at your own invitation. The Holy Spirit is in [Ur: is

nothing more than] your right mind, as He was in [Ur: was also] mine. The Bible says, "May the mind be in you that was also in Christ Jesus," and uses this as a <u>blessing</u>. It is the blessing of miracle-mindedness. It asks that you may think as I thought, joining with me in Christ thinking.

What is the invitation to the Holy Spirit? Generosity. You hold onto all of the fullness inside of you by giving it all away. This is how to have the mind in you which was also in Christ Jesus (Philippians 2:5). This is how you acquire the mind of the miracle worker.

The Holy Spirit has been mentioned only six times before now (in the original dictation) and always in passing. This paragraph begins an extended discussion of Him. One thing you should know is that these early references to the Holy Spirit bounce back and forth between describing the Holy Spirit as a "He" Who was created by God, and describing Him as an "it" that is just our own right mind, just a state of inspiration from God. I have heard (I believe from Judy Skutch) that Helen was very threatened by the idea of the Holy Spirit and had trouble taking down early references to Him. I don't know if this is true, but it is true that the later language about the Holy Spirit is definitely that of a "He" Who was created by God. For this reason, the editors rightly changed the early language to reflect that.

> 4.   The Holy Spirit is the only part of the Holy Trinity that has a symbolic function [Ur: which is symbolic]. He is referred to as the Healer, the Comforter and the Guide. He is also described as something "separate," apart from the Father and from the Son. I myself said, "If I go I will send you <u>another</u> Comforter and He will abide with you." His symbolic function makes the Holy Spirit difficult to understand, because symbolism is open to different interpretations [Ur: The Holy Spirit is a difficult concept to grasp, precisely because it *is* symbolic, and therefore open to many different interpretations]. As a man and also one of God's creations, my right thinking, which came from the Holy Spirit or the Universal Inspiration, taught me first and foremost that this Inspiration is for <u>all</u>. I could not have It myself without knowing this. The word "know" is proper in this context, because the Holy Spirit is so close to knowledge that He calls it forth; or better, allows it to come. I have spoken before of the higher or "true" perception, which is so near to truth that God Himself can flow across the little gap. Knowledge is always ready to flow everywhere, but it cannot oppose. Therefore you can obstruct it, although you can never lose it.

The Holy Spirit takes on these symbolic guises: Healer, Comforter, Guide. "He seems to be a Voice, for in that form He speaks God's Word to you. He seems to be a Guide through a far country, for you need that form of help. He seems to be whatever meets the needs you think you have" (C-6.4:5-7). Yet His real Being lies far beyond these symbolic guises.

The Holy Spirit has many gifts. He guides us, He sends us visions and revelations. But His core gift is to inspire us with *right thinking*. That is His sacred mission. This right thinking, or true perception, raises us so close to God that knowledge "can flow across the little gap." This is because true perception does not oppose knowledge. Our current perception *does* oppose knowledge, so that in order to come into our minds, knowledge would have to get into a shoving match with it. Yet the whole nature of knowledge is that it contains no opposition. "It cannot oppose." It is boundless. It is pure inclusion, pure embrace. How then could it shove its way into our minds?

The Holy Spirit's inspiration is for everyone, not just for the rare saint. He, in fact, is the teacher of those rare saints, just as He was Jesus' teacher. As He infuses their minds with His right thinking, they know what we don't—that God's gifts are spread out equally for everyone.

> 5.   The Holy Spirit is the Christ Mind which is aware of [Ur: that senses] the knowledge that lies beyond perception. He came into being with the separation as a protection, inspiring the Atonement principle [Ur: the beginning of the Atonement] at the same time. Before that there was no need for healing, for [Ur: and] no one was comfortless. The Voice of the Holy Spirit is the Call to Atonement, or the restoration of the integrity of the mind. When the Atonement is complete and the whole Sonship is healed there will be no call to return. But what God creates is eternal. The Holy Spirit will remain with the Sons of God, to bless their creations and keep them [the Sons] in the light of joy.

Before the separation, no one needed a Healer, a Comforter, a Guide. Yet after the separation, we all did. Our minds had split into a jumble of parts and levels, leaving us splintered and divided. Thus the Holy Spirit was created to guide us back home. He puts on those symbolic masks to reach we who live in a world of masks. One such mask is that of the Call. He calls us back to joy, back to an integrated mind, back to the wholeheartedness of Heaven. Yet when we have all come home, there won't be any need for a Call. The Holy Spirit can then take His masks off. "And then the Voice is gone, no longer to take form but to return to the eternal Formlessness of God" (C-6.5:8). Yet His real essence will still exist. He brought us back to the light of joy; thus, He will make sure we *stay* in the light of joy ("The Holy Spirit will remain with the Sons of God…and keep them in the light of joy").

> 6.   God honored even the miscreations of His children because they had made them. But He also blessed His children with a way of thinking that could raise their perceptions so high [Ur: until they became so lofty that] they could reach almost back to Him. The Holy Spirit is the Mind of the Atonement. He represents a state of mind close enough to One-mindedness that transfer to it is at last possible. [Ur: As you well know, transfer depends on common elements in the old learning and the new situation to which it is transferred.] Perception is not knowledge, but it can be <u>transferred</u> to knowledge, or <u>cross over</u> into it. It might even be more helpful here to use the literal meaning of transferred or "carried over," since the last step is taken by God.

Knowledge is an incredibly exalted thing. It is the rare crown jewel of spiritual experiences. It is the lofty peak of mystical experiences, reaching far above the timber-line of form and change. The Holy Spirit's job is not to pull us into knowledge, but rather to lead us into a way of perceiving that is so pure, so lofty, so perfect, that our minds no longer oppose knowledge. Then God can reach down and lift us into knowledge.

This true perception is God's gift to us. He wouldn't just knock down our towers of distorted thought. We made them, and like any good parent, our Father honors what we make. Instead of knocking them down, He sent us a gift. He gave us a way of thinking that was so perfect it could lift us back to Him.

> 7.   The Holy Spirit, the shared Inspiration of all the Sonship, induces a kind of perception in which many elements are like those in the Kingdom of Heaven itself: First, its universality is perfectly clear, and no one who attains [Ur: receives] it could believe for one instant that sharing it involves anything <u>but</u> gain. Second, it is incapable of attack and is therefore truly open. This means that although it does not engender knowledge, it does not obstruct it in any way. [Ur: There is a

point at which sufficient quantitative changes produce real qualitative differences. The next point requires real understanding, because it is the point at which the shift occurs.] Finally, it points the way beyond the healing that it brings, and leads the mind beyond its own integration toward the paths of creation. It is at this point that sufficient quantitative change occurs to produce a real qualitative shift.

This final paragraph expands on what has been mentioned already: that the Holy Spirit's true perception is such a perfect mirror of knowledge that it makes way for knowledge. How so?

First, true perception is universal—it applies to everyone without exception. And giving it to everyone involves only gain, not loss. This exactly mirrors the nature of knowledge, in which there are no exceptions and there is only increase.

Second, true perception is incapable of attack. It opposes nothing. As we have seen, knowledge also opposes nothing. Thus, true perception reflects knowledge and opens the door to it.

On our journey, we move into further and further degrees of true perception. At some point, however, we take that one last step and perception is perfected. All of the mind's splintered pieces click back into place. The mind is whole again. True perception is like a guide who has brought us to this place and now, though it can carry us no further, it "points the way" to our ultimate destination. After all of our incremental, quantitative change, we now shift into a qualitatively different place. We awaken in the realm of knowledge. There, with our whole mind intact once again, we resume our ancient function of creating with God.

This can sound very distant to us. What are we supposed to do right now? Our job now is not to acquire heavenly knowledge here on earth. Our task here is to be artists of thought, you could say, to paint the canvas of our perception with only the purest, most beautiful brushstrokes of light. Then someday, our canvas will reflect only Heaven, and our journey will be done. Our job now is to simply *desire* this, to want with all our heart to think and perceive with perfect purity. Do we want this?

II. The Voice for God
Commentary by Robert Perry

1. Healing is not creating; it is reparation. The Holy Spirit promotes healing by looking beyond it to what the children of God were before healing was needed, and will be when they have <u>been</u> healed. This alteration of the time sequence should be quite familiar, because it is very similar to the shift in the perception of time that the miracle introduces. The Holy Spirit is the <u>motivation</u> for miracle-mindedness; the decision [Ur: will] to <u>heal</u> the separation by letting it go. Your will is still [Ur: It {the Holy Spirit} is] <u>in</u> you because God placed it in your mind, and although you can keep it asleep you cannot obliterate it. God Himself keeps your will [Ur: It {the Holy Spirit}] alive by transmitting it from His Mind to yours as long as there is time. [Ur: It is partly His will and partly yours.] The miracle itself is a reflection of this [Ur: is just this fusion or] union of will between Father and Son.

If you really want to heal, you have to *look beyond healing*. You have to momentarily ignore healing, looking right past it to the eternal truth of who this person was before he needed healing, and will be when he has risen above all healing.

This can seem to be a task beyond our limited strength, and in a sense, it is. How, then, do we do it? We can only do it through the strength of the Holy Spirit in us. He is the power in us that lifts our gaze past sickness, past even healing, to timeless perfection. He "is the motivation for miracle-mindedness."

Yet He is not some outside Power that is somehow inside our minds. He came into being through the union of the Father's Will and the Son's will—our will. This, too, is why He is the source of miracles, because miracles flow from this very fusion of our will with God's.

2. The Holy Spirit is the spirit of joy. He is the Call to return with which God blessed the minds of His separated Sons. This is the vocation of the mind. The mind had no calling until the separation, because before that it had only <u>being</u>, and would not have understood the call to right thinking. The Holy Spirit is God's Answer to the separation; the

12

means by which the Atonement heals [Ur: could repair] until the whole mind returns [Ur: returned] to creating.

In the state of being, there was nowhere to go, nothing to correct, no calling to rise to. We just *were*. If someone had asked us to correct our thinking, we would have had no idea what this meant. Can you imagine such a state? Yet after the separation, we needed help to get back to this perfect state, and God blessed us with just such help. He gave us a Call that could provide us with a *calling*, a "vocation." What is this vocation? To call our brothers to return. Whatever you think your job in life is, this is your real vocation.

> 3. The principle of Atonement [Ur: The Atonement] and the separation began at the same time. When the ego was made, God placed in the mind the call to joy. This call is so strong that the ego always dissolves at its sound. That is why you must [Ur: can] choose to hear [Ur: listen to] one of two voices within you. One you made yourself, and that one is not of God. But the other is given you by God, Who asks you only to listen to it. The Holy Spirit <u>is</u> in you in a very literal sense. His is the Voice That calls you back to where you were before and will be again. It is possible even in this world to hear <u>only</u> that Voice and no other. It takes effort and great willingness to learn. It is the final lesson that I learned, and God's Sons are as equal as learners as they are as Sons.

Even traditional religions will tell you that we have two voices within us. Yet traditionally we see the higher Voice as one that commands, that calls us to sacrifice happiness for the truth, and that asks us to believe irrational things on the basis of faith. Given this, in order to side with this Voice, we have to virtually wrap our ego in a straightjacket.

Yet the truth is very different. The Voice of the Holy Spirit merely invites us to listen to it ("asks you only to listen to it"). It is the voice of our ego that is coercive. The Holy Spirit is "the call to joy." Our ego is the taskmaster who drains the joy out of life. The Holy Spirit is the Voice for sanity. Our ego is the self-made voice, the irrational ranting that flies in the face of reality. The Call of our Creator "is so strong," so respectful, so joyful, and so sane, that we don't need to restrain the ego to side with it. Our ego merely "dissolves at its sound."

It seems so hard to hear this Voice at all, yet we can learn to hear this Voice and no other. This is the very last thing that Jesus learned. He let the Holy Spirit inspire his every thought and flow through his every deed. We can learn this lesson, too, and we will. For, amazingly, our learning ability is every bit the equal of Jesus', since we were all created as equal Sons of God.

> 4.   You *are* the Kingdom of Heaven, but you have let the belief in darkness enter your mind and so you need a new light. The Holy Spirit is the radiance that you must let banish the idea of darkness. His is the glory before which dissociation falls away, and the Kingdom of Heaven breaks through into its own. Before the separation you did not need guidance. You <u>knew</u> as you will know again, but as you do not know now.

I feel a real poignancy in this paragraph. We *are* the Kingdom of Heaven. We are the Sons of God. In the beginning, we knew reality with unshakable certainty. Yet we, these exalted, eternal beings, have let darkness creep into our minds and snuff out the light of knowledge. How could we let this happen? Now we need a light not of our making. We need the glory of the Holy Spirit to shine in our mind and chase away our long, dark night. Then the Kingdom can break through into its own darkened spaces, and once again we can *know*. This reminds me of a poem by Frederich Schiller that I memorized many years ago:

> *Weep for the godlike life we lost afar—*
> *Weep!—thou and I its scattered fragments are;*
> *And still the unconquered yearning we retain—*
> *Sigh to restore the rapture and the reign,*
> > *And grow divine again.*

> 5.   God does not guide, because He can share only <u>perfect knowledge</u>. Guidance is <u>evaluative</u>, because it implies there is a <u>right</u> way and also a <u>wrong</u> way, one to be chosen and the other to be avoided. By choosing one you give up the other. [Ur: This *is* a conflict state. It *means* that knowledge has been lost, because knowledge is *sure*.] The choice for the Holy Spirit is the choice for God. [This sentence was composed by the editors.] God is not in you in a literal sense; <u>you</u> are part of <u>Him</u> [He is not in you; you are in Him]. When you chose to leave Him He gave

14

you a Voice to speak <u>for</u> Him because He could no longer share His knowledge with you without hindrance. Direct communication was broken because you had made another voice [Ur: through another will].

"God does not guide." Huh? How can that be? Well, the very need for guidance implies that there are two roads before you and you are torn between them. You don't know which way to go. Guidance then comes in and offers its evaluation, telling you which road to choose and which road to avoid. It doesn't make sense for God Himself to do this, because He offers "only perfect knowledge," and that means absolute certainty. When you are absolutely certain of the way to go, the other way does not exist for you at all.

This certainty is where we began. We started out in God, where He could directly communicate His certainty to us. But then we left His Mind. Now, for us, the other road *does* exist, and we are *not* sure which way to go. So God can no longer give us the knowledge He really wants to give. He has to give us a Voice that can provide the guidance we need, that can tell us which pathway leads us back home.

> 6.   The Holy Spirit calls you both to remember and to forget. You have chosen to be in a state of opposition in which opposites are possible. As a result, there <u>are</u> choices you must make. In the holy state the will is free, so [Ur: in the sense] that its <u>creative</u> power is unlimited and choice [Ur: but choice itself] is meaningless. Freedom to choose is the same <u>power</u> as freedom to create, but its <u>application</u> is different. Choosing depends on a split mind [Ur: Choosing *means* divided will]. The Holy Spirit is one way of choosing. [Ur: This way is in you *because* there is also another way.] God did not leave His children comfortless, even though they chose to leave [Ur: left] Him. The voice they put in their minds was <u>not</u> the Voice for His Will, for which the Holy Spirit speaks.

This is a great discussion of the difference between free will and free choice. Free will is the freedom to express yourself, totally, right? Yet this very definition shows why free *choice* is not free *will*. In the state of choice, you are divided between those different roads I discussed above. You are hamstrung between opposite poles. Thus, whichever way you go, the part of you that wants the *other* way does not get to express itself. Part of you remains bottled up. How can that be freedom?

Only in the holy state do we experience free *will*. In that state, everything in our mind is pulling in the same direction. That means that everything in us gets to express its full creative power, and that power flows forth from us without limitation. Nothing remains bottled up. We experience *unlimited* self-expression. Now *that* is freedom.

In this world we have free choice, but free choice is not freedom. Only in Heaven do we experience true freedom.

> 7. [Ur: The call to return is stronger than the call to depart, but it speaks in a different way.] The Voice of the Holy Spirit does not command, because it is incapable of arrogance. It does not demand, because it does not seek control. It does not overcome, because it does not attack. It merely <u>reminds</u>. It is compelling only because of what it reminds you *of*. It brings to your mind the <u>other</u> way, remaining quiet even in the midst of the turmoil you may make [Ur: have made for yourselves]. The Voice for God is always quiet, because it speaks of peace. Peace is stronger than war because it heals. War is <u>division</u>, not increase. No one gains from strife. What profiteth it a man if he gain the whole world and lose his own soul? [Ur: This means that] If you listen to the wrong voice you *have* <u>lost sight</u> of your soul. You <u>cannot</u> lose it, but you <u>can</u> not know it. It is therefore "lost" to you [Ur: *lost to him*] until you choose [Ur: he chooses] right.

How can we tell the two voices apart? The ego's voice commands and demands. It says, "You better do this or you are a total idiot!" Like some overbearing spouse, it tries to berate us and shame us into doing its bidding. And what is its bidding? To wage war on the world. "To the victor goes the spoils," it preaches over and over, posing as the voice of reason. Yet as we sit atop our pile of spoils, we have the horrible feeling we have lost our soul. We haven't *really* lost it, but we don't know that.

The Holy Spirit's Voice is totally different. It is not the booming Voice we think of as thundering atop Mount Sinai. Rather, it is a quiet voice; the still, small voice. It does not command, demand, control, or overcome. It merely reminds us of the truth we have forgotten. It reminds us of peace.

Though quiet, in the end this Voice is far stronger, because the truth is by nature compelling. Peace is by nature more attractive than war. This Voice, therefore, doesn't have to shout. It can afford to be quiet, because it is so secure in the compelling nature of its message, and in the inevitability of our response.

8.   The Holy Spirit is your Guide in choosing. He is in the part of your mind that <u>always</u> speaks for the right choice, because He speaks for God. He is your remaining communication with God, which you can interrupt but cannot destroy. The Holy Spirit is the way in which God's Will is [Ur: can be] done on earth as it is in Heaven. Both Heaven and earth are in <u>you</u>, because the call of both is in your mind. The Voice for God comes from your own altars to Him. These altars are not <u>things</u>; they are <u>devotions</u>. Yet you have other devotions now. Your divided devotion has given you the two voices, and you must choose at which altar you want to serve. The call you answer now <u>is</u> an evaluation because it is a <u>decision</u>. The decision [Ur: itself] is very simple. It is made on the basis of which call is worth more to you.

We seem to have separated ourselves from God completely. Where is God in this godforsaken world? Despite appearances, however, we have not cut ourselves off from God. We cannot destroy our communication with Him. The Holy Spirit is the living proof of this fact. He is our "remaining communication with God." Because He is there, God's Will *can* be done on this war-torn earth. Because of Him, there is a light in our mind that always knows which way to go, that always "speaks for God." What can we do but thank God that He is there?

So now we have two altars in our mind. One is an altar set up to our own ego. The other is an altar to God, from which the Holy Spirit speaks to us. Both of these devotions are already in us. At which altar will we serve? Which one is "worth more" to us?

Application: Imagine a situation in your life in which you feel torn between the ego and the Holy Spirit. Visualize yourself walking to a deep place in your mind. Two altars stand before you. On the left-hand altar lie symbols of your devotion to your ego in this situation. See what they are. On the right-hand altar lie symbols of your devotion to God in this situation. Now you are faced with a choice: Which altar will you kneel at?

9.   My mind will always be like yours*, because we were created as equals. It was only my <u>decision</u>* that gave me all power in Heaven and earth. My only gift to you* is to help you make the same decision [Ur: *for yourself*]. This decision is the choice to <u>share</u> it [Ur: The will for this decision is the will to *share* it], because the decision itself *is* the

17

decision to share. It is <u>made by giving</u>, and is therefore the one choice [Ur: act of mind] that resembles true creation. [Ur: You understand* the role of models in the learning process, and the importance of the models you value and choose to follow in determining what you will to learn.] I am your model for decision*. By deciding for God I showed you that this decision <u>can</u> be made, and that <u>you</u>* can make it.

Application: Please read this paragraph again, slowly, and insert your name wherever I have inserted an asterisk (*). Imagine Jesus speaking this personally to you.

What was your experience in inserting your name? I'll share mine. Normally, I feel so different from Jesus. Yet here, he speaks to me as an equal. He explains that there is only one difference between us: He made *the decision*. This decision alone is what gave him all power in Heaven and earth. Can a mere decision grant one all power? That is a decision I want to have. Yet this one seems so impossible to make. However, that's why he's here, to help me make the same decision he did. What else would he do but share it with me when the decision itself was the decision to share? Thus, just as I may have seen Martin Luther King Jr. as my model for social justice, so I should see Jesus as my model for *decision*. He showed it can be done. He proved that the seemingly impossible decision to wake up could be made, and that *I* can make it.

10. I have assured [Ur: promised] you* that the Mind that decided for me is also in <u>you</u>, and that you can let it change you just as it changed me. This Mind is unequivocal, because it hears only <u>one Voice</u> and answers in only <u>one way</u>. *You are the light of the world with me. Rest does not come from sleeping but from waking. The Holy Spirit is the call to awaken and be glad. The world is very tired, because it <u>is</u> the <u>idea</u> of weariness. Our task* is the joyous one of waking it to the Call for God. Everyone will answer the Call of the Holy Spirit, or the Sonship cannot be as one. What better vocation could there be for any part of the Kingdom than to restore it [the Kingdom] to the perfect integration that can make it whole? Hear only this through the Holy Spirit within you, and teach your brothers to listen as I* am teaching you.

Application: Again I suggest you reread the paragraph slowly and insert your name at the asterisks.

The very same Mind that decided for Jesus is also in me? I can let it change me just as it changed him? Amazing! This really brings home what he said in the last paragraph: There is no difference between him and me in *capacity*, only in *decision*. And if I exercise my capacity to decide, he and I can wake up the world together. The world is incredibly tired. It is really just a photograph of the idea of tiredness. It deeply needs rest, but that rest, paradoxically, can only come from waking up. Jesus and I are called to waken it together. In the end, we, and those who join with us, need to waken every last mind, or the Sonship cannot be whole. What better job could I ever have than to restore the wholeness of the Sonship, to reverse "the original error that shattered Heaven" (T-18.I.12:2)? I must see this as my only job while here on earth. Then I have made the same decision Jesus did.

> 11. When you are tempted by the wrong voice, call on me to remind you how to heal by sharing my decision and <u>making it stronger</u>. As we share this goal, we increase its power to attract the whole Sonship, and to bring it back into the oneness in which it was created. Remember that "yoke" means "join together," and "burden" means "message." Let us restate [Ur: reconsider the biblical statement] "My yoke is easy and my burden light" in this way; "Let us join together, for my message is Light." [Ur: I came to your minds because you had grown vaguely aware of the fact that there is another way, or another voice. Having given this invitation to the Holy Spirit, I could come to provide the model for *how to think*.]

Even in the midst of my urge to listen to the wrong voice, I can contribute to my joint function with Jesus. As I feel that urge, I can call on him, and he can help me share his decision. Since sharing ideas makes them stronger, this will make *his* decision stronger, and increase its power to draw the whole Sonship "back into the oneness in which it was created" (11:2). This is how I should see being in relationship with Jesus: not as being an ox with his yoke (however easy) around my neck, but as joining with him in his message of light.

Application: Choose some situation in which you feel heavily tempted by the wrong voice in you. Say to Jesus,

> *Jesus, remind me how to heal.*
> *Help me share your decision in this situation.*
> *I want to make your decision stronger, so that it can heal the*
>   *entire Sonship.*
> *Let us join together in your message of light.*

The last sentences, from the Urtext, are a great little account of why Jesus came to Helen and Bill. They had come to sense that there was "a better way" to think. They didn't think of it in spiritual terms, but just sensing this was an invitation to the Holy Spirit. This invitation was answered by Jesus, who came to be their model for a different way of thinking.

> 12. [Ur: Psychology has become the study of *behavior*, but no-one denies the basic law that behavior is a response to *motivation*, and motivation is will.] I have enjoined you to behave as I behaved*, but we must respond to the same Mind to do this. This Mind is the Holy Spirit, Whose Will is for God always. He teaches you how to keep me as the model for your thought*, and to behave like me as a result. The power of our joint motivation is beyond belief*, but not beyond accomplishment. *What we can accomplish together has no limits, because the Call for God is the call to the unlimited. Child of God, my message is for you, to hear and give away as you answer the Holy Spirit within you.

It is great to ask "What would Jesus do?" and then try to behave like him. He wants us to do that. But to act like he did, we have to come from the same Mind that he did. We have to think with the Holy Spirit. The motivation behind our actions has to be the Holy Spirit. An actor is always supposed to be asking himself, "What is my character's motivation?" We should be doing the same, and answering, "The Holy Spirit."

If we can reach this place, the sky is the limit. We can behave like Jesus. We can lift people out of decades of sickness and despair with a single word. And we and Jesus can join together and change the world. We may think, "Oh, the world is too hard to change." But what do you think Jesus is trying to tell us when he says, "What we can accomplish together has no limits" (12:5)? He means that together we have the power to produce undreamed of change in our world, just as he did. All it requires for us to take our part in this is a *decision*.

III. The Guide to Salvation
Commentary by Robert Perry

1.   The way to recognize [Ur: to *learn to know*] your brother is by recognizing [Ur: perceiving] the Holy Spirit in him. I have already said that the Holy Spirit is the bridge for the transfer of perception to knowledge, so we can use the terms as if they were related, because in His Mind they are. This relationship must be in His Mind because, unless it were, the separation between the two ways of thinking would not be open to healing. He is part of the Holy Trinity, because His Mind is partly yours and also partly God's. This needs clarification, not in statement [Ur: since we have said this before,] but in experience.

Earlier we were told that the way to heal a brother is to know him. How do we come to know him? By perceiving the Holy Spirit in him.

We have been told, however, that perception and knowledge are completely separate realms. How can *perceiving* the Holy Spirit in a brother lead to *knowledge* of that brother? Because the Holy Spirit is the bridge *from* perception *to* knowledge. Seeing the Holy Spirit is like climbing on a plane that is sitting in perception but is bound for knowledge.

Application: Think of a brother whom you regard as somewhat insane, and then repeat:

> *I see the Holy Spirit in you.*
> *I acknowledge a Presence in you that is perfectly sane,*
> *that is always seeking to guide you toward sanity,*
> *and that in the end will succeed.*

2.   The Holy Spirit is the idea of healing. Being thought, the idea gains as it is shared. Being the Call *for* God, it is also the idea *of* God. Since you are part of God it is also the idea of yourself, as well as of all His creations [Ur: all the parts of God]. The idea of the Holy Spirit shares the property of other ideas because it follows the laws of the Universe

of which <u>it</u> is a part. [Ur: Therefore,] It is strengthened by being given away. It increases in you as you give it to your brother [Ur: brothers]. [Ur: Since thoughts do not have to be conscious to exist,] Your brother does <u>not</u> have to be <u>aware</u> of the Holy Spirit in himself or in you for this miracle to occur. He may have dissociated the Call for God, just as <u>you</u> have. This dissociation is healed in <u>both</u> of you as you become aware of [Ur: see] the Call for God in him, and thus acknowledge its <u>being</u>.

The Holy Spirit is an *idea*—the idea of healing, of God, of yourself, and of all the parts of God. By seeing Him in your brother, then, you are really giving this idea *to* your brother. This gift has the power to make him aware of what he has forgotten, that in the depths of his mind there is a Call that never stops sounding—the Voice of God calling him home. This gift also has the power to increase your awareness of this Presence in you, since giving an idea reinforces it in your own mind. This gift, in short, is a miracle.

3. [Ur: Bill, who has made a number of vital contributions to our joint venture, made a major one a while ago, which he himself did not appreciate or even understand. If we recognize its value together, we will be able to use it together, because it is an idea, and must therefore be shared to be held. When Bill said that he was determined "*not* to see you that way," he was speaking negatively. If he will state the same idea *positively*, he will see the *power* of what he said. He had realized that there are two ways of seeing you, and also that they are diametrically opposed to one another.] There are two diametrically opposed ways of seeing your brother. They must both be in your mind, because you are the perceiver. They must also be in <u>his,</u> because you are perceiving him. [Ur: What he was really saying was that he would *not* look at you through *his* ego, or perceive *your* ego in you. State{d} positively, he would see you through the Holy Spirit in *his* mind, and perceive it in *yours*.] See him through the Holy Spirit in <u>his</u> mind, and you will recognize Him in <u>yours</u>. What you acknowledge in your brother you <u>are</u> acknowledging in yourself, and what you share you <u>strengthen</u>.

Jesus here uses a comment of Bill's in a rather brilliant way. What Bill apparently said was that he was determined not to see Helen in "that way"—meaning the ego's way. Jesus then draws out the implications of this. He says Bill was realizing there are two totally opposite ways of seeing Helen: according to the ego or the Holy Spirit. Further, he said, each way involves the ego or Holy Spirit in both the perceiver (Bill) *and* the perceived (Helen). So "I'm determined not to see you that way" actually meant, "I'm determined not to see you through my ego or perceive the ego in you." Jesus, however, implied that stating it positively would have more power: "I'm determined to see you through the Holy Spirit in my mind and perceive Him in your mind."

Jesus wanted to do all this mining for gold in Bill's original comment because he felt its contribution was too major to let it be lost. By drawing Bill and Helen's attention to it, the idea could be used and shared, he said, and therefore held and reinforced.

Notice the brilliance of what Jesus has done. He has been making two points before now: first, about the need to see the Holy Spirit in your brother; second, about the fact that sharing an idea strengthens it. He has somehow managed to weave both of these together in relation to Bill's idea. He has turned it into an idea about seeing the Holy Spirit in your brother, and he has done this so the idea can be shared and thus strengthened.

Application: Choose the person who is closest to you in space right now and say,

I am determined to see you through the Holy Spirit in my mind and perceive Him in your mind.

4.   The Voice of the Holy Spirit <u>is</u> weak in you. That is why you <u>must</u> share It. It must be <u>increased</u> in strength before <u>you</u> can hear It. It is impossible to hear It in yourself while It is so weak in your [Ur: *own*] mind. It is <u>not</u> weak in Itself, but It <u>is</u> limited by your unwillingness to hear It. [Ur: Will {willingness} itself is an idea, and is therefore strengthened by being shared.] If you make the mistake of looking for the Holy Spirit in yourself alone your thoughts will frighten you [Ur: You have made the mistake of looking for the Holy Spirit in *yourselves*, and that is why your meditations have frightened you] because, by adopting the ego's viewpoint, you are undertaking [Ur: you undertook] an ego-alien journey <u>with the ego as guide</u>. This is <u>bound</u> to produce fear. [Ur: Bill's better idea needs to be strengthened in *both* of you. Since it was *his*, *he* can increase it by giving it to you.]

Now Jesus weaves this idea of seeing the Holy Spirit in your brother together with the issue of hearing the Holy Spirit inside you. Nearly all of us complain that we cannot hear the Holy Spirit very well. The reason you can't hear Him, Jesus says, is that you have made His Voice weak in you through your unwillingness to hear. The solution is to give the idea of the Holy Spirit to your brothers (by seeing Him in them) and this will strengthen His Voice in you. By extending your willingness to see Him in others, you increase your willingness to hear Him in yourself.

If you can't hear the Holy Spirit, the solution *seems* to be to intensify the inward quest, to meditate more and longer. Jesus is all for meditation. However, he cautions us (in this early dictation) that meditation must be combined with joining with your brothers. We just saw this passage at the end of "The Rewards of God" (4.VI):

> [Meditation] *cannot* be undertaken successfully by those who disengage themselves from the Sonship....God will come to you only as you will give Him to your brothers. Learn first of them, and you will be ready to hear God as you hear them.

Now he explains more about this. If you look for the Holy Spirit in yourself alone, you will be going away from the ego ("an ego-alien journey"), yet doing so within the ego's framework of "I am the center of the universe" ("with the ego as guide"). You'll be led up the mountain by a guide who is terrified of heights. How could this not lead to fear? Helen and Bill's meditations had been causing them fear for this very reason. Better instead to follow Bill's idea: Look for Him in your brother.

> 5.   Delay is of the ego, because time is <u>its</u> concept. [Ur: Delay is obviously a *time* idea.] Both time <u>and</u> delay are meaningless in eternity. I have said before that the Holy Spirit is God's Answer to the ego. Everything of which the Holy Spirit reminds you is in direct opposition to the ego's notions, because true and false perceptions are <u>themselves</u> opposed. The Holy Spirit has the task of <u>undoing</u> what the ego has made. He undoes it at the same level on [Ur: in the same realm of discourse in] which the ego operates, or the mind would be unable to understand the change.

In truth, there is no time. In the great sweep of eternity, time means nothing and has no existence. That seems to imply "Take all the time you want." Yet delay is always of the ego. The ego is the ultimate procrastinator. Its ultimate goal is to continually put off eternity.

If you are getting guidance and it always tells you what you already wanted to hear, and your face always lights up with a serene smile as you murmur, "Yes, I knew that," then I seriously doubt you are getting the real thing. What the Holy Spirit says is directly in opposition to what your ego wants to hear. In fact, the Holy Spirit's whole job is to undo the thought system the ego has made. He is here to undo everything you think is real. He is here to challenge every value that you hold. When He's done with you, nothing will be the same.

> 6.   I have repeatedly emphasized that one level of the mind is not understandable to another. So it is with the ego and the Holy Spirit [Ur: the Soul]; with time and eternity. Eternity is an idea of God, so the Holy Spirit [Ur: the Soul] understands it perfectly. Time is a belief of the ego, so the lower mind, which is the ego's domain, accepts it without question. The only aspect of time that is [Ur: really] eternal is *now*. [Ur: That is what we *really* mean when we say that now is the only time. The literal nature of this statement does not mean anything to the ego. It interprets it, at best, to mean "don't worry about the future." This is *not* what it really means at all.]

It is crucial to read the second and third sentences in this paragraph according to the original dictation. The idea is that our ego and our Soul (or spirit) occupy two realms that can't reach each other at all. That's why we need the Holy Spirit to play the role of mediator, which we'll see in the next paragraph.

The ego is so clueless about eternity, the Soul's natural domain, that when it hears "now is the only time," it doesn't have a clue what that really means. It thinks it must mean, "Don't worry about the future," or "Savor the moment." Yet it really means, as the Course will explain later, that *literally* only this instant is real, and that if you could enter fully into the pure presence of this instant (not the *sensations* of this instant, just the blank canvas of it), you would experience eternity.

> 7.   The Holy Spirit is the Mediator between the interpretations of the ego and the knowledge of the spirit [Ur: the Soul]. His ability to deal

with symbols enables Him to work with [Ur: *against*] the ego's beliefs in its own language. His [Ur: equal] ability to look <u>beyond</u> symbols into eternity enables Him to understand the laws of God, for which He speaks. He can therefore perform the function of <u>reinterpreting</u> what the ego makes, not by destruction but by understanding. Understanding is light, and light leads to knowledge. The Holy Spirit is <u>in</u> light because He is <u>in you</u> who <u>are</u> light, but you yourself do not know this. It is therefore the task of the Holy Spirit to reinterpret you on behalf of God.

To really understand this paragraph, we have to see it as the continuation of a thread begun at the end of paragraph 5. Let me try to capture the whole thing. Our ego and our Soul do not understand each other in the slightest. Yet the ego has to be reached and undone on its own level.

That is why we need the Holy Spirit to work as a Mediator between the two realms. He has the ability to carry a perceptual reflection of the Soul's knowledge right into the ego's system. There, He can speak the speak the ego's language and uses this ability to constantly *reinterpret* the ego's symbols: "You see this symbol that you thought meant this? Well, it actually means something completely different." He can bring understanding into the very mind that a moment before was mired in the ego.

The Holy Spirit, then, sparks change on *this level*. If you tell someone that all is one and only timelessness is real and we are all divine, he may look up and say, "Aaah, how wonderful," and then go on with his ego's business. But if you say, "You need to stop thinking you are better than your next door neighbor, and you need to let go of the idea that your parents deprived you, and you need to stop verbally berating your girlfriend," that's a different story altogether.

> 8.   You cannot understand yourself alone. This is because you have no meaning apart from your rightful place in the Sonship, and the rightful place of the Sonship is God. This is your life, your eternity and your Self. It is of this that the Holy Spirit reminds you. It is this that the Holy Spirit <u>sees</u>. This vision [Ur: invariably] frightens the ego because it is so calm. Peace is the ego's greatest enemy because, according to <u>its</u> interpretation of reality, war is the guarantee of its survival. The ego becomes strong in strife [Ur: because]. If you believe there is strife you will react viciously, because the idea of danger has entered your mind. The [Ur: This] idea itself <u>is</u> an appeal to the ego. The Holy Spirit is as

vigilant as the ego to the call of danger, opposing it with His strength just as the ego <u>welcomes</u> it [Ur: with all its might]. The Holy Spirit counters this welcome by welcoming peace. Eternity and peace are as closely related as are time and war.

We are all trying to understand ourselves. This implies two things: first, that we, by ourselves, have the capacity to understand ourselves, and, second, that we can be understood by ourselves, distinct from others and from the whole. The Course is disagreeing with both of these. We have no meaning apart from our brothers and from the entire constellation of the Sonship. Who we are is therefore vast, totally transcending this tiny self. That is why we need a Mind much larger than this tiny mind to interpret us for us. This is what the Holy Spirit seeks to do: to refute the ego's constricted view of ourselves and show us a vision of our true grandeur.

This vision, being so vast, is incredibly calm and peaceful. And this frightens our ego, because our ego defines us in relation to struggle. It sees our identity as defined by response to threat. Who would we be without threats, challenges, crises, and problems to react to? The ego loves threats, it loves the "call of danger," because that call is a great excuse to respond viciously, and attack is the essence of the ego. Little do we realize that, as we give in to this viciousness, the Holy Spirit is there opposing the call of danger with His strength and inviting us to welcome peace instead.

> 9. Perception [Ur: as well as knowledge] derives meaning from <u>relationships</u>. Those you accept are the foundations of your beliefs. The separation is merely another term for a split mind. [Ur: It was not an act, but a thought. Therefore, the idea of Separation can be given away, just as the idea of unity can, and either way, it will be *strengthened in the mind of the giver*.] The ego is the symbol of [Ur: the] separation, just as the Holy Spirit is the symbol of peace. What you perceive in others you are <u>strengthening in yourself</u>. You may let your mind misperceive, but the Holy Spirit lets your mind reinterpret its own misperceptions.

I have difficulty understanding how this paragraph all ties together. Here is my best guess: Both in the realm of perception and the realm of knowledge, the meaning we give ourselves is based on our network of relationships and what we ourselves are pumping into that network, so to speak. If we pump the idea of separation into that network, seeing everyone as separate from us, that is how we will see ourselves: as separate, alone, insignificant, and deficient. If we pump the idea of peace into that network, seeing the Holy Spirit in everyone we meet, we will reinterpret ourselves. We will see ourselves in a totally new light.

> 10. The Holy Spirit is the perfect teacher. He uses only what your mind already understands to teach you that you do not understand it. The Holy Spirit can deal with a reluctant [Ur: an unwilling] learner without going counter to his mind [Ur: will], because part of it [Ur: his will] is still for God. Despite the ego's attempts to conceal this part, it is still much stronger than the ego, although the ego does not recognize it. The Holy Spirit recognizes it perfectly because it is His Own dwelling place; the place in the mind where He is at home. You are at home there, too, because it is a place of peace, and peace is of God. You who are part of God are not at home except in His peace. If peace is eternal, you are at home only in eternity.

Here we see how the Holy Spirit works. He meets you where you are; He speaks your language. And as you say, "Yes, I see…I'm following…I get what you mean," He leads you to a startling conclusion: "I have no clue who I am." Isn't this exactly how the Course itself works?

The third sentence of this paragraph is an important statement. The Holy Spirit can't work without your mind's permission, but He always has *some* permission to work. Why? Because part of your mind is still for God. That part is His home base. It is always giving Him permission. That part seems so subtle and so weak, but in the end, it will win out. I once read about a farmer in Mexico who found a tiny jet of steam escaping from a finger-sized hole on his land. It seemed like nothing. Yet what was buried beneath his farmland was more powerful than he could have imagined. Within months it was a massive volcano.

The holy part of our mind is the only place where we feel truly home. This is what the Holy Spirit sees when He looks upon us. This is what He has come here to tell us about.

> 11. The ego made the world as it perceives it, but the Holy Spirit, the reinterpreter of what the ego made, sees the world [Ur: only] as a

teaching device for bringing you home. The Holy Spirit must perceive time, and reinterpret it into the timeless. [Ur: The mind must be led into eternity *through* time, because having made time it is capable of perceiving its opposite.] He must work through opposites, because He must work with and for a mind that is in opposition. Correct and learn, and be open to learning. You have not made truth, but truth can still set you free. Look as the Holy Spirit looks, and understand as He understands. His understanding looks back to God in remembrance of me. He is in communion [Ur: Holy Communion] with God always, and He is part of you. He is your guide to salvation, because He holds the remembrance of things past and to come ["the remembrance of things past" is from Shakespeare's Sonnet 30], and brings them to the present ["brings them to the present" appears to have been inserted by the editors]. He holds this gladness gently in your mind, asking only that you increase it in His Name by sharing it to increase His joy in you.

Here we have a great example of the Holy Spirit's reinterpreting (we'll see more in Section VI). The ego made the world as evidence that only separation is real. The Holy Spirit reinterprets the world "as a teaching device for bringing you home."

That's what He does: He takes what we have made and reinterprets it, gives it an opposite meaning. All of His work is done upon the field of opposites, for that's what our mind currently is, "a battleground, where contradiction reigns and opposites make endless war" (M-27.2:7). Therefore, it's up to us to be OK with Him trying to move our perception from one opposite to another. We have to be OK with being told, "What this thing really means is the *opposite* of what you have assumed it means." We have to be open to *correction*, which means open to *learning*.

We need to take all of this from Him because of Who He is. After all, He is in holy communion with God always. He holds the remembrance of the Heaven that we left behind and that we are going to. Do we really think we know better than He does? All He wants is for us to follow His teaching so His joy in us can be increased.

IV. Teaching and Healing
Commentary by Robert Perry

This section is really about love, about *holding* it and *sharing* it. It is about letting our thoughts be purified so we have a truly loving impulse behind our behavior. And it is about extending that loving impulse to others in order to reinforce its strength within us.

1.   What fear has hidden still is part of you [This sentence appears to have been composed by the editors. What originally went here was a discussion in which Jesus mentioned that Helen defended against the Kingdom largely through dissociation, while Bill defended against it largely through repression. Because their defenses were different, they could help each other get over these defenses, and they were doing so. If they had the same defense, each would be too frightened by seeing it in the other to be helpful.]. Joining the [Ur: Joining in] Atonement [Ur: which I have repeatedly asked you to do] is the way [Ur: is *always* a way] <u>out</u> of fear. [Ur: This does not mean that you can safely fail to acknowledge anything that is true, but] The Holy Spirit will [Ur: not fail to] help you reinterpret <u>everything</u> that you perceive as fearful, and teach you that <u>only</u> what is loving is <u>true</u>. Truth [Ur: It {apparently, "what is loving"}] is beyond your ability to destroy, but entirely within your ability to accept [Ur: within your grasp]. It belongs to you because, as an extension of God, <u>you</u> created it with Him [Ur: It *belongs* to you because *you* created it]. It is yours because it is part of you, just as you are part of God because He created you. Nothing that is good can be lost because it comes from the Holy Spirit, the Voice for creation. Nothing that is not good was ever created, and therefore cannot be protected. The Atonement is the <u>guarantee</u> of the safety of the Kingdom [what follows was spliced in from later in the section], and the union of the Sonship <u>is</u> its protection. The ego cannot prevail against the Kingdom <u>because</u> the Sonship is united. In the presence of those who hear the Holy Spirit's call to be as one, the ego fades away and is undone [Ur: the ego fades away and is undone in the presence of the attraction of the parts of the Sonship which hear the call of the Holy Spirit to be as One].

31

"Joining the Atonement" was originally "Joining in Atonement," so that rather than suggesting that we as individuals should join the Atonement, it said that we should join each other *in* the Atonement. Helen and Bill each had different defenses against the awareness of the Kingdom (or the truth). This put them in an excellent position to help each other drop those defenses. If they both used the *same* defense, seeing it in the other would frighten them too much, which would impede being helpful.

Just joining another, however, is not a substitute for undoing your own defenses (I think that's what that line "This does not mean that you can safely fail to acknowledge anything that is true" means). You still have to let go of your defense against the truth and come to acknowledge it instead. The Holy Spirit will gently guide you to this place. He will teach you that the truth you've been defending against is not the fearful thing you thought it was. He will teach you that only the loving is true. How can the truth be fearful when "only what is loving is true"?

The rest of the paragraph (until the last 2 ½ sentences, which were spliced in from elsewhere) is really about this love. It refers back to Jesus telling Helen that her loving thoughts came from the Holy Spirit in her and thus are eternal. (This material, which was spliced in at the end of this section, originally came before the section began.) To make sense of these sentences, we need to posit this idea: When you have a loving thought in this world, you are actually tapping into the timeless love of Heaven. This love is beyond your ability to destroy, but entirely within your reach. It belongs to you because you actually created its timeless reality in Heaven. It is part of you forever. It can never be lost, because it came from the eternal in you. Love, then, is not the fleeting, elusive thing it appears to be. The love we experience is a small taste of a stable, eternal reality that is forever part of us.

The paragraph ends on a note of joining, just as it began. The ego cannot prevail (thank God!) "because the Sonship is united," while the ego is all about separation. The ego vanishes when the parts of the Sonship hear the call to be as one, feel the attraction to each other, and join.

2.   [Ur: Nothing that is not good was ever created, and therefore *cannot* be protected. {This was the original end of the previous paragraph.}] What the ego makes it <u>keeps to itself</u>, and so it is without

strength. Its existence is unshared. It does not die; it was merely never born. Physical [Ur: Real] birth is not a beginning; it is a <u>continuing</u>. Everything that continues [Ur: *can* continue] has already <u>been</u> born. It will [Ur: But it can] <u>increase</u> as you are willing to return the unhealed part of your mind to the higher part, returning it undivided to creation [Ur: and thus render your creating undivided. You yourself always told your patients that the real difference between neurotic and 'healthy' guilt feelings was that neurotic guilt feelings *do not help anyone*. This distinction was very wise, though incomplete. Let us make the distinction a little sharper now. Neurotic guilt feelings are a device of the ego for "atoning" without sharing, and for asking for pardon without change. The ego *never* calls for real atonement, and cannot tolerate real forgiveness, which *is* change. Your concept of "healthy guilt feelings" has great merit, but without the concept of the Atonement it lacked the healing potential it held. *You* make the distinction in terms of feelings which led to a decision not to *repeat* the error, which is only *part* of healing. Your concept therefore lacked the idea of *undoing* it. What you were really advocating, then, was adopting a policy of sharing without a real *foundation*.] I have come to give you the foundation, so your own thoughts can make you really free. You have carried the burden of unshared ideas that are too weak to increase, but having made them you did not realize how to <u>undo</u> them. You <u>cannot</u> cancel out your past errors alone. They will <u>not</u> disappear from your mind without the Atonement [Ur: remedy.], a remedy not of your making [Ur: The remedy is *not* of your making, anymore than *you* are.] The Atonement must be understood [Ur: cannot be understood except] as a <u>pure act of sharing</u>. That is what I meant when I said it is possible even in this world to listen to <u>one </u>Voice. If you are part of God and the Sonship is one, you <u>cannot</u> be limited to the self the ego sees.

What is truly good in this world, what is truly loving, is eternal. It can never be lost. In contrast, the not-good, the unloving, cannot last. It must pass away. Indeed, it was never born in the first place. This is great news, isn't it? The reason the unloving is so weak is that it is made by the ego, which refuses to share it, thus depriving it of strength. All of this is also true of the ego itself, which is never really born because it never really exists. This "never born" idea is also true of the good. We ourselves were not really born when we were born, because we already existed. And our loving thoughts were not born when we thought them. They, too, already existed, and will increase if we return our mind to Heaven.

What follows is a discussion of Helen's notion of "neurotic guilt feelings" vs. "healthy guilt feelings." Neurotic guilt is where you beat yourself up in the thought that doing so makes up for what you did. Therefore, you don't need to actually change. You don't need to replace the withholding of love—what you feel guilty for—with a real *sharing* of love. This guilt, then, is a device for "'atoning' without sharing, and for asking for pardon without change." What a line! You have supposedly atoned, but you're still the same unloving S.O.B. you were before.

Healthy guilt feelings, in Helen's view, were ones that led to a decision not to repeat the error. But Jesus said that this left out actually *undoing* the error, undoing the thought behind the behavior. In her view, you would then share—you would behave lovingly—but without the real foundation of having love in your heart, because you hadn't yet undone the unlove that was behind your former mistake.

Jesus says, "I have come to give you the foundation." Our guilt can spur us to stamp out the behavior, but we really don't know how to undo the ideas behind the behavior. The fact is that we can't undo them alone. We need the Atonement. We need Jesus. If we invite him, he can step in and cleanse our mind of that thought-pattern that was behind the compulsion to repeat the same harmful behaviors over and over. Then we can truly love. And on that solid foundation, we can truly share.

> 3.   Every loving thought held in <u>any</u> part of the Sonship belongs to every part. It is shared *because* it is loving. Sharing is God's way of creating, and also <u>yours</u>. The ego can keep you in exile <u>from</u> the Kingdom, but in the Kingdom itself it has no power. Ideas of the spirit do not leave the mind that thinks them, nor can they conflict with each other [Ur: Ideas do not *leave* the mind which thought them in order to have separate being. Nor do separate thoughts conflict with one another in space, because they do not occupy space at all.]. However, ideas of the ego [Ur: *Human* ideas] can conflict [Ur: in content] because they occur at different levels and also include opposite thoughts at the <u>same</u> level. *It is impossible to share opposing thoughts.* [Ur: The Holy Spirit does not *let* you forsake your brothers. Therefore,] You can share only the thoughts that are of God [Ur: Him] and that He [Ur: which He also] keeps for <u>you</u>. And of such is the Kingdom of Heaven. The rest remains with you until the Holy Spirit has reinterpreted them in the light of the Kingdom, making them, too, worthy of being shared. When they have been sufficiently purified He lets you give them away. The decision to share them *is* their purification.

The previous paragraph spoke of the normal human attempt to be sharing while still retaining more or less the same thoughts in you that led to you being attacking. This can't work. This paragraph clarifies that in fact you can *only* share loving thoughts, thoughts that are of the Holy Spirit. Only they can provide the basis for real sharing.

This leads into his emphatic statement, *"It is impossible to share opposing thoughts."* Why is this? Let me speculate a bit here. First, to share a thought by definition means that you and the other person both hold the same thought. The thought started with you and then was embraced by him. That is why loving thoughts can be so easily shared. Once the giver has embraced them, the receiver will readily do so as well. Hateful thoughts cannot be shared because the receiver would not want to embrace the thought "You are worthy of my hate." The giver may embrace such a thought, but the receiver will reject it. He will not want to believe that he is worthy of hate.

In other words, thoughts that see the giver pitted against the receiver will not be shared. However much the giver embraces the thought, the receiver will reject it, because it puts him in a losing position.

This paragraph, however, is talking about thoughts in which the opposition is *within* the giver's mind, not *between* giver and receiver. These thoughts are *internally* conflicted. My speculation is that these thoughts are ones in which part of the thought is on the side of the receiver and part of the thought is on the side of the giver *against* the receiver. For instance, let's say you carry this thought: "I love John, but I really do feel that he is not really worthy of me." The first part of the thought is on the side of John, but the second part is on the side of your ego against John. The two sides are in conflict, and one side is against John. Could John really share a thought like this? Could he really embrace it with you? Not wholeheartedly, surely.

Rather than holding onto these thoughts and trying to be sharing and loving anyway, we should let the Holy Spirit purify these thoughts. He purifies them, obviously, by trimming off the unloving part.

> 4. [Ur: You cannot learn *except* by teaching.] I heard one Voice because I understood that I <u>could not atone for myself alone</u>. Listening to one Voice implies the decision to share It in order to hear It yourself. The Mind that was in me is still irresistibly drawn to every mind created by God, because God's Wholeness <u>is</u> the wholeness of His Son.

[Ur: Turning the other cheek does *not* mean that you should submit to violence without protest. It means that] You cannot be hurt, and do not want to show your brother anything except your wholeness. Show him that he <u>cannot</u> hurt you and hold nothing against him, or you hold it against yourself. This is the meaning of "turning the other cheek."

The way to have love in you is to decide to give it. This is what Jesus means by, "You cannot learn except by teaching." If you want to learn love, you have to teach it, extend it, for love is extension. This is what he means by, "The decision to share them *is* their purification." If you want to have pure, loving thoughts, you have to decide to give them away, for pure thoughts are by nature *giving* thoughts. This is also what he means by "Listening to one Voice implies the decision to share It in order to hear It yourself." The decision to hear the Voice of love is also the decision to share love. Since giving is the nature of love, you can't *have* it without being willing to *give* it.

The latter part of the paragraph contains a brilliant interpretation of turning the other cheek. This is commonly interpreted as "If you want to be good, just let them keep slapping you." The message you send in this case is, "I love you even though you have wounded me and rendered me not whole," or even worse, "Look how much purer I am than you." This is the very error this section has been talking about. It is an attempt to extend love while still holding conflicting, unloving thoughts within the self. Jesus makes a similar point about the martyr's mentality in *The Song of Prayer* (see S-2.II.4). Instead of focusing on performing a radical behavior with ambivalent love within, you need to focus on having real love in your heart, and real love says to the other, "You never hurt me. You are innocent."

This is what Jesus did in the crucifixion. Rather than saying, "Look what you've done to me," his message was, "You're not doing anything to me. You are still my innocent brother."

Do you notice the visual interpretation Jesus is giving this saying? He is interpreting "turning the other cheek" as symbolic of presenting to your brother the un-wounded side of you. Turning the other cheek becomes a metaphor for showing him your wholeness.

5.   Teaching is done in many ways, [Ur: by formal means, by guidance, and] above all <u>by example</u>. [Ur: If you will to learn, you *must* will to

teach.] Teaching should be healing [Ur: Teaching is therapy], because it is the sharing of ideas and the recognition that to share ideas is to strengthen them. I cannot forget my need to teach what I have learned, which arose in me *because* I learned it. I call upon you to teach what you have learned, because by so doing you can depend on it. Make it dependable in my name because my name is the Name of God's Son. What I learned I give you freely, and the Mind that was in me rejoices as you choose to hear it.

This paragraph expands on the previous one. If you really learn love, you will be unable to resist the compulsion to teach it. That is why Jesus is so focused on teaching, because he grew to understand what love means, and love means *extending to others*. Only when you teach it will your learning of it become truly dependable. If you feel that the love in you is not dependable enough, then get out there and teach love. If you don't feel up to the task, remember that history's greatest master of love is offering you literally everything he learned, freely, right now.

How you do teach love? There are many ways, but the main way is by *example*. What is so powerful about example? It shows that you really mean it. It shows, in a way that mere words cannot, that you have really come to believe in what you teach. Here again we see the power of having the right thoughts and not just saying the right words or aping the right behavior. It's the thought behind the behavior that counts.

6.   The Holy Spirit atones in all of us by undoing, and thus lifts the burden you have placed in your mind. By following Him you are led back to God where you belong, and how can you find the way except by taking your brother with you? My part in the Atonement is not complete until you join it and give it away. As you teach so shall you learn. I will never leave you or forsake you, because to forsake you would be to forsake myself and God Who created me. You forsake yourself and God if you forsake any of your brothers. [Ur: You are more than your brother's keeper. In fact, you do {should} not *want* to keep him.] You must learn to see them as they are, and understand they belong to God as you do. How could you treat your brother better than by rendering unto God the things that are God's?

The Holy Spirit atones in us not by paying for our sins, but by undoing the unloving thoughts that caused the "sins" in the first place. This is how

He leads us back to God. But to actually make it back, we have to take our brother with us. If we forsake him, we forsake ourselves. The Bible implies that we are our brother's keeper, but we are even more than that. Rather than keeping him for ourselves, we should take him with us on the journey and deliver him back into the Hands of God. This is how we carry out the injunction of another Bible verse and "render unto God the things that are God's."

Application: Think of a cherished loved one and say the following to him or her:

> *I will never leave you or forsake you, [name] .*
> *To forsake you would be to forsake myself and God Who created me.*
> *I am more than your keeper.*
> *Rather than keeping you, my goal is to render you to God.*
> *For you belong to God, not to me.*

7.   The Atonement gives you the power of a healed mind, but the power to create is of God. Therefore, those who have been forgiven must devote themselves first to healing [others] because, having received the idea of healing, they must give it to hold it. The full power of creation cannot be expressed as long as any of God's ideas [Sons] is withheld [Ur: are withholding it {the power of creation}] from the Kingdom. The joint will of the Sonship is the only creator that can create like the Father, because only the complete can think completely, and the thinking of God lacks nothing. Everything you think that is not through the Holy Spirit *is* lacking.

Once we receive the sense that we ourselves have been forgiven, our major priority is to extend healing to others. This accomplishes two things. First, it reinforces healing in our own minds, so that we ourselves become fully healed. Second, it helps draw the whole Sonship back to the Kingdom. Only when everyone is back can the Sonship be whole, and only when it is whole can it create like our Father, the infinitely Whole. Again and again we see the theme that creation can only be performed by a whole mind, a mind in which all its parts are pulling completely in the same direction. This applies to both the individual mind and the mind of the entire Sonship. All the parts of that mind must be united in pouring all of their power in the exact same direction to create something that is eternally real.

> 8.   How can you who are so holy suffer? All your past except its beauty is gone, and nothing is left but a blessing. I have saved all your kindnesses and every loving thought you ever had [Ur: and I assure you, you have had many]. I have purified them of the errors that hid their light, and kept them for you in their own perfect [error-free] radiance. They are beyond destruction and beyond guilt. They came from the Holy Spirit within <u>you</u>, and we know what God creates is eternal [so they are eternal]. You can indeed depart in peace because I have loved you as I loved myself. You go <u>with</u> my blessing and <u>for</u> my blessing. Hold it and share it, that it may always be ours. I place the peace of God in your heart and in your hands, to hold and share. The heart is pure to hold it, and the hands are strong to give it. We cannot lose. My judgment is as strong as the wisdom of God, in Whose Heart and Hands we have our being. His quiet children are His blessed Sons. The Thoughts of God are with you.

This is such a beautiful paragraph! The third through sixth sentences were originally found in the paragraphs preceding this section. The context for them was that, according to Jesus, Helen had "learned to be a loving, wise, and very understanding therapist," except on behalf of herself. This exception deprived her, but the love that she had given would not be lost to her. That's when he breaks into those beautiful lines, "I have saved all of your kindnesses....I have purified them.... They are beyond destruction....They came from the Holy Spirit...[and are therefore] eternal."

In the remaining sentences, notice the repeated admonition to *hold* and *share*. Hold and share "my blessing"—Jesus' blessing. Hold and share "the peace of God." "The heart is pure to hold it, and the hands are strong to give [share] it." This speaks to the very core of the section, which asks us to let the Atonement purify our thoughts, so that we can hold something pure in our hearts, and then share its blessing with others. This is how we hang onto it and reinforce it for ourselves. After all of his explanation in this section, Jesus here is really sending us out on our mission as teachers of love.

Application: Read the paragraph again, very slowly (if you read it quickly, you just deprive yourself), inserting your name wherever I have placed an asterisk:

How can you * who are so holy suffer?

All your past except its beauty * is gone, and nothing is left but a blessing.

I have saved all your kindnesses * and every loving thought you ever had.

I have purified them * of the errors that hid their light, and kept them for you in their own perfect radiance.

They are beyond destruction and beyond guilt.

They came from the Holy Spirit within you *, and we know what God creates is eternal.

You can indeed depart in peace because I have loved you * as I loved myself.

You go with my blessing and for my blessing.

Hold it and share it *, that it may always be ours.

I place the peace of God in your heart and in your hands *, to hold and share [visualize this].

The heart is pure to hold it *, and the hands are strong to give it.

We cannot lose *.

My judgment is as strong as the wisdom of God, in Whose Heart and Hands we have our being.

V. The Ego's Use of Guilt
Commentary by Robert Perry

This is the real introduction of the crucial topic of guilt in the Course. Before this section, there are very few references to it, only five in the published Course. Although we think of guilt as mostly coming from actions in the world, this section focuses on guilt that comes from thinking our own thoughts, apart from God.

> 1.   Perhaps some of our concepts [Ur: Perhaps this] will become clearer and more personally meaningful if the ego's use of guilt is clarified. The ego has a purpose, just as the Holy Spirit has. The ego's purpose is <u>fear</u>, because only the fearful can be egotistic. The ego's logic is as impeccable as that of the Holy Spirit, because your mind has [Ur: all] the means at its disposal to side with Heaven or earth, as it elects. But again, remember that both are in you.

Everything the ego does has the purpose of making you afraid. Why? Because being afraid seems to give you just cause to act egotistically, to act viciously. We have been told earlier, "Frightened people are apt to be vicious," "Those who are afraid are apt to be vicious," and "You will react viciously because the idea of danger has entered your mind" (all Urtext versions). Fear is an excuse to act like an ego. No wonder fear is the ego's goal.

The ego knows that making you afraid will make you vicious, and that viciousness will bind you more closely to itself. It understands these connections because its "logic is impeccable." It makes sure that every single thing it does is consistent with its fundamental purpose. It never misses an opportunity. It is like the most focused salesman in the world, who in every situation is thinking, "How can I use this to get my commission?"

The Holy Spirit, however, is the same way. His logic is also impeccable. Do you find it strange that the Holy Spirit is said not only to be logical, but to have *impeccable* logic? For many spiritual systems this would sound incongruous, but not for the Course.

2. In Heaven there is no guilt, because the Kingdom is attained through the Atonement [Atonement being understood as the wiping away of guilt], which releases you to create [Ur: which creates in you]. The word "create" is appropriate here because, once what you have made is undone by the Holy Spirit, the blessed residue is restored and therefore continues in creation. What is truly blessed is incapable of giving rise to guilt, and must give rise to joy. This makes it invulnerable to the ego because its peace is unassailable. It is invulnerable to disruption <u>because</u> it is whole. Guilt is *always* disruptive. Anything that engenders fear is divisive because it obeys the law of division. If the ego is the symbol of the separation, it is also the symbol of guilt. Guilt is more than merely not of God. It is the symbol of [Ur: the] <u>attack</u> on God. This is a totally meaningless concept <u>except</u> to the ego, but do not underestimate the power of the ego's belief in it. This is the belief from which <u>all</u> guilt really stems.

The process begins with the Holy Spirit undoing both what we have made and the guilt for making it. But even after this undoing, there is still something left: the "blessed residue." These are our loving thoughts that have been so purified and have become so radiant that they are recognized as little sparks of eternal love. They are so blessed, so pure, that they abide in a state of perfect peace and joy, a state into which the ego's disruption can never intrude, a state in which guilt is impossible. (What would a totally guilt-free state be like?) Now they become part of our unlimited mind, which spends eternity overflowing in the act of creation.

Guilt and God are antithetical. When you are in guilt, you cannot be in God. When you are in God, you cannot feel guilty. This is so different from what we may have been taught—that it is godly to feel guilty.

Ultimately, all guilt comes from our belief that we attacked God in the separation. Each time we attack a brother and feel guilty, then, we are seeing this as a miniature repetition of the original attack on God.

Application: Think about some instance of guilt recently. While holding it in mind, say these words:

> *The real cause of these guilt feelings is that I think I have attacked God.*
> *But this is ridiculous. God cannot be attacked.*

3.   The ego <u>is</u> the part of the mind that believes in division. How could part of God detach itself [divide off from Him] <u>without</u> believing it is attacking Him? We spoke before of the authority problem as based on the concept of <u>usurping</u> God's power. The ego believes that this is what <u>you</u> did because it believes that it *is* you. [Ur: It follows, then, that] If you identify <u>with</u> the ego, you <u>must</u> perceive yourself as guilty. Whenever you respond to your ego you <u>will</u> experience guilt, and you <u>will</u> fear punishment. The ego is quite literally a fearful thought. However ridiculous the idea of attacking God may be to the sane mind, never forget that the ego is <u>not sane</u>. It <u>represents</u> a delusional system, and speaks for it. Listening to the ego's voice <u>means</u> that you believe it is possible to attack God, and that a part of Him has been torn away by you. [Ur: The classic picture of] Fear of retaliation from without [Ur: then] follows, because the severity of the guilt is so acute that it <u>must</u> be projected.

At the very heart of the ego is the thought, "I attacked God and tore myself out of His Mind. That is my identity." Whenever you identify with the ego, you are simultaneously identifying with this idea. How could that not lead to crushing guilt? And in the severity of that guilt, how could you not project this onto God, and see Him believing in your guilt as well? And what could this lead to but constant fear of His retaliation? This is how the ego fulfills its purpose of fear, by making you feel guilty. "The ego is quite literally a fearful thought" because the ego believes that its very existence is cause for unending retaliation from the Omnipotent. If you identify with the ego, you must see your very existence as a very fearful thing.

Yet all of this is a delusion of grandeur. How can we believe we can overpower God and wrench ourselves out of His Mind against His Will? What are we thinking? This idea is at the heart of all of our pain, yet upon examination, it is simply "ridiculous."

Application: Ask yourself,

> *Do I really think I can overpower God and tear myself out of His mind?*

4. Whatever you accept <u>into</u> your mind has reality for you. It is [Ur: however, only] your <u>acceptance</u> of it that makes it real. [Ur: As an extreme example of dissociation yourself, you should have little trouble in understanding that it is perfectly possible not to *accept* what *is* in your minds.] If you enthrone the ego in your mind, your allowing it to enter <u>makes it your reality</u>. This is because the mind [Ur: as God created it] is capable of creating reality or making illusions ["or making illusions" was added by the editors]. I said before that you must learn to think <u>with</u> God. To think <u>with</u> Him is to think <u>like</u> Him. This engenders joy, not guilt, because it is natural. Guilt is a sure sign that your thinking is unnatural. Unnatural [Ur: Perverted] thinking will <u>always</u> be attended with guilt, because it is the belief in sin. The ego does not perceive sin as a lack of love, but as a <u>positive act of assault</u>. This is necessary to the ego's survival because, as soon as <u>you</u> regard sin as a <u>lack,</u> you will automatically attempt to remedy the situation. And you will succeed. The ego regards this as doom, but <u>you</u> must learn to regard it as freedom.

Our entire ego-based experience of being a separate person living in a world of dangerous forms came from accepting the delusion of the ego into our minds. Can accepting one idea be this powerful? Yes, because God gave our minds the power of creating reality. As a reflection of this power, once we accept something into our minds, it becomes reality for us. Look around you and think, "This all came from accepting a single idea into my mind."

We must learn, therefore, to accept only true ideas into our minds, only God's ideas. We must learn to think with God. This is really the only natural way to think. Thinking on our own is actually unnatural. It is so unnatural, so against our nature, that Jesus called it "perverted." Imagine that: "To think on my own, to think apart from God, is so unnatural for me that it is perverted." Every self-generated thought repeats the ego's core belief: "I am on my own, having torn myself away from God." Each one is therefore attended by guilt.

Yet this is the wrong way to look at it. Instead of seeing each unloving thought and deed as a sin, we should think, "That thought (or deed) was merely lacking in love, and love is what I want, in all its fullness. I will remedy that lack."

5. The guiltless mind cannot suffer. Being sane, the mind heals the

body because *it* has been healed. The sane mind cannot conceive of illness because it cannot conceive of attacking anyone or anything. I said before that illness is a form of magic. It might be better to say that it is a form of magical <u>solution</u>. The ego believes that by punishing <u>itself</u> it will mitigate the punishment of God. Yet even in this it is arrogant. It attributes to God a punishing intent, and then takes this intent as its <u>own</u> prerogative. It tries to usurp <u>all</u> the functions of God as it perceives them, because it recognizes that only total allegiance can be trusted.

Without guilt, I "cannot suffer." What an amazing thought. All of my suffering is self-imposed punishment for presumed guilt. This includes all illness, which is punishment taken out on my body. There does appear to be some decency in this approach: "At least I'm humble enough to punish myself once I feel guilty." Yet the Course sees this in more sinister tones. First, the ego says, "If I punish myself a little, then maybe God won't step in and punish me a lot." But the arrogance actually goes much deeper. The ego is saying, "Obviously, I am guilty [arrogance], and I know God wants to punish me [arrogance], but that function is much better off in my hands [arrogance]." Every step of the way is arrogant (for a similar discussion see M-5.I.2). Real humility would ask more questions and leave the answers up to God.

6.   The ego cannot <u>oppose</u> the laws of God any more than <u>you</u> can, but it can <u>interpret</u> them according to what it wants, just as <u>you</u> can. That is why the question, "What <u>do</u> you want?" must be answered. You <u>are</u> answering it every minute and every second, and each moment of decision is a judgment that is anything <u>but</u> ineffectual. Its effects will follow automatically <u>until</u> the decision is changed. [Ur: This is a redundant statement, because you have *not* learned it. But again, any decision can be Unmade as well as made.] Remember, though, that the <u>alternatives</u> themselves are unalterable. The Holy Spirit, like the ego, is a decision. Together they constitute all the alternatives the mind <u>can</u> accept and obey. The Holy Spirit and the ego are the <u>only</u> choices open to you. God created one, and so you cannot eradicate it. <u>You</u> made the other, and so you <u>can</u>. Only what God creates is irreversible and unchangeable. What <u>you</u> made can always be changed because, when you do not think <u>like</u> God, you are not really thinking at all. Delusional ideas are <u>not</u> real thoughts [Ur: thought], although you <u>can</u> [Ur: think that you] believe in them. But you are wrong. The function of thought

comes <u>from</u> God and is <u>in</u> God. As part of <u>His</u> Thought, you *cannot* think <u>apart</u> from Him.

We cannot oppose the laws of God, but we can interpret them in the way we want (just as the ego did by seeing God's laws as laws of punishment). The real question, then, is, "What do I want?" We are actually asking and answering this question *every second*. We are answering it right now... and right now...and right now. These decisions go unnoticed, but they have huge effects, and those effects keep rolling on until we change our mind. The key is asking and answering this question *consciously*. What do I want? What do I *really* want?

Our decision, though powerful, cannot change how many alternatives there are. Though we seem to be faced with a million alternatives, when you boil them down to their essence, there are only two: the ego or the Holy Spirit. Those are the hidden alternatives within every choice.

Let's look at these two alternatives. One is created by God and is therefore "irreversible and unchangeable." The other is made by us apart from God. This means it is not only changeable, it is not even real. The ego is not a real thought at all, since it was thought apart from God. So, of our two choices, one is eternally real while the other is completely vacuous and illusory. Not much of a choice.

7.   Irrational thought is disordered thought [Ur: is a thought *disorder*]. God Himself orders your thought because your thought was created <u>by</u> Him. Guilt feelings are always a sign that you do not know this. They also show that you believe you <u>can</u> think apart from God, and <u>want</u> to. Every disordered thought [Ur: thought disorder] is attended by guilt at its inception, and <u>maintained</u> by guilt in its continuance. Guilt is inescapable by those who believe they order their <u>own</u> thoughts [Ur: thought], and must therefore obey their dictates [Ur: its orders]. This makes them feel <u>responsible</u> for their errors [Ur: mind *errors*] without recognizing that, by <u>accepting</u> this responsibility, they are reacting irresponsibly. If the sole responsibility of the miracle worker is to accept the <u>Atonement</u> for himself [Ur: accept the *Atonement*], and I assure you that it is, then the responsibility for *what* is atoned for <u>cannot</u> be yours. The dilemma [Ur: This contradiction] cannot <u>be</u> resolved except by accepting the solution of undoing. You *would* be responsible for the effects of all your wrong thinking <u>if it could not be undone</u>. The purpose of the Atonement is to save the past in <u>purified</u>

form only. If you accept the remedy <u>for</u> disordered thought [Ur: a thought-disorder], a remedy whose efficacy is beyond doubt, how can its symptoms remain? [Ur: You have reason to question the validity of symptom cure. But *no one* believes that the symptoms can remain if the underlying *cause* is removed.]

If our thoughts flowed constantly and effortlessly from God, if all of our thoughts were ordered by God Himself, how could we feel any guilt? Now, however, our thought is generated and ordered by ourselves, or rather, by our erratic ego, making our thought essentially irrational. In short, we have a *thought disorder*. This is a psychological term that can apparently refer to either disordered *content* (delusional thinking) or disordered *form* (in which our thought flows erratically from one idea to an *unrelated* idea, causing problems in speech and writing). The notion that we should be the author of our thoughts seems obvious, yet Jesus says it leads to constant guilt. For it repeats the original error of rejecting God's Authorship.

This paragraph's discussion of responsibility seems puzzling. Doesn't the Course say we are responsible for our thoughts? The solution, I believe, is to realize that "responsible" in this case means *accountable*. It means something has gone wrong and you are responsible for making it right. In this case, what has gone wrong is your thinking, and this wrong thinking has caused problems in the world. If you are in charge of your thoughts, and your thoughts derail and then cause the world to derail, who else but you should be held accountable for this?

Yet to hold yourself accountable is to merely repeat the error of thinking you are the rightful author in this situation (which is the very mistake the ego made in setting things "right" by punishing the body). If you want to react truly responsibly, then resign as author of your thoughts. Let Someone Else come in and make things right for you. Accept the Atonement. Let the Holy Spirit come in, clean up your disordered thoughts, and clean up the mess they caused in the world. Imagine how great it would feel to say,

I am responsible for causing this mess.
But I am not responsible for cleaning it up.
I let the Holy Spirit clean up my thinking.
And I trust that will automatically clean up all the effects of my
   wrong thinking.

8. The <u>continuing</u> decision [Ur: will] to remain separated is the only possible reason for continuing guilt feelings. We have said this before, but did not emphasize the destructive results of the decision [Ur: at that time]. <u>Any</u> decision of the mind will affect both behavior <u>and</u> experience. What you want you <u>expect</u>. This is <u>not</u> delusional. Your mind *does* make your future, and it will turn it [your future] back to full creation at any minute <u>if it accepts the Atonement first</u>. It [your mind] will also return to full creation the instant it has done so. Having given up its disordered thought [Ur: thought *disorder*], the proper ordering of thought becomes quite apparent.

It is all a question of "what do I want?" Do I want to stay in my ego? Do I want to remain separated? Do I want to be the author of my thoughts? Do I want to feel responsible for all the messes my thinking causes? If so, this choice will bring the unbearable weight of guilt. Indeed, I will only feel guilty if I am answering "yes" to these questions *right now*. Even if I have made terrible past mistakes, I will not feel guilty for them if I let God be responsible for making things right. When I really turn my mind over to Him, all my mistakes will be undone, and their effects will vanish with them. In an instant, I will grasp the proper ordering of thought. I will suddenly know that the proper ordering is Heaven, which is where I will now be.

VI. Time and Eternity
Commentary by Robert Perry

1.   God in His knowledge is not waiting, but His Kingdom is bereft while *you* wait. All the Sons of God are waiting for your return, just as you are waiting for theirs. Delay does not matter in eternity, but it is tragic in time. You have elected to be in time rather than eternity, and therefore believe you *are* in time [Ur: and have therefore changed your belief in your status]. Yet your [Ur: But] election is both free and alterable. You do not belong in time. Your place is only in eternity, where God Himself placed you forever.

Imagine that you are in a race, and as you near the finish line you see that literally every Son of God (and there is are an infinite number) is there, waiting for you to finish, cheering you on. Then you see this is no ordinary finish line. It is actually a gate, the gate of Heaven. The reason they are cheering is that you are returning home. You left home by your own election, but the experience was a disaster, so you have elected to return. They are cheering because they know that neither you nor the Kingdom will be whole until you are back inside.

If you held this image before you at all times, would it change the speed of your journey?

2.   Guilt feelings are the preservers of time. They induce fears of [Ur: *future*] retaliation or abandonment, and thus ensure that the future will be [Ur: remain] like the past. This is the ego's continuity. It gives the ego a false sense of security by believing [Ur: through the belief] that you cannot escape from it. But you can and must. God offers you the continuity of eternity in exchange. When you choose to make this exchange, you will simultaneously exchange guilt for joy [Ur: peace], viciousness for love, and pain for peace [Ur: joy]. My role is only to unchain your will and set it free. Your ego cannot accept this freedom, and will oppose it [Ur: your free decision] at every possible moment and in every possible way. And as its maker, you recognize [Ur: *know*] what it can do because you gave it the power to do it. [Ur: The mind does indeed know its {own} power, because the mind does indeed know God.]

49

On this race, the ego is using every device in its power to slow us down, and its power is all the power we have given it. It tells us we are guilty, and therefore our future is one of punishment, a never-ending process of trying to pay down our debt. We will always need more time to do this, so we can forget about stepping off the wheel of time. We can forget about eternity. Don't try to exercise your will to get out of the ego, it tells us; it is hopeless to try. It even tells us there is a security in this. We can feel secure in the fact that we will always be the same as we are now.

Can you relate to these thoughts? Have you succumbed to them? This is the sleep on the way to the Emerald City, on the way to Heaven's gate. Don't give in to it. Don't let your will be chained. The only thing your will desires is to reach those gates. Let it be free. Let it draw you at full speed toward the gates.

> 3.   Remember the Kingdom always, and remember that you who are part of the Kingdom cannot <u>be</u> lost. The Mind that was in me *is* in you, for God creates with perfect fairness. Let the Holy Spirit remind you always of His fairness, and let me teach you how to share it with your brothers. How else can the chance to claim it for yourself be given you? [Ur: What you do not understand is that] The two voices speak for different interpretations of the same thing simultaneously; or almost simultaneously, for the ego always speaks first. Alternate interpretations were unnecessary until the first one was [Ur: has been] made [Ur: and speaking itself was unnecessary before the ego was made].

The opening lines are urging us to not fall asleep on the way to the Kingdom. Remember the goal always. Remember that we belong in the Kingdom and can never be lost to it. We will make it. After all, Jesus made it, and we have the same Mind in us (the Holy Spirit) that brought him to the end of the race. This is a race, however, in which we have to bring our brothers with us, rather than making them eat our dust. We need to tell them about the holy Mind that is in them—the Holy Spirit, for that will strengthen His presence in us, and His Presence is the power that draws us to the end.

The line "the ego always speaks first" is usually taken to mean that when you ask for guidance, the ego will be the first voice you hear. What it actually means is that when you interpret anything, the ego will interpret it first, and then the Holy Spirit will reinterpret it, correcting the ego's interpretation. We'll see how this works in detail in the following paragraphs.

> 4.   The ego speaks in judgment, and the Holy Spirit reverses its decision [Ur: decisions], much as a higher court [Ur: the Supreme court] has the power to reverse a lower court's decisions in [Ur: about the laws of] this world. The ego's decisions are <u>always</u> wrong, because they are based on the error [Ur: on a complete fallacy which] they were made to uphold. <u>Nothing</u> the ego perceives is interpreted correctly. Not only does the ego cite Scripture for its purpose, but it even interprets Scripture as a witness for itself. The Bible is a fearful thing in the ego's judgment [Ur: to the ego]. Perceiving it as frightening, it interprets it fearfully. Being afraid [Ur: Having made *you* afraid], you do not appeal to the Higher Court because you believe its judgment would also be <u>against</u> you.

This paragraph continues the theme of the ego speaking first. What it means is that the ego immediately renders its judgments on things, judgments that are always designed to uphold the ego and fuel its fear. It judges people. It judges situations. It judges the Bible. It even judges you.

The court metaphor here is really a great one. Our job is to not rest with the ego's verdict, for this judge is always wrong. We must appeal the verdict. If we do, our case will be immediately heard by the *real* Supreme Court (the Holy Spirit), and this court will always overturn the lower court's (the ego's) verdict. Our problem is that we don't appeal the ego's decisions. This is because the lower court judge has been telling us lies about the Supreme Court and has convinced us its decision will be against us.

> 5.   There are many examples of [Ur: We need site {sic} only a few examples to see] how the ego's interpretations are misleading [Ur: have misled you. A favorite ego quotation is "As ye sow, so shall ye reap." Another is "Vengeance is mine sayeth the Lord." Still another is "I will visit the sins of the fathers unto the third and the fourth generation." And also, "The wicked shall perish." There are many others, but if you will let the Holy Spirit reinterpret these in its own light, they will suffice.], but a few will suffice to show how the Holy Spirit can reinterpret them in His Own Light.

51

Now Jesus is going to show us the principles he has been talking about in action. He's going to show us how the ego speaks first and how the Holy Spirit reverses its verdict in the specific case of Bible interpretation.

> 6. "As ye sow, so shall ye reap" He interprets to mean what you consider worth cultivating you will cultivate in yourself. Your judgment of what is worthy makes [Ur: *does* make] it worthy for you.

"As ye sow, so shall ye reap" is a farming metaphor normally interpreted to mean that if you sow sin, you will reap punishment. If you sow seeds of evil in the world, guess what harvest you'll end up reaping? That's not how the Holy Spirit sees it, however. He sees it as a *psychological* principle about farming in your mind. It says that whatever you consider worth cultivating in the field of your mind, you will. If you sow thoughts of the ego there, you will reap its painful effects. If you sow thoughts of the Holy Spirit, you will reap His joyous effects. Thus, rather than being about God paying you back, this verse is about *you* deciding what crop you want to plant in the fertile soil of your mind.

> 7. "Vengeance is mine, sayeth the Lord" is easily reinterpreted [Ur: explained] if you remember that ideas increase only by being shared. The statement emphasizes that vengeance <u>cannot</u> be shared. Give it therefore to the Holy Spirit, Who will undo it in you because it does not <u>belong</u> in your mind, which is part of God.

"Vengeance is Mine" is usually understood to mean that we shouldn't take vengeance into our own hands, but rather leave it to God. The Holy Spirit, of course, agrees with the first part, but takes the second part one step further: Don't leave the act of vengeance to God to carry out for you; rather, give the *idea* of vengeance "to the Holy Spirit, Who will undo it in you." Vengeance is one of those ideas that can't be shared. Who will share with you the notion "You deserve my wrath"? If it could be shared, God will share it with us. But because it can't, He says "It is Mine alone," and asks us to give it to Him to be cleansed from our holy minds.

> 8. "I will visit the sins of the fathers unto the third and fourth generation," as interpreted by the ego, is particularly vicious. It becomes

merely an attempt to guarantee the ego's own survival [Ur: beyond itself]. To the Holy Spirit, the statement means that in later generations He can still reinterpret what former generations had misunderstood, and thus release the thoughts from the ability to produce fear [Ur: Actually, all it really means is that the Holy Spirit in later generations retains the power to interpret *correctly* what former generations have thought, and thus release *their* thoughts from the ability to produce fear *anywhere* in the Sonship].

The ego interprets this passage to mean that the sins of one lifetime keep calling down punishment in generation after generation, thus giving the ego that committed those sins a kind of perverse immortality (guaranteeing the ego's own survival "beyond itself"). The Holy Spirit interprets this passage almost oppositely. Here, the sins are not so much evil deeds as *mistaken beliefs*. And instead of those sins calling down God's punishment on future generations, they call down the Holy Spirit's reinterpretation. This enables future generations to correct those mistaken thoughts from their ancestors, and thus release everyone from the fearful effects of those thoughts.

> 9.   "The wicked shall perish" becomes a statement of Atonement [Ur: is merely a statement of fact], if the word "perish" is [Ur: properly understood.] understood as "be undone." Every loveless thought <u>must</u> be undone, a word the ego cannot even understand [the latter half of the sentence was composed by the editors]. To the ego, to be undone means to be destroyed [Ur: Even the word "undone" is fearful to the ego, which interprets "I am undone" as "I am destroyed."]. The ego will <u>not</u> be destroyed because it is part of <u>your</u> thought, but because it is uncreative and therefore unsharing, it <u>will</u> be reinterpreted [Ur: entirely] to release you from fear. The part of your mind that you have given to the ego will merely return to the Kingdom, where your whole mind <u>belongs</u>. [Ur: The ego is a form of *arrest*, but arrest is merely delay. It does *not* involve the concept of police at all, although the ego welcomes that interpretation.] You <u>can</u> delay the completion of the Kingdom, but you <u>cannot</u> introduce the concept of fear [Ur: *assault*] into it.

Rather than, "God shall destroy wicked souls," Jesus interprets this verse to mean, "The Holy Spirit will undo your wicked thoughts, particularly your wicked ego." The ego sees being undone as being destroyed, but in fact it will not be destroyed, but merely "reinterpreted entirely." This will free your mind to return to the Kingdom and resume its function of creating. The ego has arrested your mind, held it back from the Kingdom. The ego, as usual, sees this as your mind being under arrest for breaking God's law. But that is not how the Kingdom works.

We have now looked at all four examples of how the ego interprets certain biblical passages and how the Holy Spirit reinterprets them. Now we can see exactly what the Course means by "the ego always speaks first." The ego jumped in and interpreted every single passage fearfully. And in each case it saw the fear coming from the same source: God's punishment for our sins. The ego's judgment of things in the world is, at heart, a hidden judgment of *us*. It sees us as surrounded by danger as an implicit statement that we deserve danger, given how sinful we are.

In each case, the Holy Spirit then reinterpreted the biblical passage as being about what we might call "mental housecleaning," about the importance of what we let into our minds, and about the Holy Spirit's ability to release us from what we *shouldn't* have let into our minds. Rather than punishing us for our misdeeds, the Divine is pictured as *releasing* us from our *misthoughts*. What a difference!

All of this is not to say that the Holy Spirit's interpretation is what the biblical writers really intended. I think what they meant was closer to the ego's interpretation. But that doesn't matter. Whatever the original intent of a symbol was, the Holy Spirit can see it as a container of His truth.

> 10. You need not fear the Higher Court will condemn you [Ur: The Higher Court will not condemn you.]. It will merely dismiss the case against you. There can be no case against a child of God, and every witness to guilt in God's creations is bearing false witness to God Himself. Appeal everything you believe gladly to God's Own Higher Court, because it speaks for Him and therefore speaks truly. It will dismiss the case against you, however carefully you have built it up. The case may be fool-proof, but it is not God-proof. The Holy Spirit [Ur: The voice for God] will not hear it [Ur: at all], because He can only witness truly. His verdict will always be "thine is the Kingdom," because He was given to you to remind you of what you are.

Now we see the real heart of the Holy Spirit's reinterpretation. The

Holy Spirit is here to reverse the ego's judgment of you. He is here to reinterpret *you*.

Application: Picture yourself being led, with feet and hands in shackles, into a courtroom, God's Own Higher Court. As you are seated, you remember that you have already been convicted by a lower court of crimes against humanity and God. You, however, have appealed this conviction to God's Higher Court. This is your appeal.

In front of you stands the prosecuting attorney, the lawyer in the case against you. To your astonishment, the lawyer looks exactly like you. You realize that the lawyer is you, in a sense—the false you. It is your ego, the part of your mind that is bent on tossing you in jail and throwing away the key.

In his/her hands, the lawyer holds the case against you. He approaches the bench. Behind the bench is the judge, but the judge is simply a large radiant light. You realize that this is the Holy Spirit appearing in a form you can understand. You might see the form of Jesus in this light.

The prosecuting attorney—your ego—begins his/her case, holding the case against you in the air, declaring it fool-proof, and placing it in front of the Judge.

Out of the radiant light that is the judge, you hear a voice. Picture it sounding however you think God's Voice would sound. He speaks directly to you:

"This case may be fool-proof, but it is not God-proof.
Every witness to your guilt is bearing false witness against Me.
Although you have built this case up very carefully, I will not hear it.
I am dismissing the case against you.
My verdict is,

"THINE IS THE KINGDOM."

You hear Him say, "This court is adjourned." The case against you vanishes, as you hear a single pounding of the gavel.

11. When I said "I am come as a light into the world," I meant that I came to share the light with you. Remember my reference to the ego's

dark glass [4.IV.1], and remember also that I said, "Do not look there." It is still true that where you look to find yourself is up to you.

These sentences originally came at the beginning of the previous paragraph. Jesus has not come as a being of special illumination. He has come to share the light with us, to show us the light in us. We don't have to accept the ego's judgment of us. We don't have to look in its funhouse mirror. We can appeal to God's Higher Court to find out who we are.

> Your patience with your brother is your patience with yourself. Is not a child of God worth patience? I have shown you infinite patience because my will is that of our Father, from Whom I learned of infinite patience. His Voice was in me as It is in you, speaking for patience towards the Sonship in the Name of Its Creator.
> 12. Now you must learn [Ur: What you need to learn now is] that only infinite patience produces [Ur: *can* produce] immediate effects. This is the way in which time is exchanged for eternity. Infinite patience calls upon infinite love, and by producing results *now* it renders time unnecessary. [Ur: To say that time is temporary is merely redundant.] We have repeatedly said that time is a learning device to be abolished when it is no longer useful. The Holy Spirit, Who speaks for God in time, also knows that time is meaningless. He reminds you of this in every passing moment of time, because it is His special function to return you to eternity and remain to bless your creations there. He is the only blessing you can truly give, because He is [Ur: so] truly blessed. Because He has been given you freely by God, you must give Him as you received Him.

This is beautiful material on patience, and is rightly loved by Course students. To understand it, we have to realize that it is all about being patient with our brothers. Let me try to paraphrase it.

If you want to be patient with yourself, remember that you can only be as patient with yourself as you are with your brother. Your brother is a child of God, and isn't a child of God worth patience? What I'm asking you to give your brother is the very thing I have given you. I have shown you infinite patience. No matter how long I have to wait for you to learn your lessons, my love for you will remain completely unaffected. It was God's Voice in me that taught me to be infinitely patient towards you, and this same Voice is in you, calling you to be patient with your brothers. What you need to learn now is that only infinite patience with your brothers can instantly produce the effects you have been waiting for in them. For infinite patience is infinitely loving, and that love calls on your brothers to respond immediately. Perhaps you feel that only impatience will get them moving, but love is what will draw them to itself, and *patience* is *love*. Because infinite patience will produce results now, time becomes unnecessary. The whole purpose of time is to bring you and your brothers to the end of learning's journey, and that is exactly what infinite patience does. Its love carries you both to the end of the road.

VII. The Decision for God
Commentary by Robert Perry

1.   Do you <u>really</u> believe you can make a voice that can drown out God's? Do you really believe you can devise a thought system that can separate you from Him [Ur: His]? Do you <u>really</u> believe you can plan for your safety and joy better than He can? You need be neither careful nor careless; you need merely cast your cares upon Him because He careth for <u>you</u> [1 Peter 5:7]. You <u>are</u> His care because He loves you. His Voice reminds you always that all hope is yours <u>because</u> of His care. You <u>cannot</u> choose to escape His care because that is not His Will, but you <u>can</u> choose to accept His care and use the infinite power <u>of</u> His care for all those He created <u>by</u> it.

Application: When Jesus asks us questions like those that open this paragraph, he really wants us to ask them of ourselves. So let's do that. Ask each question separately, and then give yourself time to ponder your answer.

> *Do I really believe I can make a voice that can drown out God's?*
> *Do I really believe I can devise a thought system that can separate me from Him?*
> *Do I really believe I can plan for my safety and joy better than He can?*

Application: The final sentences of this paragraph are so beautiful. I'd like to put them in first person (with some minor editing) and have us read them in that form:

> *I need be neither careful nor careless;*
> *I need merely cast my cares upon Him because He careth for me.*
> *I am His care because He loves me.*
> *All hope is mine because of His care.*
> *I cannot escape His care because that is not His Will,*
> *but I can choose to accept His care*

and use the infinite power of His care to serve all those He created
   by it.

2.   There have been many healers who did not heal themselves. They
have not moved mountains by their faith because their faith was not
<u>whole</u>. Some of them have healed the sick at times, but they have not
raised the dead. Unless the healer heals <u>himself,</u> he cannot [Ur: does
not] believe that there is no order of difficulty in miracles. He has not
learned that <u>every</u> mind God created is equally worthy of being healed
because <u>God created it whole</u>. You are merely asked to return to God
the mind as <u>He</u> created it. He asks you only for what He gave, knowing
that this giving will heal <u>you</u>. Sanity <u>is</u> wholeness, and the sanity of
your brothers <u>is</u> yours.

This is the Course's first discussion of the unhealed healer. This is
the healer who believes healing applies to others but not to himself. The
effects of this one exclusion are quite dramatic. It means he believes in
an order of difficulty in miracles; he believes miracles are harder when
it comes to him because he is not "equally worthy of being healed." It
means his faith is "not whole," for it leaves him out. For these reasons,
he cannot do the really big miracles. He cannot move mountains. He
cannot raise the dead. What he needs to do is give his mind back into the
Hands of God, which means acknowledge his mind as it really is in truth.
This will make him a healed healer.

3.   Why should you listen to the endless insane calls you think are
made upon you, when you can know [Ur: when you *know*] the Voice
for God is in you? God commended His Spirit to you, and asks that you
commend yours to Him. He wills to keep it in perfect peace, because
you are of one mind and spirit with Him. Excluding yourself from
the Atonement is the ego's last-ditch defense of its own existence. It
reflects both the ego's need to separate, and your willingness to side
with its separateness. This willingness means that <u>you do not want to
be healed</u>. [Ur: When I told Bill that there is "just one more thing," he
heard me very well. I hope he will hear me as well now. His intelligent
mis-hearing of "river" as "rivet" showed that, even though he wanted
release, he was not able to cope with it at the time.]

God's Voice is in us, calling to give our mind back to Him, calling us to commend our spirit to Him, calling us to give ourselves to the Atonement and return to perfect peace. Yet what are we doing? We are holding ourselves apart from the Atonement, thinking that surely it doesn't apply to us. Instead of listening to God's Call, we are running around like a crazy person, ordered to and fro by the "endless insane calls" that come to us from the world. As a result, we don't have time to turn aside and listen to God's Voice. Though hard to face, what this means is that we don't want to be healed. It means we want to remain an unhealed healer.

The final part refers to a Freudian slip Bill made, apparently in hearing the phrase—presumably from Jesus—"one more river." Based on the subtle hints in the Urtext, my guess is that Jesus said something like "There is just one more river that must be dealt with on the way to God." (Later, Jesus explained that this "one more river" related to the sex impulse.) Bill, however, heard "rivet" instead of "river." Jesus said this slip actually came not from the ego-based unconscious but from the superconscious, and "was an expression of a Soul gaining enough strength to request freedom from prison. It will ultimately *demand* it." Perhaps in the mindset of the slip, the sentence meant, "There is just one more rivet to be removed before you're out of prison." I don't know. But now Jesus is saying that the slip had a negative side as well as a positive one. The positive side was that Bill's Soul was requesting freedom from prison. The negative side was that he wasn't able to cope with freedom at that time. If he had been, he would have *demanded* it. There wouldn't have been even *one* rivet left.

> 4.   But the time is now. You have not been asked to work out the plan of salvation yourself because, as I told you before, the remedy could not be of your making. God Himself gave you the perfect Correction for everything you made that is not in accord with His holy Will. I am making [Ur: I have made] His plan perfectly explicit to you, and will also tell [Ur: have also told] you of your part in it, and how urgent it is to fulfill it. [Ur: There is time for delay, but there need not be.] God weeps at the "sacrifice" of His children who believe they are lost to Him. [Ur: The "one more thing" that Bill must learn is merely that he is *not* the one more. He is both *one* and *at one*. If he will learn this *now*, he will be willing in accord with the last judgment, which is

really only the Biblical reminder of the inevitability of self-*inclusion*. This is what "Physician, heal thyself" really means. Bill has frequently observed for *himself* that this is hard to do. He has, however, been perfectly aware of *just* what *you* should do about it. You might ask him for me whether he does not think he might be dissociating *himself* from his own awareness, since he is so clear about the remedy for *you*. You might also remind him that to whatever extent he separates himself from you, he is separating himself from *me*. This *is* a collaborative venture. Let me therefore return his own ideas to him, so that you can share them and thus help each other to help me.]

This paragraph is clearly addressed to Bill. When he made his Freudian slip, he wasn't ready to cope with freedom, but that was weeks before this point. Now is the time to lay hold of that freedom. ("But the time is now.") God has given Bill "the perfect Correction" for all of the beliefs that made up the walls of his prison. He needs to accept this Correction because God urgently needs him to take his place in the Great Crusade to bring correction to the whole world. He can delay, but why would he want to? God yearns to alleviate the pain of His children who believe that they will never belong to Him again.

What does Bill need to do? He needs to overcome the fallacy of the unhealed healer. "The 'one more thing' that Bill must learn is merely that he is *not* the one more"—he is not the exception to the universal rule of healing. He is not the exception to the Kingdom; he is part of it, one with it. He needs, in other words, to apply the old adage "Physician, heal thyself." This looks too hard to him. What should he do? What is the remedy? It all seems beyond him. Yet Jesus reminds Bill that he is totally clear what *Helen* should do in this regard. This is the classic unhealed healer scenario, isn't it? Who of us can't relate to knowing what someone else should do but being totally at a loss when it comes to our own healing? The fact that he is so clear about the remedy for Helen shows that he can see the remedy, he just chooses to hold himself apart from it. He is dissociating himself from his own awareness. Jesus is calling him to snap out of it.

5.   [Ur: But let me first remind you of something I told you myself.] Whenever you are not wholly joyous, it is because you have reacted with a lack of love to one of God's creations [Ur: to some Soul which

61

God created]. Perceiving this as "sin" you become defensive because you <u>expect attack</u>. The decision to react in this way is <u>yours,</u> and can therefore be undone. It <u>cannot</u> be undone by repentance in the usual sense, because this implies guilt. If you allow yourself to feel guilty, you will reinforce the error rather than allow it to be undone <u>for</u> you.

Jesus here is reminding us of what he said back in "This Need Not Be" (4.IV):

When your mood tells you that you have willed wrongly, and this is so whenever you are not joyous, then *know* this need not be. In every case you have thought wrongly about some Soul that God created, and are perceiving images your ego makes in a darkened glass. (T-4.IV.2:2-3 Urtext version)

In the current paragraph, he is going into more detail about how perceiving someone lovelessly leads to lack of joy: You view your judgmental perception of this person as a sin, so you then expect to be attacked as the just recompense for your sinfulness. This, of course, is not a joyous state. Now here's the remarkable thing: This is what is going on *whenever* you are not wholly joyous. In every case, the real cause is not *their* loveless treatment of *you*, but *your* loveless perception of *them*. All lack of joy, then, comes down to pangs of conscience over unkind perception, over those scraps of meanness.

Of course, since your lack of joy comes down to guilt, trying to solve things through repenting in the sense of feeling guilty just reinforces the whole scenario.

6. Decision [Ur: Decisions] <u>cannot</u> be difficult. This is obvious, if you realize that you must <u>already</u> have decided <u>not</u> to be wholly joyous if that is how you feel. Therefore, the first step in the undoing is to recognize that <u>you actively decided wrongly,</u> <u>but can as actively decide otherwise</u>. Be very firm with yourself in this, and keep yourself fully aware that the <u>undoing</u> process, which does <u>not</u> come from you, is nevertheless <u>within</u> you because God placed it there. <u>Your</u> part is merely to return your thinking to the point at which the error was made, and give it over to the Atonement in peace. Say this to yourself [Ur: Say to yourselves the following,] as sincerely as you can, remembering that the Holy Spirit will respond fully to your slightest invitation:

> *I must have decided wrongly, because I am <u>not</u> at peace.*
> *I made the decision myself, but I can also decide otherwise.*
> *I want [Ur: **will**] to decide otherwise, because I **want** to be at peace.*
> *I do <u>not</u> feel guilty, because the Holy Spirit will undo all the consequences of my wrong decision <u>if I will let Him</u>.*
> *I choose [Ur: **will**] to let Him, by allowing Him to decide for God for me.*

This is an extremely powerful practice. I remember that Marianne Williamson used to call it "a page 83" (which is where it appeared in the First Edition). I highly recommend memorizing it. However, its specific meaning is easy to miss, unless you read the preceding two paragraphs carefully. Let me restate this important practice in a way that clarifies what it means. Before you read my restatement, however, choose someone to apply it to, someone whom you have perceived as dragging down your mood.

> *I must have decided to see [name] unlovingly, because I am not wholly joyous. My mood must be dragged down by the dispiriting influence of guilt.*
> *I actively decided wrongly, but I can just as actively decide otherwise. Since I made one decision I can surely make another.*
> *I **will** to make another decision, because I want my mood to be joyous. I am very firm with myself about this.*
> *I do not feel guilty (which will only reinforce the problem anyway), because if I let the Holy Spirit undo my unloving perception of [name], then He will also undo whatever harm that perception caused him/her.*
> *I will to let Him. I let Him heal my unloving perception of this brother. Holy Spirit, decide for me how I will see [name]. Let me see him/her through Your eyes.*

Commentaries on Chapter 6

THE LESSONS
OF LOVE

Introduction
Commentary by Robert Perry

1.   The relationship of anger to attack is obvious, but the relationship [Ur: inevitable association] of anger to <u>fear</u> is not always so apparent. Anger <u>always</u> involves <u>projection of separation</u>, which must ultimately be accepted as [Ur: entirely] one's own responsibility, rather than being blamed on others [this final phrase was apparently composed by the editors]. Anger cannot occur unless you believe that you have <u>been</u> attacked, that your attack is <u>justified</u> in return [Ur: the attack {on you} was justified], and that you are in no way responsible for it [the attack on you]. Given these three wholly irrational premises, the equally irrational conclusion that a brother is worthy of attack rather than of love must follow. What can be expected from insane premises <u>except</u> an insane conclusion? The way to undo an insane conclusion is to consider the sanity of the premises on which it rests. You cannot *be* attacked, attack *has* no justification, and you *are* responsible for what you believe.

Editing changes have unfortunately changed the original meaning of this paragraph. It begins by saying we all understand how anger leads to attack, but we probably don't understand how anger leads to fear. Here's how: To begin with, anger is always an act of projection—projecting onto others the responsibility for your separated condition, your condition of being alone and deprived. You yourself caused this condition, but then you projected this causation onto others. You see them as attacking you (first premise). You unconsciously see their attack as justified (second premise)—otherwise, why would you give it any power? And you see their attack as an objective fact, rather than a belief chosen by you (third premise). In this view, your fear of them is totally justified, and this is how anger/projection leads to fear. In this view, your attack on them is totally justified as well. Indeed, the idea that attack is justified is the only conclusion one can derive from those three premises.

Yet the paragraph ends by saying that this conclusion must be insane because all three premises are irrational. First, no one can attack you. (We'll see why later.) Second, their attack on you is totally unjustified—

so why give it any power? And third, you—not your attacker—are responsible for your belief that you have been attacked. The real conclusion? This person deserves only love, not attack.

> 2.   You have been asked to take me as your model for learning, since [Ur: and we have often said that] an extreme example is a particularly helpful learning device. <u>Everyone</u> teaches, and teaches all the time. This is a responsibility you inevitably assume the moment you accept any premise at all, and <u>no one</u> can organize his life without some [Ur: *any*] thought system. Once you have developed a thought system of any kind, you live by it and teach it. Your capacity for allegiance to a thought system may be misplaced, but it is still a form of faith and can be redirected. [Ur: You have been chosen to teach the Atonement precisely *because* you have been *extreme* examples of allegiance to your thought systems, and therefore have developed the capacity *for* allegiance. It has indeed been misplaced. Bill had become an outstanding example of allegiance to apathy, and you have become a startling example of fidelity to variability. But this *is* a form of faith, which you yourselves had grown willing to redirect. You cannot doubt the *strength* of your devotion when you consider how faithfully you observed it. It was quite evident that you had *already* developed the ability to follow a better model, if you could *accept* it.]

The three premises and their inevitable conclusion are basic pillars of our thought system. Once we embrace this thought system, we can't help but teach it, with our every word and deed. We can't help but act as enthusiastic salesmen for it in every interaction. Perhaps we thought we could keep such ego-based beliefs to ourselves, but we can't.

Jesus stands forth as a model for a different thought system. What is great about adopting him as a model is that he is such an extreme example. Extreme examples are wonderful, because even if they pull you only partway toward them, they pull you far from where you are now.

We may feel too committed to our current thought system, but that very commitment is a power we have employed and can redirect. We can give it to a whole new thought system. This is Jesus' point about Helen and Bill. Bill was "an outstanding example of allegiance to apathy," while Helen was "a startling example of fidelity to variability." Notice the irony in being zealously committed to apathy and unwaveringly faithful to variability! It's a situation that cries out for solution, and this solution was in their power. Having developed the capacity for allegiance, they could redirect it by following a better model. And so can we.

I. The Message of the Crucifixion
Commentary by Robert Perry

1. For learning purposes, let us consider the crucifixion again [this sentence appears to have been composed by the editors]. I did not dwell on it [Ur: the crucifixion] before because of the [Ur: its] fearful connotations you may associate with it ["you may associate with it" was added by the editors]. The only emphasis laid upon it so far has been that it was <u>not</u> a form of punishment. Nothing, however, can be [Ur: But we know that nothing can be really] explained in negative terms only. There is a positive interpretation of the crucifixion that is wholly devoid of fear, and therefore wholly benign in what it teaches, if it is properly understood.

Now he launches into his reconsideration of the crucifixion. He discussed it quite passionately in the opening paragraphs of "Atonement Without Sacrifice" (3.I). There, however, all he was doing was negating its "fearful connotations." He was saying the crucifixion was not a case of him taking on the punishment for humanity's sins to appease an angry God. I can never get over the irony of us spending centuries tearfully thanking Jesus for his great sacrifice on our behalf, and then, after all that time, he steps forward and calmly states that we have gotten it all wrong.

All he did in that previous discussion, however, was explain what the crucifixion did *not* mean. Now, having laid that groundwork, he is ready to tell us what it *did* mean.

2. The crucifixion is nothing more than an extreme example. Its value, like the value of any teaching device, lies solely in the kind of learning it facilitates. It can be, and has been, misunderstood. This is only because the fearful are apt to perceive fearfully. I have already told you that you can always call on me to share my decision, and thus <u>make it stronger</u> [5.II.11:1]. I have also told you that the crucifixion was the last useless [Ur: foolish] journey the Sonship need take, and that it represents [Ur: it should means {sic}] <u>release</u> from fear to anyone who understands it [4.In.3:1-2]. While I emphasized only the resurrection before, the purpose of the crucifixion and how it actually

70

led to the resurrection was not clarified then. Nevertheless, it has a definite contribution to make to your own life, and if you will consider it <u>without</u> fear, it will help you understand your own role as a teacher.

Already the difference between his way of looking at the crucifixion and the traditional way is apparent. In the traditional view, the crucifixion was a one-time transaction with God that paid for mankind's sins. Here, however, the crucifixion is "nothing more than an extreme example." He also calls it a "teaching device." Those two phrases imply a basic orientation to the crucifixion, one that is fundamentally different than the traditional view.

Let's look at that difference. Rather than being a ritualistic transaction with God designed to change God's Mind, the crucifixion had nothing to do with God. It was a public display put on for us, designed to change *our* minds. It was not some magical act meant to alter our status in God's eyes. It was an example we were meant to follow, a teaching device we were meant to learn from. It represented a decision we were meant to share.

Yet our ego has done with it exactly what it did with those Bible verses in 5.VI. It has interpreted it fearfully, as evidence of a God Who wants to punish us for our sins. On this issue, the ego has indeed spoken first. But now the Holy Spirit offers us another interpretation.

> 3.   You have probably [Ur: You have] reacted for years <u>as if</u> you were being crucified. This is a marked tendency of the separated, who <u>always</u> refuse to consider what they have done to <u>themselves</u>. Projection means anger, anger fosters assault, and assault promotes fear. The real meaning of the crucifixion lies in the *apparent* intensity of the assault of some of the Sons of God upon another [Ur: a brother]. This, of course, is impossible, and must be fully understood *as* impossible. Otherwise, [Ur: In fact, unless it *is* fully understood as *only* that,] I cannot serve as a [Ur: real] model for learning.

We really need to see this paragraph as another version of the discussion in the first paragraph of the Introduction. We have projected onto others the responsibility for our own separated condition. This angry act of blame provokes others to assault us, and interprets them as doing so ("anger fosters assault"). And this makes us afraid ("assault promotes fear"). We now seem to be surrounded by people who are crucifying us. Clearly they are responsible for our miserable condition. Yet we are just assigning them the blame for what we have done to ourselves.

The crucifixion was designed to address this very situation. It was designed to be an extreme mirror of the condition we already see ourselves in: one person surrounded by a ring of vicious attackers. In this utterly familiar situation, Jesus modeled a different response, one that sees being assaulted as actually *impossible*. This is how we must see Jesus as our model. Rather than emulating his choice to let himself be crucified for a higher good, we need to emulate his choice to see himself as *invulnerable* to crucifixion.

> 4.   Assault can ultimately be made <u>only</u> on the body. There is little doubt that one <u>body</u> can assault another, and can even destroy it. Yet if destruction <u>itself</u> is impossible, <u>anything</u> that is destructible cannot be real. Its destruction, therefore, does <u>not</u> justify anger. To the extent to which you believe that it <u>does</u>, you are accepting false premises and <u>teaching them to others</u>. The message the crucifixion was intended to teach was that it is not necessary to perceive <u>any</u> form of assault in persecution, because you cannot *be* persecuted. If you respond with anger, you <u>must</u> be equating yourself with the destructible, and are therefore regarding yourself insanely.

If you are a mind, formless and without boundary, how can you be attacked? Only a form can be attacked and wounded. An egg is easy to crush, but how can you crush something that has no form? This is why only the body can be assaulted. You as a mind are invulnerable.

Yet the body is not real, and so its destruction cannot be real, either. "Its destruction, therefore, does not justify anger." What a line! This means that you are not justified in getting even a little annoyed with someone who is murdering your body. If you think you are, then you are believing that you *are* a body, which means you are "regarding yourself insanely" and teaching this insanity to others. We, of course, have made teaching this into our full-time job.

The crucifixion was designed to show us a radical alternative. Jesus realized that he was not a body and that his mind was unassailable. And so, even as his body was being murdered, from his perspective he was not being assaulted. Nothing was being done to *him*.

5.   I have made it perfectly clear that I am like you and you are like me, but our fundamental equality can be demonstrated only through joint decision. You are free to perceive yourself as persecuted if you choose. When you <u>do</u> choose to react that way, however, you might remember that I <u>was</u> persecuted as the world judges, and did not share this evaluation for myself. And because I did not share it, I did <u>not</u> strengthen it. I therefore offered a <u>different</u> interpretation of attack, and one which I want to share with you. If you will <u>believe</u> it, you will help me <u>teach</u> it.

Jesus has told you that you and he are equals, but this equality only comes out when you make the same decision. How can you do that? When you feel persecuted, remember what he demonstrated in the crucifixion. Remember that he did not perceive himself as being persecuted. If you can share this perception, you will undermine the global belief in vulnerability to attack, just as he did ("I did not strengthen it"). And you will help him teach the world the real message of the crucifixion: that we are all immune to attack.

Application: Think of a situation in which you feel persecuted or attacked in some way. Now dwell on these lines:

Let me remember what Jesus demonstrated in the crucifixion.
Like him, I will refuse to see myself as being attacked
I will join him in his decision and thereby strengthen it.
I will help him teach the world that we are all immune to attack.

6.   As I have said before, "As you teach so shall you learn." If you react as if you are persecuted, you <u>are</u> teaching persecution. This is not a lesson a Son of God should <u>want</u> to teach if he is to realize [learn] his own salvation. Rather, teach your own perfect immunity, which <u>is</u> the truth in you, and realize [Ur: *know*] that it cannot *be* assailed. Do not try to protect it yourself, or you are believing that it <u>is</u> assailable. You are not asked to <u>be</u> crucified, which [Ur: because that] was part of my own teaching contribution. You are merely asked to follow my example in the face of much less extreme temptations to misperceive, and <u>not</u> to accept them as false justifications for anger. There can <u>be</u> no justification for the unjustifiable. Do not believe there is, and do not <u>teach</u> that there is. Remember always that what you believe you will teach. Believe with me, and we will become equal as teachers.

Notice the recurring trio of *believe* then *teach* then *learn*.

"Believe with me." Believe with him that you are perfectly immune and therefore that you never have any cause for anger. In how you see your tiny crucifixions each day, follow the example he laid down in his vastly more extreme crucifixion.

"Teach your own perfect immunity." Teach others your belief that you can't be attacked. How? By being free of anger in the face of attack, and by being defenseless, by refusing to protect yourself. If you believe with Jesus, you can be every bit as powerful a teacher as him ("we will become equal as teachers"). What a promise!

Learn: "As you teach so shall you learn." If you teach that you are perfectly immune, you will learn that your being transcends the threats of time and space. You will learn you are saved.

> 7. <u>Your</u> resurrection is your reawakening. I am the model for rebirth, but rebirth itself is merely the dawning on your mind of what is already in it. God placed it there Himself, and so it is true forever. I believed in it, and therefore accepted it as true [Ur: made it true forever] for me. Help me to teach it to our brothers in the name of the Kingdom of God, but first believe that it is true for you, or you will teach amiss. My brothers slept during the so-called "agony in the garden," but I could not be angry with them because I knew I could not *be* abandoned. [Ur: Peter swore he would never deny me, but he did so three times. It should be noted that he did offer to defend me with the sword, which I naturally refused, not being at all in need of bodily protection.]

This section is really about how Jesus got to the resurrection and how we can get there. Resurrection is rising to a life that is above all the damaging winds of this world. Resurrection is the full realization of that perfectly immune core in you. It is "the dawning on your mind of what is already in it." Jesus needs you to join him in teaching everyone that this liberating invulnerability lies in each of us. But to teach it, you have to believe it yourself. For you teach it most powerfully not by your words but by your example, just as he taught it by his.

The final part of the paragraph shows that he taught it not just in the crucifixion, but also in the events leading up to the crucifixion. He taught it in the garden of Gethsemane, by not being in agony over the fate that awaited him. He knew that fate was merely a teaching demonstration to put on for his brothers. He taught it in that same garden by not being angry with his disciples for abandoning him. He knew he couldn't be abandoned. And he taught it by refusing Peter's offer to protect him with a sword. He knew that protecting his body was unnecessary, since his reality was eternally safe.

> 8.   I am sorry when my brothers do not share my decision to hear [Ur: (and be)] only one Voice, because it weakens them as teachers and as learners. Yet I know they cannot really betray themselves or me, and that it is still on them that I must build my church. There is no choice in this, because only you can be the foundation of God's church. A church is where an altar is, and the presence of the altar is what makes the church holy [Ur: makes it a church]. A church that does not inspire love has a hidden altar that is not serving the purpose for which God intended it. I must found His church on you, because those who [Ur: you, who] accept me as a model are literally my disciples. Disciples are followers, and [Ur: but] if the model they follow has chosen to save them pain in all respects, they are [Ur: probably] unwise not to follow him.

We need to see the opening remarks as following directly on his comments about the disciples abandoning him in the garden of Gethsemane and Peter denying him during the trial. His response is beautiful: "I'm sorry when they do that—not for my sake, but for their sake, because it weakens them. Yet the fact remains that they cannot really betray me. And the fact remains that I still depend on them to be the foundation of my church." Can you sense the profound forgiveness in these words?

The comments about building his church are fascinating. He is saying that the real foundation of his church must be followers who have a true inner devotion (altars symbolize our inner devotion) to following him as their model. Then he switches from the disciples being this foundation to Helen and Bill being this foundation (or presumably part of this foundation).

Yet the Christian church is not founded on devotion to following him as our model, but on belief in him as our savior. And Helen and Bill were not part of the Christian church and were certainly not about to become foundation stones in it. What he is calling "my church" must therefore *not* be the Christian church. His church must be an invisible community, a community without walls, composed of those who are really attempting to follow his teachings. Many of these, I'm sure, are within the walls of the Christian church, and many, no doubt, are on the outside. Are we part of this church? He is calling us not only to join it, but to be pillars of it.

> 9.   I elected, [Ur: both] for your sake <u>and</u> mine, to demonstrate that the most outrageous assault, as judged by the ego, does [Ur: did] not matter. As the world judges these things, but <u>not</u> as God knows them, I was betrayed, abandoned, beaten, torn, and finally killed. It was clear that this was only because of the projection of others onto me, since I had not harmed anyone and had healed many.

Here is a beautiful encapsulation of the message of the crucifixion: "to demonstrate that the most outrageous assault...does not matter." Later, Jesus will say to us: "*Recognize what does not matter*, and if your brothers ask you for something 'outrageous,' do it *because* it does not matter" (T-12.III.4:1). Has it occurred to us that the crucifixion was the ultimate example of this teaching?

Notice the comment about projection. Those who crucified him were engaging in the very process he mentioned earlier (see In.1 and I.3). Their own angry projection led them to interpret Jesus as attacking them, as a threat to them, as someone to be feared, even though nothing of the kind was true.

> 10.   We are still equal as learners, although we do not need to have equal experiences. The Holy Spirit is glad when you can learn from mine, and [Ur: when you can learn enough from *mine* to] be reawakened by them. That is [Ur; was] their only purpose, and that is the only way in which I can be perceived as the way, the truth and the life. When you hear only one Voice you are never called on to sacrifice. On the contrary, by being able [Ur: by enabling *yourselves*] to hear the Holy Spirit in others you can learn from their experiences, and can gain from them <u>without</u> experiencing them directly yourself. That is because the Holy Spirit <u>is</u> one, and anyone who listens is inevitably led to demonstrate His way for <u>all</u>.

Even though we are equal to him as learners, we don't need to undergo all the experiences that he himself learned from. Thank God! That last one was a doozy.

I often get the impression in New Age circles that our own personal experience is paramount, yet here Jesus takes a very different angle. If others are following the Holy Spirit and demonstrating His way, and if we are willing to hear the Holy Spirit in them, then we can learn from their experiences without having to have those experiences ourselves. Notice how greatly this expands our learning opportunities!

This, says Jesus, is the only value of his experiences. They weren't rituals that magically tipped the cosmic scales. They were simply public demonstrations we could all observe and learn from. He is the way, the truth, and the life not because his blood tore the curtain in two and opened up access to God, but merely because he was such an effective demonstrator.

> 11. You are not persecuted, nor was I. You are not asked to repeat my experiences [Ur: experience] because the Holy Spirit, Whom we <u>share</u>, makes this unnecessary. To use my experiences constructively, however, you must still follow my example in how to perceive them. My brothers and yours are constantly engaged in justifying the unjustifiable. My one lesson, which I must teach as I learned it, is that no perception that is out of accord with the judgment of the Holy Spirit <u>can</u> be justified. I undertook to show this was true in an [Ur: a very] extreme case, merely because it would serve as a good teaching aid to those whose temptation to give in to anger and assault would not be so extreme. I will with God [Ur: I will, with God Himself,] that none of His Sons should suffer.

We can learn from Jesus' experiences, but to do this, we have to see them like he did. We need to see the crucifixion not as a call to martyrdom, but as a demonstration that even under the most extreme persecution, anger and retaliation are not justified because the persecution is not real.

He keeps mentioning the extremity of it, calling it "an extreme example" (2:1), "the most outrageous assault, as judged by the ego" (9:1), and "a very extreme case," and mentioning the "*apparent* intensity of the assault" (3:4). Why all this focus on the extremity of it? Quite simply, it is because we think these principles stop applying at a certain level of extremity. His goal was to show us that they still apply even at the level of the most extreme attack imaginable. And if they apply at that level, then surely they must apply at the far milder levels we face. Getting across this very message was the whole point of the crucifixion.

> 12. The crucifixion <u>cannot</u> be shared because it is the symbol of projection, but the resurrection <u>is</u> the symbol of sharing because the reawakening of every Son of God is necessary to enable the Sonship to know its wholeness. Only this <u>is</u> knowledge.

I have puzzled over this brief paragraph for years. In trying to solve its puzzle I have collected a number of related passages (T-7.VIII.3:2; T-11.VI.2:1, 4:9; T-19.IV(D).17:5; T-20.I.2:9). Here is what I have come up with thus far:

"Do not join me in the crucifixion, because the whole point of the crucifixion was that it was a solitary experience, in which others stood on one side and I stood on the other, with them projecting blame onto me, punishing me, and inducing me to undergo the private experience of death. How can you join me in a situation in which, by its very nature, I was separate and alone?

"But do join me in the resurrection, because resurrection is an experience that ultimately all must enter into. Everyone must resurrect— must awaken—for the Sonship to know its wholeness. And the Sonship must know its wholeness, for only that *is* knowledge."

> 13. The message of the crucifixion is [Ur: very simple and] perfectly clear:

> *Teach only love, for that is what you are.*

We know this line already, perhaps because *Teach Only Love* was the title of one of Jerry Jampolsky's books. But did we realize that this is the Course's interpretation of the *crucifixion*? And what an original interpretation! Only Jesus could come up with something this original. We look at the crucifixion and our eyes are rooted on the blood and guts. Yet he looks at the same thing and sees only his loving response in the face of the blood and guts.

He has prepared us for this interpretation, by saying that anger is insane even when the body is destroyed, by saying that the truth in us is unassailable, by saying that our responses teach the thought system behind them, and by saying that nothing out of accord with the Holy Spirit is justified no matter how extreme the temptation. Now he puts all of this in a new, condensed form: No matter how extreme the attack appears to be, teach *only* love, for that is the truth in you.

In one breath, he has moved the crucifixion from being a distant mythological act for the sake of abstruse theological consequences, to being a radical challenge to our whole response to an attacking world. In the face of every attack, we should remember these immortal words: "I will teach *only* love, for that is what I am."

> 14. If you interpret the crucifixion in any other way, you are using it as a weapon for assault rather than as the call for peace for which it was intended. The Apostles often misunderstood it, and [Ur: always] for the same reason that anyone misunderstands it [Ur: that makes anyone misunderstand anything]. Their own imperfect love made them vulnerable to projection, and out of their own fear they spoke of the "wrath of God" as His <u>retaliatory</u> weapon. Nor could they speak of the crucifixion entirely without anger, because their [Ur: own] sense of guilt had made them angry.

The traditional interpretation of the crucifixion ends up taking what was intended as a call for peace and using it as a weapon of assault. And isn't that what it has become—an assault on the Jews who were deemed responsible, an assault on the martyrs who felt called to emulate Jesus, and an assault on sinful humanity whose sins required Jesus to undergo this horrible death?

His own disciples misinterpreted, he says, yet did so for the same reason the crucifiers saw Jesus as a threat (9:3), for the same reason we interpret Bible passages fearfully (5.VI.4-9), for the same reason any of us misinterprets anything. We take our own act of throwing God away and project this onto the world. Now we see the world taking God from us. (This is presumably why the disciples were angry; the world had taken away the light of their lives.) And we see the world as delivering our just deserts; we see its attacks as vehicles of divine justice.

> 15. These are some of the [Ur: There are two glaring examples] examples of upside-down thinking in the New Testament, although its gospel is really [Ur: whose whole Gospel is] only the message of love.

[Ur: These are not at all like the several slips into impatience which I made, because I had learned the Atonement prayer, which I also came to teach, too well to engage in upside down thinking myself.] If the Apostles had not felt guilty, they never could have quoted me as saying, "I come not to bring peace but a sword." This is clearly the opposite of everything I taught. Nor could they have described my reactions to Judas as they did, if they had really understood me. I could not [Ur: They could not have believed that I could] have said, "Betrayest thou the Son of Man with a kiss?" unless I believed in betrayal. The whole message of the crucifixion was simply that I did not. The "punishment" I was said to have called forth upon Judas was a similar mistake [Ur: reversal]. Judas was my brother and a Son of God, as much a part of the Sonship as myself. Was it likely that I would condemn him when I was ready to demonstrate that condemnation is impossible?

To appreciate this paragraph, it helps to divide it up into two major points. The first point is that Jesus did not say "I come not to bring peace but a sword," and that he did not see Judas as betraying him. He did not condemn Judas or call down punishment on him. Instead, he saw Judas as his beloved brother, as much a Son of God as Jesus himself. (What a statement!)

The second point is that the Apostles mistakenly attributed these threatening, punitive things to Jesus because of the process of projection we have already discussed. As we saw in discussing those biblical passages, when we feel guilty, we unconsciously interpret things in the world as vehicles of divine retribution. If, then, the disciples saw Jesus as divine, how else would their guilt interpret his actions?

I really appreciate Jesus' comments about his own "slips into impatience." He says that he had several such slips, presumably over people not getting it more quickly. But he also characterizes these as mere slips, saying that he had come too far to engage in genuine upside down thinking. He handles his own ego with the same objectivity he handles that of others, which of course is the very mark of egolessness.

16. [Ur: I am very grateful to the Apostles for their teaching, and fully aware of the extent of their devotion to me. But] As you read the teachings of the Apostles, remember that I told them myself that there was much they would understand later, because they were not wholly ready to follow me at the time. [Ur: I emphasize this only

because] I do not want you to allow <u>any</u> fear to enter into the thought system toward which I am guiding you. I do <u>not</u> call for martyrs but for <u>teachers</u>. [Ur: Bill is an outstanding example of this confusion, and has literally believed for years that teaching *is* martyrdom. This is because he thought, and still thinks at times, that teaching leads to crucifixion rather than to re-awakening. The upside down nature of this association is so obvious that he could only have made it *because* he felt guilty.] No one is punished for sins, and the Sons of God are not sinners. <u>Any</u> concept of punishment involves the projection of blame, and <u>reinforces</u> the idea that blame is justified. The result [Ur: The behavior that results] is a <u>lesson in blame</u>, for [Ur: just as] all behavior teaches the beliefs that motivate it. The crucifixion was the result of [Ur: was a complex of behaviors arising out of] clearly opposed thought systems; [Ur: As such, it is] the perfect symbol of the "conflict" between the ego and the Son of God. This conflict seems just as real now, and its lessons must be learned now as well as then. [Ur: It was as much intrapersonal as interpersonal then, just as it is now, and it is still just as real. But *because* it is just as real now, its lesson, too, has equal reality *when it is learned*.]

Jesus is clearly warning us here that the Apostles didn't fully understand him, and that we therefore need to exercise discernment in reading their teachings (which I assume refers to the New Testament). Otherwise, we may mix their fear into the new thought system he is teaching us. (We can extend this to our reading of any spiritual teaching, I believe) He is not asking us to be martyrs, but teachers.

Bill had confused these two. He thought teaching was martyrdom, because his guilt made him think God would use his students to enact the crucifixion he deserved. The martyr has the same basic assumption; he just responds to it differently. Whereas Bill sought to escape his punishment, the martyr seeks it out, in the belief he can only be pure again by voluntarily facing the music. Again and again Jesus focuses on this mindset. He points it out in Bill, in the disciples, in the martyr, in those who crucified him. This mindset says, "I project onto you my decision to throw God away. Consequently, I see you as to blame for my God-deprived condition and/or I see you as the instrument by which God punishes me."

The crucifixion represented the meeting of this mindset with Jesus' completely opposite mindset. His mindset said, "Since my reality is unassailable, I cannot be hurt by you. Since my reality is love, my only natural response is to extend love to you." These two thought systems met in the crucifixion, but they meet every day inside of us. Which will we choose?

> 17. I do not need gratitude [Ur: any more than I needed protection.], but you need to develop your weakened ability to be grateful, or you cannot appreciate God. He does not need your appreciation, but *you* do. You cannot love what you do not appreciate, for [Ur: and] fear makes appreciation impossible. When you are afraid of what you are you do not appreciate it, and will therefore reject it. As a result, you will teach rejection.

I have a hard time following the logic here. Let me try to recreate it to the best of my ability:

Jesus does not need your gratitude for the crucifixion, but you need to develop the capacity to be grateful, so you can appreciate God. He does not need your appreciation; *you* need it, and as you give it to Him, you simultaneously give it to yourself, your real Self. And as you appreciate yourself, you will then love yourself. Right now, you are afraid of yourself, which leads to not appreciating yourself, which leads to rejecting yourself. And when you reject yourself, you will reject others. "You will teach rejection."

> 18. The power of the Sons of God is present [Ur: operating] all the time, because they were created as creators. Their influence on each other is without limit, and must be used for their joint salvation. Each one must learn to teach that all forms of rejection are [Ur: utterly] meaningless. The separation is the notion of rejection. As long as you teach this you will [Ur: *you* still] believe it. This is not as God thinks, and you must think as He thinks if you are to know Him again.

This paragraph says what the whole section has implied: Don't just pay attention to what you believe. Pay attention as well to what you *teach*. For as a Son of God, you are incredibly powerful, and your influence on the other Sons of God "is without limit." If you teach rejection, you will reinforce the separation, both for them and for yourself.

These are strong words, and they cut against the grain of the usual assumption of the Course student that it's only about what we believe, not about how we influence others.

> 19.   Remember that the Holy Spirit is the communication link between God the Father and His separated Sons. If you will listen to His Voice you will know that you cannot either hurt or be hurt, and [Ur: but] that many need your blessing to help them hear this for themselves. When you perceive only this need in them, and do not respond to any other, you will have learned of me and will be as eager to share your learning as I am.

Our job is to hear the Holy Spirit telling us His beautiful message of liberation, that we can neither hurt nor be hurt. Others, however, will not be able to hear this directly from Him. Instead, our blessing will be the messenger that delivers to them this message from the Holy Spirit. With everyone we meet, even when they seem to be attacking us, we need to realize that hearing this message is their only need. Then we need to somehow give this message, give them the feeling that they can neither hurt nor be hurt. When we have reached this place, we will finally have learned from what Jesus modeled in the crucifixion. We will finally be following in his footsteps.

II. The Alternative to Projection
Commentary by Robert Perry

1.   Any split in mind <u>must</u> involve a rejection of part of it, and this *is* the belief in separation. The wholeness of God, which <u>is</u> His peace, cannot be appreciated <u>except</u> by a whole mind that recognizes the wholeness of God's creation [Ur: and *by* this recognition knows its Creator]. By this recognition it knows its Creator. Exclusion and separation are synonymous, as are separation and dissociation. We have said before that the separation was and is dissociation, and that once it occurs projection becomes its main defense, or the device that <u>keeps it going</u>. The reason, however, may not be so obvious [Ur: as clear] as you think.

The separation was not us physically splitting off from God. It was us psychologically splitting off from part of our own mind, the part that knows God. Now we are like severely brain-damaged people—we have to run on only part of our mind. Until we again think with our whole mind, we cannot begin to grasp the wholeness of God.

So separation is the same as dissociation—excluding something from our awareness, from our sense of who we are. Once we do this, the main device that protects it is projection, which, as we'll see, is simply another form of pushing something out of our mind.

2.   What you project you disown, and therefore <u>do not believe is yours</u>. [You believe it is someone else's.] You are [Ur: therefore] <u>excluding</u> yourself [Ur: from it] by the very judgment [Ur: by the very statement you are making] that you are <u>different</u> [Ur: from someone else.] from the one on whom you project. Since you have also judged <u>against</u> what you project, you continue to attack it because you continue to keep it separated [Ur: you attack it because you have already attacked it *by* rejecting it]. By doing this <u>unconsciously</u>, you try to keep the fact that you attacked yourself out of awareness, and thus imagine that you have made yourself safe.

This paragraph is a brief description of the mechanics and the

84

insidiousness of projection. You start out with something you hate within yourself. Let's use the classic case of the homophobic male, who hates his own latent homosexual tendencies. To cope with this, he disowns those tendencies in him. Now they are no longer his. Instead, he sees them in others. This makes those others seem so very different than himself. He attacks the homosexual tendencies in others, because the whole process began with him attacking them in himself. What he doesn't realize is that what he is attacking out there is still within. He is therefore attacking himself, even though he believes he has made himself safe by disowning this hated part of him.

Application: Ask yourself what one of the main things you despise in others is. Then ask yourself: "Is it possible that I despise this thing in myself and have disowned it by projecting it onto others?" You may well have *less* of this attribute than most others, but as long as you hate its presence in yourself, you will focus on it in them, exaggerate it in them, and attack it in them, all to get yourself off the hook.

3.   Yet projection will always hurt you. It reinforces your belief in your own split mind, and its only purpose is to keep the separation going. It is solely a device of the ego to make you feel different from your brothers and separated from them. The ego justifies this on the [Ur: wholly spurious] grounds that it makes you seem "better" than they are, thus obscuring your equality with them still further. Projection and attack are inevitably related, because projection is always a means of justifying attack. Anger without projection is impossible. The ego uses projection only to destroy [Ur: distort] your perception of both yourself and your brothers. The process begins by excluding something that [Ur: you think] exists in you but which you do not want, and leads directly to excluding you [Ur: yourself] from your brothers.

Seen in this light, projection is a brilliant ego strategy. First, you separate from the awareness of God in your own mind. Then you hate yourself for doing this. Since self-hatred is unbearable, the ego tells you to disown it, to project it onto others. Now you look out and see a world full of ungodly people, people who are constantly separating from God. But not you; you are the godly one, the spiritual one, the one who wants only the truth. Why are they so different from you? You don't know. All you know is that they are beneath you. Given how ungodly they are, they are clearly worthy of your attack, rather than your love. Just as clearly, they cannot be part of you, nor you of them; just look at the gulf that lies between you.

Little do we realize that the ungodliness we see in them is really in us. (It may be in them, too, but we focus on it in them, exaggerate it, and hate it, all because we hate it in ourselves.) Even less do we realize that we have projected it onto them ostensibly to relieve the pain of the separation, but really to perpetuate the separation. After all, the net effect of projecting onto them is to separate from them. Now they are different, inferior, worthy of attack, all of which adds up to one thing: They are *separate*.

> 4.   We have learned, however, that there *is* an alternative to projection [Ur: there is another use of projection]. Every ability of the ego has a better use [Ur: counterpart], because its abilities are directed by the mind, which has a better Voice. The Holy Spirit extends and the ego projects. As their goals are opposed, so is the result.

Projection as described here is so ugly, such a dirty device of the ego, it is hard to believe there can be a holy use of it. Yet the Holy Spirit can use everything we make for His holy purpose. Whereas the ego projects, the Holy Spirit extends. It is the same basic dynamic. (Indeed, in this early part of the dictation, both were called "projection.") but used in an opposite way, with an opposite goal, and opposite results.

> 5.   The Holy Spirit begins by perceiving <u>you</u> as perfect. <u>Knowing</u> this perfection is shared He <u>recognizes</u> it in others, thus strengthening it in both. Instead of anger this arouses love <u>for</u> both, because <u>it establishes inclusion</u>. Perceiving equality, the Holy Spirit perceives equal needs. This invites Atonement automatically, because Atonement <u>is</u> the one need in this world that is universal. To perceive <u>yourself</u> this way is the <u>only</u> way in which you can find happiness in the world. That is because it is the acknowledgment that you are <u>not</u> in this world, for the world *is* unhappy.

The Holy Spirit starts from a completely different foundation than we do with projection. Rather than seeing something hated in you, He sees only the perfect in you. Rather than disowning this and seeing it in others instead, He maintains the awareness of your perfection and then extends this perception to others, seeing perfection in them, too. In this sight, you are both the same, rather than different. You are both equal, rather than you being "better." You are both joined in the same perfection, rather than being separate. And you both love each other, rather than hating and attacking each other. This is the opposite of the way we see now, yet it is the only way to be happy in this unhappy world.

> 6. How else can you find joy in a joyless place except by realizing that you are not there? You cannot be anywhere God did not put you, and God created you as part of Him. That is both where you are and what you are. It [Ur: This] is completely unalterable. It is total inclusion. You cannot change it now or ever. It is forever true. It is not a belief, but a Fact. Anything that God created is as true as He is. Its truth lies only in its perfect inclusion in Him Who alone is perfect. To deny this [Ur: in any way] is to deny yourself and Him, since it is impossible to accept one without the other.

The Holy Spirit's way of seeing implies that you are not here, not in this world. Why? Because it sees only the perfect in you and the perfect in your brothers. Yet nothing in this world is perfect. If you are perfect, then, you must *not be in this world.* Realizing this is the only way to be happy in this miserable world.

That is exactly what the Course teaches, that we are not really here. How could we be? God established us in Heaven. Can we change that? Can we overpower God?

Application: Repeat the following lines to yourself.

> *God created me as part of Him.*
> *"Part of Him" is **what** I am and **where** I am.*
> *This is completely unalterable.*
> *It is total inclusion.*
> *It is forever true.*
> *It is not a belief but a Fact.*
> *My truth lies only in my perfect inclusion in Him Who alone is perfect.*

7.   The perfect equality of the Holy Spirit's perception is the reflection [Ur: counterpart] of the perfect equality of God's knowing. The ego's perception has no counterpart in God, but the Holy Spirit remains the bridge between perception and knowledge. By enabling you to use perception in a way that reflects [Ur: *parallels*] knowledge, you will ultimately remember it [Ur: ultimately meet it and *know* it]. The ego would prefer to believe that this memory is impossible, yet it is *your* perception the Holy Spirit guides. Your perception will end where it began. [These last two sentences were largely composed by the editors.] [Ur: The ego prefers to believe that parallel lines do not meet, and conceives of their meeting as impossible. You might remember that the human eye perceives them as if they *do* meet in the distance, which is the same as *in the future*, if time and space are one dimension. The later mathematics support the interpretation of ultimate convergence of the parallel theoretically.] Everything meets in God, because everything was created by Him and in Him.

The discussion of parallel lines is just great. I wish the editors had left it in. The idea is that the Holy Spirit's perception is one line and God's knowing is the other line. These lines are not the same, but they do parallel each other. Both are all about the total equality of every Son of God. Our goal is to get on the Holy Spirit's line, and if we do, we will ultimately meet God's line.

Now we were all taught in school that parallel lines never meet. But in this case, they do. (Jesus even asserts that recent developments in mathematics say this is theoretically possible.) Just as the eye sees parallel lines meeting in the distance, so these two parallel lines (God's knowing and the Holy Spirit's perceiving) will meet in the future. After all, everything meets in God.

For me, the upshot is this: You don't need to climb directly onto the line of God's knowledge. Instead, climb onto the line of the Holy Spirit's true perception. Be content with riding that line. Be content with a pure way of seeing yourself and everyone else. And trust that that line will one day converge with the line of God's knowledge. For all things meet in God.

8.   God created His Sons by extending His Thought, and retaining the extensions of His Thought in His Mind. All His Thoughts are thus perfectly united within themselves and with each other [Ur: because

they were created neither partially nor in part]. The Holy Spirit enables you to <u>perceive this wholeness</u> *now.* [Ur: You can no more pray for yourselves alone than you can fine {sic} joy for yourself alone. Prayer is a re-statement of *inclusion,* directed by the Holy Spirit under the laws of God.] God created you to create. You cannot <u>extend</u> His Kingdom until you <u>know</u> of its wholeness.

Not only does the Holy Spirit extend, but God does, too. He created His Kingdom by *extending* His Thought, not projecting it, not hurling it outside. Those Thoughts, therefore, are still in His Mind. And because He created each part completely whole, those Thoughts are united within themselves *and* with each other. How else could they be whole?

All of this is what God knows, and this knowledge is beyond this world. However, the Holy Spirit has a parallel to this knowledge and you can climb onto His parallel line. In His perception, you can see a reflection of this wholeness now. Rather than seeing yourself surrounded by a bunch of inferior bozos, you need to see yourself and others as equally whole. Rather than seeking joy for yourself alone, you need to see yourself and others as equal parts of a larger Whole.

9.   Thoughts begin in the mind <u>of the thinker,</u> from which they reach outward. This is as true of God's Thinking as it is of yours. Because your mind is split, you can perceive as well as think. Yet perception cannot escape the basic laws of mind. You perceive <u>from</u> your mind and project your perceptions outward. Although perception of any kind is unreal [Ur: unnecessary], <u>you</u> made it and the Holy Spirit can therefore use it well. He can <u>inspire</u> perception and lead it toward God [Ur: by making it *parallel* to God's way of thinking, and thus guaranteeing their ultimate meeting]. This convergence <u>seems</u> to be far in the future <u>only</u> because your mind is <u>not</u> in perfect alignment with the idea, and therefore <u>does not want it now</u>.

By splitting our mind in two, we have made ourselves capable of perceiving. Yet we cannot make our perception work in a way that's contrary to the laws of mind. No matter what we do, our perceptions will always start within and be projected (or extended) outward. In other words, our own attitudes, values, and beliefs will always be the guiding force behind how we see the world, rather than it being the other way around. Yet we can make this into a holy blessing or an unholy terror.

The Holy Spirit can take perception and so inspire it that it parallels God's way of thinking. And as we have seen, these parallel lines will one day meet. This meeting seems so far off in the future only because we want to put it off. If we didn't, those parallel lines would meet now.

> 10. The Holy Spirit <u>uses</u> time, but does <u>not</u> believe in it. Coming from God He uses <u>everything</u> for good, but He does not <u>believe</u> in what is not true. Since the Holy Spirit <u>is</u> in your mind, your mind can also [Ur: *must* be able to] believe <u>only</u> what is true. The Holy Spirit can speak only for this, because He speaks for God. He tells you to return your whole mind to God, <u>because it has never left Him</u>. If it has never left Him, you need only perceive it <u>as it is</u> to <u>be</u> returned. The full awareness of the Atonement, then, is the recognition that *the separation never occurred.* The ego <u>cannot</u> prevail against this because it is an explicit statement that the <u>ego</u> never occurred.

The Holy Spirit uses time, but only because we want to take our time. He doesn't actually believe in time. And we don't actually believe in it, either. We certainly seem to, but we don't believe in it with all our heart. Somewhere deep-down, we have serious doubts about this whole time thing. We sense that what time is all about—which is things arising out of the blue and changing into what they are not—just doesn't make sense.

Though the Holy Spirit works within our beliefs, He speaks only for the truth. And what is the truth? That we should return our mind to God because in fact it never left. It is in God now, merely dreaming that it's living on a planet called Earth. To return it to God, therefore, all we need to do is perceive it *as it is*.

The fact that our mind never left God means something very profound. It means "*the separation never occurred.*" This is an extremely important statement in the Course. It is called "the full awareness of the Atonement." Atonement has to do with God and His children reconciling, with the children returning to the Father. In Christianity, of course, the children are able to return once Jesus has paid for their sins. Here, the children return merely by realizing they never left in the first place.

If the ego objects to this rather radical idea, we can simply say to it, "Excuse me, but this idea means that *you* never occurred either. So why should I bother listening to you?"

11. The ego can accept the idea that <u>return</u> is necessary because it can so easily make the idea seem difficult. Yet the Holy Spirit tells you that even <u>return</u> is unnecessary, because what never happened cannot be difficult [Ur: *cannot* involve *any* problem]. However, you can [Ur: But it does *not* follow that *you* cannot] *make* the idea of return both necessary and difficult. [Ur: God made nothing either necessary *or* difficult. But *you* have perceived both *as if* they were part of His perfect creations.] Yet it is surely clear that the perfect <u>need</u> nothing, and you <u>cannot</u> [Ur: and cannot] experience perfection as a difficult accomplishment, because that is what you [Ur: they] <u>are</u>. This is the way in which you <u>must</u> perceive God's creations, bringing all of your perceptions into the one [Ur: parallel] line the Holy Spirit sees. This line is the direct line of communication with God, and lets <u>your</u> mind converge with <u>His</u>. There is <u>no conflict anywhere</u> in this perception, because it means that <u>all</u> perception is guided by the Holy Spirit, Whose Mind is fixed on God. <u>Only</u> the Holy Spirit can resolve conflict, because <u>only</u> the Holy Spirit is conflict-free. He perceives <u>only</u> what is true in your mind, and extends outward <u>only</u> to what is true in other minds.

When I first got into the Course, I was vaguely annoyed at its notion that even return was unnecessary. I preferred the notion that our soul was going through a process of returning via perfecting itself. This made more sense to me. I didn't realize that the notion that we have to undergo a real return, through a real process of perfecting our genuinely imperfect nature, made it all seem so incredibly difficult and lengthy. In this scenario, it takes longer because we carry the concept that it *has* to take so long. We have built into the concept of our being this idea of *necessary, difficult return*.

Yet if we are already perfect, then all we need do is remember what we are. If our brothers are already perfect, all they need do is the same. This is the concept we need to carry of ourselves and our brothers. We need to see that all we are doing is taking off the blankets under which we have hidden our perfection. There are a lot of these blankets (the Sufis speak of 70,000 veils), but they are really all the same one in different forms.

If we can see everyone in this way, as just peeling off layers that have covered their perfection, we have climbed onto the line of the Holy Spirit's perception. And we are well on the way to our mind converging with God's.

Only the Holy Spirit's perception contains no conflict. Why? Because His mind is fixed on God, in Whom all things meet. This gives Him the ability to see any situation, even the most contentious, in such a way that no one's interests conflict.

> 12. The difference between the ego's projection and the Holy Spirit's extension is very simple. The ego projects to exclude, and therefore to deceive. The Holy Spirit extends by recognizing Himself in every mind, and thus perceives them as one. Nothing conflicts in this perception, because what the Holy Spirit perceives is all the same. Wherever He looks He sees Himself, and because He is united He offers the whole Kingdom always. This is the one message God gave to Him and for which He must speak, because that is what He is. The peace of God lies in that message, and so the peace of God lies in you. The great peace of the Kingdom shines in your mind forever, but it must shine outward to make you aware of it.

The ego projects to exclude—to exclude everyone from you. You see a world full of out-of-control egos, while, in contrast, your ego is strangely civilized, safely under control. Projection has made everyone seem different than you. Everyone's on the outside.

The Holy Spirit's perception, as we have seen, is just the opposite. "Wherever He looks He sees Himself." This is a phenomenal line when you think about it. When He looks at your spouse, He sees only Himself. When He looks at your child, He sees only Himself. When He looks at your obnoxious neighbor, He sees only Himself. When He looks at you, He sees only Himself. And when you look at these people through Him, you see what He sees. Can you imagine that?

This is His message: "See Me everywhere, in everyone, and I will offer you the whole Kingdom." This is the message God sent Him to give us, and since God's peace is in this message, God's peace is in *us*.

> 13. The Holy Spirit was given you with perfect impartiality, and only by recognizing [Ur: perceiving] Him impartially can you recognize [Ur: perceive] Him at all. The ego is legion, but the Holy Spirit is one. No darkness abides anywhere in the Kingdom, but [Ur: so] your part is only to allow no darkness to abide in your own mind. This alignment with light is unlimited, because it is in alignment with the light of the world. Each of us is the light of the world, and by joining our minds in this light we proclaim the Kingdom of God together and as one.

II. The Alternative to Projection

To claim the Holy Spirit's message, however, we have to see Him *impartially*. We have to fully accept that He is just as much in Hitler as in Jesus, just as much in our first spouse as in our current spouse, just as much in that complete stranger as in our mother. For He is not carved up into pieces. He is one. And that same One is fully present in every single person. If we refuse to see Him in our worst enemy, then we refuse to see *Him*.

Every single member of the Kingdom is filled with His light. We don't need to make sure His light finds its way inside all our friends and neighbors. We just need to make sure His light is turned on inside of *us*. Then we will see that all is light. Then we will be aligning ourselves with the light of the world. Then we will realize we *are* the light of the world. And then we will take our place alongside all of those who have realized the same thing and will join with them in lighting up the world.

III. The Relinquishment of Attack
Commentary by Robert Perry

1.   [Ur: We have used many words as synonymous which are not ordinarily regarded as the same. We began with having and being, and recently have used others. Hearing and being is an example, to which we can also add teaching and being, learning and being, and, above all, *projecting* {or extending} and being. This is because,] As we have already emphasized, every idea begins in the mind of the thinker [Ur: and extends outward]. Therefore, what extends from the mind is still in it, and from *what* it extends it knows itself [its being]. [Ur: This is its natural talent.] The word "knows" is correct here, [Ur: even though the ego does *not* know, and is not concerned with *being* at all.] because ["because" was added by the editors] the Holy Spirit still holds knowledge safe in your mind through His impartial perception. By attacking nothing, He presents no barrier to the communication of God. Therefore, being is never threatened. Your Godlike mind can never be defiled. The ego never was and never will be part of it, but through the ego you can hear and teach and learn [Ur: and project] what is not true. You have taught yourself to believe that you are not what you are. You cannot teach what you have not learned, and what you teach you strengthen in yourself because you are sharing it. Every lesson you teach you are learning.

This brief section is an extremely important exploration of a core principle in the Course: As you teach so shall you learn. The Course places this principle at the very center of its path to God.

The paragraph begins with a list of synonyms for "being," eventually saying that projecting and being are synonymous. Bear in mind, though, that at this point in the dictation, "projection" is a term that covers both projection and extension. In this case, I think, the accent is more on extension. We can take this equation, therefore, to mean: You extend your being, and your being is extension. Put differently, what you are, you extend, and what you extend, you are.

This leads into a discussion of the fact that we *learn* what we are through what we extend or project. If we extend love, we come to *know* (used in the technical sense) our true Self. If we project anger, we become convinced that we are someone else, someone we are not. We can see this principle operating all the time. Our self-concept is shaped on a moment-by-moment basis by the thoughts, words, and deeds that come out of us, and by their effect on others. In the state of perception, we cannot see ourselves directly. We can only see the effects we produce, and from those effects, we surmise what the cause must be, what *we* must be. If our effects are loving, we surmise that we must be innocent. If our effects are harmful, we surmise that we must be sinful.

This is why what we teach others is so important. Everything we put out toward them is simultaneously teaching us what we are (or what we are not). This is why most people's self-concept lies in ruins.

> 2.   That is why you must teach only <u>one</u> lesson. If you are to be conflict-free yourself, you must learn <u>only</u> from the Holy Spirit and teach <u>only</u> by Him. You <u>are</u> only love, but when you deny [Ur: denied] this, you make [Ur: made] what you <u>are</u> something you must <u>learn</u> to remember. I said before that the message of the crucifixion was, "Teach <u>only</u> love, for that is what you <u>are</u>." This is the <u>one</u> lesson that is perfectly unified, because it is the only lesson that <u>is</u> one. Only <u>by</u> teaching it can <u>you</u> learn it. "As you teach so will you learn." If that is true, and it is true indeed, do not [Ur: you must never] forget that what you teach is teaching you. And what you project or extend you believe [Ur: What you project you *believe*].

We are only love, but we have forgotten this and need to remember it. But how? The most obvious approach is through inward experience, through the direct experience of our true nature. Strangely, though, this paragraph is saying that we won't really learn it this way. "Only by teaching it can you learn it." What a remarkable statement. The only way to become really convinced that you are love is by *extending love*.

Therefore, we must teach only this one lesson. Right now, we teach conflicting lessons—both love and attack. As a result, we have taught ourselves that our very being is split in two.

> 3.   The only [Ur: *real*] safety lies in extending the Holy Spirit, because as you see His gentleness in others your own mind perceives <u>itself</u> as totally harmless. Once it can accept this fully, it sees no need to <u>protect</u>

itself. The protection of God then dawns upon it, assuring it that it is perfectly safe forever. The perfectly safe <u>are</u> wholly benign. They bless because they know that they <u>are</u> blessed. Without anxiety the mind is wholly kind, and because it extends beneficence it <u>is</u> beneficent. Safety is the <u>complete relinquishment of attack</u>. No compromise is possible in this. Teach attack in any form and <u>you have learned it, and it will hurt you</u>. Yet this learning is not immortal, and you can unlearn it <u>by not teaching it</u>.

These sentences are so beautiful and evocative. Let's imagine them being true for you. Imagine extending the Holy Spirit to whomever you meet, so that in everyone you see only His gentleness. Because you are harming no one, because only love is coming out of you, your mind perceives itself as totally harmless. Try to imagine that. Now, because you are harmless, you no longer believe you deserve harm in return. You therefore see no need to protect yourself. Feel your defenses dropping. Feel yourself relaxing. In this state of total defenselessness, feel the protection of God dawn upon your mind. Hear Him assuring you that you are perfectly safe forever. You abide in this blanket of perfect protection, and you know that you will abide there forever. You feel totally, immeasurably blessed. What can you do but bless others? You have lost all anxiety, all concern for your safety. What can you be but wholly kind? Your every word, even your mere glance, radiates beneficence. It streams from you like blossoms blowing off a tree in spring. How could you not be convinced that what you are is pure beneficence?

How do we reach this place of bottomless safety? There is only one way: the complete relinquishment of attack. *The complete relinquishment of attack.*

4.　Since you cannot *not* teach, your salvation lies in teaching the exact opposite of <u>everything the ego believes</u>. This is how <u>you</u> will learn the truth that will set you free, and will keep you free as others learn it of <u>you</u>. The only way to <u>have</u> peace is to <u>teach</u> peace. By teaching peace you must learn it yourself [Ur: By learning it through projection {extension}, it becomes part of what you *know*], because you cannot teach what you still dissociate. Only thus can you win back the knowledge that you threw away. An idea that you <u>share</u> you <u>must have</u>. It awakens in your mind through the <u>conviction</u> of teaching it. [Ur: It awakens in you through the *conviction* of teaching. Remember that if teaching is being and learning is being, then teaching is learning.] <u>Everything</u> you teach <u>you</u> are learning. Teach only love, and learn that love is yours and <u>you</u> are love.

He couldn't put it any clearer than this. This is the only way out of our suffering, to teach the opposite of what the ego believes, to teach peace, to teach only love. Why is this the way out? We can boil it down to two reasons. First, teaching an idea—extending it to others through our attitudes and behavior—proves that the idea must be within us. Teaching therefore strengthens an idea's presence in us. The idea grows stronger in our mind.

Second, as the first paragraph said, what we teach reveals our nature to us. By the effects we produce, we learn the nature of their cause— ourselves. When we teach an idea, then, we are really teaching ourselves that our nature is characterized by that idea, is one with that idea. We learn that we *are* that idea.

To put these two together, by teaching an idea, we prove to ourselves that that idea is in us, and *is* us. This, of course, is what that beautiful final line says, "Teach only love, and learn that love is yours [the idea is in you] and you are love [the idea *is* you]."

If you want to win back knowledge, pure non-dual awareness of God, then teach others that they are lovable by giving your love to them.

Application: Think of a recent incident in which you thought about or treated someone harshly or unkindly.

> Can you see that you were teaching the idea of attack?
>
> Can you see how, by teaching that idea, you taught yourself that that idea was in you? How does it feel to believe that attack is in you?
>
> Can you see how, by teaching that idea, you taught yourself that idea *is* you? How does it feel to believe that you *are* attack?
>
> Now think of a recent incident in which you thought about or treated someone genuinely lovingly.

Can you see that you were teaching the idea of love?

Can you see how, by teaching that idea, you taught yourself that that idea was in you? How does it feel to believe that love is in you?

Can you see how, by teaching that idea, you taught yourself that idea *is* you? How does it feel to believe that you *are* love?

In light of this exercise, is it possible that the quality of your thoughts (in terms of love or attack) is the prime force in teaching you who you are?

IV. The Only Answer
Commentary by Robert Perry

This section contrasts the ego's poisonous relationship with us with God and the Holy Spirit's empowering relationship with us. The ego sees us as its enemy, conspires against us, and undermines us with its questions and uncertainty. God, however, does not respond by blotting the ego out. Rather, He affirms our ability to get out of it ourselves. He sends us the Holy Spirit, Who answers the questions raised by the ego. Rather than commanding us, the Holy Spirit affirms our role as commander. Rather than disempowering us, He helps us develop our powers until we return to our inherent perfection.

> 1.   Remember that the Holy Spirit is the <u>Answer</u>, not the question. The ego always speaks first [Ur: because it is capricious…]. It is capricious and does <u>not</u> mean its maker well. [Ur: This is because] It believes, and correctly, that its maker may withdraw his support from it at any moment. If it meant you well it would be glad, as the Holy Spirit will be glad when He has brought you home and you no longer need His guidance. The ego does <u>not</u> regard itself as part of you. Herein lies its primary [Ur: perceptual] error, the foundation of its whole thought system.

We have already seen (in 5.VI) that "the ego always speaks first" means the ego always *interprets* things first. Now, we get a look behind the scenes. The ego speaks first because it does not mean us well. It resents the fact that we may withdraw our support from it at any time. Its relationship with us is analogous to a really sick relationship between a dishonest charitable institution and its major donor. The institution wants to make sure it keeps this donor's checks coming. At the same time, it hates him for the fact that he may choose to withdraw his support. And so, whenever anything happens, this institution makes sure it is the first one to speak to the donor, guiding his perception of what has happened in ways that keep him faithful while simultaneously hurting and draining him.

Yet if the ego really meant us well, it would be happy when we no longer feel we need it. This is the Holy Spirit's attitude. When we no longer need His guidance, He will celebrate, for He is not in this to be the hero. All He wants is to lead us to joy.

> 2.   When God created you He made you part of Him. That is why attack <u>within</u> the Kingdom is impossible. [Ur: But] <u>You</u> made the ego without love, and so it does not love <u>you</u>. You could not remain <u>within</u> the Kingdom without love, and since the Kingdom *is* love, you believe that you are <u>without</u> it. This enables the ego to regard itself as <u>separate and outside its maker</u>, thus speaking for the part of your mind that believes *you* are separate and outside the Mind of God. The ego, then, raised the first question that was ever asked, but one it can never answer. That question, "What are you?" was the beginning of doubt. The ego has never answered any questions since, although it has raised a great many. The most inventive activities of the ego have never done more than <u>obscure the question</u>, because you <u>have</u> the answer and *the ego is afraid of you.*

The way God created us determines everything about us. He created us in such great love that He made us part of Himself. Since everything in the Kingdom is part of God, there's no room for attack, only love. How can we attack when we're all one with each other?

Likewise, the way we made the ego determined everything about it, especially the way it regards us. We made the ego without love, and so it doesn't love us. This loveless act seemingly placed us outside the love of the Kingdom, outside the Mind of God. For this reason, encoded in the thought of the ego is the idea of effect being outside its cause. As a result, the ego (an effect) sees itself as outside of *its* cause (us).

Being outside of our true nature, the ego doesn't have a clue what we are. In this ignorance, it raised the primordial question, the root of all questioning and all uncertainty ever since: "What are you?" It tries to answer, but it mainly tries to obscure the question. It is afraid of us asking the question clearly and directly, because *we* have the answer.

> 3.   You cannot understand the conflict until <u>you</u> fully understand the basic fact that the ego cannot know anything [Ur: does not know]. The Holy Spirit does not speak first, *but He always answers.* <u>Everyone</u> has called upon Him for help at one time or another and in one way or

another, <u>and has been answered</u>. Since the Holy Spirit answers truly He answers <u>for all time</u>, which means that <u>everyone has the answer</u> *now*.

Now "the ego speaks first" seems to mean that the ego raises the question, a question it can't answer because it doesn't know. The Holy Spirit, however, always answers. Since everyone has asked Him for help, this means that *everyone* has been answered. And since He answers for all time, that means His answer is present in every moment of time, and therefore everyone has the answer *now*.

Have you ever known anyone who always answered your every call for help? If you have, you know that it inspires such a feeling of trust and safety. That is the feeling we ought to have in relation to the Holy Spirit. Even if we aren't listening, He is always answering.

4. The ego cannot hear the Holy Spirit, but it <u>does</u> believe that part of the [Ur: same] mind that made it is <u>against</u> it. It interprets this [Ur: wholly] as a justification for <u>attacking</u> its maker. It believes that the best defense is attack, and <u>wants</u> *you* <u>to believe</u> it. Unless you <u>do</u> believe it you will not side with it, and the ego feels badly in need of allies, though not of brothers. Perceiving something alien to itself in your <u>mind</u>, the ego turns to the body [Ur: *not* the mind] as its ally, because the body is *not* [Ur: *because* the body is not] part of you. This makes the body the ego's friend. It is an alliance frankly based on separation. If you side with this alliance you <u>will</u> be afraid, because you are siding with an alliance <u>of</u> fear.

Although the ego can't hear the Holy Spirit, it senses that there is a Presence in your mind that is against it. The ego is a disease and it senses that you carry within you the cure. You, therefore, become the enemy. In its war against you, the ego joins with the body. The two make natural allies because both are outside of your real nature. Having gained this ally, the ego says to you, "Pssst. You want to join our little club here?" It doesn't tell you that you are joining a club of fear, nor that the club's bylaws are all about destroying the threat of *you*. Then it says, "If you want to join, all you need to do is attack your brothers." It doesn't tell you that inducing you to attack your brothers is its way of attacking you.

5. The ego uses the body to [Ur: The ego and the body] conspire <u>against</u> your mind, and because the ego realizes that its "enemy" <u>can</u>

end them both merely by recognizing they are not part of you, they join in the attack together. This is perhaps the strangest perception of all, if you consider what it really involves. The ego, which is not real, attempts to persuade the mind, which *is* real, that the mind is the ego's learning device; and further, that the body is more real than the mind is. No one in his right mind could possibly believe this, and no one in his right mind does believe it.

You've joined the club, but you don't realize that the other two members—the ego and the body—are having secret meetings in which they conspire against you. When you actually do meet with them, they try to convince you that you are the lowest on the totem pole. They tell you that you are just a device to be used by one of them (the ego) and that you are less real than the other (the body). This masks the essential fact that, of the three, the only one that is real is you.

6. Hear, then, the one answer of the Holy Spirit to all the questions the ego raises: You are a child of God, a priceless part of His Kingdom, which He created as part of Him. Nothing else exists and only this is real. You have chosen a sleep in which you have had bad dreams, but the sleep is not real and God calls you to awake. There will be nothing left of your dream when you hear Him, because you will awaken [Ur: *will* be awake]. Your dreams contain many of the ego's symbols and they have confused you. Yet that was only because you were asleep and did not know. When you wake you will see the truth around you and in you, and you will no longer believe in dreams because they will have no reality for you. Yet the Kingdom and all that you have created there will have great reality for you, because they are beautiful and true.

Please read this paragraph again, very slowly, inserting your name at some logical point in each sentence. Note your reactions while you read.

Here are my reactions: The ego has been whispering "What are you?" in my ear for as long as I can remember. I've tried answering this question in so many different ways. Yet now I have the real answer, the Holy Spirit's answer. His answer is that I am a whole different kind of creature than I think I am, and He is speaking to the creature I am, not the creature I seem to be. This world that seems to define me, He tells me, is just a dream. In this dream, I am surrounded by dream symbols of the ego, symbols that speak of the reality of separation. These symbols have lulled me into thinking that I am defined by the dream, that I am a creature of the dream. In my waking state, however, I am someone else entirely. I am a child of God, not a human being. And I live in God's Kingdom, not in this world. When I finally wake up, nothing that I see now will be real to me. It will vanish like a dream from my mind.

> 7. In the Kingdom, where you are and what you are is perfectly certain. There is no doubt [Ur: there], because the first question was never asked. Having finally been wholly answered, it *has never been*. *Being* alone lives in the Kingdom, where everything lives in God without question. The time spent on questioning in the dream has given way to creation and to its eternity. <u>You</u> are as certain as God because you are as true as He is, but what was once certain in your mind has become only the <u>ability</u> for certainty.

Once I awaken in the Kingdom, I will be "perfectly certain" about *what* I am and *where* I am. There will be no doubt because there will be no question. The question—"What am I?"—has been so completely answered that there is not a trace of it left. I don't even remember it was ever asked. The uncertainty of earth life has been replaced by *being* ("*Being* alone lives in the Kingdom"), by *knowing* ("In the Kingdom… you are…perfectly certain"), and by *creating* ("questioning in the dream has given way to creation"). All three of these words suggest a total lack of ambivalence, uncertainty, or division. Our whole mind is completely united. Nothing in it is held back. Nothing in it is divided or uncertain. It simply *is*.

> 8. The introduction of abilities into being was the beginning of <u>uncertainty</u>, because abilities are <u>potentials</u>, not accomplishments. Your abilities are useless in the presence of God's accomplishments, and also of yours. Accomplishments are <u>results</u> that <u>have been</u> achieved. When they are perfect, abilities are meaningless. It is curious that the perfect must now be perfected. In fact, it is impossible. Remember, however, that when you put yourself in an impossible situation you believe that the impossible *is* possible.

We have been talking about the uncertainty introduced by questions. Now we are switching to the uncertainty introduced by abilities. We have already visited this concept, in the first paragraph of 3.IV and of 3.V.

There, what was said was that our abilities are open to question and doubt because we are not certain how we will use them. Here, virtually the same point is made. Abilities are associated with uncertainty because they are potentials, not accomplishments, and potentials are uncertain. You may know what a potential *can* do, but you don't know what it *will* do. Having an ability thus means being in a state of uncertainty.

To perfect an ability means to bring it closer and closer to its potential. When it finally reaches that potential, it stops being an ability. It becomes pure accomplishment. This is the goal we are after. How paradoxical that the perfect must now perfect themselves (their abilities). Yet this is the strange position in which we've placed ourselves.

> 9.   Abilities must be <u>developed</u> before you can use them. This is not true of anything that God created, but it is the kindest solution possible for what <u>you</u> made. In an impossible situation, you can develop your abilities to the point where they <u>can get you out of it</u>. You have a Guide to how to develop them, but you have no commander <u>except yourself</u>. This leaves <u>you</u> in charge of the Kingdom, with both a Guide to <u>find</u> it and a <u>means</u> to keep it [we keep it by giving it away; for another "find/keep" pairing, see 6.III.4:2]. You have a model to follow who will strengthen your command, and never detract from it in any way. You therefore retain the central place in your imagined enslavement, which in <u>itself</u> demonstrates that you are <u>not</u> enslaved.

God would not create us in a state of potential, for that would not be loving. We placed ourselves in this state. Now, the kindest way out of the crippling uncertainty of potential is to develop our potential, to perfect our abilities. That is how we get back to God.

On this journey, we are in charge. The Holy Spirit will guide us in developing our abilities. Jesus will model the way for us. Yet both will work to strengthen our role as commander of our own ship. They are there to advise and help, not to take the wheel out of our hands. If we really get this, if we fully understand that we are in charge, we will be catapulted ahead to the end of the journey. For the journey's goal is to realize that we are not a disempowered slave. The whole journey is about reclaiming the power we gave away when we entered a state of mere potential.

10. You are in an impossible situation only because you think it is possible to be in one. You *would* be in an impossible situation if God showed you your perfection, and <u>proved</u> to you that you were wrong. This would demonstrate that the perfect are inadequate to bring <u>themselves</u> to the awareness of their perfection, and thus side with the belief that those who have everything need help and are therefore helpless. This is the kind of "reasoning" in which the ego engages. God, Who <u>knows</u> that His creations are perfect, does <u>not</u> affront [Ur: insult] them. This would be as impossible as the ego's notion that it has affronted [Ur: insulted] Him.

Each of the last three paragraphs has said that we are in an "impossible situation." This and other Course passages define an impossible situation as one that is so insane that it cannot work and cannot even *be*. Impossible situations are disempowering. Because they can't work, they give you the message that all your efforts are futile, that you are powerless. Yet *this* situation is actually a testament to our power, for that's what got us into it. We are only in this impossible situation because *we* decided that "it is possible to be in one." If we had the power to get into it, we must also have the power to get out, and getting out is the only real solution to an impossible situation.

The situation, however, would be so impossible that we *couldn't* get out if God came in and disempowered us. This would happen if He didn't let us perfect ourselves; if He forced on us the awareness of our perfection and showed us how wrong we have been about ourselves. This would prove that we ourselves don't have the power to get out. By doing this, God would be doing exactly what Jesus and the Holy Spirit refrain from doing. He would be taking away the role of commander of our own journey. He would be insulting the very power in us that one day can and will get us out of this impossible situation. Do we really want to ask Him to do that?

11. That is why the Holy Spirit <u>never</u> commands. To command is to assume <u>inequality</u>, which the Holy Spirit demonstrates does not exist. Fidelity to premises [in this case, the premise of equality] is a law of mind, and everything God created [including the Holy Spirit] is faithful to His laws. Fidelity to other laws is also possible, however, not because the laws are true, but because <u>you made them</u>. What would be gained if God proved to you that you have thought insanely? Can God lose

His Own certainty? I have frequently said that what you teach you <u>are</u>. Would you have God teach you that you have sinned? If He confronted the self you made with the truth He created <u>for</u> you, what could you be but afraid? You would doubt your right mind [Ur: sanity], which is the only place where [Ur: which is the one thing in which] you can <u>find</u> the sanity He gave you.

This paragraph continues the same theme. Neither the Holy Spirit nor God will step in and abort our journey. The Holy Spirit won't belittle us by issuing commandments. God won't confront our illusory self with the truth of who we are and show us how insane we've been. Since you learn what you teach, by teaching us that we had defiled ourselves, God would lose His Own certainty of our sinless purity. Rather than drawing out our inherent sanity, this would make us feel like there was no sanity in us whatsoever. At that point, how could we ever find sanity?

These paragraphs address a common complaint along the spiritual journey: Why won't God just step in and do it for us? Why does He just let me sit here and suffer? The answer: He is always there to help, but this journey is one of reclaiming the power in you, reclaiming the sanity in you. If He just did it all for you, He would disempower you and prove to you that you are fundamentally hopeless. If you gave a child a puzzle to solve, but then grabbed the puzzle and solved it for the child, what message would you send that child?

12. God does not teach. To teach is to imply a lack, which God <u>knows</u> is not there. God is not conflicted. Teaching aims at change, but God created <u>only</u> the changeless. The separation was not a loss of perfection, but a failure in <u>communication</u>. A harsh and strident form of communication arose as the ego's voice. It could not shatter the peace of God, but it <u>could</u> shatter *yours*. God did not blot it out, because to eradicate it would be to attack it. Being questioned, He did not question. He merely gave the Answer. His Answer <u>is</u> your Teacher.

Unlike the Holy Spirit, God does not teach. For God to teach would be to imply that we are lacking, that we are imperfect, that we need real change. Yet God knows us only as changelessly perfect. We didn't lose that perfection in the separation, we merely cut off communication with God. We let the ego speak for us, and it flat out refused to communicate with Him. If God were to blot it out, that would treat it as real, treat it as *us*. All He did was note the ego's question—"What are you?"—and then give an Answer, an Answer so perfect and all-encompassing that It could answer every last uncertainty in our minds and until we returned to knowledge.

V. The Lessons of the Holy Spirit
Commentary by Robert Perry

1.   Like any good teacher, the Holy Spirit knows more than you do now, but He teaches only to make you equal with Him. [Ur: This is because] You had already taught yourself wrongly, having believed what was not true. You did not believe in your own perfection. Would [Ur: Could] God teach you that you had made a split mind, when He knows your mind only as whole? What God does know is that His communication channels are not open to Him, so that He cannot impart His joy and know that His children are wholly joyous. Giving His joy is an ongoing process, not in time but in eternity. God's extending outward, though not His completeness, is blocked when the Sonship does not communicate with Him as one. So He thought, "My children sleep and must be awakened."

The Holy Spirit does know more than we do, but any possible sense of humiliation this may induce is erased by two additional facts. First, He teaches only to make us equal with Him (the Course says several times that this is the goal of any good teacher). Second, what He knows that we don't is that *we are perfect*.

The rest of the paragraph says that God does not know your mind as actually split, but He *does* know that your mind fell asleep and stopped communicating with Him. This paragraph (along with 4.VII.6) is one of the most important statements in the Course about God's awareness of the separation. The two paragraphs, in fact, say virtually identical things. If you look at them side by side, the parallels are quite striking:

T-4.VII.6.4-7	T-6.V.1.5-8
"And this He does know."	"What God does know"
"His channels are closed"	"His communication channels are not open"
"[your joy] is incomplete. And this He does know."	"so that He cannot...know that His children are wholly joyous."

continued on page 109

T-4.VII.6.4-7	T-6.V.1.5-8
"The constant going out of His Love"	"Giving His joy is an ongoing process"
"His Love is blocked...when the minds He created do not communicate fully with Him"	"God's extending outward...is blocked when the Sonship does not communicate with Him"

2.   How can you wake children in a more kindly way than by [Ur: in a better and more kindly than with] a gentle Voice That will not frighten them, but will merely remind them that the night is over and the light has come? You do not inform them that the nightmares that frightened them so badly are not real, because children <u>believe</u> in magic. You merely reassure them that they are safe *now*. Then you train them to <u>recognize the difference</u> between sleeping and waking, so they will understand they need not be afraid of dreams. And so when bad dreams come, they will <u>themselves</u> call on the light to dispel them.

On the literal level, this paragraph is talking about dealing with very small children. When they are caught in nightmares, it says, you just tell them that night is over, the light has come, and they are safe *now*. You don't tell them their nightmare wasn't real, because they wouldn't relate to this. They think their dream actually happened, since they are not old enough to distinguish their dreams from their waking experience. However, as they grow, you gradually train them to make this distinction. Now, when they have nightmares, they can realize they are just caught in a dream and call on the light themselves.

Of course, what this is really talking about is how the Holy Spirit deals with us. We are the cosmic equivalent of two-year-olds who don't realize their nightmares aren't real. So at first, with infinite gentleness, He merely says to us, "It's OK, you're safe now." Yet as we develop more, He starts to school us in the difference between illusion and truth. Eventually, we are able to recognize our nightmares *as* nightmares, and call on the light within us ourselves. When we become truly adept at this, we no longer dream at all, and, being awake, we no longer need the Holy Spirit.

3.   A wise teacher teaches through approach, not avoidance. He does not emphasize what you must avoid to escape from harm, but [Ur: as much as] what you need to learn to have joy. [Ur: This is true even of the world's teachers.] Consider the fear and confusion a child would experience if he were told, "Do not do this because it will [Ur: might] hurt you and make you unsafe; but if you do that instead [Ur: but if you do *that*], you will escape from harm and be safe, and then you will not be afraid." It is surely better to use [Ur: All of this could be included in] only three words: "Do only that!" This simple statement is perfectly clear, easily understood and very easily remembered.

This paragraph is a great window onto Jesus' own style of teaching. He does recognize the value of teaching through avoidance, but his primary emphasis is clearly on teaching through approach. When he at one point gives Helen and Bill a long discourse on the mistakes they made during a single day, he carefully prefaces his remarks by saying that this is a one-time thing he is doing, and that what he is interested in are not the particular mistakes but how typical they are. He then says, "The whole value of this section rests *only* in showing you what *not* to do. The more constructive emphasis is, of course, on the positive approach"—which he explains to be mind-watching.

Jesus also gives his share of explanations that sound like the longer statement ("Do not do this because…"). However, he also takes care to boil these down to very simple, positive, easy-to-remember statements. In fact, "Do only that" sounds a great deal like his condensation of the message of the crucifixion: "Teach only love."

4.   The Holy Spirit never itemizes errors because He does not frighten children, and those who lack wisdom *are* children. Yet He always answers their call, and His dependability makes them more certain. Children *do* confuse fantasy and reality, and they are frightened because they do not recognize the difference. The Holy Spirit makes no distinction among dreams. He merely shines them away. His light is always the call to awaken, whatever you have been dreaming. Nothing lasting lies in dreams, and the Holy Spirit, shining with the Light from God Himself, speaks only for what lasts forever.

Lists of what we have done wrong are always a scary thing. The idea of such lists, whether they be God's or Santa's, have a tremendous hold on our minds for just this reason. This is why the Holy Spirit doesn't confront us with lists of our errors (just as we shouldn't confront our children—or spouses or parents—with such lists). Instead, His message is, "There's no difference among your errors. Dreams are dreams. There is nothing lasting in any dream, even good ones. Let Me give you the light that shines away all dreams, and then together we will find what lasts forever." Along the way, He carefully builds your trust and sense of security by answering every call you make to Him.

A. To Have, Give All to All

1.   When your body and your ego and your dreams are gone, you will know that <u>you</u> will last forever. Perhaps you [Ur: Many] think this is accomplished through death, but <u>nothing</u> is accomplished through death, because death is nothing. <u>Everything</u> is accomplished through life, and life is of the mind and in the mind. The body neither lives nor dies, because it cannot contain you who <u>are</u> life. If we share the same mind, <u>you can overcome death because I did</u>. Death is an attempt to resolve conflict by not deciding at all. Like any other impossible solution the ego attempts, it *will not work*.

Nothing in this dream lasts forever. Yet when all of it is gone—your body, your ego, your dreams—you will know that there is one thing that does last forever: *you*. We may hope that this will happen when we die. Yet how can dying accomplish anything? The body is just an illusion and illusions are always coming and going. The only change that really changes things is a change of *mind*. What we need is not for the body to die, but for the mind to awaken to its own eternal life. The mind has to make a *decision*, the same decision Jesus did. Death, oddly enough, is the avoidance of this decision. It is the attempt to get out of the conflict of life on earth by physically leaving, rather than by changing our mind. Yet what we discover on the other side is that we still have an ego and we still have dreams. We are still faced with the only question there is: Will we change our minds?

2.   God did not make the body, because it is destructible, and therefore not of the Kingdom. The body is the symbol of <u>what you think you are</u>. It is clearly a separation device, and therefore does not exist. The Holy

111

Spirit, as always, takes what you have made and translates it into a learning device [Ur: *for* you]. Again as always, He reinterprets what the ego uses as an argument <u>for</u> separation into a demonstration [Ur: an argument] <u>against</u> it. If the mind can heal the body, but the body cannot heal the mind, then the mind <u>must be stronger</u> than the body. Every miracle demonstrates this.

God did not make the body. It is not holy and spiritual. Neither is it sinful and evil. It is just a symbol, a dream symbol of what we think we are. Yet we know the Holy Spirit has the job of reinterpreting the ego's symbols. He points out that the mind can heal the body—which is what happens in miracles—but the body cannot heal the mind. This shows the mind is stronger, more real, which argues for a dramatic conclusion: the body does not have the power to impose separation on the mind.

Application: Look down at your body and say, *"This body is just a dream symbol of what I think I am, nothing more."*

3.   I have said that the Holy Spirit is the <u>motivation</u> for miracles. [Ur: This is because] He <u>always</u> tells you that <u>only</u> the mind is real, because only the mind <u>can be shared</u>. The body <u>is</u> separate, and therefore <u>cannot</u> be part of you. To be of one mind is meaningful, but to be one body is meaningless. By the laws of mind, then, the body <u>is</u> meaningless.

The Holy Spirit gives us another argument against the body's reality. According to the laws of mind, only what can be shared is real. This is something we innately know. We know that if we have an idea like "With this hand I can crush Jupiter," no one else can really share that and so its content must be unreal. What exists in the bubble of one solitary mind and cannot be shared must be untrue. But do we realize that bodies are just like that crazy idea? They cannot be shared. By the laws of mind, then, *they* cannot be real.

4.   To the Holy Spirit, <u>there is no order of difficulty in miracles</u>. This is <u>familiar</u> enough to you by now, but it has not yet become believable. Therefore, you do not understand it and cannot <u>use</u> it. We have too much to accomplish on behalf of the Kingdom to let this crucial

concept slip away. It is a real foundation stone of the thought system I teach and want you to teach. You cannot perform miracles without believing it, because it is a belief in perfect equality. Only one equal gift can be offered to the equal Sons of God, and that is full appreciation. Nothing more and nothing less. Without a range, order of difficulty is meaningless, and there must be no range in what you offer to your brother.

"The Holy Spirit is the motivation for miracles" (Paragraph 3) because He teaches that the mind can heal *any* bodily illness, since the mind is real and the body is unreal. This is another way of stating the first principle of miracles, that there is no order of difficulty among them. Jesus understands exactly where we are in relation to this principle: We are familiar with it but do not yet believe it. He is calling us higher, for without real belief in this principle we cannot perform miracles. This is because a miracle offers every receiver the exact same message: "You deserve total appreciation, just as much as anyone else." Yet unless you believe in the first principle of miracles you don't believe this. For beneath every belief that a certain person is harder to heal is the belief that that person is less *deserving* of healing.

5.   The Holy Spirit, Who leads to God, translates communication into being, just as He ultimately translates perception into knowledge. You do not lose what you communicate. The ego uses the body for attack, for pleasure and for pride. The insanity of this perception makes it a fearful one indeed. The Holy Spirit sees the body only as a means of communication, and because communicating is sharing it [communication] becomes communion. Perhaps you think [Ur: You might argue] that fear as well as love can be communicated; and therefore can be shared. Yet this is not so real as it may appear [Ur: as it sounds]. Those who communicate fear are promoting attack, and attack always breaks communication, making it [Ur: and therefore makes communion] impossible. Egos do join together in temporary allegiance, but always for what each one can get *separately*. The Holy Spirit communicates only what each one can give to all. He never takes anything back, because He wants you to keep it. Therefore, His teaching begins with the lesson:

To *have*, *give* all *to* all.

113

The Holy Spirit wants you to communicate, because communication is sharing (the sharing of ideas), sharing is communion, and communion is oneness. This is how He will ultimately get you back to the oneness of knowledge, through getting you to truly communicate with other minds. This, therefore, is the only purpose he sees in the body: to be a means of communication—a mechanism for giving ideas that can be shared.

The ego has very different plans for the body. It "uses the body for attack [to verbally and physically force our world into the shape we want], for pleasure [no explanation needed] and for pride [to make us look good]." Let's be honest: this is it, isn't it? This is what we see the body as being—a getting mechanism. This may even seem compatible with the Holy Spirit's purpose, since it looks like you can communicate fear and even join together around fear. Yet ultimately you can't, for the state of fear is ultimately about looking out for number one. Thus, a joining that is produced by fear is always a temporary illusion in which each person is really in it for themselves.

The Holy Spirit is coming from precisely the opposite place. He wants each person to be in it for everyone. He wants you to give to everyone, to communicate love to everyone, for only thus do you truly gain. The gifts you withhold or take back, you lose. That is why His teaching begins with the simple but radical lesson, "To have, give all to all."

> 6.   This is a very preliminary step, and the only one you must take for [Ur: *must take*] yourself. It is not even necessary that you complete the step yourself, but it is necessary that you turn in that direction. Having chosen to go that way, you place yourself in charge of the journey, where you and only you must remain. This step may appear [Ur: *appears*] to exacerbate conflict rather than resolve it, because it is the beginning step in reversing your perception and turning it right-side up. This conflicts with the upside-down perception you have not yet abandoned, or the change in direction would not have been necessary. Some [Ur: people] remain at this step for a [Ur: very] long time, experiencing very acute conflict. At this point they may [Ur: Many] try to accept the conflict, rather than take the next step towards its resolution. Having taken the first step, however, they will be helped. Once they have chosen what they cannot complete alone, they are no longer alone.

Now we can see that he has begun to describe the spiritual journey. The lesson we just saw—"To have, give all to all"—is now revealed as the first step in that journey. The Holy Spirit is calling you out of your old ways, in which you assumed that having came from getting. He is asking you to head toward a higher destination, in which you realize that having comes from giving.

This first step may sound incredibly advanced, but you don't actually complete the lesson at this point. You just set your direction toward it. You just decide to leave behind the familiar ways of your ego. Now *you* are in charge of the journey. Yet this is a journey you can't complete alone, and this very fact calls upon a Power beyond yourself to help you complete it.

After the rosy glow of the initial choice, you slowly realize that you are in total conflict. You have chosen a new way, but you are still heavily invested in the old way. This sense of being torn between two opposite ways is the place that nearly all of us are. We want to forgive and we want to avenge. We want to give and we want to get. Most of us, however, have managed in one way or another to live with the conflict, usually by masking it over, by trying to obscure the contrast between the two ways. Yet this just draws the process out. The thing to do is to take the next step.

> [Ur: You, Helen, had taken this step, and because you believed in it, you taught it to Bill, who still believed in the solution of sleep. You were not consistent in teaching it, but you did so often enough to enable him to learn it. Once *he* learned it, he could teach *you* how to become more consistently awake, and thus begin to waken *himself.* This placed him, too, in command of the journey. His recognition of the direction it must take was perfectly stated when he *insisted on collaboration.* You, Helen, had taken a giant step *into* conflict, but Bill turned you both forwards *toward the way out.* The more he teaches this, the more he will learn it.]

In this additional paragraph, we can see that Jesus was actually talking about a journey that both Helen and Bill were taking together, in which leadership was passing back and forth. First, Helen decided to learn the way of giving. This woke Bill out of his slumber, and once he learned the lesson from her, he began to return it to her, so she could be more consistently awake. This, in turn, strengthened his own learning. He then grasped the direction they had to go in. He realized they had to go *together.* This was their way out.

115

B. To Have Peace, Teach Peace to Learn It

1.   All who believe in separation [Ur: All the separated ones] have a basic fear of retaliation and abandonment. [Ur: This is because] they believe in attack and rejection, so that is what they perceive and teach and learn. These insane ideas are clearly the result of [Ur: their own] dissociation and projection. What you teach you are, but it is quite apparent that you can teach wrongly, and can therefore teach yourself wrong. Many thought I was attacking them, even though it was apparent I was not. An insane learner learns strange lessons. What you must recognize is that when you do not share a thought system, you are weakening it. Those who believe in it therefore perceive this as an attack on them. This is because everyone identifies himself with his thought system, and every thought system centers on what you believe you are. If the center of the thought system is true, only truth extends from it. But if a lie is at its center, only deception proceeds from it.

This paragraph really hearkens back to the cycle of perception that played such an important role in "The Message of the Crucifixion" (6.I). The point here is that we believe in attack and rejection. Then we teach attack and rejection—we attack and reject others. Then (through projection) we anticipate receiving the "natural" response to our actions. We anticipate *retaliation* for our attack, and *abandonment* for our rejection. And so we expect and fear these things, simply because we have taught ourselves that this is what we *deserve,* given what we *are.* Our attack and rejection have taught us a wrong view of what we are.

As a result, we imagine we are being attacked even when no one's doing a thing to us. That is what happened with Jesus. He was clearly perceived as an attacker, or else why would they kill him? Yet he was attacking no one. Ironically, this is why he made such a good projection screen, because he wasn't playing into their expectations of retaliation and abandonment. He wasn't confirming their image of themselves as guilty sinners who deserved punishment. Thus, he wasn't sharing their thought system, and his lack of agreement with it was perceived as weakening it. Therefore, because he was so totally benign, he was perceived as an attacker so dangerous that he had to be killed.

2.   All good teachers realize that only fundamental change will last, but they do not begin at that level. Strengthening motivation for

change is their first and foremost goal. It is also their last and final one. Increasing motivation for change in the learner is all that a teacher need do to guarantee change. Change in motivation is a change of mind, and this will inevitably produce fundamental change because the mind *is* fundamental.

I've always found this to be a very interesting remark—that all good teachers aim first and foremost at strengthening motivation for change. This is why motivational speakers are so highly prized in our culture. What this implies is that if we were only sufficiently motivated, we could do everything the Course asks us to do. We could forgive anyone, we could heal any illness, we could even let go of our entire ego. We are capable of all these things right now. All we lack is the motivation.

3.   The first step in the reversal or undoing process is the undoing of the getting concept. Accordingly, the Holy Spirit's first lesson was "To have, give all to all." I said that this is apt to increase conflict temporarily, and we can clarify this still further now. At this point, the equality of *having* and *being* is not yet perceived. Until it is, *having* appears to be the opposite of *giving*. Therefore, the first lesson seems to contain a contradiction, since it is being learned by a conflicted mind. This means conflicting motivation, and so the lesson cannot be learned consistently as yet. Further, the mind of the learner projects its own conflict [Ur: split], and thus does not perceive consistency in the minds of others, making him suspicious of their motivation. This is the real reason why, in many respects, the first lesson is the hardest to learn. Still strongly aware of the ego in yourself, and responding primarily to the ego in others, you are being taught to react to both as if what you do believe is not true.

Now we revisit the first lesson. Its whole aim, we are told, is to undo the concept that *having* comes through *getting*. It aims to teach us instead that having comes through giving. Yet this lesson puts us in a bind. We don't yet know that having and being are the same. We think that what we have are things that are separate and detachable from us, things that can be gained or lost. If we realized that what we have is our *being*, then we would also realize that we can't lose this by giving. How can you lose your being?

Now, however, we feel a pull towards giving and we feel a pull towards having, and we see these two pulls as totally in contradiction. Thus, when we are told "To have, give all to all," what we hear is, "Give all in order to be good, even though you'll have nothing left." Understandably, we feel conflicting motivation about learning such a lesson, and conflicting motivation is the death of learning.

Further, when we look out at the world, we see the same conflicting motivation in others, because we have projected it onto them. As a result, we think they want to give, but we are sure they want to get. If they can't be trusted, how can our giving lead to having? The more we give, we think, the more those vultures out there will just pick our bones clean. Therefore, to see only the motive to give in others, and to come only from this motive in us, seems like suicide.

> 4.   Upside down as always, the ego perceives the first lesson as insane. In fact, this is its only alternative since the other possibility, which would be much <u>less</u> acceptable to it, would obviously be that *it* is insane. The ego's judgment, here as always, is predetermined by what it <u>is</u> [Ur: though not more so than is any other product of thought]. The fundamental change will still occur with the change of mind <u>in the thinker</u>. Meanwhile, the increasing clarity of the Holy Spirit's Voice makes it impossible for the learner <u>not to listen</u>. For a time, then, he <u>is</u> receiving conflicting messages <u>and accepting both</u>.

So part of us—our ego—sees the first lesson as completely insane. Isn't this true? "To have, give all to all" sounds like insanity, doesn't it? This is because either it is insane, or our ego is insane, and the latter possibility is not very savory. On the other hand, we genuinely feel drawn to listen to the Holy Spirit. His message of total giving sounds so freeing, so loving, so holy. We almost can't *not* listen to this message.

In other words, we are listening to both. Both the ego and the Holy Spirit are making persuasive cases to us. Isn't this exactly where we are? Isn't this why our motivation to learn the Course is weak? And doesn't this leave us seriously divided inside, with no firm ground on which to stand?

> 5.   The way out of conflict between two opposing thought systems is clearly <u>to choose one and relinquish the other</u>. If you identify <u>with</u> your thought system, and you cannot escape this, and if you accept two

thought systems which are in <u>complete</u> <u>disagreement</u>, peace of mind <u>is</u> impossible. If you <u>teach</u> both, which you will surely do as long as you <u>accept</u> both, you are teaching conflict and <u>learning</u> it. Yet you <u>do</u> want peace, or you would not have called upon the Voice for <u>peace</u> to help you. Its <u>lesson</u> is not insane; the <u>conflict</u> is.

Jesus is not describing some abstract theory. He is describing our current condition exactly. He has us totally pegged: We are divided inside, and this is extremely uncomfortable. As we vacillate back and forth, we are actually teaching conflict to others. Have we thought about that? We are identifying with two opposing thought systems, and what does that imply about our identity? What kind of mutant hybrid does that make us? As this mutant hybrid, how can we be at peace? Yet we long for peace. That's why we called on the Holy Spirit in the first place.

How, then, can we have peace? We cannot have it through working out a reasonable truce between the two sides, which is what most of us try to do. We can only have it through choosing one side and getting rid of every last vestige of the other.

6. There can <u>be</u> no conflict between sanity and insanity. Only one is true, and therefore only <u>one</u> is <u>real</u>. The ego tries to persuade you that it is up to <u>you</u> to decide which voice is true, but the Holy Spirit teaches you that truth was created by God, and <u>your</u> decision <u>cannot</u> change it. As you begin to realize the quiet power of the Holy Spirit's Voice, and <u>Its perfect consistency</u>, it <u>must</u> dawn on your mind that you are trying to undo a decision that was irrevocably made <u>for</u> you. That is why I suggested before that you remind yourself to allow the Holy Spirit to decide for God for <u>you</u>.

We think that the outcome of this conflict is up to us, awaiting our final decision of which voice is true. What we don't realize is that it was never up to us. It's a completely done deal. We begin to sense this as we listen to the Holy Spirit. We notice that the quietness of His Voice comes from an infinite certainty in His message. We sense that no matter what we do, we will never be able to make Him waver, that He is unflappably consistent. We begin to suspect, in other words, that one side is unalterably true and the other is utterly false. And this means there is no conflict, for you can't have conflict between two things when one

119

of them isn't there. The whole conflict that we are experiencing, then, is nothing but our own delusion. We don't need to make a superhuman decision to be good and say no to all temptation. We just need to wake up from a conflict that isn't there.

> 7. You are <u>not</u> asked to make insane decisions, although you can [Ur: you are free to] <u>think</u> you are. It <u>must</u>, however, be insane to believe that <u>it is up to you</u> to decide what God's creations <u>are</u>. The Holy Spirit perceives the conflict <u>exactly as it is</u>. Therefore, His second lesson is:

> To *have* peace, <u>*teach*</u> peace to <u>*learn*</u> it.

We think we are being asked to insanely give everything away so that we have nothing left, but that's not what we are being asked. We think that the nature of ourselves and our brothers (as pure givingness) is up to us, but in truth it is up to God. We are seeing the conflict insanely, because we are insane. Only the Holy Spirit can see it objectively. Therefore, He gives us our second lesson: *"To have peace, teach peace to learn it."*

> 8. This is still a preliminary step, since *having* and *being* are still not equated. It is, however, more advanced than the first step, which is really only the beginning of the thought reversal [Ur: really only a thought *reversal*]. The second step is a positive affirmation of <u>what you want</u>. This, then, <u>is</u> a step in the direction <u>out</u> of conflict, since it means that alternatives have been considered, and <u>one</u> has been chosen as <u>more desirable</u>. Nevertheless, the term "more desirable" still implies that the desirable has degrees. Therefore, although this step is essential for the ultimate decision, it is clearly <u>not</u> the final one. [Ur: It should be clear that] Lack of order of difficulty in miracles has not yet been accepted, because <u>nothing</u> is difficult that is *wholly* <u>desired</u>. To desire wholly is to <u>create</u>, and creating <u>cannot</u> be difficult if God Himself created you <u>as</u> a creator.

The way out of the conflict and into peace is to choose the Holy Spirit's side. This resolves the conflict for two reasons: first, by choosing only one of the two sides, we are obviously choosing to end the conflict between them, and, second, the Holy Spirit's side *is* peace.

This helps us understand the second lesson. Its call to teach peace is, quite simply, a call for us to teach only the Holy Spirit's side. Right now, we are teaching both sides and thus teaching—*and learning*—conflict. If we want out of the conflict, we must express only one side in our interactions with others.

This lesson entails, therefore, a decision that the Holy Spirit's alternative is more desirable than the ego's. Since learning comes from motivation, this decision will make our learning far easier. Yet it will still not be totally easy, for we are not yet motivated in only one direction. If our motivation was completely single-minded, nothing would be impossible. We could do any miracle with equal ease. We could even go beyond that and create in Heaven. All of our difficulty comes from lack of motivation, "because nothing is difficult that is *wholly* desired."

> 9.   The second step, then, is still perceptual, although it is a giant step toward the unified perception that reflects [Ur: parallels] God's knowing. As you take this step and hold this direction, you will be pushing toward the center of your thought system, where the <u>fundamental</u> change will occur. [Ur: You are only beginning this step now, but you have started on this way by realizing that *only one way is possible*. You do not yet realize this consistently, and so your progress is intermittent,] At the second step progress is intermittent, but the second step is easier than the first because it follows. Realizing that it *must* follow [Ur: The very fact that you have accepted *that*] is a demonstration of a growing awareness that the Holy Spirit <u>will</u> lead you on.

The second step isn't all the way there, because the mind is still not completely unified. But it's on the way to being unified. In the first step, you were torn between getting and giving. Now, however, you realize that only one way is possible. This acceptance makes the process easier. You have more confidence that there is only one destination and that the Holy Spirit will keep on leading you until you reach it. And what is the destination? "Fundamental change." We will find out what that means in the third lesson.

The Urtext material in the middle of this paragraph depicts Helen (or maybe both she and Bill) as being basically at the beginning of the second lesson. She realizes that only one way is possible (the essence of the second lesson), but does not realize this consistently.

Application: To get in touch with how accurately Jesus is describing your condition, you may want to fill out the following questionnaire.

Do You Have CGD (Conflicting Goals Disorder)?

Give yourself a score of 0-3 for each item. 0 = never true. 1 = seldom true. 2 = sometimes true. 3 = often or always true. At the end, add up your scores. Score of 20 or over = CGD.

___1. You feel conflict between your needs and the requirements of the path.

___2. You feel asked to sacrifice your own best interests on behalf of truth.

___3. You feel as if you are being taught to respond as if what you believe (about yourself and others) is not true.

___4. You find yourself alternating between expressing your right mind (the "good") and your ego (the "bad").

___5. You vow to permanently express only the "good," leaving the "bad" unexpressed.

___6. You ping-pong back and forth between the above two strategies.

___7. You feel unsure of who you are, whether you are of Heaven or of the earth.

___8. Realizing you are torn between God and the ego, and can therefore serve neither well, you feel depressed by the thought that you will neither reach God nor truly satisfy your ego.

___9. You feel like a failure at both the worldly life and the spiritual life.

___10. You feel confused about whether to devote any particular chunk of time to things of God or things of the ego.

___11. You feel that before you were on the path you were more sure of who you were, where you were going, and what you wanted from life.

___12. Watching yourself spend part of your time pursuing God and part of your time feeding your ego, you feel confused about what your life is about.

___13. You sometimes feel as if there are two different people locked up inside of you, one an angel and the other a devil.

___14. You sometimes feel as if there is a fault line running down the very center of you.

___15. Because you stand for different things at different moments (attack one moment and love the next), you feel as if you do not *really* stand for anything.

___16. You have grown accustomed to having to deal with different impulses pulling you in opposite directions in any given situation.

C. Be Vigilant Only for God and His Kingdom

1.   [Ur: For your own salvation you *must* be critical, because *your* salvation *is* critical to the whole Sonship.] We said before that the Holy Spirit <u>is</u> evaluative, and <u>must</u> be. [Ur: In *your* mind, and your mind *only*, He sorts out the true from the false,] He sorts out the true from the false in your mind, and teaches you to judge every thought you allow to <u>enter</u> it in the light of what God <u>put</u> there. Whatever is <u>in accord</u> with this light He retains, to strengthen the Kingdom in <u>you</u>. What is <u>partly</u> in accord with it He accepts and purifies. But what is <u>out of accord</u> <u>entirely</u> He rejects by judging against. This is how He keeps the Kingdom perfectly consistent and perfectly unified. Remember, however, that what the Holy Spirit <u>rejects</u> the ego <u>accepts</u>. This is

because they are in fundamental disagreement about everything, being in fundamental disagreement about <u>what you are</u>. The ego's beliefs on this crucial issue vary, and that is why it promotes different moods. The Holy Spirit <u>never</u> varies on this point, and so the <u>one</u> mood He engenders is joy. He <u>protects</u> it by rejecting everything that does <u>not</u> foster joy, and so He alone can keep you wholly joyous.

This paragraph uses words like "critical," "evaluative," "rejects," "judge," and even "judging against." Despite what we may expect, they are all used *positively*. Their positive use highlights a crucial difference in how we should treat our own thoughts vs. the thoughts of others. While in relation to the thoughts of others we are not meant to judge or be critical, in relation to our own thoughts, we *are*. Remember (from 3.VI) that judgment primarily refers not to condemnation, but to measuring something against a standard and consequently accepting or rejecting it. We are supposed to be critical (in the sense of "exercising… careful judgment or judicious evaluation"—Merriam-Webster) about the thoughts we let into our mind. We are supposed to judge (in the sense of measuring them against the standard of right-thinking). We are supposed to do this because our "salvation *is* critical to the whole Sonship."

Actually, the Holy Spirit is already carrying this process out, largely outside of our awareness. He measures each thought against the standard of the light God put in our mind. If a thought measures up, He accepts it. If it partly measures up, He purifies it. If it doesn't at all measure up, He rejects it. Our goal is to get in touch with this process He is carrying out and join Him in it. This, in fact, is exactly what we do in practicing Lesson 151 in the Workbook.

The ego is carrying out its version of this same process, only its standards are opposite. Our problem is that, by and large, we have joined with the ego as evaluator of our thoughts, rather than the Holy Spirit. This is a major mistake, for at the heart of everything the ego does is a collection of varying views of who we are, and none of them makes us happy. In contrast, the Holy Spirit always carries the same view of us, one which leads to a constantly joyful mood.

2. The Holy Spirit does not teach you to judge others [Ur: does not teach your mind to be critical of others minds], because He does not want you to teach error and learn it yourself [Ur: to teach your

124

errors and *learn them yourselves*]. He would hardly be consistent if He allowed you to <u>strengthen</u> what you must learn to avoid. In the mind of the <u>thinker</u>, then, He *is* judgmental, but only in order to unify the mind so it can perceive <u>without</u> judgment. This enables the mind to <u>teach</u> without judgment, and therefore to learn to *be* without judgment. The <u>undoing</u> is necessary only in <u>your</u> mind, so that you [Ur: cannot *project* it {judgment}.] will not project, instead of extend. God Himself has established what you can extend with perfect safety. Therefore, the Holy Spirit's third lesson is:

> *Be vigilant <u>only</u> for God and <u>His</u> Kingdom.*

We may find it odd that we are asked to be critical in relation to our thoughts yet not in relation to the thoughts of others. Yet this double standard is literally the only way we can refrain from judging others. To say it plainly, *unless we watch our own thoughts with a critical eye, we will constantly allow in thoughts of judgment about others.* The only way to keep from judging others, then, is to police our own thoughts, to critically evaluate exactly what we allow into our mind. This is the goal of the Holy Spirit's activity in our mind. He aims to cleanse the mind of judgment so that we don't project judgment onto others. While reflecting on this, what came to me was this: "It doesn't matter what's in their mind. It only matters what's in *mine*." This doesn't mean I shouldn't care about them and respond to their needs. It just means that I shouldn't be concerned with how in line with God their thoughts are. I should only be concerned with how in line with God *my* thoughts are. By judging the alignment of their thoughts, I am throwing my own thoughts *out of* alignment.

Application: Think of someone whose thoughts you have judged and say to him or her:

> *It is not my place to evaluate your thoughts.*
> *It is only my place to evaluate my own.*
> *My only question must be: Is there love in my mind?*

The third and final lesson, then, is about this very policing of our mind. It is a call for mental vigilance, a call to allow only right-minded thoughts into our mind.

125

3.   This is a major step toward <u>fundamental</u> change. Yet it still has an aspect of thought <u>reversal,</u> since it implies that there is something you must be vigilant *against*. It has advanced far from the first lesson, which is merely the beginning of the thought reversal [Ur: which was *primarily* a reversal], and also from the second, which is essentially the identification of what is <u>more</u> desirable. This step, which follows from the second as the second follows from the first, emphasizes the <u>dichotomy</u> between the desirable and the <u>un</u>desirable. It therefore makes the <u>ultimate</u> choice inevitable.

This paragraph sketches the broad sweep of the spiritual journey. We start with an emphasis on reversal, on going *away* from our old thought system. The emphasis, in other words, is primarily negative (in the sense of negating). As we continue, our next step begins to emphasize the positive, the desirable, what we are going *toward*. Yet this step still includes going away from the undesirable. Finally, the third step is almost totally positive: Allow into your mind *only* the desirable. There is still an element of reversal; there is a focus on excluding the last vestiges of the undesirable. But the focus is mainly on "Do only that!" (V.3:4).

4.   While the first step seems to <u>increase</u> conflict and the second may still entail [Ur: still *entails*] conflict to some extent, this step calls for <u>consistent</u> vigilance [Ur: effort] <u>against it</u>. I have already told you that you can be as vigilant <u>against</u> the ego as for it. This lesson teaches not only that you can be [Ur: not that you *can* be], but that you *must* be. It does not concern itself with order of difficulty, but with <u>clear-cut priority for vigilance</u>. This lesson is unequivocal in that it teaches <u>there must be no exceptions,</u> although it does <u>not</u> deny that the temptation to <u>make</u> exceptions will occur. Here, then, your consistency is called on <u>despite</u> chaos. Yet chaos and consistency <u>cannot</u> coexist for long, since they are <u>mutually exclusive</u>. As long as you must be vigilant against <u>anything,</u> however, you are not recognizing this mutual exclusiveness, and still believe that you can choose either one. By teaching *what* to choose, the Holy Spirit will ultimately teach you that <u>you need not choose at all</u>. This will finally liberate your mind [Ur: will] from choice, and direct it towards creation within the Kingdom.

In this third step, we are emerging from the conflict, from being torn between two opposing sides. The goal is no longer to realize that the one side is more desirable. It is to realize that the one side is *totally* desirable and the other is totally *undesirable*. The goal is to be as vigilant against the ego as we used to be for it. The goal is to stand firm in allowing only light into our mind, even while darkness is knocking at the door and banging at the windows. If we can be consistent in this, despite the chaos swirling around the house, that chaos will eventually go. At this stage, we still carry the illusion that the choice between the two is up to us. Yet at least we are not concerned with how difficult it is. How can choosing between the totally desirable and totally undesirable be difficult? This means we are just a step away from learning that this "choice" is no choice at all. We are on the way to being liberated from choice itself. We are close to the total reunification of our mind.

> 5. Choosing through the Holy Spirit will [Ur: only] lead you to the Kingdom [Ur: *to* it]. You create by your true being, but what you are you must learn to remember. The way to remember it is <u>inherent</u> in the third step, which brings together the lessons implied in the others, and goes beyond them towards real integration. If you allow yourself to <u>have</u> in your mind only what God put there, you are acknowledging your mind as God created it. Therefore, you are accepting it <u>as it is</u>. Since it <u>is</u> whole [not divided, not conflicted], you are teaching peace *because* you believe in it. The final step will still be taken <u>for</u> you by God, but by the third step the Holy Spirit has <u>prepared</u> you <u>for</u> God. He is <u>getting you ready</u> for the translation of *having* into *being* by the very nature of the steps you must take <u>with</u> Him.

Now we see where these three steps are leading: to the final step, in which God lifts us back into knowledge. That is the fundamental change he keeps talking about. We also see how the three steps lead us there. Their progression is one in which we started out including only the ego's thoughts and end up including only God's. The resulting state of purity, in which we have in our mind only what God put there, is an acknowledgment of our mind as it really is. This state of wholeness, in which our mind is no longer a war zone between the two sides, is a reflection of the peace of our true nature. The three steps, in other words, lead us into a state that very closely reflects our true being. We are now ready to remember our being. That is what happens in the final step.

6.   You learn first that *having* rests on giving, and not on getting. Next you learn that you learn what you teach, and that you want to learn peace. This is the condition for identifying with the Kingdom, since it is the condition *of* the Kingdom. You have believed that you are without the Kingdom, and have therefore excluded yourself from it in your belief. It is therefore essential to teach you that you must be included, and that the belief that you are not is the only thing that you must exclude.

Notice that he keeps wanting to convey a sense of the entire sweep of the journey outlined by the three steps. The first step is about learning that having comes from giving, not getting. This places you in conflict between the impulse to give and the urge to get. Therefore, in the next lesson, you learn that what you really want is to be out of this conflict. You want peace, and the way to have this peace is by giving it to others, by teaching peace.

Teaching peace means demonstrating only one thought system (the Holy Spirit's) in your interactions with others. By teaching peace, you learn that peace is yours, and since peace is the condition of the Kingdom, you learn that the *Kingdom* is yours. Now you feel included in it, no longer on the outside. Yet there are still remaining shreds of your belief in being excluded from it. And so, in the third step, you focus on allowing none of those shreds into your mind. They are no longer invited in.

7.   The third step is thus one of protection for your mind, allowing you to identify only with the center, where God placed the altar to Himself. Altars are beliefs, but God and His creations are beyond belief because they are beyond question. The Voice for God speaks only for belief beyond question, which is the preparation for *being* without question. As long as belief in God and His Kingdom is assailed by any doubts in your mind, His perfect accomplishment is not apparent to you. This is why you must be vigilant on God's behalf. The ego speaks against His creation, and therefore engenders doubt. You cannot go beyond belief until you believe fully. [Ur: No one can *extend* a lesson he has *not learned fully*. Transfer, which *is* extension, is the measure of learning because it is the *measurable result*. This, however, does *not* mean that what it transfers *to* is measurable. On the contrary, unless it transfers to the whole Sonship, which is immeasurable because it was created *by* the Immeasurable, the learning itself *must* be incomplete.]

In the third step, then, we focus on total protection of our mind. We identify only with thoughts of the Kingdom. We are vigilant to exclude all other thoughts, just as in the summer we in Arizona are vigilant to not let the hot outside air into our air-conditioned homes. As Lesson 236 says, "Father, my mind is open to Your Thoughts, and closed today to every thought but Yours." In previous steps it was natural for our mind to be assailed by doubts. Yet now it is imperative that we allow no doubts to even enter. We have to reach a place where we believe without doubt, without question. Only then can we "go beyond belief." Only then can we return to "*being* without question."

The test of whether we have reached this place is our ability to extend it to others. The test of whether we have truly grasped any lesson is *transfer*: Can I apply what I have learned in one setting to a new and novel setting? When we extend our thoughts to others, that is what we are doing. We are transferring them to a new setting—in this case, another person—and thus proving that we have truly learned them. However, our learning is not really complete until we can extend it completely—meaning, to everyone, to the immeasurable totality of the Sonship.

> 8.   To teach the whole Sonship without exception demonstrates that you perceive its wholeness, and have learned that it is one. Now you must be vigilant to hold its oneness in your mind because, if you let doubt enter, you will lose awareness of its wholeness and will be unable to teach it. The wholeness of the Kingdom does not depend on your perception, but your awareness of its wholeness does. It is only your awareness that needs protection, since being cannot be assailed. Yet a real sense of being cannot be yours while you are doubtful of what you are. This is why vigilance is essential. Doubts about being must not enter your mind, or you cannot know what you are with certainty. Certainty is of God for you. Vigilance is not necessary for truth, but it is necessary against illusions.

Extension, as we saw, is the test of learning. If we can extend peace to the whole Sonship, without exception, this is the test that we have learned what the Sonship is. It shows we have learned it is one, rather than a collection of disparate fragments. Having reached this place, our focus must be on letting no doubts about its oneness enter our mind. After all, our goal is to return to being, and being is unequivocal. It is absolutely certain. Being just *is*. To *be* what it is and to *doubt* what it is are mutually exclusive. In the state of being, then, there is no doubt. How can we return to being, then, while a single sliver of doubt remains in our mind?

> 9.   Truth is <u>without</u> illusions and therefore <u>within</u> the Kingdom. Everything <u>outside</u> the Kingdom <u>is illusion</u>. When you threw truth away you [Ur: But you must learn to *accept* truth because *you threw it away*. You therefore] saw yourself <u>as if</u> you were <u>without</u> it. By making another kingdom that [Ur: *which*] <u>you valued</u>, you did <u>not</u> keep *only* the Kingdom of God in your mind, and thus placed part of your mind <u>outside</u> it. What you made has [Ur: thus *divided*] imprisoned <u>your will</u>, and given you a sick mind that <u>must</u> be healed. Your vigilance <u>against</u> this sickness <u>is</u> the way to heal it. Once <u>your</u> mind is healed it radiates health, and thereby <u>teaches</u> healing. This establishes you as a teacher who teaches <u>like</u> me. Vigilance was required of me as much as of you, and those who choose to teach the same thing <u>must</u> be in agreement about what they believe.

We have thrown the truth out of our minds, thus making our minds sick. Now the only solution is to let the truth back in and throw out the illusion. This heals our mental illness. Our minds then radiate health to others. We become teachers of health who teach like Jesus. Yet to reach this place, we need to do what he did: We need to exercise vigilance. He needed to be vigilant just as much as we do. (Imagine that!) We need to be critical about what we let into our mind, for our salvation is critical to the whole Sonship.

> 10.   The third step, then, is a statement of what you <u>want</u> to believe, and entails a willingness to <u>relinquish everything else</u>. [Ur: I told you that you were just beginning the second step, but I also told you that the third one *follows* it.] The Holy Spirit <u>will</u> enable you to take this step [Ur: *will* enable you to go on], <u>if you follow Him</u>. Your vigilance is the sign that you *want* Him to guide you. Vigilance <u>does</u> require effort, but only until you learn [Ur: but only to teach you] that effort <u>itself</u> is unnecessary. You have exerted <u>great</u> effort to preserve what you made <u>because</u> it was <u>not</u> true. Therefore, you must now turn your effort <u>against</u> it. Only this can cancel out the <u>need</u> for effort, and call upon the <u>being</u> which you both *have* and *are*. <u>This</u> recognition is wholly

<u>without</u> effort since it is <u>already</u> true and needs no protection. It is in the perfect safety of God. Therefore, inclusion is total and creation is <u>without limit</u>.

It is, of course, very hard to say where each one of us is in these steps. Maybe we are on the first step. Maybe, like Helen, we are just beginning the second. Maybe we are further along. No matter where we are in this progression, however, the Holy Spirit will lead us on, *if we follow Him.* How do we do that? Through being vigilant.

Yes, vigilance does require effort, but only because we have poured so much effort into establishing the illusion in our mind. Now that illusion uses the energy we have poured into it to call to us, to pull us toward it. We need to instead use that same energy to cancel it out. Once we have used our effort to cleanse the illusion from our mind, we are ready to return to the state of being, a state free of effort and strain, a state of pure, effortless grace.

This echoes a theme we find throughout this section. We need to choose well in order to go beyond choice. We need to believe fully in order to go beyond belief. We need to exert effort in order to reach the eternally effortless.

The real challenge in this section, though, I believe is this: Are we willing to be critical about what we let into our minds? Are we willing to evaluate each thought in light of what God placed in our minds? Are we willing to be vigilant *only* for God and *His* Kingdom?

Commentaries on Chapter 7

THE GIFTS OF
THE KINGDOM

I. The Last Step
Commentary by Greg Mackie

The previous section laid out the spiritual journey, which culminates in the "fundamental change" from perception to knowledge, the "final step" taken by God Himself (see T-6.V(C).5:7). This section tells us "something about this last step" and about the limitless loving extension of creation in Heaven, which we remember in the last step.

> 1.   The creative power of [Ur: both] God <u>and</u> His creations is limitless, but they are [Ur: it is] <u>not</u> in reciprocal relationship. You [Ur: *do*] communicate fully <u>with</u> God, as He does with <u>you</u>. This is an ongoing process in which you <u>share</u>, and <u>because</u> you share it, you are inspired to create <u>like</u> God. Yet in creation you are <u>not</u> in a reciprocal relation <u>to</u> God, since He created <u>you</u> but you did <u>not</u> create Him. I have already told you that only in this respect your creative power differs from His. Even in this world there is a parallel. Parents give birth to children, but children do <u>not</u> give birth to parents. They <u>do</u>, however, give birth to their children, and thus give birth <u>as</u> their parents do.

The Course often talks about our oneness with God, but here Jesus reminds us of the one crucial distinction between God and us: our creative power is not "reciprocal" ("Reciprocal" = "given…by each toward the other; mutual.") Communication between God and us *is* reciprocal, a two-way street in which each gives to the other. But creation goes only one way—from God to us: "He created you but you did not create Him."

Creation in Heaven is thus similar to a familiar one-way phenomenon in this world: a family tree. God is our Father, He created us as His Sons, and we in turn create our own sons. In this way, just as successive generations increase the family line of Smith or Jones, we increase the family line of God.

> 2.   If you created <u>God</u> and He created you, the <u>Kingdom</u> could not increase through its <u>own</u> creative thought. Creation would therefore be limited, and you would <u>not</u> be co-creator [Ur: co-creators] <u>with</u> God. As God's creative Thought proceeds <u>from</u> Him <u>to</u> you, so must <u>your</u>

creative thought proceed <u>from</u> you to <u>your</u> creations. Only in this way can <u>all</u> creative power <u>extend outward</u>. God's accomplishments are <u>not</u> yours, but yours are <u>like</u> His. <u>He</u> created the Sonship and <u>you</u> increase it. You <u>have</u> the power to <u>add</u> to the Kingdom, though <u>not</u> to add to the Creator <u>of</u> the Kingdom. You claim this power when you become vigilant only for God <u>and</u> His Kingdom. <u>By accepting</u> this power as <u>yours</u> you have learned to remember what you <u>are</u>.

One reason that distinction between God and us is crucial is that if creation *were* reciprocal, it would be a closed system with no increase, as if two people were constantly exchanging the same Christmas gift. The one-way nature of creation extending from God to us to our sons ensures that the family line of God will move *outward*. It will increase without limit, just as a single set of parents can start a family that can, in time, produce millions of offspring in this world. How can we get in touch with this limitless power of creation? By perfecting the last lesson of the Holy Spirit: being vigilant *only* for God and His Kingdom.

> 3. <u>Your</u> creations belong in <u>you</u>, as <u>you</u> belong in God. You are part of God, as your sons are part of His Sons. To create is to love. Love extends outward simply because it cannot be contained. Being limitless it <u>does not stop</u>. It creates forever, but <u>not</u> in time. God's creations have <u>always been</u>, because <u>He</u> has always been. <u>Your</u> creations have always been, because you can create only as God creates. Eternity is yours, because He created you eternal.

"To create is to love" (third sentence). What a beautiful thought! Creation extends in Heaven because the very nature of love is to extend outward, to share, to increase. Think of how you feel when you are in love: walking on air, beaming at total strangers, passionately describing your beloved to anyone who will listen. Moreover, you and your beloved may extend your love by producing children. One way or another, love just has to spill out and encompass everything. If this is so even with limited earthly love, think of how eager God is to extend His *limitless* Love, and how eager we must truly be to extend it to our own creations.

Application: This paragraph is not just abstract metaphysics; it is about *you*. To let that sink in, try reading it in the first person: "My creations belong in me as I belong in God..."

4.   The ego, on the other hand, always demands <u>reciprocal</u> rights, because it is competitive rather than loving. It is always willing to strike a bargain [Ur: make a deal], but it cannot understand that to be <u>like</u> another means that no bargains [Ur: deals] are possible. To gain you must <u>give</u>, not bargain. To bargain is to <u>limit</u> giving, and this is <u>not</u> God's Will. To will <u>with</u> God is to create like <u>Him</u>. God does not limit <u>His</u> gifts in <u>any</u> way. <u>You</u> *are* His gifts, and so your gifts must be like <u>His</u>. Your gifts <u>to</u> the Kingdom must be like His gifts to <u>you</u>.

In Heaven, the one-way, nonreciprocal nature of creation ensures that everyone in the family line is of the same nature: like Father, like Son, like sons. One aspect of this nature is the ability to extend outward without limit, so Heaven is a place of limitless giving, limitless increase. God is unlimited in His giving to us, so our gifts to our own creations are equally limitless.

The ego, however, demands reciprocal rights. (Another definition of "reciprocal" is "given or done in return for something else.") It wants to play "Let's make a deal." When you make a deal or bargain, the assumption is that you are different: each party wants different things and has different things to give in exchange. A bargain is also a closed system, like the Christmas present exchange I described above. If you exchange one thing for another thing, you're just passing the same old stuff back and forth. The "giving" is very limited; there is no increase.

Since you are a creation of God and not an ego, "Your gifts to the Kingdom must be like His gifts to you." This is a statement of fact about Heaven, but I think it also suggests an injunction for our life on earth: our gifts to fellow members of the Kingdom here on earth ought to be reflections of the gifts of Heaven. Instead of ego bargains, our gifts to one another should be free extensions of love, earthly versions of God's gifts to us.

5.   I gave <u>only</u> love to the Kingdom because I believed that was what I <u>was</u>. What you believe you are <u>determines</u> your gifts, and if God created you by extending <u>Himself as</u> you, you can only extend <u>yourself</u> as He did. Only joy increases forever, since joy and eternity are <u>inseparable</u>. God extends outward beyond limits and beyond time, and you who are co-creator [Ur: co-creators] with Him extend His Kingdom forever and beyond limit. Eternity is the indelible stamp of creation. The eternal are in peace and joy forever.

The first sentence is a subtle reference to the message of Jesus' crucifixion: "Teach only love, for that is what you are" (T-6.I.13:2). Indeed, "What you believe you are determines your gifts." If we believe we are egos, we will give the "gifts" of the ego, making bargains with everyone and everything. But if we believe we are love, as Jesus did, we will give love. We will give limitless gifts of joy and peace, gifts that reflect the eternal Kingdom. By doing this, we will get in touch with a joy that "increases forever." Can you imagine what that must feel like?

Application: Say, "What I believe I am determines my gifts. I am a Son of God, not an ego. Therefore, I must extend myself as God did. I already do this in Heaven. To recognize this on earth, I must extend limitless gifts that reflect the eternal love, peace, and joy of Heaven, just as Jesus did."

> 6. To think like God is to share His certainty of <u>what you are</u>, and to <u>create</u> like Him is to share the perfect Love He shares with <u>you</u>. To this the Holy Spirit leads you, that your joy may be complete because the Kingdom of God is whole. I have said that the last step in the reawakening of knowledge is taken by God. This is true, but it is hard to explain in words because words are symbols, and nothing that is true need [Ur: *needs* to] be explained. However, the Holy Spirit has the task of translating the use<u>less</u> into the use<u>ful</u>, the meaning<u>less</u> into the meaning<u>ful</u>, and the temporary into the time<u>less</u>. He <u>can</u> therefore tell you something about this last step, [Ur: although this one {this one last step} you must know yourself, because *by* it you know what you are. This *is* your being].

Through learning the lessons of the Holy Spirit, we are led to the point where we are ready for God's last step. God will lift us back to the state of creation in Heaven, to recognition of "His certainty of what you are" and "the perfect Love He shares with you." Now, finally, we will be told a little bit about what this "last step" really is.

> 7. God does not take steps, because His accomplishments are <u>not</u> gradual. He does not teach, because His creations are changeless. He does nothing <u>last</u>, because He created <u>first</u> and <u>for always</u>. It must be

understood that the word "first" as applied to Him is <u>not</u> a time concept. He is first in the sense that He is the First in the Holy Trinity Itself. He is the Prime Creator, because <u>He</u> created His co-creators. Because He <u>did</u>, time applies neither to Him <u>nor</u> to what He created. The "last step" that God will take was therefore true in the beginning, is true now, and will be true forever. What is timeless i<u>s always there</u>, because its <u>being</u> is eternally changeless. It does <u>not</u> change by increase, because it was forever created <u>to</u> increase. If you perceive it as <u>not</u> increasing you do not know what it <u>is</u>. You also do not know Who created it [Ur: what created it, or who *He* is]. God does not <u>reveal</u> this to you because it was never hidden. His light was never obscured, because it is His Will to <u>share</u> it. How can what is fully shared be withheld and then revealed?

What a mind-bending paragraph! Jesus wasn't kidding when he said in the last paragraph that "it is hard to explain [the last step] in words." This paragraph is full of paradoxes, and I'm not even going to pretend I understand it all. (I don't think Jesus expects us to understand it all.) Let's sort it out as best we can.

In talking about the last step, Jesus says a lot about what the last step is *not*:

1. It is not really a step. God doesn't take steps. His accomplishments are not gradual, and the idea of steps implies a gradual progression.
2. It is not really last. God does everything first. And even "first" does not mean first in time, but (I'm guessing) something like "first in the chain of causation."
3. It is not taught. God doesn't teach, because teaching implies change, and His creations are changeless.
4. It is not the revelation of a secret truth. God does not withhold anything. His Will is only to share everything He has.

What, then, *is* the last step? In some inscrutable sense, the last step is the *first* step, God's original act of creating us. It is that same extension and increase that has been going on since the beginning. (Notice here a resolution to the paradox of being changeless and increasing at the same time: the nature of creation is to increase, so it is by increase that creation retains its changeless nature.) Later in the Course we read: "Yet the last step must be taken by God, because the last step in your redemption, which seems to be in the future, was accomplished by God in your creation" (T-13.VIII.3:2). Jesus has tied the last step into the main theme of the section: the nature of creation in Heaven. Somehow, the last step and creation are one and the same thing.

Therefore, the last step has always been there. To experience it, all we need to do is follow those lessons of the Holy Spirit to the point where we are vigilant only for God and His Kingdom. And one major aspect of being vigilant for God and His Kingdom is giving to our brothers on earth—our fellow members of the Kingdom—in a way that reflects creation in Heaven. Since this giving reflects creation and the last step *is* creation, giving to our brothers on earth prepares our minds for God's last step.

II. The Law of the Kingdom
Commentary by Greg Mackie

1.   To heal is the <u>only</u> kind of thinking in this world that resembles the Thought of God, and because of the elements they <u>share</u>, can transfer easily <u>to</u> it. When a brother perceives himself as sick, he <u>is</u> perceiving himself as <u>not whole</u>, and therefore <u>in need</u>. If you, too, see him this way, you are seeing him as if he were <u>absent</u> from the Kingdom or separated <u>from</u> it, thus making the Kingdom <u>itself</u> obscure to <u>both of you</u>. Sickness and separation are not of God, but the Kingdom <u>is</u>. If you obscure the Kingdom, you are perceiving <u>what is not of God</u>.

The previous section discussed God's last step, the final stage of the spiritual journey in which our minds are returned to full awareness of the Kingdom. Here, we see that extending healing to others is the earthly version of extending creation in the Kingdom ("the Thought of God"), and is therefore what we must do to prepare our minds for God's last step.

How do we heal others? We *don't* heal them by perceiving them as really, truly sick. Of course, it's perfectly fine to acknowledge that a person is exhibiting symptoms of sickness on an earthly level, but we must not see the sickness as *real*. When we think someone is horribly sick, we aren't seeing that person as she really is: a holy being who is totally invulnerable to sickness. We are evicting her from the Kingdom, and thus find ourselves out on the street as well.

2.   To heal, then, is to correct perception in your brother <u>and</u> yourself by <u>sharing the Holy Spirit with him</u>. This places you both <u>within</u> the Kingdom, and restores <u>its</u> wholeness in your mind [Ur: minds]. This reflects [Ur: *parallels*] creation, because it <u>unifies by increasing</u> and <u>integrates by extending</u>. What you project or extend is real for you [Ur: *What you project you believe*]. This is an immutable law of the mind in this world as well as in the Kingdom. However, the content is different in this world [Ur: its *content* is somewhat different in this world from what it *really* is], because the thoughts it governs are <u>very</u> different from the Thoughts in the Kingdom. Laws must be adapted to circumstances

if they are to maintain order. The outstanding characteristic of the laws of mind as they operate in this world is that by obeying them, and I assure you that you <u>must</u> obey them, you can arrive at diametrically opposed results. This is because the laws have been adapted to the circumstances of this world, in which diametrically opposed outcomes seem possible because you can respond to two conflicting voices [Ur: in which diametrically opposed outcomes are *believed* in. The laws of mind govern thoughts, and you *do* respond to two conflicting voices].

The way to heal others is to share the Holy Spirit with them. This means *perceiving* the Holy Spirit *in* them, whatever symptoms of sickness the body may be manifesting. Seeing the Holy Spirit in a sick person reveals that she has never been evicted from the Kingdom, and this brings us back in off the street as well. Since this vision reflects the extension and increase of creation in Heaven, it brings God's last step one step closer.

Application: Think of someone you know who is sick. Say mentally to him or her, "I don't want to see you as truly sick, because this means I am seeing both of us as outside God's Kingdom. Let me look beyond your symptoms and see the Holy Spirit in you instead. This places us both within God's Kingdom, where we belong."

This is an application of a basic law of mind: "What you project or extend is real for you." This law of the Kingdom is adapted by the Holy Spirit to "maintain order" in this perceptual world. It will lead to "diametrically opposed results" depending on whether the ego or the Holy Spirit uses it. I'll talk a little more about those results in the next paragraph.

3. <u>Outside</u> the Kingdom, the law that prevails <u>inside</u> is <u>adapted</u> to "What you project you believe." This is its <u>teaching</u> form, because outside the Kingdom [Ur: teaching is mandatory because] learning is essential. This form [Ur: of the law clearly] implies that you will learn what <u>you</u> are from what you have projected onto others, and therefore believe <u>they</u> are. <u>In</u> the Kingdom there is no teaching <u>or</u> learning, because there is no <u>belief</u>. There is only <u>certainty</u>. God and His Sons, in the surety of being, <u>know</u> that what you extend [Ur: project] you <u>are</u>. That form of the law is <u>not</u> adapted at all, being the law of creation. God Himself created the law by creating *by* it. And His Sons, who create

<u>like</u> Him, follow it gladly, knowing that the <u>increase</u> of the Kingdom depends on it, just as <u>their</u> own creation did.

Now we have a complete picture of the law of the Kingdom, how the Holy Spirit has adapted it for use on earth, and the two ways of using it on earth:

1. *The law of the Kingdom: "What you extend you are."* This is the pure, non-adapted law of Heaven, the law of creation.

2. *The law adapted to this world: "What you project you believe."* When our minds left the Kingdom and fell into perception, we forgot what we are, so now we need a form of the law that can *teach* us what we are. If in Heaven what you extend you are, on earth what you project you *believe* you are. Or, to paraphrase the third sentence: Whatever you project onto others you will believe *they* are, and this will teach you what *you* are.

3. *Two different voices interpreting the law adapted to this world, with diametrically opposed results.* The two voices are the ego and the Holy Spirit, and we've already seen a good example of their diametrically opposed results. In the ego's usage, we project sickness onto our brothers—we see them as truly sick. This leads us to believe that they are outside of the Kingdom, which teaches us that we are outside the Kingdom as well. In the Holy Spirit's usage, we extend the Holy Spirit to our brothers—we see Him in them instead of sickness. This leads us to believe that they are within the Kingdom, which teaches us that we are within the Kingdom as well.

Application: Let's try out the "teaching form" of this law. Think of someone whom you believe to be deficient in some way. This is your projection onto him or her. (He may actually lack certain things in a worldly sense, but the idea that he is *truly* deficient is your projection.) Now, look within: Underneath your surface feelings, can you get in touch with the belief that *you too* are deficient? This is what your belief in the other person's deficiency is teaching you about yourself. You might want to try this same process with a person you believe to be truly holy and loving. How does this affect your belief about yourself?

4. Laws must be communicated if they are to be helpful. In effect, they must be <u>translated</u> for those who speak different languages [Ur: a different language]. Nevertheless [Ur: But], a good translator, although he <u>must</u> alter the <u>form</u> of what he translates, <u>never</u> changes the meaning. In fact, his whole <u>purpose</u> is to change the form <u>so that</u> the original meaning <u>is</u> retained. The Holy Spirit <u>is</u> the translator of the laws of God to those who do <u>not</u> understand them. <u>You</u> could not do this yourself because a conflicted mind <u>cannot</u> be faithful to one meaning, and will therefore <u>change the meaning to preserve the form.</u>

The Holy Spirit translates the laws of God into a form that we who speak the very different "language" of perception can understand. Like any good translator, the Holy Spirit translates those laws in a way that changes the form but preserves the meaning. The law of God discussed here is essentially the law of loving extension—that is its meaning—and He translates it into an earthly form of loving extension: healing. If we use the law to extend the Holy Spirit to our brothers, we will learn that we are of the Kingdom.

Because our minds are torn between the Holy Spirit and the ego, we ourselves would be very poor translators, because we can't stick to one meaning. We would tend to translate as the ego does, in a way that changes the meaning but preserves the form. The form here is essentially the idea that whatever comes out of you provides evidence for what you are. The ego takes that form and uses it to reinforce an idea totally antithetical to God's meaning: sickness. If we use the law to project sickness onto our brothers, we will learn that we are *not* of the Kingdom.

5. The Holy Spirit's purpose in translating is [Ur: naturally] <u>exactly</u> the opposite. He translates <u>only</u> to preserve the original meaning in <u>all</u> respects and in <u>all</u> languages. Therefore, He <u>opposes</u> the idea that differences in form are meaningful [Ur: He *opposes* differences in form as meaningful], emphasizing always that *these differences do not matter*. The meaning of His message is <u>always</u> the same; <u>only</u> the meaning matters. God's law of creation [Ur: in perfect form] does <u>not</u> involve the <u>use</u> of truth to convince His Sons <u>of</u> truth. The <u>extension</u> of truth, which *is* the law of the Kingdom, rests only on the knowledge of <u>what truth is.</u> This is your <u>inheritance</u> and requires no learning at all, but when you <u>dis</u>inherited yourself [Ur: *yourselves*] you <u>became</u> a learner of necessity [Ur: you *became* learners].

144

Again, the Holy Spirit translates in a way that changes the form but preserves the original meaning "in all respects and in all languages." I'm struck by this emphasis on preserving the original meaning. It has huge implications for how we interpret the Course. There is this idea in Course circles that different interpretations of the Course are equally valid. But if the Holy Spirit aims to preserve the original meaning of everything, our task as Course interpreters must be to do our absolute best to find the original meaning Jesus put there. The most valid interpretation is the one that is truest to this meaning.

The last three lines of the paragraph reiterate why the Holy Spirit needed to translate the laws of God into an earthly form. In the Kingdom, we don't need to be convinced of the truth, because we already *know* the truth with certainty. But such convincing *is* necessary on earth—because we have disinherited ourselves from the Kingdom, we must now learn the truth that we formerly knew with certainty.

> 6. No one questions the [Ur: intimate] connection of learning and memory. Learning is impossible <u>without</u> memory since it must be consistent to be remembered [Ur: Learning is impossible *without* memory, because it *cannot* be consistent *unless* it is remembered]. That is why the Holy Spirit's teaching <u>is</u> a lesson in remembering [Ur: That is why the Holy Spirit *is* a lesson in remembering]. I said before that He teaches remembering and <u>forgetting</u>, but the forgetting [Ur: aspect] is only <u>to make the remembering consistent</u>. You forget in order to <u>remember better</u>. You will <u>not</u> understand His translations while you listen to two ways of interpreting [Ur: perceiving] them. Therefore you must forget or relinquish one to <u>understand</u> the other. This is the only way you can <u>learn</u> consistency, so that you can finally *be* consistent.

This paragraph really echoes the lessons of the Holy Spirit. If you'll recall, the first lesson of the Holy Spirit engenders an intense conflict between His way and our way, the way of the ego. In our section here, that conflict takes the form of listening to two opposed ways of interpreting the Holy Spirit's translations of the laws of God. Learning His lessons is a process of resolving the conflict by choosing only His way and letting the other go entirely.

Here, the idea is that we learn to replace the conflict with *consistency* through a process of remembering and forgetting:

- In order to learn what the Holy Spirit teaches us consistently, we must remember it. Only if we remember what He teaches us can we measure our subsequent learning by His standard. That's why He is a lesson in remembering.
- In order to remember His lessons more consistently, we must forget the ego's lessons. That's why He teaches us both remembering and forgetting.
- Through this remembering and forgetting, we will learn consistently from the Holy Spirit.
- Through learning consistently from the Holy Spirit, we will finally *be* consistent.

> 7.   What can the perfect consistency of the Kingdom <u>mean</u> to those who are confused? It is [Ur: *must* be] apparent that confusion <u>interferes</u> with meaning, and therefore <u>prevents the learner from appreciating it</u>. There is <u>no</u> confusion in the Kingdom, because there <u>is</u> only one meaning. This meaning comes from God and *is* God. Because it is also <u>you</u>, you share it and <u>extend</u> it <u>as your Creator did</u>. This needs no translation because it is perfectly understood, but it <u>does</u> need extension because it *means* extension. Communication [Ur: here] is perfectly direct and perfectly united. It is totally free [Ur: without strain], because nothing discordant <u>ever</u> enters. That is why it <u>is</u> the Kingdom of God. It belongs to Him and is therefore <u>like</u> Him. That <u>is</u> its reality, and nothing <u>can</u> assail it.

The confusion of listening to two ways of interpreting the earthly form of God's laws blocks us from appreciating the true meaning of those laws. But in the Kingdom this confusion does not exist. In the Kingdom, there is only one meaning, a meaning inseparable from God Himself, which is shared by all the Sonship through perfect, direct communication. Regardless of what we try to do to distort God's laws and disrupt communication, the reality of the Kingdom can never be assailed. Thank God!

Though I think the extension referred to here is mainly extension in the Kingdom, I think the clear implication is that we must extend healing on earth. After all, we were told in the very first sentence of this section that healing is the way we return to the Kingdom. Through earthly extension, the Holy Spirit's translation of Heavenly extension, we prepare ourselves for God's last step, in which He lifts us back to the Kingdom. Through healing, we rediscover our eternal wholeness.

III. The Reality of the Kingdom
Commentary by Greg Mackie

1.   The Holy Spirit teaches one lesson, and applies it to <u>all</u> individuals in <u>all</u> situations. Being conflict-free, He maximizes <u>all</u> efforts and <u>all</u> results. By teaching the power of the Kingdom of God Himself, He teaches you that <u>all power is yours</u>. Its application does not matter. It is <u>always</u> maximal. Your vigilance does <u>not</u> establish it as yours, but it <u>does</u> enable you to use it <u>always</u> and in <u>all ways</u>. When I said "[Ur: Behold] I am with you always," I meant it literally. I am not absent to <u>anyone</u> in <u>any</u> situation. <u>Because</u> I am always with you, *you* are the way, the truth and the life. <u>You</u> did not make this power, any more than I did. It was created to <u>be</u> shared, and therefore cannot be meaningfully perceived as <u>belonging</u> to anyone <u>at the expense</u> of another. Such a perception makes it mean<u>ingless</u> by eliminating or overlooking its real and <u>only</u> meaning.

In an Urtext discussion that precedes this paragraph, Jesus says the ego developed abilities as "potentials for excelling," means of being better than others. The Holy Spirit sees those same abilities as "potentials for *equalizing*," means of affirming everyone's inherent equality. He applies all abilities maximally to teaching His one lesson: the equality of everyone who shares "the power of the Kingdom of God."

We normally think the situations in our lives present many different lessons to learn, so our minds are all over the place. But we are called to commit ourselves, through our mental vigilance for God and His Kingdom, to devote everything in our lives to teaching and learning the Holy Spirit's one lesson. This commitment will release the power of the Kingdom in *us* to be used maximally for everyone in every situation. We may think such miracle-working power belongs only to great masters like Jesus, but the Holy Spirit's very lesson is that it is equally shared by all the Sonship. All power is ours; like Jesus, we can use the power of the Kingdom "always and in all ways."

Application: Jesus is eager to share the power of the Kingdom with us. Imagine him saying these words to you: *"I am literally with you* *always. I am not absent to anyone in any situation. Because I am with you, **you** are the way, the truth, and the life."*

2.   God's meaning waits in the Kingdom, because that is where He placed it. It does not wait in time. It merely rests in the Kingdom because it belongs there, as you do. How can you who are God's meaning perceive yourself as absent from it? You can see yourself as separated from your meaning only by experiencing yourself as unreal. This is why the ego is insane; it teaches that you are not what you are. That is so contradictory it is clearly impossible. It is therefore a lesson you cannot really learn, and therefore cannot really teach. Yet you are always teaching. You must, therefore, be teaching something else [Ur: as well], even though the ego does not know what it is. The ego, then, is always being undone, and does suspect your motives. Your mind cannot be unified in allegiance to the ego, because the mind does not belong to it. Yet what is "treacherous" to the ego is faithful to peace. The ego's "enemy" is therefore your friend.

Deep down, underneath the ego's lies, we really know that we belong to the Kingdom and share its power. At our core, we *are* fully committed to the Kingdom. Because of this, we cannot wholeheartedly believe we are separate from it. As Lesson 182 says, "A memory of home keeps haunting you" (W-pI.182.1:3). Our current state feels vaguely unreal and insubstantial. We feel like strangers in a strange land; like Neo early on in *The Matrix*, we suspect that our reality is much more than it seems.

So, even as we teach and learn that we are egos in a separate world, we can't quite pull the wool completely over our eyes. Our reality asserts itself and teaches the truth silently, even as we deny it with our lips. This terrifies the ego, because it senses that our mind does not really belong to it, and is therefore an "enemy" that can wise up and undo it at any time. We want peace, and only committing fully to our true mind, our reality, can give it to us.

3.   I said before that the ego's friend is not part of you, because the ego perceives itself [Ur: as] at war and therefore in need of allies. You who are not at war must look for brothers and recognize all whom you see as brothers, because only equals are at peace. Because God's equal Sons have everything, they cannot compete. Yet if they perceive any

of their brothers as anything <u>other</u> than their perfect equals, the <u>idea</u> of competition <u>has</u> entered their minds. Do not underestimate your need to be vigilant *against* this idea, because <u>all</u> your conflicts come <u>from</u> it. It *is* the belief that conflicting interests are possible, and therefore you have accepted the <u>im</u>possible as true. Is that different from saying you perceive <u>yourself</u> as unreal?

When we identify with the ego, we set up a seeming war within between truth and illusion, and a seeming war without between ourselves and others. Others seem to have "conflicting interests" with us, forcing us to do constant battle with them for limited resources. The ego's primary ally in this war is its "friend," the body (see T-6.IV.4-5), the ultimate limited resource. But we are not *really* at war, and to recognize this we must see those "enemies" out there as *brothers*, our true allies, equal members of the Kingdom of God who have everything, just as we do. If everyone has everything, what need is there for competition? If our interests never conflict, what could there be but peace?

Application: Think of a situation where you are competing with someone. Say: *"The idea of competition has entered my mind, and I must be vigilant against this idea. All of my conflicts, including this one, come from it. Let me see this person as an equal brother who has everything, as I do. When I do this, I will know we are at peace."*

4.   To be <u>in</u> the Kingdom is merely to focus your full attention <u>on</u> it. As long as you believe you can <u>attend</u> to what is <u>not</u> true, you are accepting conflict as your <u>choice</u>. <u>Is it really a choice</u>? It <u>seems</u> to be, but seeming and reality are hardly the same. You who *are* the Kingdom are not concerned with seeming. Reality is yours because you <u>are</u> reality. This is how *having* and *being* are ultimately reconciled, not in the Kingdom, but <u>in your</u> mind [Ur: *minds*]. The altar there is the <u>only</u> reality. The altar is <u>perfectly</u> clear in thought [Ur: It is *perfectly* clear in its thought], because it is a reflection of <u>perfect</u> Thought. Your right mind [Ur: It {the altar}] <u>sees</u> only brothers, because it sees <u>only</u> in its own light.

We normally focus our attention on a million different things. But if we want to recognize our reality, we must focus our full attention on the *Kingdom*—we must be vigilant only for it. This means we must see our brothers as equal members of the Kingdom, not competitors with conflicting interests. In practical terms, the choice to see the Kingdom can be something as simple as forgiving your brother for leaving the toilet seat up.

This is really our only choice—the "choice" for the ego and the conflict it engenders is a choice for something impossible, which is not a choice at all. It is like saying, "I choose to live on the planet Vulcan." The only option truly open to us is our *reality*, the Kingdom of God, which is both what we *have* and what we *are*. Deep in our minds is the altar God placed there in the beginning, at which we and all our brothers are gathered together in communion. This is where we must focus our attention.

> 5.   God has lit your mind [Ur: minds] Himself, and keeps your mind [Ur: minds] lit <u>by</u> His Light because His Light is <u>what your</u> mind is [Ur: *minds are*]. This is <u>totally</u> beyond question, and when <u>you</u> question it you are answered [Ur: when *you* questioned it you *were* answered]. The Answer [Ur: answer] merely <u>undoes</u> the question by establishing the fact that to <u>question</u> reality is to question <u>meaninglessly</u>. That is why the Holy Spirit <u>never</u> questions. His sole function is to <u>un</u>do the questionable and thus <u>lead to certainty</u>. The certain are perfectly calm, because they are not in doubt. They do <u>not</u> raise questions, because <u>nothing questionable enters their minds</u>. This holds them in perfect serenity, because this is what they <u>share</u>, <u>knowing</u> what they are.

"To question reality is to question meaninglessly." We've seen this theme throughout this section. When we question the reality of the Kingdom, we are questioning meaninglessly, believing in impossible things. What a reversal! Even if we are spiritual seekers, we normally think that our egos and our world are essentially real, while trying to reach the exalted state the Course describes feels like believing in the impossible. But in truth, it is the other way around. In our frantic attempts to believe that we are what we are not, we are like the Queen in Lewis Carroll's *Through the Looking Glass*:

Alice laughed: "There's no use trying," she said; "one can't believe impossible things." "I daresay you haven't had much practice," said the Queen. "When I was younger, I always did it for half an hour a day.

Why, sometimes I've believed as many as six impossible things before breakfast."

We've had lots of practice believing impossible things, but Jesus says, "There's no use trying." Our constant questioning of reality reflects our belief in impossible things, which means our questions aren't real questions at all. They are simply expressions of insanity, evidence that we've lost touch with reality. The Holy Spirit has answered them, but He has done more than that: He has *undone* them. If we accept His undoing of our questions by directing our full attention to the Kingdom, we will be led to the certainty that has always been there deep in our minds. The whole time we've been questioning reality and fighting the ego's war and trying to believe the impossible, we have been immersed *in* our reality, sharing perfect peace with our brothers in the Kingdom of God.

IV. Healing as the Recognition of Truth
Commentary by Greg Mackie

Before we begin the section proper, I want to comment briefly on two paragraphs that precede it in the Urtext:

> Healing is both an art and a science, as has so often been said. It is an art because it depends on inspiration in the sense that we have already used the term. Inspiration is the opposite of dis-spiriting, and therefore means to make joyful. The dis-spirited are depressed because they believe that they are literally "without the Spirit," which is an illusion. You do not *put* the Spirit in them by inspiring them, because that would be "magic," and therefore would not be real healing. But you *do* recognize the Spirit that is *already there*, and thereby *reawaken it*. This is why the healer is part of the Resurrection and the *Life*. The *Spirit* is not asleep in the minds of the sick, but the part of the mind that can perceive it and be glad *is*.

Healing is an art because just as art depends on the inspiration of the artist and inspires the person who partakes of the artist's work, healing depends on the inspiration of the healer and inspires the recipient of the healing. Earlier, Jesus said that "to be inspired is to be in the spirit" (T-4. In.1:6). But healing isn't establishing the spirit in the recipient yourself; that would be magic. Instead, healing is recognizing the spirit that is already there, which reawakens it in the recipient.

> Healing is also a science because it obeys the laws of God, whose laws are true. *Because* they are true, they are perfectly dependable, and therefore universal in application. The real aim of science is neither prediction nor control, but *only understanding*. This is because it does *not* establish the laws it seeks; *cannot* discover them through prediction, and has *no* control over them at all. Science is nothing more than an approach to *what already is*. Like inspiration, it can be misunderstood as magic, and *will* be whenever it is undertaken as *separate* from what already is, and perceived as a means for *establishing* it. To believe this is possible is to believe *you can do it*. This can *only* be the voice of the ego.

153

This discussion parallels the one about healing as an art. Healing is a science because the proper aim of science is to understand universal laws that must be obeyed, and healing obeys the universal laws of God. But healing isn't establishing the laws yourself; that would be magic. Instead, healing is recognizing the laws that are already there, which are the vehicle for reawakening spirit in the recipient.

> 1.   Truth can only *be* <u>recognized</u> and *need* only be recognized. Inspiration is of the Holy Spirit [Ur: Inspiration is of the Spirit], and certainty is of God according to His laws. Both, therefore, come from the same Source, since inspiration comes from the Voice <u>for</u> God and certainty comes from the laws <u>of</u> God. Healing does not come <u>directly</u> from God, Who knows His creations as perfectly whole. Yet healing is still [Ur: nevertheless] <u>of</u> God, because it proceeds from His Voice and from His laws. It is their <u>result</u> [the result of His Voice and His laws], in a state of mind that does not know Him. The <u>state</u> [of mind that does not know Him] is unknown to Him and therefore does not exist, but those who sleep are <u>unaware</u>. <u>Because</u> they are unaware, <u>they do not know</u>.

In the discussions of healing as art and healing as science, we saw that in both cases, healing comes from recognizing a truth that is already there. Healing is based on the inspiration that comes from recognizing the spirit and the certainty that comes from recognizing God's laws. Healing does not come directly from God, because He is in the state of knowledge and therefore knows that we are perfectly whole. Yet healing does come *indirectly* from God, because it comes from the Holy Spirit's translation of His laws into earthly forms (which was discussed in T-7.II).

> 2.   The Holy Spirit must work *through* you to teach you He is *in* you. This is an intermediary step toward the knowledge that <u>you</u> are in God <u>because you are part of Him</u>. The miracles the Holy Spirit inspires <u>can</u> have no order of difficulty, because every part of creation <u>is</u> of one order. This is God's Will <u>and</u> yours. The laws of God <u>establish</u> this, and the Holy Spirit reminds you <u>of</u> it. When you heal, you are <u>remembering the laws of God</u> and <u>forgetting</u> the laws of the ego. I said before that forgetting is merely a way of <u>remembering better</u>. It is therefore <u>not</u> the opposite of remembering when it is properly perceived. Perceived improperly, it induces a perception of <u>conflict with something else,</u> as

all incorrect perception does. <u>Properly</u> perceived, it can be used as a way <u>out</u> of conflict, as all proper perception

Healing of our brothers occurs when we let the Holy Spirit work miracles *through* us. This proves that He is *in* us because it demonstrates that there is something in us that is far more holy and powerful than we currently imagine ourselves to be. Forrest Gump famously said, "Stupid is as stupid does." In like manner, love is as love does. If I manage to do something only the Love of God could do, it must mean that His Love is in me.

There is no order of difficulty in miracles because they are based on God's laws. His laws give us all power; affirm that all sickness is pure illusion; and proclaim the absolute equality, shared nature, and infinite worth of every brother, "every part of creation." Since all this is true, how could there be any difficulty at all?

What makes miracles *seem* difficult is our obstinate belief in the limiting laws of the ego. Fortunately, the very act of healing through the Holy Spirit helps us remember God's laws and forget the ego's. (The earlier reference to forgetting so we can remember better was T-7.II.6:5.) In the Holy Spirit's hands, forgetting is not the opposite of remembering; instead, forgetting false laws is a way of *helping* us remember true ones.

3.   The ego does <u>not</u> want to teach everyone all it has learned, because that would <u>defeat</u> its purpose [Ur: in learning]. Therefore it does not <u>really</u> learn at all. The Holy Spirit teaches <u>you</u> to use what the ego has made, to <u>teach</u> the opposite of what the ego has "<u>learned</u>." The <u>kind</u> of learning is as irrelevant as is the particular ability that was applied <u>to</u> the learning. All you need do is make the effort to learn, for the Holy Spirit has a unified goal for the effort. If different abilities are applied long enough to one <u>goal</u>, the abilities <u>themselves</u> become unified. This is because they are channelized in one direction, or in one <u>way</u>. Ultimately, then, they all contribute to <u>one result</u>, and by so doing, their <u>similarity</u> rather than their differences is emphasized. [Ur: You can *excel* in many *different* ways, but you can *equalize* in *one way only*. Equality is *not* a variable state, by definition.]

The material in this paragraph was moved from the beginning of T-7.III, and is part of a longer Urtext discussion. As I mentioned in my commentary on that section, that discussion points out that the ego developed abilities as "potentials for excelling," means of being better than others. That's why it doesn't want to teach everyone everything it has learned. Like a scientist who withholds critical research results from his colleagues so he can publish them himself and win a Nobel Prize, the ego uses its knowledge to inflate itself. The last thing it wants to do is share everything with everyone and thereby make everyone equal.

The Holy Spirit, however, wants to do the very thing the ego wants to avoid. He sees those same abilities as "potentials for *equalizing*," means of affirming everyone's inherent equality as Sons of God, members of His Kingdom. Whatever abilities we have and however ego-based our original learning purpose for them may have been, He can transform them all from vehicles for various ways of excelling into vehicles for His unified goal of healing—so much so that if they are used in this way long enough, "the abilities themselves become unified."

Helen's scribing of the Course was an example of this principle in action. Jesus told her that "the Holy Spirit has taken very diversified areas of *your* past learning, and has applied them to a *unified* curriculum." He took Helen's psychic abilities, her knowledge of psychology, her love of logic, her penchant for Shakespearean iambic pentameter, etc., and wove them into a masterpiece. Indeed, there seems to be no ability that can't be used by the Holy Spirit; even Bill's punning ability had a potentially miraculous use in Jesus' eyes.

> 4.   All abilities should therefore be given over to the Holy Spirit, Who understands how to use them properly. He uses them only for healing, because He knows you only as whole. By healing you learn of wholeness, and by learning of wholeness you learn to remember God. You have forgotten Him, but the Holy Spirit understands [Ur: still knows] that your forgetting must be translated into a way of remembering [Ur: and *not* perceived as a *separate* ability which *opposes an opposite*. This is the way in which the ego tries to use *all* abilities, because its goal is *always* to make *you* believe that *you* are in opposition].

Again, there seems to be no ability that can't be used by the Holy Spirit. Even our unfortunate ability to forget God can be transformed by Him into the ability to forget the ego. Therefore, we should give *all* of our abilities to the Holy Spirit. If we let Him apply them all to

His one goal of healing, the rewards are great. We will recognize our wholeness, and this will enable us to achieve the ultimate goal of the spiritual journey: to remember God. So, what is *your* masterpiece? What power might be unleashed in you if you got all your sled dogs pulling in the same direction, if you committed every ability you have to the Holy Spirit's goal of healing?

Application: Think of an ability of yours that you feel is a real strength, but which you have used mostly for your ego, mostly to excel. Say to the Holy Spirit: *"I give my ability for _____ to You. Only you understand how to use it. I want to let You use it for healing so I can awaken to my own wholeness and remember God."*

> 5. The ego's goal is as unified as the Holy Spirit's, and it is <u>because</u> of this that their goals can <u>never</u> be reconciled in <u>any</u> way or to <u>any</u> extent. The ego <u>always</u> seeks to divide and separate. The Holy Spirit <u>always</u> seeks to unify and <u>heal</u>. As you heal [others] you <u>are</u> healed, because the Holy Spirit sees <u>no order of</u> difficulty in <u>healing</u>. Healing <u>is</u> the way to undo the belief in differences, being the <u>only</u> way of perceiving the Sonship as one [Ur: undo the belief in differences, because it is the *only* way of perceiving the Sonship *without* this belief]. This perception is therefore <u>in</u> accord with the laws of God, even in a state of mind that is <u>out</u> of accord with His. [Ur: But] The strength of right perception is so great that it brings the mind <u>into</u> accord with His, because it serves His Voice, Which <u>is</u> in all of you.

Just as the Holy Spirit is totally committed to the goal of unifying and healing, the ego is totally committed to the goal of dividing and separating. There's no way any relationship between the two will work out; this is truly a case of "irreconcilable differences." For this reason, as those lessons of the Holy Spirit in Chapter 6 emphasized, we must commit ourselves totally to God and send the ego packing. To do this, we must commit ourselves to the function this "course in miracles" is training us to do: working miracles, extending healing to our brothers. This is the only way to heal ourselves, to undo the belief in differences, to perceive the Sonship as one, and to bring our minds back into accord with the laws of God.

6.   To think you can oppose the Will of God is [Ur: To oppose the pull or the will of God is not an ability but] a real delusion. The ego believes that it can [Ur: *has* this ability], and that it can offer you its own "will" [Ur: offer this ability to *you*] as a gift. *You do not want it.* It is not a gift. It is nothing at all. God has given you a gift that you both *have* and *are*. When you do not use it, you forget [Ur: do not know] that you have it. By not remembering it [Ur: not knowing this], you do not know what you are. Healing, then, is a way of approaching knowledge by thinking in accordance with the laws of God, and recognizing their universality. Without this recognition, you have made the laws meaningless to you. Yet the laws are not meaningless, since all meaning is contained by them and in them.

This section has spoken of how the ego developed abilities for the purpose of excelling. But there is one ability the ego has *never* developed, because it is quite simply impossible: the ability to "oppose the pull or the will of God." It dangles this "ability" before our eyes and tells us that we want it and can really have it, but in fact it is totally undesirable because "It is nothing at all." Thank God! I'm so glad we can't *really* oppose the pull of God. It makes the spiritual journey feel much easier.

When we *think* we've opposed God, all we've done is forgotten Him and His gifts. This forgetting is exacerbated by letting our healing ability fall into disuse. Just as the Holy Spirit working through us teaches us that He is in us, so not letting Him work through us leads to forgetting that He is in us. The laws of God become meaningless to us, and not using the gift we *have* causes us to forget what we *are*. Letting Him work through us—extending healing to others—helps us to remember what we have forgotten. It realigns our minds with God's laws and restores our awareness of the gift of God we both *have* and *are*.

Application: Bring to mind some grievance you are holding against a brother right now. This grievance is a temptation of the ego, the ego's attempt to offer you the "gift" of the ability to oppose the pull or Will of God. Say to yourself: *"I do not want it. It is not a gift. It is nothing at all. God has given me a gift that I both **have** and **am**. Let me use this gift to extend healing my brother, and thus remember what I am."*

7.   Seek ye first the Kingdom of Heaven, because that is where the

laws of God operate truly, and they can operate <u>only</u> truly because they are the laws of truth. But <u>seek this only</u>, because you can <u>find</u> nothing else. There *is* nothing else. God is All in all in a very literal sense. All being is in Him Who is [Ur: because He *is*] all Being. <u>You</u> are therefore in Him since [Ur: because] <u>your</u> being <u>is</u> His. Healing is a way of <u>forgetting</u> the sense of danger the ego has induced in <u>you</u>, by not recognizing its existence in your brother [Ur: brothers]. This strengthens the Holy Spirit in <u>both</u> of you, because it is a <u>refusal to acknowledge fear</u>. Love needs only this invitation. It comes freely to <u>all</u> the Sonship, being what the Sonship <u>is</u>. By your awakening <u>to</u> it, you are merely forgetting what you are <u>not</u>. This enables you to remember what you <u>are</u>.

The first two sentences here present another version of the Holy Spirit's third lesson: "Be vigilant only for God and His Kingdom" (T-6.V(C).2:8). There is really nothing else to seek and find; in reality, there is nothing *but* God and His Kingdom. Seeking the Kingdom may sound metaphysical and abstract, but as we've seen, the way we do it is quite down to earth: healing others. Extending healing undoes the fearful sickness and suffering in our brother, which undoes fear in ourselves as well. Dropping the wall of fear strengthens the awareness of the Holy Spirit in both of us, and this is all the invitation love needs. Love comes streaming not only into our minds, but into every mind in the Sonship. When we awaken to love, we forget what we are not and remember what we are.

V. Healing and the Changelessness of Mind
Commentary by Greg Mackie

1.   The body is nothing more than a framework for developing abilities [Ur: It is therefore a means for developing potentials], which is quite apart from what they are [Ur: the potential is] used <u>for</u>. *That* is [Ur: This *is*] a decision. The effects of the ego's decision in this matter are so apparent that they need no elaboration, but the Holy Spirit's decision to use the body <u>only</u> for communication has such a direct connection with healing that it <u>does</u> need clarification. The unhealed healer <u>obviously</u> does not understand his own vocation.

Remember the previous discussion about abilities: the ego developed them as "potentials for excelling" and the Holy Spirit transformed them into "potentials for equalizing." Now a new element enters the discussion: the body, "a framework for developing abilities" and thus "a means for developing potentials." The body is simply a neutral tool; we can use it to develop whatever potentials we like. We're already all too familiar with using the body for excelling—that's what people use it for every day (recent Exhibit A: the Olympics). But we aren't quite so familiar with how the Holy Spirit uses it for equalizing. We need clarification on this, because it has a direct connection with our calling to be healers.

2.   <u>Only</u> minds communicate. Since the ego <u>cannot</u> obliterate the impulse to communicate because it is also the impulse to <u>create</u>, it can only teach you that the <u>body</u> can both communicate <u>and</u> create, and therefore <u>does not need the mind</u>. The ego thus tries to teach you that the body can <u>act</u> like the mind, and <u>is</u> therefore self-sufficient. Yet we have learned that behavior is <u>not</u> the level for either teaching <u>or</u> learning, since you <u>can</u> act in accordance with what you do <u>not</u> believe. To do this, however, will weaken you as a teacher <u>and</u> a learner [Ur: teachers *and* learners] because, as has been repeatedly emphasized, you teach what you *do* believe. An inconsistent lesson <u>will</u> be poorly taught <u>and poorly learned</u>. If you teach both sickness *and* healing, you are both a poor teacher and a poor learner.

160

We all think the body can communicate and create. We think real communication happens when it says or writes something, and real creation happens when it produces a work of art or a baby. But in truth, communication and creation are of the mind. Whatever we seem to be communicating with our behaviors, what we really communicate and really create is what the mind really *believes*. Ideally, our behavior should reflect what we believe—indeed, using the body to communicate healed beliefs is what the Course is talking about when it says the Holy Spirit uses the body only for communication. But everyone knows we can also behave in a way that doesn't reflect what we really believe.

When we do this, we're sending mixed messages. We've all experienced mixed messages: we speak of someone not "walking her talk" and we've heard those dreaded words, "Do as I say, not as I do." In this paragraph, the mixed message is that our beliefs communicate one thing while our behavior communicates another. This is what the unhealed healer does; this is why he "does not understand his own vocation." An unhealed healer is a person who tries to heal others without having the core beliefs that produce real healing. He may be teaching "healing" with his words and deeds, but the unhealed thoughts in his mind are still teaching sickness. How likely is this to produce real healing?

> 3. Healing is the one ability everyone <u>can</u> develop and <u>must</u> develop if he is to <u>be</u> healed. Healing <u>is</u> the Holy Spirit's form of communication in this world, and <u>the only one He</u> accepts [Ur: *knows*]. He recognizes no other, because He does <u>not</u> accept the ego's confusion of mind and body. Minds <u>can</u> communicate, but they <u>cannot</u> hurt. The body in the service of the ego can hurt other <u>bodies,</u> but this <u>cannot</u> occur <u>unless</u> the body has <u>already</u> been confused <u>with</u> the mind. This situation [Ur: fact], too, can be used either for healing or for magic, but you must remember [Ur: realize] that magic always involves [Ur: is *always*] the belief that healing is <u>harmful</u>. This belief is its totally insane premise, and so it proceeds accordingly.

If we want healing for ourselves, we must develop the ability to heal others—we must become miracle workers. This is an amazing statement. Whatever we may be called to do on a form level, the inner content—the true vocation of literally every person on earth—is "healer." Healing, in fact, is the only thing that really qualifies as "communication." The

Holy Spirit doesn't buy into our silly notion that bodies communicate by themselves.

Application: Say to yourself, *"Healing others is the one ability I can develop and must develop if I want to be healed myself."*

This paragraph contains the first statement of the important Course principle that minds cannot attack. The idea is that minds cannot really hurt each other, because they are not separate from each other—they are totally one. Bodies *can* hurt each other, but this can only happen when we've bought the ego's lie and convinced ourselves that we are bodies, not minds.

The final two sentences here have always baffled me. Here's my best shot at interpreting them: The fact that the body can be *confused* with the mind implies that this confusion is a *decision* of the mind—we aren't imprisoned by the body. Therefore, we have two options to choose from, with two different results. One, we can choose to retain the confusion of body and mind. If we do this, all of our attempts at healing others will be magic, some attempt to fix the body instead of healing the mind. We'll resort to magic because we'll feel threatened by real healing, which undoes the body-mind confusion we're trying to hold on to. Two, we can choose to give up this confusion. If we do this, we will develop the ability to extend real healing, the very ability we must develop if we want to be healed ourselves.

> 4. Healing <u>only strengthens</u>. Magic always tries to weaken. Healing perceives <u>nothing</u> in the healer that everyone else does not share <u>with</u> him. Magic <u>always</u> sees something "special" in the healer, which he believes he can offer as a gift to someone who does <u>not</u> have it. He may believe that the gift comes from God <u>to</u> him, but it is quite evident that he does <u>not</u> understand God if he thinks <u>he</u> has something that others lack.

The magical healer appears to possess some special power that she bestows on the poor, pathetic sick person to "heal" him. This weakens the patient, because it pictures the patient as a deficient person who doesn't have the special power the healer has. But the true healer recognizes that God doesn't give special powers to anyone; all are equal recipients of

His gifts. The true healer sees the same power and holiness in both the patient and herself. This recognition of equality in God—an example of the Holy Spirit using abilities as "potentials for equalizing"—is how true healing happens.

> [Ur: You might well ask why *some* healing *can* result from this kind of thinking, and there is a real reason for this.
>
> However misguided the "magical healer" may be, and however much he may be trying to strengthen his ego, *he is also trying to help.* He *is* conflicted and unstable, but *at times* he is offering *something* to the Sonship, and the *only* thing the Sonship can *accept is* healing. When the so-called healing "works," then, the impulse both to help and *be* helped have coincided. This is co-incidental, because the healer may *not* be experiencing *himself* as truly helpful at the time, and the belief that he *is*, in the mind of *another, helps him.*]

I love this Urtext paragraph and wish the editors hadn't taken it out. We may wonder: Why does *some* healing come even from magical healers who are trying to strengthen their egos? The answer is that even the magical healer is *trying to help.* As he's bumbling along trying to help in his misguided and ego-driven way, the pure impulse to be truly helpful might pop up and meet the patient's desire to be helped. The patient's very belief in the healer increases the odds that this meeting will come about. And whenever true helpfulness meets the desire to be helped, healing occurs (for another excellent discussion of this phenomenon, see the *Psychotherapy* supplement, P-3.II.3).

This, however, is unreliable, because it depends on the off chance that a genuine healing impulse might break through the healer's ego interference and meet the patient's desire to be helped. It's so unreliable that Jesus calls it a "so-called healing."

> 5.   The Holy Spirit does not work by chance, and healing that is of Him *always* works. Unless the healer <u>always</u> heals <u>by</u> Him the results <u>will</u> vary. Yet healing itself <u>is</u> consistent, since <u>only</u> consistency is conflict-free, and only the conflict-free <u>are</u> whole. By accepting exceptions and acknowledging that he can <u>sometimes</u> heal and <u>sometimes</u> not, the healer is <u>obviously</u> accepting <u>in</u>consistency. He is therefore <u>in</u> conflict, and is <u>teaching</u> conflict. Can <u>anything</u> of God <u>not</u> be for all and for always? Love is incapable of <u>any</u> exceptions. Only if there is fear

does the [Ur: whole] idea of exceptions [Ur: of any kind] seem to be meaningful. Exceptions are fearful because they are made by fear. The "fearful healer" is a contradiction in terms, and is therefore a concept that only a conflicted mind could possibly perceive as meaningful.

Why is spiritual healing so inconsistent and unreliable? Why doesn't it always work? Because the healer isn't relying only on the Holy Spirit—his healing relies to a large degree on the "chance" described in that last Urtext paragraph. When the healer sometimes relies on the Holy Spirit and sometimes doesn't, he is being inconsistent and is therefore teaching conflict. Inconsistency and conflict both imply a split of some sort, and this is the very antithesis of healing, which is the recognition of wholeness.

A healer who accepts inconsistency and conflict isn't reliable because he makes *exceptions*. Making exceptions means that his mind is not in a state of love—since love makes no exceptions—and must therefore be in a state of fear. Perhaps he's afraid that he's not a good enough healer. Perhaps he's afraid that this patient's illness is too "serious" to be healed. Perhaps he's afraid that this person is too great a sinner to deserve healing. But whatever exceptions his fear leads him to make, he is now a "fearful healer," which is a complete contradiction in terms.

6. Fear does not gladden. Healing does. Fear always makes exceptions. Healing never does. Fear produces dissociation, because it induces separation. Healing always produces harmony, because it proceeds from integration. It is predictable because it can be counted on. Everything that is of God can be counted on, because everything of God is wholly real. Healing can be counted on because it is inspired by His Voice, and is in accord with His laws. Yet if healing is consistent it cannot be inconsistently understood. Understanding means consistency because God means consistency. Since that is His meaning, it is also yours. Your meaning cannot be out of accord with His, because your whole meaning and your only meaning comes from His and is like His. God cannot be out of accord with Himself, and you cannot be out of accord with Him. You cannot separate your Self from your Creator, Who created you by sharing His Being with you.

If you think about it, isn't inconsistency fearful? We're afraid because we never know what we're going to get next. All of our rules have exceptions. The only constant is change. We can't count on anything. Our dearest friends can betray us. The house we've lived in for fifty years can be flattened by a hurricane in an instant. The abusive parent can hug us one minute and slap us the next. And, as we've seen here, our attempts at healing can produce miracles but can just as easily do more harm than good.

How refreshing, then, to be told that the very meaning of God and our true Self is *consistency*. How joyful to learn that "everything that is of God can be counted on." In truth, there is no way that we can ever be out of accord with the absolute consistency of the Being God shares with us. For this reason, we can become healers who extend miracles to everyone, every time, without exception. To accomplish this, all we must do is consistently understand the laws of God and be consistently inspired by His Voice. If we consistently affirm consistency, healing is guaranteed.

> 7.   The unhealed healer wants gratitude <u>from</u> his brothers, but he is <u>not</u> grateful to them. That is because he thinks he is giving something <u>to</u> them, and is <u>not</u> receiving something equally desirable in return. His <u>teaching</u> is limited because he is <u>learning</u> so little. His <u>healing</u> lesson is limited by his own ingratitude, which is a lesson in <u>sickness</u>.

Lack of gratitude is a major characteristic of the unhealed healer. A big reason he's in the healing business is simply to get his ego stroked. He thinks he's making a sacrifice, so the recipient had better pay up. This is an attitude of demand and resentment rather than love, and therefore a lesson in sickness that limits whatever healing he may give. The healed healer, on the other hand, recognizes that when he extends healing, he benefits as much as the patient does. Therefore, he is able to give freely with a truly loving and grateful heart.

> True learning is constant, and so vital in its power for change that a Son of God can recognize his power in one instant and change the world in the next. That is because, by changing his mind, he has changed the most powerful device that was ever given him [Ur: created] <u>for</u> change. This in no way contradicts the changelessness of mind as <u>God</u> created it, but <u>you</u> think that you <u>have</u> changed it as long as you learn through the ego. This places [Ur: *does* place you] you in a position of needing to

learn a lesson that <u>seems</u> contradictory; - you must learn to change your mind <u>about</u> your mind. Only by this can you learn that it *is* changeless.
8.   When you heal, that is exactly what you *are* learning [Ur: (doing)]. You are recognizing the changeless mind in your brother by realizing [Ur: perceiving (knowing)] that he could <u>not</u> have changed his mind. That is how you perceive the Holy Spirit in him. It is <u>only</u> the Holy Spirit in him that never changes His Mind. He himself may [Ur: must] think he <u>can,</u> or he would not perceive himself as sick. He therefore does not know what his Self <u>is</u>. If <u>you</u> see only the changeless in him you have not really changed him [Ur: at all]. By changing your mind about <u>his</u> *for* him, you help him undo the change his ego thinks it has made in him.

This is a fascinating discussion of the whole idea of "changing your mind" and its relation to healing. The key to resolving the apparent contradiction referred to at the end of the first paragraph here is to recognize that there are two senses of the phrase "change your mind": 1) change your thinking, and 2) change your mind's basic nature. Therefore, the "lesson that seems contradictory" means: "You must learn to change your mind's thinking about your mind's basic nature." We think we changed our mind's nature when we apparently separated from God. We must change our thinking about this. We must learn that our apparent separation from God did not change our mind's nature in the least. It is still one with God.

The way to heal another person is to change our thinking about *his* mind's basic nature. He too thinks that he changed his mind's nature when he apparently separated from God. He must think that, or he wouldn't be sick. As long as we think his sickness is real, we are agreeing that he really changed his mind's nature. But we heal him when we choose to see that however things may appear, his apparent separation from God did not change his mind's basic nature in the least. It too is still one with God.

This is how we perceive the Holy Spirit in him, because the Holy Spirit in him also recognizes that he has not changed his nature. Obviously, seeing the changeless mind in our brother doesn't really change him— in fact, it is the recognition that he *cannot* be changed. We are simply helping him see the fact that his mind's nature cannot be changed.

Application: Think of someone in your life who needs healing. Realize that to some degree you see this person as truly sick. That means you think this person succeeded in changing his mind's nature from one that is whole and complete to one that can get sick. Now, silently say to this person, *"Let me change my mind about you, [name]. Let me recognize the changeless mind in you, and know that you could never have changed your changeless Self. Let my vision of you help you undo the change your ego thinks it has made in you."*

9.   As you can hear two voices, so you can see in two ways. One way shows you an image, or [Ur: better,] an idol that you may worship out of fear, but will never love. The other shows you only truth, which you will love because you will <u>understand</u> it. Understanding is <u>appreciation</u>, because what you understand you can identify <u>with</u>, and by making it part of <u>you</u>, you have accepted it with love. That is how God Himself created <u>you</u>; in understanding, in appreciation and in love. The ego is totally unable to understand this, because it does <u>not</u> understand what it makes, does <u>not</u> appreciate it and does <u>not</u> love it. It incorporates to <u>take away</u>. It literally believes that every time it deprives someone of something, <u>it</u> has increased. I have spoken often of the <u>increase</u> of the Kingdom by <u>your</u> creations, which can only <u>be</u> created as <u>you</u> were. The whole glory and perfect joy that *is* the Kingdom lies in you to give. Do you not <u>want</u> to give it?

We can see through the eyes of the ego or the Holy Spirit. The ego's eyes picture a world in which our holy brothers are reduced to idols, false gods from whom the ego tries to extract its happiness. Taking is what the ego is all about. It tries to increase itself by sucking others dry. When we see our brothers as nothing more than a food supply for the ego—and who knows if they'll fill us up or not?—what could we do but fear them? How could we possibly regard them with understanding, appreciation, and love?

The Holy Spirit's eyes reveal the truth in our brothers, which we *will* love because we will understand it. This understanding leads us to identify with them, and therefore love and appreciate them. This is a reflection of how God created all of us: in understanding, appreciation, and love. And this vision is revealed when we choose to give instead of take. In Heaven, we increase ourselves not by taking away, but by giving our very being in creation. On earth, we are called to give to our brothers in a way that reflects creation—we are called to heal. Do you not want to give the whole glory and perfect joy of the Kingdom?

> 10.   You <u>cannot</u> forget the Father because I am with you, and <u>I cannot</u> forget Him. To forget <u>me</u> is to forget yourself and Him Who created you. Our brothers <u>are</u> forgetful. That is why they need your remembrance of me and of Him Who created me. Through this remembrance, you can change <u>their</u> minds about themselves, as I can change <u>yours</u>. Your mind is so powerful a light that you can look into theirs and enlighten them, as I can enlighten yours. I do not want to share my <u>body</u> in communion because this is to share nothing. Would I try to share an illusion with the most holy children of a most holy Father? Yet I do want to share my <u>mind</u> with you because we <u>are</u> of one Mind, and that Mind <u>is</u> ours. See <u>only</u> this Mind everywhere, because only this <u>is</u> everywhere and in everything. It <u>is</u> everything because it encompasses all things within <u>itself</u>. Blessed are you who perceive only this, because you perceive only what is true.
>
> 11.   Come therefore unto me, and learn of the truth in <u>you</u>. The mind <u>we</u> share <u>is</u> shared by all our brothers, and as we see them truly they <u>will</u> be healed. Let <u>your</u> mind shine with mine upon their minds, and by our gratitude to them make <u>them</u> aware of the light in <u>them</u>. This light will shine back upon <u>you</u> and on the whole Sonship, because this <u>is</u> your proper gift to God. He will accept it and give it to the Sonship, because it is acceptable to Him and therefore to His Sons. This is true communion with the Holy Spirit [Ur: the true communion of the Spirit], Who sees the altar of God in everyone, and by bringing it to <u>your</u> appreciation, He calls upon you to love God and His creation. You can appreciate the Sonship <u>only</u> as one. This is part of the law of creation, and therefore governs <u>all</u> thought.

Jesus remembers the Father always. Therefore, if we remember him, we will remember the Father too. Then we can pass this memory on to our forgetful brothers. By extending this memory of Jesus and our Father to them—by seeing in them the Mind that all of us share—we can change their minds and heal them. God Himself accepts the light of gratitude we have shined into their minds and shines it back into ours, illuminating the entire Sonship. This is true communion: not consuming Jesus' blood and body in the form of wine and a wafer, but letting him share his mind with us so we can see the one Mind that is everything, appreciate the altar of God in everyone, and love God and His creation as one. Blessed are those who perceive only this.

Application: These last two paragraphs are great paragraphs to personalize. I recommend reading them as a personal message from Jesus to you, inserting your own name at appropriate points.

VI. From Vigilance to Peace
Commentary by Robert Perry

1.   [Ur: You can think of the Sonship *only* as one. This is part of the law of Creation, and therefore governs *all* thought.] Although you can love the Sonship only as one [the beginning of this sentence was apparently composed by the editors], you can perceive it [Ur: *perceive the Sonship*] as fragmented. It is impossible, however, to see something in part of it that you will not attribute to all of it. That is why attack is never discrete, and why it must be relinquished entirely. If it is not relinquished entirely it is not relinquished at all. Fear and love [Ur: are equally reciprocal. They] make or create, depending on whether the ego or the Holy Spirit begets or inspires them, but they *will* return to the mind of the thinker and they will affect his total perception. That includes his concept of God, of His creations and of his own. He will not appreciate any of them if he regards them fearfully. He will appreciate all of them if he regards them with love.

If you think that you can love selectively, that you can feel different things for different people, that you can love your mother while hating Osama Bin Laden, this paragraph has news for you: "You can think of the Sonship *only* as one." Yes, you can see it divided up into countless different fragments, but here is the crucial point: What you see in one fragment you will see in all of them. You cannot see something in Hitler that you will not then see in your most cherished loved one, in yourself, and even in God. When you have attack thoughts about one person, you have darkened your view of everyone. Therefore, in deciding how you see each person, you are deciding how you see the entire Sonship.

"That is why attack is never discrete." We are so afraid of our own attack, our own destructiveness, that it only feels safe to attack if we can restrict it to specially targeted people. What if we can't? If you had a gun and knew that if you pulled the trigger, millions of bullets would fly in all directions at once and hit literally everyone on earth, would you do it?

Application: Think of someone you have been having attack thoughts toward, and repeat this:

In deciding how I see [name], I am deciding how I see everyone.

2. The mind that accepts attack <u>cannot</u> love. That is because it believes it can <u>destroy</u> love, and therefore does not understand what love <u>is</u>. If it does not understand what love <u>is,</u> it <u>cannot</u> perceive itself as loving. This loses the awareness of being, induces feelings of unreality and results in utter confusion. Your thinking has done this because of its power, but your thinking can also save you <u>from</u> this because its power is not of your making. Your ability to <u>direct</u> your thinking as you choose <u>is</u> part of its power. If you do not believe you can do this, you have <u>denied</u> the power of your thought, and thus rendered it power<u>less</u> in your belief.

If you attack, you are thinking that you can destroy not only the other person; you are thinking you can destroy love, at least in this situation. "I have shattered whatever love may have been here," you think. But you are wrong. The love is still there, invisible but present, silently enveloping both you and your "victim." Thinking you can destroy love doesn't make it so; it just means that you don't understand what love is. And if you don't know what love is, how can you be loving? And then how can you *see yourself* as loving? And if you don't see yourself as loving, this paragraph says, you will lose the awareness of your true being. You will begin to feel more like a ghost than a real person.

These results are dramatic, and they have all come from using the power of your mind for attack rather than love. Yet you can put just as much power into relinquishing attack. To do this, however, you have to reclaim the power of your mind. To muster the power required to stop yourself from attacking, you have to cease feeling so powerless.

3. The ingeniousness of the ego to preserve itself is enormous, but it stems from the very power of the mind <u>the ego denies</u>. This means that the ego attacks <u>what is preserving it</u>, which <u>must</u> result in [Ur: *must* be a source of] extreme anxiety. That is why the ego <u>never</u> recognizes [Ur: knows] what it is doing. It is perfectly logical but clearly insane. The ego draws upon the one source that is totally inimical to its existence *for* its existence. Fearful of perceiving the <u>power</u> of this source, it is forced to <u>depreciate</u> it. This threatens its <u>own</u> existence, a state which it finds intolerable. Remaining logical but still insane, the ego resolves

171

this completely insane dilemma in a completely insane way. It does not perceive *its* existence as threatened by projecting the threat onto *you*, and perceiving your <u>being</u> as <u>non</u>existent. This ensures <u>its</u> continuance if you side <u>with</u> it, by guaranteeing that you will <u>not</u> know your <u>own</u> Safety [Ur: safety].

The ego is in a very uncomfortable position. It totally relies on the power of your mind, the power of your belief. It relies on your intelligence to hatch its ingenious schemes to preserve itself. It is a program that runs using the power of your processor. At the same time, this exact same power makes it feel severely threatened, for this power could easily throw it away. So it tells you that you have no power, that you are powerless in the face of your addiction to it. It says, "Who are you to think you can get rid of me? You are just a ghost, a hollow person. I'm the one with real substance here."

To appreciate this, we must apply it to ourselves. Do you feel powerless to overcome your ego, to step out of its old habits of thought and feeling and behavior? If so, that is not because you really are powerless. It is because you are believing the seductive voice of your ego, which tells you that you are powerless because it is *afraid* of your power. Your belief that you have no power, then, is actually indirect evidence *of* your power.

Application: Think of some way in which you feel powerless in the face of your ego's impulses or patterns, then dwell on these lines:

> *I believe that I am powerless in the face of my ego.*
> *This is because I am listening to my ego, which fears my power.*
> *My belief in my powerlessness is therefore a testament to my*
> *   ego's fear of my power,*
> *And therefore a testament to my power.*

4.   The ego <u>cannot afford to know anything</u> [and cannot afford you knowing your safety—see the end of paragraph 3]. Knowledge is total [which means knowing anything equals knowing totality], and the ego <u>does not believe in totality</u>. This unbelief is its origin, and while the ego does not love <u>you</u> it *is* faithful to its own antecedents, begetting as it was begotten. Mind <u>always re</u>produces as it was produced. Produced by

fear, the ego reproduces fear. This is its allegiance, and this allegiance makes it treacherous to love because you *are* love. Love is your power, which the ego must deny. It must also deny everything this power gives you *because* it gives you everything. No one who has everything wants the ego. Its own maker, then, does not want it. Rejection is therefore the only decision the ego could possibly encounter, if the mind that made it knew itself. And if it recognized [knew again] any part of the Sonship, it *would* know itself.

The ego was born from fear, "produced by fear": fear of love, fear of totality, fear of the Everything. This makes it afraid of you, for you have and are all of these things. It therefore has to keep you unaware of yourself. It has to keep you down. It has to tell you that you are small, that you are insignificant, that you are petty, that you have no love inside you. Do you have a voice in your head that whispers these things? Then you know the sound of the ego's voice.

The instant you realize the grandeur that you have and are, you will have no idea why you ever wanted the ego. I remember talking to a guy who claimed his guru came to him (non-physically) and took him out of his body. He said he looked back at his body and it was like an ocean looking at a grain of sand and saying, "I live in *that*?" That is how we will look back at the ego when we remember who we are.

And how do we come to know who we are? We come to know *one part* of the Sonship, and then we will regain all knowledge, for "knowledge is total." Knowing one brother, then, is the little bit of knowledge the ego has to keep us from.

> 5.   The ego therefore opposes all appreciation, all recognition, all sane perception and all knowledge. It perceives their threat as total, because it senses that all commitments the mind makes are total. Forced, therefore, to detach itself from you [Ur: who *are* mind], it is willing to attach itself to anything else. But there *is* nothing else. [Ur: It does *not* follow, however, that the mind cannot make illusions.] The mind can, however, make up illusions, and if it does so [Ur: But it *does* follow that if it makes illusions] it will believe in them, because that is how it made them.

Have you ever felt an unbridled appreciation of someone arise in your mind, and then felt yourself recoil from it? That was because your ego knew that this appreciation really implied a *total* appreciation of *everyone*, and it couldn't stand for that. The nature of mind is that each idea it accepts in a particular instance then spreads out and covers everything. Each commitment it makes becomes total.

The ego wants to carve things up into little segments and sectors and hide within those cubicles. Yet the nature of mind is that it ignores these walls. What it does in one room immediately spreads to all rooms. The ego, therefore, has to distance itself from mind, "from you who *are* mind." It has to attach itself instead to mindless illusions, and that is what it does. As a result, we spend our little lives celebrating, worshipping, and worrying about all kinds of mindless forms, not realizing that in doing so we are betraying the nature of ourselves as mind.

> 6.   The Holy Spirit undoes illusions without attacking them, [Ur: merely] because He cannot perceive them at all. They therefore do not exist for Him. He resolves the <u>apparent</u> conflict they engender by perceiving <u>conflict</u> as meaningless. I have said before that the Holy Spirit perceives the conflict <u>exactly as it is</u>, and it *is* meaningless. The Holy Spirit does not want you to <u>understand</u> conflict; He wants you to realize that, <u>because</u> conflict is meaning<u>less,</u> it is not understandable. As I have already said, understanding brings appreciation and appreciation brings love. Nothing else <u>can</u> be understood, because nothing else is real and therefore nothing else <u>has</u> meaning.

We have split ourselves between pure mind and mindless illusions. We want to contemplate God, and we want to shop till we drop. One way to try to resolve this conflict is to try to *understand* it. "It is understandable that I want both sides because God gave me a mind to contemplate with and a body to shop with. To honor both sides is to honor the dance of creation and the oneness that weaves through it all. I have therefore come to appreciate and even love the many different facets of my being. It's all good." The Holy Spirit, however, resolves the conflict much more simply. He says, "What conflict? I don't understand the conflict because I don't see any conflict. Only one side is real. How, then, can there be a conflict?"

> 7.   If you will keep in mind what the Holy Spirit offers you, you cannot be vigilant for anything *but* God and His Kingdom. The <u>only</u>

reason you may find this hard to accept is because you may still think there is something else. Belief does not require vigilance unless it is conflicted. If it is, there are conflicting components within it that have led to [Ur: engendered] a state of war, and vigilance has therefore become essential. Vigilance has no place in peace. It is necessary against [Ur: *only against*] beliefs that are not true, and would never have been called upon by the Holy Spirit if you had not believed the untrue. [Ur: But you *cannot* deny that] When you believe something, you have made it true for you. When you believe what God does not know, your thought seems to contradict His, and this makes it appear as if you are attacking Him.

This paragraph revisits "The Lessons of the Holy Spirit," particularly the third lesson, "Be vigilant only for God and His Kingdom." The Holy Spirit may realize that the conflict is not real, but we don't. If we truly knew that only one side was real, there would be no need for vigilance. Because we still believe in both sides, we *must* exercise vigilance. For us right now, the highest form of acknowledgment of truth is not to say, "I know that the ego is not real, so why be vigilant?" Rather, it is to say, "I am committed to learning that only God and His Kingdom are real, and so I am constantly vigilant against all other thoughts."

8. I have repeatedly emphasized that the ego does believe it can attack God, and tries to persuade you that you have done this. If the mind cannot attack, the ego proceeds perfectly logically to the belief that you must be a body [Ur: to the position that *you* cannot be mind]. By not seeing you as you are, it can see itself as it wants to be. Aware of its weakness the ego wants your allegiance, but not as you really are. The ego therefore wants to engage your mind in its own delusional system, because otherwise the light of your understanding would [Ur: *will*] dispel it. It wants no part of truth, because the ego itself is not true [Ur: because the truth is that *it* is not true]. If truth is total, the untrue cannot exist. Commitment to either must be total; they cannot coexist in your mind without splitting it. If they cannot coexist in peace, and if you want peace, you must give up the idea of conflict entirely and for all time. This requires vigilance only as long as you do not recognize what is true. While you believe that two totally contradictory thought systems share truth, your need for vigilance is apparent.

"Mind cannot attack" is a central principle in the Course, mentioned many times. If mind has no form, if all mind is one, how can one part of that formless oneness attack another? There are no boundaries to collide. The ego tells us that we have attacked God, but since mind cannot attack, the ego must also tell us that we are not really mind. And basically, we have believed it. We act like forms whose entire lives are about acquiring, moving around, interacting with, getting close to, and consuming other forms. "The ego wants your allegiance," but it wants the allegiance of a you that is ensnared in its web of delusions, a you that is lost in its fog and has lost sight of the truth. For if you found the truth, you would discover that "the truth is that *it* [the ego] is not true."

Right now, we are committed to both sides. Our mind is split between God's truth and the ego's untruth. And a split mind cannot be at peace. Being constantly vigilant may not *feel* peaceful, but it's the only road to real peace.

> 9. Your mind is dividing its allegiance between two kingdoms, and you are totally committed to neither. Your identification with the Kingdom is totally beyond question except by you, when you are thinking insanely. What you are is not established by your perception, and is not influenced by it at all. Perceived problems in identification at any level are not problems of fact. They are problems of understanding, since their presence implies a belief that what you are is up to you to decide [Ur: They *are* problems of *understanding*, because they *mean* that you perceive *what* you can understand as *up to you to decide*]. The ego believes this totally, being fully committed to it. [Ur: But] It is not true. The ego therefore is totally committed to untruth, perceiving in total contradiction to the Holy Spirit and to the knowledge of God.

To really appreciate this paragraph, it is important to realize it is not talking about somebody else's predicament. It is talking directly about *ours*. Our mind *is* "dividing its allegiance between two kingdoms," between God and ego. On one side is a truth that is eternally true, beyond our ability to change. It just is what it is. On the other side is a realm in which everything seems up to us. We decide what that table is for. We decide what that friend is for. We decide what that co-worker is really all about. And most of all, we decide what we ourselves are. Indeed, in this state, we limit our perception of ourselves to what we can readily think is up to us. We emphasize our body, which we can shape, our abilities, which we can control, our possessions, which we can acquire or throw away, and our life situations, which we can manipulate. We thus shut out our awareness of a Self that timelessly *is*, regardless of what we think or do.

Believing that the truth is up to us means being in a state of *untruth*. It really is a childish state. It is like believing that if we put our hands over our eyes, everything goes away. The ego "is totally committed" to this childish position. And that puts us at a kind of disadvantage, for it means that we, with our *divided* commitment, are trying to pull away from a voice that is 100% committed all the time.

> 10.   You can be perceived with meaning <u>only</u> by the Holy Spirit because your being *is* the knowledge of God. <u>Any</u> belief you accept <u>apart</u> from this <u>will</u> obscure God's Voice in you, and will therefore obscure God <u>to</u> you. Unless you perceive His creation truly you <u>cannot</u> know the Creator, since God and His creation <u>are not separate</u>. The oneness of the Creator and the creation <u>is</u> your wholeness, your sanity and your limitless power. This limitless power is God's gift to you, because it is <u>what you are</u>. If you dissociate your mind <u>from</u> it you are perceiving the most powerful force in the universe <u>as if</u> it were weak, because you do <u>not</u> believe <u>you</u> are part of it.

As the previous paragraph said, we think that what we are is up to us. We think that we can arrive at accurate opinions of ourselves. Yet only the Holy Spirit is in a position to perceive us accurately, because only He is in touch with God's knowledge of our being. Therefore, all the opinions of ourselves that we generate apart from Him just obscure our true being. They also obscure God, since we are one with Him. Finally, they obscure our oneness with Him, and this is something we don't want to hide. We should regard it as the single most treasured thing we have.

Application: Think of some opinion you have of yourself, and notice how it pictures you as separate and apart from God. Then say,

> *The oneness of my Creator and myself is my wholeness, my*
> *sanity, and my limitless power.*
> *I will not dissociate my mind from it.*

11. Perceived <u>without</u> your part <u>in</u> it, God's creation <u>is</u> seen as weak, and those who <u>see</u> themselves as weakened <u>do</u> attack. The attack <u>must</u> be blind, however, because there is nothing <u>to</u> attack. Therefore they make up images, perceive them as unworthy and attack them for their unworthiness. That is all the world of the ego is. <u>Nothing</u>. It has no meaning. It does not exist. Do not <u>try</u> to understand it because, if you do, you are believing that it <u>can</u> be understood and is therefore capable of being appreciated and loved. That <u>would</u> justify its existence, which <u>cannot be</u> justified. <u>You</u> cannot make the meaning<u>less</u> meaning<u>ful</u>. This can <u>only</u> be an insane attempt.

Let me see if I can follow the logic here. We've all pulled out of the Sonship. The members have quit. Hence, the Sonship as a collective feels very weak. In this state of perceived weakness, the Sons want to attack, but there is nothing real that is worthy of attack. So they make up unworthy images and attack *them.*

Now for the punch line: "That is all the world of the ego is." That is all *this* world is. Just a bunch of unworthy images we made up to give us something to attack. Just a bunch of old rusty cans we set up to give us something to shoot at. This may sound like a bizarre account of the origin of the universe, yet it does line up with our everyday experience. After all, we do look around and see lots and lots of unworthy images, don't we? And these images inspire our constant disappointment, complaint, and attack, don't they?

Jesus tells you to refrain from trying to understand this world, because that will make you think it is meaningful, that it can be appreciated and even loved. After watching umpteen science programs on the wonders of nature and the cosmos, I can tell you that this is absolutely true.

12. Allowing <u>insanity</u> to enter your mind means that you have not judged sanity <u>as wholly desirable</u>. If you <u>want</u> something else you <u>will</u> <u>make</u> something else, but because it <u>is</u> something else, it <u>will</u> attack your thought system and divide your allegiance. You <u>cannot</u> create in this divided state, and you <u>must</u> be vigilant <u>against</u> this divided state because only peace <u>can be</u> extended. Your divided mind is blocking the extension of the Kingdom, and its extension <u>is</u> your joy. If you do not extend the Kingdom, you are <u>not</u> thinking with your Creator and creating as He created.

Again and again in these early chapters we hear the message: Don't allow your mind to split. A split mind is a mind divided against itself. It cannot express its true power because each side is canceling out the other. Yet expressing our power is what we yearn for. We want to extend our peace without limit. We want to experience what Jesus called "the vast radiation range of [our] own inner illumination." We want to do the unthinkable and actually extend the scope of the Kingdom of God. This is our heart's desire. Yet this is what we are totally *unable* to do in our divided state. ("You cannot create in this divided state.")

Application: Think of your ambivalence about loving a certain person in your life. Think of how you feel the pull to love and to judge, to forgive and to hold a grudge. Then say,

> *My divided mind is blocking the extension of the Kingdom,*
> *And its extension is my joy.*

13. In this depressing state the Holy Spirit reminds you gently that you are sad because you are not fulfilling your function as co-creator with God, and are therefore depriving yourself [Ur: *yourselves*] of joy. This is not God's choice [Ur: Will] but yours. If your mind could be [Ur: If your will is] out of accord with God's, you would be [Ur: *are*] willing without meaning. Yet because God's Will is unchangeable, no conflict of will is possible. This is the Holy Spirit's perfectly consistent teaching. Creation, not separation, is your will *because* it is God's, and nothing that opposes this means anything at all. Being a perfect accomplishment, the Sonship can only accomplish perfectly, extending the joy in which it was created, and identifying itself with both its Creator and its creations, knowing they are one.

If you were to ask yourself in one of your sadder moments, "Why am I sad?" would you ever come up with the Holy Spirit's answer? He says you are sad because you are not co-creating with God in Heaven, which is the real function for which you were created.

Application: Think of something recent that seemed to make you sad, and say,

I am sad because I am not fulfilling my function as co-creator with God in Heaven.
I am therefore depriving myself of joy.

We may have chosen this state of not creating, but our choice is an empty one. As with many of the choices we have forced ourselves to make, we are trying to will without meaning. Our heart is not really in it. Our real will is still to co-create with God. It is impossible that our true will could conflict with God's Will, for He created it. The only thing we really want to do is join with Him in "extending the joy" of the Kingdom.

VII. The Totality of the Kingdom
Commentary by Robert Perry

This section is both practical and profound. It says that our response to each individual, especially an attacking individual, determines our perception of totality and of ourselves.

> 1.   Whenever you deny a blessing to a brother *you* will feel deprived, because denial is as total as love. It is as impossible to deny part of the Sonship as it is to love it in part. Nor is it possible to love it totally <u>at times</u>. You <u>cannot</u> be totally committed <u>sometimes</u>. [Ur: Remember a very early lesson,—"never underestimate the power of denial".] Denial has no power in <u>itself</u>, but <u>you</u> can give it the power of <u>your</u> mind, whose power is without limit [Ur: of *any* kind]. If you use it to deny reality, reality is <u>gone for you</u>. *Reality cannot be partly appreciated.* That is why denying any part of it means you have lost the awareness of <u>all</u> of it. [Ur: That is the negative side of the law as it operates in this world.] Yet denial is a defense, and so it is as capable of being used positively as well as negatively [Ur: used positively as it is of being used destructively]. Used negatively it <u>will</u> be destructive, because it will be used for attack. But in the service of the Holy Spirit, it can help you recognize part of reality, and thus appreciate all of it [Ur: But in the service of the Holy Spirit, the law becomes as beneficent as all of the laws of God. Stated positively, the law requires you only to recognize *part* of reality to appreciate *all* of it]. Mind [a decision of the mind] is too powerful to be subject to exclusion. You will <u>never</u> be able to exclude yourself from your thoughts [Ur: from what you project {or extend}].

The basic idea in this paragraph is that, because of the immense power of your mind, your mind will take whatever you do in one case and generalize it to all cases. This means that however you see one person, you will see everyone, including yourself. When you deny a blessing to a brother, you yourself will feel deprived of blessing. When you deny one brother's reality, you blind yourself to *all* of reality. You may assume that you can think ill of someone and confine that negative intent to that one person. But that overlooks the power of the mind. That attack thought is so powerful that it simply can't be confined to that one person. It will ripple out and affect your perception of everyone and everything, including yourself.

The law, however, works positively as well. The positive side of this is that you only need to "recognize *part* of reality to appreciate *all* of it." Just as one brother seen as sinful taints all of reality in your eyes, so one brother seen as holy causes everything to shine.

Application: Think of someone you are currently seeing in a negative way, someone you see as mistreating you or not appreciating you. Ask yourself, "How am I seeing this person?" Try to boil it down to one word and then insert that one word in the four spaces below. Now repeat to yourself,

> *Because I see him as_____I will see everyone as_____.*
> *Because I see him as_____I will see myself as_____.*
> *But if I bless him, I will see myself as blessed.*
> *If I recognize his reality, I will appreciate all of reality.*

2.   When a brother acts insanely, he is offering you an opportunity to bless him. His need is <u>yours</u>. <u>You</u> need the blessing you can offer him. There is no way for you to have it <u>except</u> by giving it. This <u>is</u> the law of God, and it <u>has no exceptions</u>. What you deny you <u>lack</u>, not because it <u>is</u> lacking, but because you have denied it in another and are therefore not aware of it in yourself. Every response you make is determined by what you think you <u>are</u>, and what you <u>want</u> to be *is* what you think you are. What you <u>want</u> to be, then, must determine every response you make.

When a brother behaves insanely, we all know the normal responses—to be outraged, to try to set him straight, to fix him, to retaliate, to mobilize group opinion against him. Actually, says this paragraph, we should see him as offering us a gift—the opportunity to bless him. This is a gift to us because we ourselves need blessing and the only way we can have it is by blessing him. This is called here the "law of God" and is called later in the Text and Workbook the "law of love" (see Lesson 344). In truth, we already have the blessing we seek—we are *eternally* blessed—but we will not know this if we deny blessing to a brother.

Apparently, we do this on purpose. The final lines emphasize that our response to our brother is actually determined by what we ourselves want to be. Something in our mind understands the cause-and-effect connection between what we give our brother and what we learn that we are. Thus, we unconsciously *choose* our response to him based on what we *want* to teach ourselves. In other words, if I treat my brother as if he's not worthy of being blessed, my unconscious reason for doing that is that I want to teach myself that *I'm* unworthy of being blessed. And it works.

Application: Pick four people you expect to encounter today, and say this line silently to each one: *"I need the blessing I can offer you, [name]."*

3.   You do <u>not</u> need God's blessing because that you have forever, but you <u>do</u> need <u>yours</u>. The ego's picture of you [Ur: The picture you see of yourselves] is deprived, unloving and vulnerable. You <u>cannot</u> love this. Yet you can very easily escape <u>from</u> this image by leaving it behind. You are <u>not</u> there and that is not <u>you</u>. Do not see this picture in anyone, or you <u>have</u> accepted it *as* [Ur: as] you. <u>All</u> illusions about the Sonship are <u>dispelled</u> together as they were <u>made</u> together. Teach no one that <u>he</u> is what <u>you</u> would not want to be. Your brother is the mirror in which you see the image of yourself as long as perception lasts. And perception <u>will</u> last until the Sonship knows itself as whole. You <u>made</u> perception and it <u>must</u> last as long as you <u>want</u> it.

We all carry around a fairly pitiful picture of ourselves. The Course uses three words to describe that picture: deprived, unloving, and vulnerable. Doesn't each word describe a major chunk of our self-perception? These three adjectives are so universally believed in that self-esteem usually means learning to esteem ourselves in spite of them. Yet the Course here flatly denies that this is possible: "You cannot love this." The only way to really love ourselves is to escape from this image. We need to *give* it up, not *shine* it up. We have to realize, "You are not there and that is not you."

How do we realize this? We need to not see this picture in anyone. We need to not teach anyone that he is deprived, unloving, and vulnerable. We teach others that they are deprived by taking things from them. We teach them that they are unlovable by withdrawing love from them. We teach them that they are vulnerable by hurting them. *This* is the source of our low self-esteem. It wasn't our parents or teachers or friends who taught us we are deprived, unlovable, and vulnerable. We taught ourselves that we are this by teaching *others* that they are this.

> 4.   Illusions are investments. They will last as long as you value them. Values are relative, but they are powerful because they are <u>mental judgments</u>. The only way to dispel illusions is to withdraw <u>all</u> investment from them, and they will <u>have</u> no life for you because you will have put them <u>out of your mind</u>. While you include them <u>in</u> it, you are <u>giving</u> life to them. Except there is nothing there to receive your gift.

Perception will last as long as we want it to because that is the nature of illusions—they last as long as we value them. We are the ones who give life to them, yet, ironically, we are giving life to something that is not there. The only way to be rid of illusions is to withdraw our investment in them. And we do that by *not seeing them in our brother*.

> 5.   The gift of life is yours to give, because it was given <u>you</u>. You are unaware of <u>your</u> gift <u>because</u> you do not give it. You <u>cannot</u> make nothing live, since nothing cannot <u>be</u> enlivened. Therefore, you are not extending the gift you both *have* and *are*, and so you do <u>not</u> know your being. All confusion comes from not extending life, because that is <u>not</u> the Will of your Creator. You <u>can</u> do nothing apart from Him, and you do do nothing apart from Him. Keep His way to remember yourself, and teach His way [Ur: Ways] lest you forget yourself. Give only honor to the Sons of the living God, and count yourself among them gladly.

God gave us the gift of life. We don't know we have this gift for one reason: because we don't give it. Instead of giving life to our brothers, we are too busy trying to give life to our illusions (which, remember, are illusions of ourselves as deprived, unloving, and vulnerable). While we are busy trying to "make nothing live"—an impossibility—we are not extending the gift of life that we both have and are. And thus we do not know our being, because we can only know it by extending it.

The only solution, says the paragraph in its concluding sentence, is to "give only honor to the Sons of the living God." To give honor is to give *respect* and *esteem*.

Application: Select someone you have seen as pitiable and say silently to him or her,

> *I refuse to see you as deprived, unlovable, and vulnerable.*
> *I give you only honor as a Son of the living God.*

6.   <u>Only</u> honor is a fitting gift for those whom God Himself created worthy of honor, and whom He honors. Give them the appreciation God accords them always, because they are His beloved Sons in whom He is well pleased. You <u>cannot</u> be apart from them because you are not apart from Him. Rest in His Love and protect your rest by loving. But love <u>everything</u> He created, of which <u>you</u> are a part, or you cannot learn of His peace and accept His gift <u>for</u> yourself and <u>as</u> yourself. You <u>cannot</u> know your own perfection until you have honored all those who were created <u>like</u> you.

We often feel too good, too important, to give honor to the "undeserving" individuals we see around us. But if God created them worthy of honor, and if He Himself honors them, why are *we* too good to honor them? He always accords them appreciation, "because they are His beloved Sons in whom He is well pleased." What a remarkable line! That, of course, is what God reportedly spoke to Jesus at his baptism. In fact, however, God is constantly speaking that line to everyone, even to our worst enemies.

The final sentences make a challenging point: If we want to rest in God's Love, if we want accept His gift for ourselves, if we want to learn of His peace, if we want to know our own perfection, we need to do one thing: We need to love, honor, and appreciate everyone He created.

Application: Go through a variety of people and say silently to each one, *"You are God's beloved Son in whom He is well pleased."* You might even imagine this person being baptized by John the Baptist in the river Jordan. As this person comes out of the water, you see a white dove descend on him or her, and you hear a loud voice from Heaven proclaim "This is My Beloved Son in whom I am well pleased." See how it makes you feel about them.

> 7. One child of God is the only teacher sufficiently worthy to teach another. One Teacher is in all minds and He teaches the same lesson to all. He always teaches you the inestimable worth of <u>every</u> Son of God, teaching it with infinite patience born of the infinite Love for which He speaks [Ur: born of the Love of Him for whom He speaks]. Every attack is a call for His patience, since His patience can translate attack into blessing. Those who attack <u>do not know they are blessed</u>. They attack <u>because they believe they are deprived</u>. Give, therefore, of <u>your</u> abundance, and teach your brothers <u>theirs</u>. Do not share their illusions [Ur: delusions] of scarcity, or you will perceive <u>yourself</u> as lacking.

The Holy Spirit has one lesson He teaches: "the inestimable worth of every Son of God." That is the real essence of all the lessons He has ever taught you. He teaches this lesson in the mind of every Son of God, but in many cases, He must teach one Son of God through another. When someone attacks you, that person hasn't yet learned this lesson. The Holy Spirit within him responds to his slow learning with infinite patience. Yet chances are that the person himself will not be aware of this. It's therefore up to you to be the Holy Spirit's messenger. Be the communicator of His infinite patience. Rather than thinking, "I can't believe this guy still doesn't get it," you need to think, "He'll get it someday, and God is infinitely patient with him." Give him your blessing. Give him of your abundance. Don't see yourself here as the one in need; see your attacker as the one in need. For it is only because he feels needy and deprived that he attacks. If you respond from your own feeling of need, you will reinforce your belief in lack. If you respond with blessing, however, his attack will have been transformed into a blessing for both of you.

> 8. Attack could never <u>promote</u> attack unless you perceived it as a means of depriving you of <u>something you want</u>. Yet you cannot lose <u>anything</u> unless <u>you</u> do not value it, and therefore <u>do not want it</u>. This makes you feel <u>deprived</u> of it, and by projecting <u>your</u> own rejection you

then believe that others are <u>taking it from you</u>. You <u>must</u> be fearful if you believe that your brother is attacking you to tear the Kingdom of Heaven from you. This is the ultimate basis for <u>all</u> the ego's projection.
9.   Being the part of your mind that does <u>not</u> believe it is responsible for <u>itself</u>, and being without allegiance to God, the ego is incapable of trust. Projecting its insane belief that <u>you</u> have been treacherous to <u>your</u> Creator, it believes that your brothers, who are as incapable of this as you are, are out to <u>take God from you</u>. Whenever a brother attacks another, that [Ur: *this*] *is* <u>what he believes</u>. Projection <u>always</u> sees <u>your</u> wishes in others. If you choose to separate <u>yourself</u> from God, that is what you will think others are doing <u>to</u> you.

Paragraph 7 taught that you need to respond to attack with patience and with blessing. These two paragraphs explain why you usually *don't*. You respond to attack with attack because you see the other person's attack as a "as a means of depriving you of something you want." Your attack in return, then, becomes a means of self-defense. However, the Course here tells you that "you cannot lose anything unless you do not value it." So someone's attack can only deprive you of something when you yourself have already thrown it away. But we generally don't want to own up to this choice. So we project it onto someone else. Now we think *they* are the ones who have taken it from us. This is what projection does. "Projection always sees your wishes in others."

Application: Think of three people who, in your eyes, took something from you, and then fill in their names and what you think they took from you (try to boil it down to one word). Then repeat the following lines to yourself.

> *I think that _____ took _____ from me.*
> *But in fact I threw it away, and then projected my wishes onto him/her.*
> *I think that _____ took _____ from me.*
> *But in fact I threw it away, and then projected my wishes onto him/her.*
> *I think that _____ took _____ from me.*
> *But in fact I threw it away, and then projected my wishes onto him/her.*

There is a deeper dimension to this. The ultimate thing that you believe your brothers are taking from you is the Kingdom of Heaven, or, as Paragraph 9 puts it, God Himself. If you think about it, whatever you wrote in the above spaces probably amounts to aspects of God, aspects of Heaven. If you think someone stole love from you, that's an aspect of the experience of God. If you think someone stole self-esteem from you, that too is an aspect of the experience of God. If you think someone stole a particular person from you, that person, of course, is an aspect of God. Ultimately, you see others as stealing the Kingdom of God from you.

Application: Let's take the same three people and apply the following:

I believed you were out to take God from me.
But the fact is that I threw Him away, and then blamed my loss
on you.

10. You *are* the Will of God. Do not accept anything else <u>as your</u> will, or you <u>are</u> denying what you are. Deny <u>this</u> and you <u>will</u> attack, believing [Ur: because you believe] you have <u>been</u> attacked. But see the Love of God in you, and you will see it everywhere because it *is* everywhere. See His abundance in everyone, and you will know that you are in Him <u>with</u> them. They are part of you, as you are part of God. <u>You</u> are as lonely without understanding this as God Himself is lonely when His Sons do not know Him. The peace of God <u>is</u> understanding this. There is only one way out of the world's thinking, just as there was only one way <u>into</u> it. Understand totally by understanding <u>totality</u>.

This paragraph presents two scenarios. In the first scenario, you deny that your will is the same as God's. You thereby throw God away, and with Him the awareness of what you are, since "you *are* the Will of God." Now you feel lonely and deprived. And once you have conveniently blamed your loss of God on others, you will attack them.

In the second scenario, you acknowledge that God's Love is in you, that His abundance is in you. And then you see His Love and abundance in everyone. If you do that, you will know that not only are they in God, but that *you* "are in Him with them." This will take all of your sense of loneliness and loss away.

11. Perceive <u>any</u> part of the ego's thought system as wholly insane, wholly delusional and wholly undesirable, and you have <u>correctly evaluated all of it</u>. This correction enables you to perceive <u>any</u> part of creation as wholly real, wholly perfect and <u>wholly desirable</u>. Wanting this <u>only</u> you will *have* this only, and giving this only you will *be* only this. The gifts you offer to the ego are <u>always</u> experienced as sacrifices, but the gifts you offer to the Kingdom are gifts to <u>you</u>. They will always be treasured by God because they belong to His beloved Sons, who belong to Him. All power and glory are yours because the Kingdom is His.

This is how you understand totality—by seeing one part of it truly. Because of the power of the mind, you need only see part of a whole accurately in order to see the whole accurately. Thus, if you see part of the ego's thought system as completely insane and undesirable, you will see all of the ego's thought system for what it is. This will free you up to see part of creation—which means a brother—as "wholly real, wholly perfect, and wholly desirable," which will cause you to see *all* of creation for what it is. And to see yourself for what *you* are. The gift you give to creation is given you, and this gift is therefore treasured by God Himself, for all He wants is your happiness.

Application: Say to a series of people,

> *I acknowledge you as wholly real, wholly perfect, and wholly desirable.*
> *And I thereby acknowledge the perfection in myself.*

VIII. The Unbelievable Belief
Commentary by Robert Perry

1.   We have said that without projection there can be no anger [see 6.In.1:2], but it is also true that without extension [Ur: projection] there can be no love. These reflect [Ur: Projection is] a fundamental law of the mind, and therefore one that <u>always</u> operates. It is the law by which you create and were created. It is the law that unifies the Kingdom, and keeps it in the Mind of God. To the ego, the law is perceived as a means of getting <u>rid</u> of something it does <u>not</u> want. To the Holy Spirit, it is the fundamental law of sharing, by which you give what you value in order to keep it in your mind. To the Holy Spirit it is the law of extension. To the ego it is the law of deprivation. It therefore produces abundance or scarcity, depending on how you choose to apply it. This choice <u>is</u> up to you, but it is <u>not</u> up to you to decide whether or not you will <u>utilize</u> the law. Every mind <u>must</u> project or extend, because that is how it lives, and every mind <u>is</u> life.

What the Course calls a fundamental law here was, at this point in the dictation, just called projection, but later was called projection and extension. This law is absolutely basic to everything in the Course. Without understanding it, the entire Course becomes inscrutable. As this paragraph says, the ego and the Holy Spirit use this same law completely differently. The Holy Spirit uses it to extend outward what you value in your mind. By sharing it with others, you then reinforce its presence in you and thus feel more abundant. The ego, in contrast, uses it to throw outside yourself what you despise within yourself ("getting rid of something it does not want"). As a result, you see your own self-destructive choices acted out on you by others, so that they seem to be depriving you. You therefore feel both deprived and angry.

Our only choice is *how* we will use this law, not *if* we will use it. For it is the nature of mind to express outwardly what is within it. The only question is: Will we use it to spread the light in us or to smear the world with our darkness?

2.   The ego's use of projection must be fully understood before the inevitable association between projection and anger can be finally

undone. The ego <u>always</u> tries to preserve conflict. It is very ingenious in devising ways that <u>seem</u> to diminish conflict, because it does <u>not</u> want you to find conflict [Ur: to find it {the ego}] so intolerable that you will <u>insist</u> on giving it up. The ego therefore tries to persuade you that *it* can free you <u>of</u> conflict, lest you give the ego [Ur: give *it*] up and free <u>yourself</u>. Using its own warped version of the laws of God, the ego utilizes the power of the mind <u>only</u> to defeat the mind's real purpose. It projects conflict <u>from</u> your mind to <u>other</u> minds, in an attempt to persuade you that you have gotten <u>rid</u> of the problem [Ur: *rid* of it {conflict}].

Remember that in these sections, the conflict is still the same one that was discussed in "To Have, Give All to All" (6.V(A))—the conflict between the two thought systems within you. If you recall, the Holy Spirit resolves this conflict by having you extend to others only one side of the conflict—His side. The ego responds with its own plan. It too is eager to relieve your sense of conflict, for it is afraid that you'll seek the Holy Spirit's resolution, which involves seeing the ego as responsible for the conflict and therefore getting rid of it.

The ego's solution is ingenious. Rather than having you extend to others the peace that comes from being conflict-free, it has you project onto others the conflict itself. Now it is not your conflict; it is theirs. Now you aren't the one torn between God and the ego; *they* are. Jesus has already spoken of this: "Further, the mind of the learner projects its own conflict, and thus does not perceive consistency in the minds of others, making him suspicious of their motivation" (T-6.V(B).3:8).

3.   There are two major errors involved in this attempt [Ur: This has a number of fallacies which may not be so apparent]. First, strictly speaking, conflict cannot <u>be</u> projected [in the sense of "extended"] <u>because</u> it cannot be [Ur: fully] shared. Any attempt to keep <u>part</u> of it and get rid of <u>another</u> part does not really mean <u>anything</u>. Remember that a conflicted teacher is a poor teacher <u>and a poor learner</u>. His lessons are confused, and their transfer value is [Ur: severely] limited <u>by</u> his confusion. The second error [Ur: fallacy] is the idea that you can <u>get rid</u> of something you do not want <u>by</u> giving it away. <u>Giving</u> it is how you *keep* it. The belief that by seeing it outside [Ur: by giving it *out*] you have excluded it from <u>within</u> is a complete distortion of the power of <u>extension</u>. That is why those who project [Ur: from the ego] are vigilant

for their <u>own</u> safety. <u>They are afraid that their projections will return and hurt them</u>. Believing they have blotted their projections from their <u>own</u> minds, they also believe their projections are trying to creep back in. Since [Ur: This is because] the projections have <u>not</u> left their minds, they are forced [Ur: and this, in turn, forces them] to engage in constant [Ur: compulsive] activity in order <u>not</u> to recognize this.

Let's take these two fallacies one at a time. The correction for the first fallacy is that conflict cannot really be projected, or perhaps more accurately, *extended*, because it cannot fully be shared. We have discussed how thoughts of the ego can't really be shared before, but to understand the idea in this particular case we need to understand what's being projected a bit more fully.

You aren't just seeing in others the same conflict between God and ego that you have in yourself. It's more complicated than that. You are seeing in them *responsibility for your conflict*. You do this by projecting the *ego side* of your inner conflict (which is what is meant by "keep part of it and get rid of another part"). As a result, when you look without, you mainly see the ego side of the conflict, and when you look within, you mainly see the God side. Your experience in life now becomes one of the ego *in others* attacking the light *in you*. Now the conflict is not between the light and darkness in you (as it really is), but between the beautiful little candle in you and the cyclonic forces of darkness in the world.

This, I think, is why your conflict cannot be shared. What you are projecting is the idea, "You are responsible for my sense of conflict," and who is going to share that idea with you?

The correction for the second fallacy is that by projecting this conflict you are not getting rid of it; you are *keeping* it. That's because the law is that what you extend outward you reinforce in yourself. For example, the preacher who rails against all the immorality in the world is trying to convince himself that his own demons aren't in there. Yet the more he projects them onto the world, the more he reinforces his secret belief that they lurk within, and the more he fears that they will one day rise up and take control.

Questions for reflection: In your relationships, do you tend to feel in a state of conflict in which the light in you is under attack by the darkness in others? If so, can you consider that this is an illusion conjured up by your projection? Is it possible that the conflict you see is your attempt to displace onto them your own conflict between light and darkness, thus making it their responsibility, not yours? Is it possible that in actuality there is no conflict between you and them?

> 4.   You cannot perpetuate an illusion about another <u>without</u> perpetuating it about yourself. There is no way out of this, because it is <u>impossible</u> to fragment the mind. To fragment is to break into pieces, and mind <u>cannot</u> attack or be attacked ["or be attacked" seems to have been added by the editors]. The belief that it <u>can</u>, an error the ego <u>always</u> makes, underlies its whole use of projection. It does not understand what mind <u>is</u>, and therefore does not understand what *you* are. Yet <u>its</u> existence <u>is</u> dependent on your mind, because the ego is your <u>belief</u>. The ego is [Ur: therefore] a confusion in identification [Ur: which never had a consistent model, and never developed consistently]. Never having had a consistent model, it never developed consistently. It is the product of the misapplication of the laws of God by distorted minds that are misusing their power.

You can't project an illusion onto others without reinforcing illusions about yourself. Like that preacher, you can't project your demons onto others without becoming even more convinced of the demons in you. That, as we have seen in the previous two sections, is simply part of the nature of mind. What it sees in one part it will see in the whole. The evil we see in others will automatically infect all our perception, including our self-perception.

The ego is in total denial about this. "It does not understand what mind is" and how it works. Yet it depends on mind. To think you are an ego, therefore, is for the mind to believe that its nature (as ego) is alien to its nature (as mind). Talk about "a confusion in identification"!

What does it mean to say that the ego never had a consistent model? I am not sure, but a model is basically an authority-figure to whom you look to model yourself after, and the ego recognizes no authority but itself. With its own whim as its only authority, of course the ego would develop in some rather erratic ways.

> 5.   *Do not be afraid of the ego.* It depends [Ur: *does* depend] on your mind, and as you made it by believing in it, so you can dispel it by

withdrawing belief <u>from</u> it. Do <u>not</u> project the responsibility for your belief in it onto <u>anyone</u> else, or you will <u>preserve</u> the belief. When you are willing to accept sole responsibility for the ego's existence [Ur: *yourself*,] you will have laid aside all anger and all attack, because they <u>come</u> from an attempt to <u>project responsibility for your own errors</u>. But having <u>accepted</u> the errors as yours, <u>do not keep them</u>. Give them over quickly to the Holy Spirit to be undone completely, so that <u>all</u> their effects will vanish from your mind and from the Sonship <u>as a whole</u>.

Currently, we *are* afraid of our ego. We are afraid of our inner demons. That is why we project them onto others. This causes us to see others as raging egos who force us to respond with anger and judgment, who bring out the ego in us against our will. Seeing others as responsible for our own ego may feel good momentarily, but in the end it just reinforces our ego, *and* places it outside our control. Instead, we must reclaim our role as the one in charge. From this standpoint, we can then refuse to fear the ego. And we can accept sole responsibility for it, and then give it over "quickly" to the Holy Spirit, to be cleansed from our mind.

Application: Think of someone who you believe has strengthened the anger and judgment and shame and fear within you. Then repeat these words:

I will not project responsibility for my ego onto [name].
I accept sole responsibility for my ego's existence.
And I give it quickly over to the Holy Spirit,
So that He may undo it completely,
That all of its effects may vanish from my mind and from the
    Sonship as a whole.

6. The Holy Spirit will teach you to perceive <u>beyond</u> your belief, because truth <u>is</u> beyond belief and His perception <u>is</u> true. The ego can be completely forgotten at <u>any</u> time, because it is [Ur: because it was always] a totally incredible belief, and no one can <u>keep</u> a belief he has judged to be unbelievable. The more you learn <u>about</u> the ego, the more you realize that it cannot <u>be</u> believed. The incredible cannot <u>be</u> understood because it <u>is</u> unbelievable. The [Ur: utter] meaninglessness of [Ur: *all*] perception based on the unbelievable is [Ur: *must* be] apparent, but it may not be recognized as being [Ur: but it is *not*]

beyond belief, because it is [Ur: was] made *by* belief.

The Holy Spirit's perception and the ego's perception are both beyond belief, but in totally different ways and for totally different reasons. The Holy Spirit's perception is beyond belief because it is the perception of the truth, and truth is an objective certainty which transcends subjective belief. The ego's perception, on the other hand, is based on belief in the ego, and the ego is beyond belief because it is nonsense. True, we believe in it because we made it by belief, but when we *really* look at it, we see more and more how utterly nonsensical it is. It is not evil, it is just nonsense. Do you feel that the Course is slowly leading you to this realization?

> 7.   The whole purpose of this course is to teach you that the ego is unbelievable and will forever be unbelievable. You who made the ego by believing the unbelievable cannot make this judgment alone. By accepting the Atonement for yourself, you are deciding against the belief that you can be alone, thus dispelling the idea of separation and affirming your true identification with the whole Kingdom as literally part of you. This identification is as beyond doubt as it is beyond belief. Your wholeness has no limits because being is infinity [Ur: its being is in Infinity].

However unbelievable the ego is, we are not in a position to realize this by ourselves ("you...cannot make this judgment alone"). We are like the alcoholic who is unable to see how crazy his condition is. He cannot see it from the vantage point of the other side of addiction. Just as the alcoholic needs to reach beyond himself for help, so do we. This reaching beyond ourselves is implicit in the act of accepting the Atonement, for accepting the Atonement means we are accepting the idea that we can never be alone, that we are part of something much larger. Indeed, we are accepting the fact that "the whole Kingdom [is] literally part of" us, which means that our wholeness is infinite. In such a state, how could the ego appear even remotely believable?

IX. The Extension of the Kingdom
Commentary by Robert Perry

This section is unusually metaphysical. It primarily addresses our function of extension or creation in Heaven, whereby we extend our being outward and bring into being our "creations." This concept often confuses students, yet in truth it is very simple: Our creations are simply the extension of our being, and therefore they share the same nature that we do. They are pure spirit, formless, timeless, boundless, eternal, and perfect. The value of this section, in my view, is that it makes our creativity in Heaven more than just an abstract metaphysical concept. It makes it both relevant and deeply desirable.

> 1.   Only you can limit your creative power, but God wills to release it. He no more wills you to deprive yourself of your creations [the product of your creative power] than He wills to deprive Himself of His. Do not withhold your gifts to the Sonship [I think this refers to our creations], or you withhold yourself from God! Selfishness is of the ego, but Self-fullness is of spirit [Ur: the Soul] because that is how God created it. The Holy Spirit is in the part of the mind that lies between the ego and the spirit [Ur: the Soul], mediating between them <u>always in favor of</u> the spirit [Ur: *the Soul*]. To the ego this is partiality, and it responds as if it were [Ur: the part that is] being sided <u>against</u>. To spirit [Ur: the Soul] this is truth, because it knows its fullness and cannot conceive of <u>any</u> part from which it is excluded.

Notice how this paragraph tries to motivate us in regard to our heavenly function of creating. It says that while we are not creating, we are limiting our creative power, depriving ourselves of our creations and withholding ourselves from God. Do we want to limit our power? Do we want to deprive ourselves of the perfect heavenly children we created? Do we want to withhold ourselves from God? We have a choice: Do we want to be self*ish* or Self-*full*?

The Holy Spirit mediates between our ego and our spirit, but He is not an impartial mediator. He always favors our spirit. That makes our ego feel sided against, and we can see the evidence of this. For instance, doesn't your ego wish that the Course would back it up more? Our spirit, on the other hand, is so full, so complete, that it knows it can't be sided against because it knows that in truth there *is* no other side.

> 2. Spirit [Ur: The soul] <u>knows</u> that the awareness of all its brothers is included in its own, as <u>it</u> is included in God. The power of the whole Sonship <u>and of its Creator</u> is therefore spirit's <u>own</u> fullness, rendering its creations [Ur: its Creation and its creating] equally whole and equal in perfection. The ego cannot prevail against a totality that includes God, and any totality *must* include God. Everything He created is given <u>all</u> His power, because it is part of Him and shares His Being <u>with</u> Him. Creating is the <u>opposite</u> of loss, as blessing is the opposite of sacrifice. Being *must* be extended. That is how it retains the knowledge of it<u>self</u>. Spirit [Ur: The Soul] yearns to share <u>its</u> being as <u>its</u> Creator did. Created <u>by</u> sharing, its will is to create. It does <u>not</u> wish to <u>contain</u> God, but wills to <u>extend His Being</u>.

This paragraph describes the fullness of our spirit. That fullness includes being simultaneously aware of every one of the infinite number of our brothers, because awareness of them is an inherent part of our own awareness. Just try to imagine that. That fullness also includes the awareness of all of God's Being and the possession of all of His power. Our fullness, in other words, includes all of the fullness of God. How could any earthly fullness compare? How could a full stomach or a full bank account or a full dance card even remotely measure up? And how could the ego ever prevail against a fullness that is so vast that it includes God Himself?

This fullness must be extended. It must overflow in the joyous act of creation. The creative act that produced our spirit stamped itself onto the *nature* of our spirit. Our spirit was produced by sharing, so its nature is to share. Our spirit was produced as an extension of God's Being, so its nature is to further "extend His Being." And because our nature is to extend, to share, we have to do these things in order to *know* our nature. ("That is how it retains the knowledge of itself.") For all these reasons, in our true state, we yearn to share our being. Think of that. We *yearn* to share our being.

> 3. The extension of God's Being is spirit's only function. <u>Its</u> fullness cannot be contained, any more than can the fullness of its Creator. Fullness <u>is</u> extension. The ego's whole thought system <u>blocks</u> extension,

and thus blocks <u>your only function</u>. It therefore blocks your joy, so that [Ur: and *this* is why] you perceive yourself as unfulfilled. Unless you create you *are* unfulfilled, but God does <u>not</u> know unfulfillment and therefore you <u>must</u> create. <u>You</u> may not know your own creations, but this can no more interfere with their reality than your unawareness of your spirit [Ur: Soul] can interfere with its being.

Most of us know what it's like to feel so full that you just can't contain yourself. You have to express it. Your fullness has to overflow, and this overflowing is integral to your joy. Now imagine that something came along and forced you to keep it all secret. You had to keep it bottled up. Wouldn't that block your joy? All of this is an earthly version of what goes on in Heaven. In Heaven, we are so full that we have to overflow. Yet the ego "blocks extension." It keeps our very being bottled up.

Function is the action for which a thing is designed and for which it exists. If you don't do the thing for which you are designed, the thing for which you exist, how can you be happy? We have many notions of what our function is, most resting on the concept that we are needy minds inside needy bodies. Yet our real and only function is to extend God's Being. That is what were designed for. That is what we exist for. In Heaven, we are still doing that ("you must create"), but on earth we are not. And *this* is why we are unfulfilled, not because we have failed to successfully fill our needy minds or needy bodies.

> 4.   The Kingdom is forever extending because it is in the Mind of God. <u>You</u> do not know your joy because you do not know your own Self-fullness. Exclude <u>any</u> part of the Kingdom <u>from</u> yourself and you are <u>not</u> whole. A split mind <u>cannot</u> perceive its fullness, and needs the miracle <u>of</u> its wholeness to dawn upon it and heal it. This reawakens the wholeness <u>in</u> it, and restores it to the Kingdom because of its <u>acceptance</u> of wholeness. The full appreciation of the mind's Self-fullness makes selfishness impossible and extension inevitable. That is why there is perfect peace in the Kingdom. Spirit is [Ur: Every Soul *is*] fulfilling its function, and <u>only</u> complete fulfillment <u>is</u> peace. [Ur: Insanity *appears* to add to reality, but no-one would claim that what it adds is true. Insanity is therefore the *non*extension of truth, which blocks joy because it blocks Creation and therefore blocks self-*fulfillment*. The unfulfilled *must* be depressed, because their self-fulness is *unknown* to them.]

We have no clue about our fullness. How can we, when our fullness includes all of our brothers, and we have shut so many of them out of our heart? And how can we know our fullness when our mind is split? How can we know the full extent of the house when we have locked ourselves inside the broom closet? We need the miracle of our wholeness to dawn on our mind. Realizing our fullness will make "selfishness impossible and extension inevitable." It will cause us to once again overflow, and to return to the Kingdom where all is peace because *everyone* is overflowing ("every Soul *is* fulfilling its function").

Right now, we are adding to reality, in a sense, but not by extending reality; rather, by adding our insanity *onto* reality. The man who hallucinates snakes crawling up the walls is *obscuring* truth, not *extending* truth. We all have our own snakes that we imagine, and this blocks us from extending. It thus blocks our joy and makes our Self-fullness unknown to us.

> 5.   Your creations are protected <u>for</u> you because the Holy Spirit, Who is in your mind, knows of them and can bring them <u>into</u> your awareness whenever you will let Him. They <u>are</u> there as part of your own being, because <u>your</u> fulfillment <u>includes</u> them. The creations of every Son of God are yours, since every creation belongs to everyone, being created for the Sonship as a whole.

Our creations are part of our fullness ("your fulfillment includes them"), just as the creations of a painter are part of his. With a painter, however, only *his* paintings are his, whereas with creation, "the creations of every Son of God are yours." Imagine a painter's joy if he could look upon every great painting ever produced as equally his. A far greater joy can be ours, because we can know our creations, and mere paintings pale before these masterpieces. The Holy Spirit can bring them into our awareness whenever we want.

> 6.   You have not failed to increase the inheritance of the Sons of God, and thus have not failed to secure it for yourself. Since it was the Will of God to give it [your inheritance] to you, He gave it forever. Since it was His Will that you have it forever, He gave you the means for keeping it. *And you have done so.* Disobeying God's Will is meaningful only to the insane. In truth it is impossible. Your Self-fullness is as boundless as

God's. Like His, It extends forever and in perfect peace. Its radiance is so intense that It creates in perfect joy, and only the whole can be born of Its wholeness.

After all of this talk about failing to fulfill our function and thereby being joyless and depressed, here is the good news. Only the earthly part of our split mind is failing to fulfill our function. In Heaven, we have never stopped creating (which is the meaning of "*And you have done so*"), and thus have succeeded in keeping the inheritance God gave us. Would a loving Father give us an inheritance that we could lose?

Application: Repeat the following lines, and while you do, try your best to imagine being in the state they so beautifully describe:

> *My Self-fullness is as boundless as God's.*
> *Like His, mine extends forever and in perfect peace,*
> *The radiance of my Self-fullness is so intense that It creates forever and in perfect joy.*
> *And only the whole can be born of Its wholeness.*

7.   Be confident that you have never lost your Identity and the extensions which maintain It in wholeness and peace. Miracles are <u>an expression of this confidence</u>. They are reflections of both your proper identification <u>with</u> your brothers, and of your awareness that <u>your</u> identification <u>is</u> maintained by extension. The miracle is <u>a lesson in total perception</u>. By including <u>any</u> part of totality in the lesson, you <u>have</u> included the whole.

Application: Repeat the following with real gladness:

> *I am confident that I have never lost my Identity.*
> *I am confident that I have never lost the extensions of my Identity which maintain It in wholeness and peace.*

This metaphysical talk is inspiring, thought-provoking, and important for grasping the thought system of the Course. Yet how does it really help us? This paragraph explains how. If we really grasp what this section has taught us, then we will be confident that we have never lost our perfect, pristine, and infinitely whole Identity. And we will also be confident that we have never lost the extensions—our creations—which keep It infinitely whole and at peace.

And if we really have this confidence, we will do what? We will perform miracles. We will realize that, if our Self is constantly overflowing in Heaven, in order to remember it we must overflow on earth. We must extend miracles to our brothers. We will also realize that the fullness of our Self comes from everyone being included in It. Therefore, we will treat everyone as if he or she is our very own Self. And this means, again, we will extend miracles to our brothers. It means treating their need as our own, for it *is* our own.

Thankfully, we don't need to give a miracle to every single person on earth, for every person contains the whole. By giving a miracle to one person, then, we "have included the whole."

Miracles are dream reflections of heavenly realities. In Heaven, we extend. Therefore, to *remember* Heaven, we must extend; we must give miracles to our brothers here on earth. The value of a section like this is that when we truly understand heavenly realities, we will act out their reflections in the dream.

X. The Confusion of Pain and Joy
Commentary by Robert Perry

1. [Ur: You have said that, when you write of the Kingdom and your own creations which belong to it, you are describing *what you do not know*. This is true in a sense, but no more true than your failure to acknowledge the whole result of the ego's premises.] The Kingdom is the result of premises, just as this world is. You may have [Ur: You *have*] carried the ego's reasoning to its logical conclusion, which is <u>total confusion about everything</u>. [Ur: But you do not really *believe* this [that the ego's premises inevitably lead to total confusion about everything], or you could not *possibly* maintain it.] If you <u>really</u> saw this result, you <u>could</u> not want it. The <u>only</u> reason you could possibly want <u>any</u> part of it is because <u>you do not see the whole of it</u>. You <u>are</u> [Ur: therefore *are*] willing to look at the ego's premises, but <u>not</u> at their logical outcome. Is it not possible that you have done the same thing with the premises of God? Your creations <u>are</u> the logical outcome of His premises. <u>His</u> thinking has established them for <u>you</u>. They are <u>exactly</u> where [Ur: They are therefore *there, exactly* where] they belong. They belong in [Ur: to] your mind, as part of your identification with <u>His,</u> but your state of mind and your recognition of <u>what is in</u> it [Ur: *what is in your mind*] depend [Ur: at any given moment,] on what you believe <u>about</u> your mind. Whatever these beliefs may be, they are the premises that will determine <u>what you accept into your mind</u>.

I find this paragraph fascinating. Its overall theme is that we have a remarkable capacity to deny the logical results of premises, results that are there in our minds but that we refuse to see. There are two examples of this theme.

One example is that we won't acknowledge the result of the ego's premises. That result is "total confusion about everything," a result we are definitely experiencing. But we won't look at this result. We won't acknowledge that our confusion is the inevitable result of accepting the ego's premises. Strangely, we will look at those premises, "but not at their logical outcome." We won't face the fact that that outcome fills and defines our emotional condition. If we did, we would automatically give up the ego's premises, which would mean giving up the ego itself.

X. The Confusion of Pain and Joy

The other example is that we won't acknowledge the results of God's premises, which are our creations. Helen claimed that when she wrote of her creations, she was describing what she did not know. Our own reaction is probably quite similar. Course students in general react to the notion of our creations as if it is something strange and unfamiliar. Jesus, however, claims the idea that we do not know them is true only "in a sense," since our creations are in our minds right now. How, then, could we not know them? However, we have defined our minds in such a way that those creations simply could not be in them. This blots them from our consciousness, but not from our minds.

Do you think you have this trait—of refusing to acknowledge results that are actually in your mind? Might you even be willing to acknowledge the premises in your mind that cause those results, while still refusing to look at the results themselves? This paragraph implies that changing this one trait could change everything. It would lead to banishing the ego from your mind and accepting your creations in its place.

> 2. It is surely clear that you can both accept into your mind what is <u>not</u> [Ur: really] there, and <u>deny what is</u>. [Ur: Neither of these possibilities requires further elaboration, although both are clearly indefensible even if *you* elect to defend them.] Yet the function [of creation] God Himself <u>gave</u> your mind through His you may <u>deny</u>, but you <u>cannot</u> prevent. It is the logical outcome of what you <u>are</u>. The ability to <u>see</u> a logical outcome depends on the <u>willingness to see it</u>, but its <u>truth</u> has nothing to do with your willingness. Truth is <u>God's</u> Will. <u>Share</u> His Will [by creating] and you [Ur: will] share what He <u>knows</u>. Deny His Will <u>as yours</u>, and you are denying His Kingdom *and* yours [your Kingdom being your creations].

Jesus makes an undeniable point here: Your refusal to see a logical outcome doesn't affect it at all. That outcome is still true. And if it is already in your mind, then it is *still* in your mind, whether you see it there nor not. So it is with your creations. Your denial of them doesn't make them cease to exist. They are, after all, "the logical outcome of what you are." Thus, they are still in your mind. All your denial does is blind you to the real nature of your will—you no longer realize that your will is one with God's—and cause your Kingdom to vanish from your awareness, leaving you kingdom-less.

3. The Holy Spirit will direct you <u>only</u> so as to avoid [Ur: all] pain. [Ur: The *undoing* of pain must *obviously* avoid this.] Surely no one would <u>object</u> to this goal <u>if he recognized it</u>. The problem is <u>not</u> whether what the Holy Spirit says is true, but whether you want to <u>listen</u> to what He says. You no more recognize what is painful than you know what is joyful, and are, in fact, very apt to confuse the two. The Holy Spirit's main function is to teach you to <u>tell them apart</u> [Ur: However strange it may seem that this is necessary, it obviously *is*. The reason is equally obvious]. What is joyful to you <u>is</u> painful to the ego, and as long as you are in doubt about what <u>you</u> are, you <u>will</u> be confused about joy and pain. This confusion is the cause of the whole idea of sacrifice. Obey the Holy Spirit, and you <u>will</u> be giving up the ego. But you will be <u>sacrificing</u> nothing. On the contrary, you will be gaining <u>everything</u>. [Ur: *But*] If you <u>believed</u> this, there would <u>be</u> no conflict.

One of our primary experiences of guidance from the Holy Spirit is that it seems to ask sacrifice of us. It seems to call upon us "to sacrifice [our] own best interests on behalf of truth" (M-4.I.A.5:5). Yet according to this paragraph, the real truth of the matter is entirely different. Yes, the Holy Spirit does ask us to give up the ego. But the ego is nothing, and rather than being a *neutral* nothingness, it is a *painful* nothingness. Thus, by following the Holy Spirit, "you will be sacrificing nothing," and moreover, "you will be gaining everything." If we only understood this, we could follow the Holy Spirit wholeheartedly and effortlessly. As Jesus says, "There would be no conflict."

So why do we think He asks for sacrifice? For one simple reason: We have confused pain and joy. We think pain is joyful, and joy is painful. This stems from a deeper confusion: We have confused our self with the ego. Our joy "is painful to the ego," and conversely, the ego enjoys things that are painful to us.

Imagine, for example, that you confused yourself with a vampire, so that you became truly convinced on an emotional level that you were a vampire. You would, as a result, feel an overpowering urge to kill people and drink their blood. Yet you wouldn't actually *be* a vampire, and so afterwards you would react to what you had done according to your own nature. You would feel excruciating guilt and profound disgust with yourself.

Now imagine that there was someone who saw who you really are, and was trying to deliver you from those horrible pangs of guilt. As long as you still believed you were a vampire, that someone's counsel (such as, "Stop biting people"), however practical and loving, could only seem like a threat and a call to sacrifice.

> 4. That is why you need to <u>demonstrate the obvious to yourself</u>. It is <u>not</u> obvious to you. You [Ur: *really*] believe that doing the opposite of God's Will <u>can</u> be better for you. You also believe that it is <u>possible</u> to *do* the opposite of God's Will. Therefore, you believe that an impossible choice <u>is</u> open to you, and one which is both [Ur: very] fearful [because we are going against God] and [Ur: very] desirable. Yet God <u>wills</u>. He does <u>not</u> wish. <u>Your</u> will is as powerful as His because it *is* His. The ego's wishes do not mean anything, because the ego wishes for the impossible. You <u>can</u> wish for the impossible, but you can <u>will</u> only with God. This is the ego's weakness and <u>your</u> strength.

We are always thinking that doing the opposite of God's Will can be better for us. We think that being special can make us happy. We think condemning a brother can protect our self-image. We think that esteeming our body equals *self*-esteem. We think that sending an e-mail instead of doing our hourly Workbook practice can lead to a happier day. The list could go on and on.

"Yet," says the Course, "God wills. He does not wish." If God wills, that means His decision is unequivocal. It has all of His undivided power behind it. And can anything stand against all the power of God? Hence, we cannot really do the opposite of God's Will. When we try to, we are just acting in a dream in which nothing real is being done.

Furthermore, in such vacuous actions, we are not following our will, but rather the ego's wishes. They are mere *wishes* (which suggests lack of power) because they go against our nature. This prevents us from putting all of our mind and heart behind them. As a result, they are divided, uncertain, *wishy*-washy. That, too, is why they cause nothing real. They not only go against the full force of God's power, they also lack the full force of *our* power. Because our nature is God's, we can only put all of ourselves into something when we will with God. "This is the ego's weakness and your strength."

> 5. The Holy Spirit always sides with <u>you</u> and with your <u>strength</u>. As long as you avoid His guidance in any way, you <u>want to be weak</u>. Yet

weakness <u>is</u> frightening. What else, then, can this decision mean except that you <u>want</u> to be fearful? The Holy Spirit <u>never</u> asks for sacrifice, but the ego <u>always</u> does. When you are confused about this [Ur: *very* clear] distinction in motivation, it <u>can</u> only be due to projection. Projection [Ur: of this kind] <u>is</u> a confusion in motivation, and given <u>this</u> confusion, <u>trust</u> becomes impossible. No one gladly obeys a guide he does not trust, but this does not mean that the <u>guide</u> is untrustworthy. In this case, it <u>always</u> means that the <u>follower is</u>. However, this, too, is merely a matter of his own belief. Believing that <u>he</u> can betray, he believes that everything can betray <u>him</u>. Yet this is <u>only</u> because he has <u>elected to follow false guidance</u>. Unable to follow <u>this</u> guidance <u>without</u> fear, he associates fear <u>with</u> guidance, and refuses to follow <u>any</u> guidance at all. If the result of this decision is confusion, this is hardly surprising.

Your strength, as we saw, only comes out when you will with your nature—when you will with God. The Holy Spirit's guidance, therefore, "always sides with *you* and with your *strength*" (emphasis from Urtext). Thus, when you avoid His guidance, you are siding with your weakness, you are going with your ego's weak, divided wishes. But isn't it frightening to be weak? Thus, avoiding the Holy Spirit's guidance means that you are choosing a weak, divided, frightened image of yourself, and choosing this over the powerful, whole, secure self you really are. How smart is that?

The middle of the paragraph gives the real reason we don't trust the Holy Spirit: *projection.* We are projecting the ego onto the Holy Spirit. The ego has been our main experience of a guide, and our experience has been that it is a slippery, untrustworthy guide that constantly asks us to sacrifice. Based on that, we think that's what guides are like, and therefore the Holy Spirit must be like that, too. Thus, when we view the Holy Spirit with suspicion, it is only because we are superimposing the ego's face onto Him.

We are also projecting our *own* face onto Him. We note that we have been terrible followers. Since we have been following such a harsh taskmaster (the ego), we have chafed under its authority and have often rebelled. We have, in other words, betrayed our guide. Now we project this image of ourselves as betrayers onto the Holy Spirit, and assume that He will be like us—He, too, will betray.

This leaves us in a real predicament. We don't trust the Holy Spirit, we don't fully trust the ego, and we don't even trust ourselves. There is no one's guidance we regard without suspicion. And since we have no firm guide for how to understand anything, we are confused about everything.

> 6. The Holy Spirit is perfectly trustworthy, as <u>you</u> are. God Himself trusts you, and therefore your trustworthiness <u>is</u> beyond question. It will always remain beyond question, however much you may question it. [Ur: I trust *my* choices *only* because they *are* God's Will.] I said before that <u>you</u> are the Will of God. His Will is not an idle wish, and your identification <u>with</u> His Will is not optional, since it <u>is</u> what you are. Sharing His Will <u>with</u> me is not really open to choice [Ur: at all], though it may <u>seem</u> to be. The whole separation lies in this error [Ur: fallacy]. The <u>only</u> way out of the error [Ur: fallacy] is to decide that <u>you do not have to decide anything</u>. Everything has been given you by <u>God's</u> decision. That <u>is</u> His Will, and you can<u>not</u> undo it.

What wonderful news: "Your trustworthiness is beyond question." Isn't our happiness constantly undermined by our belief that we can't trust ourselves, and that no one else can, either? True, we may have behaved in an untrustworthy fashion, but as the previous paragraph said, that is only because we have been following a bad guide. Our own nature remains "perfectly trustworthy," because we *are* the Will of God, and how can the Will of God be untrustworthy?

All right, we may think, that is my nature, but how do I *realize* this nature? How do I bring it into consciousness? The answer is that you simply accept that your perfectly trustworthy nature is an unalterable fact. It is outside your power. It is "not really open to choice at all" (Urtext version). You cannot undo it. In acknowledgment of this, you just "decide that *you do not have decide anything*." You simply rest in *what is*.

> 7. Even the relinquishment of your false decision-making prerogative, which the ego guards so jealously, is not accomplished by your wish. It was accomplished <u>for</u> you by the Will of God, Who has not left you comfortless. His Voice <u>will</u> teach you how to distinguish between pain and joy, and will lead you out of the confusion <u>you</u> have made. There <u>is</u> no confusion in the mind of a Son of God, whose will <u>must</u> be the Will of the Father, because the Father's Will *is* His Son.

Even after we hear all that this section has said, we can still be left thinking, "How can I give up this idea that my nature hangs on my decision? And how can I straighten out my confusion of pain and joy?" But the answer is what we have already seen: Your nature does not contain "your false decision-making prerogative," not does it contain any confusion. These things are absolutely absent from what you really are. You don't have to banish them, for in a very real sense, they are already gone from you. And the Holy Spirit will lead you to this realization.

> 8. Miracles are <u>in accord</u> with the Will of God, Whose Will you do <u>not</u> know because you are confused about what *you* will. This <u>means</u> that you are confused about what you are. If you <u>are</u> God's Will and do <u>not</u> <u>accept</u> His Will, [Ur: you can *only* be not accepting what you are. But if your joy *is* what you are,] you <u>are</u> denying joy. The miracle is therefore a lesson in <u>what joy is</u>. Being a lesson in <u>sharing</u> it is a lesson in love, which *is* joy. Every miracle is thus a lesson in truth, and by <u>offering</u> truth <u>you</u> are learning the difference between pain and joy.

If the Holy Spirit leads us to the realization of our true nature, then surely there is something we can do to *let* Him lead us there. The situation we are in now is this: We are denying God's Will. This means that we are denying our own true will and indeed denying our own true nature, since we *are* God's Will. And since our nature is joy, we are also denying joy.

The answer then, is to do God's Will, which means to share miracles with our brothers. Sharing miracles is the way to express our true nature. It therefore means identifying with the joy that is our true nature. It also means sharing love, and love, as we all know, is joyous. In summary, then, in doing miracles, we finally learn what joy is.

This, then, is the answer to everything in this section. This is how we stop confusing joy and pain. This is how we stop denying God's Will. This is how we stop mistrusting the Holy Spirit's guidance. And this is how stop mistrusting ourselves. We do the miracles the Holy Spirit asks us to do, and thus we learn what joy really is and what our will really is.

XI. The State of Grace
Commentary by Robert Perry

1. The Holy Spirit will <u>always</u> guide you truly, because <u>your</u> joy <u>is</u> His. This is His Will for everyone because He speaks for the Kingdom of God, which *is* joy. Following Him is therefore the easiest thing in the world, and the only thing that <u>is</u> easy, because it is <u>not</u> of the world. It is therefore <u>natural</u>. The world goes <u>against</u> your nature, being [Ur: because it is] out of accord with God's laws. The world perceives orders of difficulty in <u>everything</u>. This is because the ego perceives nothing as wholly desirable. By <u>demonstrating</u> to yourself <u>there is no order of difficulty in miracles</u>, you will convince yourself that, in your <u>natural</u> state, there <u>is</u> no difficulty at all *because* it is a state of grace.

Every bit of the Holy Spirit's guidance is about getting you to joy. That's all He cares about. He cares about it so much that the Course can make the amazing statement that "your joy is His." Yet how else would He be? He is, after all, the messenger of a realm of eternal joy. If you realized this, following Him would be easier and more natural than anything in this world, for everything in you would be attracted to His guidance, seeing no drawbacks in it, seeing nothing but pure joy there.

This paragraph makes the odd claim that, apart from following the Holy Spirit, nothing in this world is either easy or natural. Really? How can the "natural world" not be natural? Because, Jesus tells us, it "goes against your nature." And because of that, there is nothing here that we find wholly desirable. That, in turn, is why nothing here is easy. Things are not difficult in themselves. They *seem* difficult because we don't find them desirable enough to draw out of us the full force of our will. In our eyes, they just aren't worth the effort. A ten-pound weight can seem like a ton if you see so little value in it that you put none of your strength into lifting it.

This is why "demonstrating to yourself there is no order of difficulty in miracles" is so valuable. Doing what appear to be incredibly difficult miracles with complete ease will teach you that there *is* a state that is natural, easy, and wholly desirable, that there is a state other than this world.

2. Grace is the natural state of every Son of God. When he is <u>not</u> in a state of grace, he <u>is</u> out of his natural environment and does <u>not</u> function well. Everything he does becomes a strain, because he was not created for the environment that he has made. He therefore <u>cannot</u> adapt to it, nor can he adapt <u>it</u> to <u>him</u>. There is no point in trying. A Son of God is happy <u>only</u> when he knows he is <u>with</u> God. That is the only environment in which he will not experience strain, because that is where he belongs. It is also the only environment that is worthy of him, because his own worth is beyond <u>anything</u> he can make.

Every time I read this paragraph, it makes me aware just how much I take it for granted that life is a condition of strain. I am in the odd position of my "natural environment" (this world) not feeling very natural to me. I feel like a fish out of water. Since I don't really fit my environment, I am in constant friction with it, constantly straining to adjust to it and get it to adjust to me. Everything is an uphill struggle. Everything is so hard. Yet what can I do? This is just the way things are.

This paragraph, however, gives me the liberating message that this is *not* the way things are. This world is not my natural environment. God did not create it, nor did He create me for it. Rather, I made it, and I did a damn poor job of it. In fact, this environment that I made is not worthy of me, simply because my own worth is beyond anything I can Instead, my true natural environment is "a state of grace." The word "grace" signifies that it is a state in which everything is freely given me, without my having to work for it, without my having to put out any effort whatsoever. Because there is a perfect fit between this environment and me, because I truly *belong* there, nothing is difficult. Nothing is a strain. It is all ease. It is all given. Because I am with my Father.

3. Consider the kingdom [Ur: *which*] <u>you</u> have made and judge its worth fairly. Is it worthy to be a home for a child of God? Does it protect his peace and shine love upon him? Does it keep his heart untouched by fear, and allow him to give always, without any sense of loss? Does it teach him that this giving <u>is</u> his joy, and that God Himself thanks him for his giving? That is the only environment in which you can be happy. You cannot make it, any more than you can make yourself. [Ur: But] It has been created for you, as you were created for it. God watches over His children and denies them nothing. Yet when they deny Him they do <u>not</u> know this, because <u>they</u> deny themselves everything. You

who could give the Love of God to everything you see and touch and remember, are literally denying Heaven to yourself.

Jesus really wants us to look at the world as we would look at a piece of merchandise, "and judge its worth fairly." So let's use the questions he provides to do just that. Please consider each question separately, and answer it as honestly as you can.

• Is this world worthy to be a home for a child of God?

Realize that the questions that follow are specific breakdowns of the first, and assume that you are that child of God.

• Does this world protect your peace and shine love upon you?
• Does it keep your heart untouched by fear?
• Does it allow you to give always, without any sense of loss?
• Does it teach you that this giving is your joy, and that God Himself thanks you for your giving?

How can we possibly answer yes to these questions? And thus what can we conclude but that this world is *not* a worthy home for a child of God?

Now glance through these questions again and realize that there is a home that with each question would compel a "yes." With each question, then, try to imagine what it would be like to live in such a home. Then realize that this home actually exists. "It has been created for you, as you were created for it."

We have denied this perfect home in favor of the painful one we made, where everything is difficult. Why in God's name would we want to do that?

> 4. I call upon you [Ur: again] to remember that I have chosen you to teach the Kingdom *to* the Kingdom. There are no exceptions to this lesson, because the lack of exceptions *is* the lesson. Every Son who returns to the Kingdom with this lesson in his heart has healed the Sonship and given thanks to God. Everyone who learns this lesson has become the perfect teacher, because he has learned it of the Holy Spirit [Ur: who wants to teach him everything He knows].

211

What does it mean to "teach the Kingdom *to* the Kingdom"? It means to teach all the members of the Kingdom—all the Sons of God—that the home described in this section awaits them and was created for them. Or, to use the language from the previous paragraph, it means to "give the Love of God to everything you see and touch and remember." When it says, "There are no exceptions to this lesson, because the lack of exceptions *is* the lesson," I believe it means that there is no one who does not deserve the Kingdom—*no one*—because the very nature of the Kingdom is that it is all-inclusive. Unless it embraced everyone, it wouldn't be that perfect home.

Do you see this as your job—to teach everyone that he or she belongs in a perfect home, in a state of grace, in which everything is easy? If you did, how would you go about doing that?

> 5. When a mind has only light, it <u>knows</u> only light. Its own radiance shines all around it, and extends out into the darkness of other minds, transforming them into majesty. The Majesty of God is there, for <u>you</u> to recognize and appreciate and <u>know</u>. Recognizing [Ur: Perceiving] the Majesty of God <u>as</u> your brother is to accept your <u>own</u> inheritance. God gives only equally. If you recognize His gift in anyone [Ur: *else*], you have acknowledged what He has given <u>you</u>. Nothing is so easy to recognize [Ur: perceive] as truth. This is the recognition [Ur: perception] that is immediate, clear and natural. You have trained yourself <u>not</u> to recognize [Ur: see] it, and this <u>has</u> been very difficult for you.

The first two sentences are so beautiful. Imagine being in that state, in which your mind "knows only light." This light is so bright and so pure that it cannot be contained. See it naturally radiating outward in all directions, radiating even "into the darkness of other minds, transforming them into majesty."

You wouldn't, of course, be actually *changing* your brothers' minds into majesty. You would be seeing the Majesty of God as present in them already, and by seeing it, you would draw it up to their awareness. And since "God gives only equally," when you see His Majesty in someone else, that automatically affirms that He gave it to you, too.

So the crucial part is seeing it in your brother. This sounds so hard, yet we are assured, "Nothing is so easy to recognize as truth. This is the recognition that is immediate, clear and natural." We have already done

XI. The State of Grace

the hard thing. We have trained ourselves not to see what is so clearly there. Having done the hard thing, why can't we now do the easy thing?

Application: Think of someone you have been less than pleased with today and repeat,

> *Recognizing the Majesty of God as [name] is to accept my **own** inheritance.*

6. <u>Out</u> of your natural environment you may well ask, "What is truth?" since truth <u>is</u> the environment by which and for which you were created. You do not know yourself, because you do not know <u>your</u> Creator. You do not know <u>your</u> creations because you do not know your brothers, who created them <u>with</u> you. I have already said that only the whole Sonship is worthy to be co-creator with God, because only the whole Sonship can create <u>like</u> Him. Whenever you heal a brother by recognizing his worth, you are acknowledging <u>his</u> power to create and <u>yours</u>. <u>He</u> cannot have lost what <u>you</u> recognize, and you <u>must</u> have the glory you see in <u>him</u>. He is a co-creator with God with <u>you</u>. Deny his creative power, and you are denying yours <u>and that of God Who created you</u>.

If our natural environment is truth, then when we are *outside* that environment, as we are now, then we lose touch with truth. The lights go out. We don't know anything—not God, our brothers, our creations, or ourselves. No wonder we are so clueless in this world!

The bulk of this paragraph is an argument for why giving miracles to a brother is a way to remember our own creative power in Heaven. Miracles heal, and we heal another by recognizing his worth. What we recognize, however, is not the conventional worth of measuring up to human standards. Rather, this worth is a Divine idea, one that also includes power and glory. Thus, giving a brother a miracle is an implicit acknowledgment of his Divine power. And if an impartial God gave him that power, then that same God must have given us power as well.

We are not really talking, though, about separate parcels of power held by each of us individually. As this paragraph points out, we don't create in Heaven separately. Creation is a joint process that we all carry out together. We are thus talking about a single power owned and exercised by the entire Sonship as one. Therefore, when we give a miracle to a brother in acknowledgment of his power, we are getting back in touch with that single, universal power.

> 7. You cannot deny part of truth. You do not know your creations because you do not know their creator. You do not know yourself [Ur: *yourselves*] because you do not know yours. Your creations cannot establish your reality, any more than you can establish God's. But you can *know* both. Being is known by sharing. Because God shared His Being with you, you can know Him. But you must also know all He created, to know what they have shared. Without your Father you will not know your fatherhood. The Kingdom of God includes all His Sons and their children, who are as like the Sons as they are like the Father. Know, then, the Sons of God, and you will know all creation.

This is a difficult paragraph to pull together. The umbrella theme seems to be that when we deny any part of the chain of creation, all of our knowledge goes dark. When we deny any member of the family of God, we cease to know the entire family.

However, the specific thrust here seems to be not denying a brother. When the first sentence tells us not to "deny part of truth," it really means do not reject any brother. If you read the end of the previous paragraph, you'll see that. And the last sentence here is about the same basic theme. Since the Sons are like both their Father and their children (their creations), then all you need do is know the Sons and you will know everything. Yet you cannot exclude even one Son and truly know any of them. Here is how Allen Watson has put it in commenting on this paragraph:

> It's a very simple teaching, really, and yet a very challenging one. Exclude no one. Put no one out of your heart. Deny no one their birthright as a child of God. Only in opening your heart wide enough to include every child of God can you ever come to know *all* of creation, including your own.

Commentaries on Chapter 8

THE JOURNEY BACK

I. The Direction of the Curriculum
Commentary by Robert Perry

1.　[Ur: You are hampered in your progress by your demands to know what you do not know. This is actually a way of hanging on to deprivation. You cannot reasonably object to following instructions in a course *for* knowing, on the grounds that you do not know. The need for the course is implicit in your objection.] Knowledge is not the motivation for learning this course. <u>Peace</u> is. [Ur: As the *prerequisite* for knowledge, peace *must* be learned.] This is the prerequisite for knowledge [Ur: This is] <u>only</u> because those who are in conflict are not peaceful, and peace is the <u>condition</u> of knowledge because it is the condition of the Kingdom. Knowledge can be restored only when <u>you</u> meet its conditions. This is not a bargain made by God, Who makes no bargains [Ur: at all]. It is merely the result of your misuse of His laws on behalf of an imaginary will that is not His. Knowledge *is* His Will. If you are <u>opposing</u> His Will, how <u>can</u> you have knowledge? I have told you what knowledge <u>offers</u> you, but perhaps you do <u>not</u> yet regard this as wholly desirable. If you did you would not be so ready [Ur: would hardly be willing] to throw it away [Ur: so readily] when the ego asks for your allegiance.

The first lines (deleted in the published Course) give this paragraph some context. Someone—who I assume to be Helen—has been demanding to know. Based on the hints contained here, I think her line of thought probably went something like this: "You [Jesus] are telling me to follow all these instructions, so that I can get to truth. But I don't really know what the truth is, so how can I know if following your instructions will get me there? Maybe the truth is altogether different from what you are saying. Given that I just don't know what truth is, why should I invest my time and energy in following your instructions?"

Jesus' response is brilliant: "The whole point of the Course is to return you to real knowing. Therefore, the fact that you don't know now is a reason to *do* the Course, not a reason to *not* do it. In light of this, your demand to know before you do it is really just a way to keep yourself deprived of knowing."

In fact, the immediate goal of the Course is not knowledge; it is peace. The Course will lead to knowing, but it is not a course *in* knowing. It is a course in getting out of the inner conflict (between the two thought systems) and at last finding peace. When we have reached total peace, we will be in a state that so closely mirrors knowledge that we will finally remember it.

We need, in other words, to meet the conditions of knowledge. This is not about God withholding knowledge from us until we meet His conditions; it is about us depriving ourselves of knowledge by choosing against it. We may be inspired by Jesus' descriptions of knowledge in the Course, but if we *really* desired it, we wouldn't be so willing to choose against it when our ego tells us its latest plan and asks us for our support.

> 2.   The distractions of the ego may seem to interfere with your learning, but the ego has no power to distract you unless you give it the power to do so. The ego's voice is an hallucination. You cannot expect it [Ur: the *ego*] to say "I am not real." [Ur: Hallucinations *are* inaccurate perceptions of reality.] Yet you are not asked to dispel your hallucinations alone. You are merely asked to evaluate them in terms of their results to you. If you do not want them on the basis of loss of peace, they will be removed from your mind for you.

Learning peace comes from getting out of the inner conflict, which means giving up the ego side of the conflict. We all want to do this, yet the ego's voice keeps talking to us, asking us to judge, to be afraid, to pursue external salvation. And it sounds so reasonable. How can we just lay it aside? The answer is to face that voice directly and realize it is an auditory hallucination and then refuse to give it power. The ego itself will never come out and say, "I am not real." That statement about it has to come from *us*. The best analogy I know for this is the story of John Nash as told in the movie *A Beautiful Mind*. He saw hallucinations and continued to see them, yet he learned to rigorously deny their reality, no matter how real they seemed.

And that is all we need to do with our hallucinations—deny their reality. Once we do, the Holy Spirit will come and remove them from our mind.

> 3.   Every response to the ego is a call to war, and war does deprive you of peace. Yet in this war there is no opponent. This is the reinterpretation

of reality that you must make to secure peace, and the <u>only</u> one you need ever make. Those whom you <u>perceive</u> as opponents are <u>part</u> of your peace, which <u>you</u> are giving up by attacking them. How can you have what <u>you</u> give up? You <u>share</u> to have, but you do <u>not</u> give it up yourself. When you <u>give up</u> peace, you are <u>excluding</u> yourself <u>from</u> it. This is a condition so <u>alien</u> to the Kingdom that you <u>cannot</u> understand the state that prevails <u>within</u> it.

When the ego asks for our allegiance (paragraph 1), when it tries to distract us (paragraph 2), it is always calling us to make war on someone. As we saw in 7.VIII, the ego projects our inner war outward, so that now the war seems to be between us and our brothers. No wonder the ego deprives us of peace! And no wonder we end up feeling outside God's Kingdom of peace.

Application: Think of someone you see as an opponent of some sort. Be honest—the Course says that we see *everyone* as an opponent to some degree. Now ask yourself, "Does seeing this person as my opponent affect my peace?" And then repeat the following to yourself:

This person is not my opponent; I have no opponent.
*This person is **part** of my peace.*
By attacking him/her, I am giving up my peace.

4. Your past learning <u>must</u> have taught you the wrong things, simply because it has not made you happy. On this basis alone its value should be questioned. If learning aims at <u>change,</u> and that is <u>always</u> its purpose, are you satisfied with the changes your learning has brought you? Dissatisfaction with learning outcomes is a sign of learning failure, since it means that you did <u>not</u> get what you wanted.

When you think about "your learning," what you should be thinking about is not learning about facts and concepts, but learning about what things *mean*. For instance, is your brother your opponent or is he part of your peace? What is his meaning in your eyes? That's the kind of learning Jesus is talking about here.

Application: Ask yourself the following questions as sincerely as you can:

> *Has my past learning made me happy?*
> *Am I satisfied with the changes my learning has brought me?*
> *If not, am I willing to question the value of my learning?*
> *Am I willing to admit that my learning has been a failure?*

5.   The curriculum of the Atonement <u>is</u> the opposite of the curriculum you have established for yourself, but <u>so is its outcome</u>. If the outcome of yours has made you unhappy, and if you <u>want</u> a different one, a change in the curriculum is obviously necessary. The first change to be introduced is a change in <u>direction</u>. A meaningful curriculum <u>cannot</u> be inconsistent. If it is planned by two teachers, each believing in diametrically opposed ideas, it <u>cannot</u> be integrated. If it is carried out by these two teachers simultaneously, <u>each one merely interferes with the other</u>. This leads to fluctuation, but <u>not</u> to change. The volatile <u>have</u> no direction. They cannot choose one because they <u>cannot</u> relinquish the other [Ur: others], <u>even if it does</u> [Ur: *the others do*] <u>not exist</u>. Their conflicted curriculum teaches them that *all* directions exist, and gives them no <u>rationale</u> for choice.
6.   The total senselessness of such a curriculum must be fully recognized before a real change in direction becomes possible. You <u>cannot</u> learn simultaneously from two teachers who are in <u>total disagreement about everything</u>. Their joint curriculum presents an <u>impossible</u> learning task. They are teaching you <u>entirely</u> different things in <u>entirely</u> different ways, which might be possible except that both are teaching you about <u>yourself</u>. Your <u>reality</u> is unaffected by both, but if you <u>listen</u> to both, your mind will be split about <u>what your reality is</u>.

Now we discover the problem with our learning: We have been trying to learn two curricula at once. Imagine that you are in school and your curriculum is made up of two classes, both of which have the exact same title: "Who You Are 101." Each morning you attend one class and then the other. The first one teaches you that you are an intelligent animal in a dog-eat-dog world, that you are surrounded by opponents and that you must use every tool at your disposal to do unto them before they do unto you, for life is a deadly competition which you must win at all costs.

The second teaches you that you are in reality a limitless spirit who only appears to be a body, that you are surrounded by friends and brothers, and that your job is to forgive, not compete, for you are here to wake up, not win, and to take all of your brothers with you.

Even the teachers themselves are totally different. The teacher of the first class is slick and entertaining, but also intimidating and heartless. He is the embodiment of the values he teaches. The second teacher is kind, gentle, and encouraging. He clearly cares first and foremost about your welfare as the student.

You understandably find yourself completely torn between these two classes. You go to one and it all seems to make sense. Then you go to the other and hear the total opposite of what you heard in the first class, but now *this* makes sense. Each day you find yourself fluctuating back and forth between the two.

If someone said to you, "You *must* learn this curriculum" (the curriculum consisting of both classes), you would surely respond, "That's impossible! How can I possibly learn both at once? One negates the other." That's what you need to say now, for this, of course, is the situation you are living in right now.

Application: Seriously reflect on the following question: Can I succeed in learning the lessons of both the ego and the Holy Spirit? Then reflect on this one: If I feel like a failure as a learner, might this be why?

II. The Difference between Imprisonment and Freedom

Commentary by Robert Perry

1.   There *is* a rationale for choice. Only <u>one</u> Teacher <u>knows</u> what your reality is. If learning to remove the obstacles to that knowledge [Ur: If learning that] is the <u>purpose</u> of the curriculum, you <u>must</u> learn it of Him. The ego does <u>not know what it is trying to teach</u>. It is trying to teach you what you are <u>without knowing</u> [Ur: *it*] what you are. It is expert <u>only</u> in confusion. It does not understand <u>anything else</u>. As a teacher, then, the ego is totally confused and <u>totally confusing</u>. Even if you could disregard the Holy Spirit entirely, which is [Ur: quite] impossible, you could still learn nothing from the ego, because the ego knows nothing.

This paragraph continues the discussion from the previous section, in which our current curriculum consists of learning the same thing (what we are) from two diametrically opposed teachers—a clearly impossible situation. We have to choose one or the other, but how? The choice should be easy, for only one teacher knows what he's talking about. Both teachers are teaching you what you are, but only one teacher—the Holy Spirit—*knows* what you are. The ego doesn't have a clue. Imagine a teacher whose words sound reasonable, and who is constantly making exciting promises and issuing veiled threats, thus keeping you hanging on his every word. Yet, after a while, you figure out that this guy is actually totally confused about his subject matter. Would you want him as your teacher?

The ego's confusion is reflected in the fact that it is constantly telling you different things about what you are. It tells you that you are a spiritual hero and a spiritual zero, that you are totally special and disappointingly ordinary, that you are a rare find and a complete loser. No wonder you are confused about yourself.

2.   Is there <u>any</u> possible reason for choosing a teacher such as this? Does the <u>total</u> disregard of <u>anything</u> it teaches make anything <u>but</u> sense?

222

Is <u>this</u> the teacher to whom a Son of God should turn to find <u>himself</u>? The ego has never given you a sensible answer to anything. Simply on the grounds of your own experience with its teaching, should not this alone disqualify it as your future teacher? Yet the ego has done more harm to your learning than this alone. Learning is joyful if it leads you along your natural path, and facilitates the development of <u>what you have</u>. When you are taught <u>against</u> your nature, however, you will lose by your learning because your learning will <u>imprison</u> you. Your will is *in* your nature, and therefore <u>cannot</u> go <u>against</u> it.

Application: Reflecting on the fact that the ego doesn't know anything, and therefore has never given you any truly sensible answers, ask yourself the following questions as sincerely as you can:

> *Is there any possible reason for following my ego as my teacher?*
> *Does the total disregard of anything it teaches make anything but sense?*
> *Is this a teacher to whom I, a Son of God, should turn to find myself?*

There are two things that should disqualify the ego as our teacher. The first is that it doesn't know anything and therefore cannot give us sensible answers. The second is that the ego teaches us against our nature and therefore imprisons our nature. It keeps our nature from freely expressing itself. It keeps our true will pent up.

Imagine, for instance, training a bird to behave like a snake. Every time the bird crawls along the ground in a zigzag line, you reward it. But every time it tries to sing or to fly, you severely punish it. After a while, its natural impulses as a bird will become imprisoned. That's what has happened to us. We have been taught against our nature and so our natural impulses as a Son of God have become imprisoned.

3.   The ego cannot teach you anything as long as your will is free, because you <u>will not listen to it</u>. It is <u>not</u> your will to be imprisoned <u>because</u> your will is free. That is why the ego <u>is</u> the denial of free will. It is <u>never</u> God Who coerces you, because He <u>shares</u> His Will <u>with</u> you. His Voice teaches <u>only</u> in accordance with His Will, but that is not the Holy Spirit's lesson because that is what you *are*. The <u>lesson</u> is that

your will and God's <u>cannot</u> be out of accord because they <u>are</u> one. This is the <u>undoing</u> of <u>everything</u> the ego tries to teach. It is not, then, only the <u>direction</u> of the curriculum that must be unconflicted, but also the <u>content</u>.

We tend to see the ego as representing unbridled expression of our will, while we see God as representing the reining in of our will for the sake of a higher good. God seems to be one huge lesson in impulse control, does He not? Yet we have it backwards. Our will is in our nature and our nature is that we are God's Son. All our will longs to do, therefore, is to express our nature as God's Son. This means that the ego is the one who is suppressing our will (as the bird analogy said). God is *unleashing* our will. This is what the Holy Spirit's is trying to teach us—that God's Will is always on the side of our will, because the two are one.

By choosing the Holy Spirit as our Teacher, then, we not only get a curriculum whose direction is unconflicted, but one whose *content* is also unconflicted. For in His content, the fundamental conflict the ego sees—that between God and us—is simply not there.

4. The ego tries to teach that you want to <u>oppose</u> God's Will. This unnatural lesson <u>cannot</u> be learned, and the <u>attempt</u> to learn it is a violation of your own freedom, making you <u>afraid</u> of your will *because* it is free. The Holy Spirit opposes <u>any</u> imprisoning of the will of a Son of God, <u>knowing</u> that the will of the Son <u>is</u> the Father's. The Holy Spirit leads you steadily along the path of freedom, teaching you how to disregard or look beyond <u>everything</u> that would hold you back.

The ego's content is inherently conflicted, being founded on the idea that your will is by nature in conflict with God's. In its view, your will is innately wayward and selfish, like a wild horse that God wants to tame, to break. All this idea does, however, is cover up your true will, which wills only to love and to join. Under the ego, you become like that bird who has been so fully trained to be like a snake that it ends up fearing its own natural impulses. The Holy Spirit is trying to reverse this. He is not coercing you; He is gently trying to lead you away from the ego's imprisonment of your will and toward the free expression of what you are.

5.   We have said that the Holy Spirit teaches you the difference between pain and joy. That is the same as saying He teaches you the difference between imprisonment and freedom. <u>You cannot make this distinction without Him</u> [Ur: That is] because you have taught <u>yourself</u> that imprisonment <u>is</u> freedom. Believing them to be the same, how can you tell them apart? Can you ask the part of your mind that taught you to believe they <u>are</u> the same, to teach you how they are different [Ur: teach you the *difference*]?

As we have seen, we think that the expression of our false, wayward, selfish will is the very definition of freedom, when in fact this imprisons our true will. And we think that the freeing of our true will is actually imprisonment, for this doesn't allow our false will to have its way. In other words, we have totally confused imprisonment and freedom. How, then, can we be the ones who teach ourselves how to tell them apart? It is like asking someone who is color blind to teach herself the difference between red and green.

Our only choice is to trust the Holy Spirit. His guidance will sound like imprisonment—it usually does. But we have to trust that when He tells us to do something, it will actually result in the unleashing of our will, even if it doesn't look that way to us.

6.   The Holy Spirit's teaching takes only *one* direction and has only *one* goal. His direction is freedom and His goal is God. Yet He cannot conceive of God without <u>you</u>, because it is not God's Will to *be* without you. When you have learned that your will <u>is</u> God's, you could no more will to be without Him than He could will to be without <u>you</u>. This <u>is</u> freedom and this <u>is</u> joy. Deny <u>yourself</u> this and you <u>are</u> denying God His Kingdom, because He created you <u>for</u> this.

The further the Holy Spirit takes you, the freer you become. And when you finally reach the goal of God, you discover that God's Will is only for Him to be with you. Even more surprising, you discover that your will is only to be with Him. In your natural state, you are no more capable of wanting to be outside of God than you are capable of wanting to be out in a blizzard naked. At the end of the road, you realize that His free Will and your free will want exactly the same thing: to be together.

7.   When I said, "All power and glory are yours because the Kingdom is His," [7.VII.11:6] this is what I meant: The Will of God is without limit, and all power and glory lie within it. It is boundless in strength and in love and in peace. It has no boundaries because its extension is unlimited, and it encompasses all things because it <u>created</u> all things. By creating all things, it made them <u>part of itself</u>. <u>You</u> are the Will of God because that is how you were created. Because your Creator creates only like Himself, you <u>are</u> like Him. You are part of Him Who <u>is</u> all power and glory, and are therefore as unlimited as He is.

This paragraph is simply an extended explanation of the sentence, "All power and glory are yours because the Kingdom is His." The line of reasoning goes something like this:

- God's Will is boundless in power, glory, strength, love, and peace.
- It is boundless because it extends without limit.
- It covers everything because it created everything.
- When it creates, it makes what it creates part of itself.
- It created you.
- You are thus part of God's Will and therefore part of God and like God.
- Hence, your power and glory are as unlimited as His.

In summary, God contains all power and glory. What He creates becomes part of Him and thus shares in His power and glory. He created you. You thus possess His power and glory as much as He does.

Application: Repeat to yourself:

> *I am part of God Who is all power and glory*
> *Therefore I am as unlimited as He is.*
> *All power and glory are mine because I am His.*

8.   To what else <u>except</u> all power and glory can the Holy Spirit appeal to restore God's Kingdom? His appeal, then, is merely to what the Kingdom is, and for its own acknowledgment of what it is. When

you acknowledge <u>this</u> you bring the acknowledgment automatically to everyone, because <u>you</u> *have* <u>acknowledged everyone</u>. By your recognition you awaken theirs, and through theirs <u>yours</u> is extended. Awakening runs easily and gladly through the Kingdom, in answer to the Call for [Ur: of] God. This is the natural response of every Son of God to the Voice for his Creator, because It is the Voice for <u>his</u> creations and for his own extension.

God appeals to you to restore His Kingdom. You may think He has picked the wrong person. Yet why wouldn't He give you the job if you *are* His Kingdom and if you have all of His power and glory? All He is asking you is to acknowledge what you are. In doing that, you acknowledge all the members of the Kingdom and awaken that acknowledgment in them. Waves of awakening ripple out from you and spread throughout the Kingdom. In saying yes to God's appeal, you have given Him the natural response, since all He seeks is to restore your freedom. And now that you have said yes, why wouldn't the rest of the Kingdom give Him the same natural response? Why wouldn't your awakening become *everyone's* awakening?

III. The Holy Encounter
Commentary by Robert Perry

1. Glory to God in the highest, and to <u>you</u> because He has so willed it. Ask and it shall be given you, because it has already *been* given. Ask for light and learn that you *are* light. If you <u>want</u> understanding and enlightenment you <u>will</u> learn it, because your decision [Ur: will] to learn it is the [Ur: your] decision to listen to the Teacher Who <u>knows</u> of light, and can therefore <u>teach it to you</u>. There is no limit on your learning because there is no limit on your <u>mind</u>. There is no limit on His teaching [Ur: will to teach] because He was created [Ur: by unlimited Will in *order*] to teach. Understanding [Ur: *Knowing*] His function perfectly He [Ur: wills to fulfill] fulfills it perfectly, because that is His joy <u>and yours</u>.

We are all seeking enlightenment. Enlightenment is a great word, because it can signify both a state of supreme spiritual liberation and a simple condition of inner clarity and understanding. Yet enlightenment can seem so difficult, even impossible, to lay hold of. This paragraph is a series of wonderful reassurances, explaining why we are guaranteed to lay hold of it.

First, God has already given us light. He has already willed us glory. Indeed, this light is not something we have (and could thus conceivably lose), but something we *are*.

Second, our Teacher, the Holy Spirit, is unbelievably able. He knows the light and has an undivided will to teach it to us. In fact, God created Him for this very purpose—to teach us enlightenment. This is His function, and "He wills to fulfill it perfectly, because that is His joy" (Urtext version).

Third, our ability to learn is actually limitless. This may be difficult to believe, but how could it really be otherwise? Learning is of the mind and "there is no limit on your mind." If our minds are limitless, how can their ability to learn not also be limitless? (See, by the way, T-12.V.9:1.)

2. To fulfill the Will of God perfectly is the only joy and peace that can be fully <u>known,</u> because it is the only function that can be <u>fully experienced</u>.

When this is accomplished, then, there is no other experience. Yet the wish for other experience will block its accomplishment [Ur: this], because God's Will cannot be forced upon you, being an experience of total willingness. The Holy Spirit understands how to teach this, but you do not. That is why you need Him, and why God gave Him to you. Only His teaching will release your will to God's, uniting it with His power and glory and establishing them as yours. You [Ur: will] share them as God shares them, because this is the natural outcome of their being.

Notice the phrases that refer to fulfilling the Will of God perfectly (which means performing our true function of creating in Heaven): "fully known," "fully experienced," "total willingness." There is, in other words, nothing halfway about this function. Everything in us is unchecked and uncorked. Every fiber of our being is expressing. Our will is released and flows outward without the slightest impediment.

Even on earth, everyone wants a function. Everyone wants to be useful, to make some kind of contribution. What this is saying, though, is that there is a function for us in Heaven that is so perfect that we can give it our all; we can give it *total willingness*. In this function, we fully share the power and glory God gave us. In doing so, we fully experience this function. And as a result, we fully know joy and peace. Clearly, there is nothing in this world that can so completely activate everything in us.

We can't return ourselves to this function. We don't know how. That is why we need the Holy Spirit. We need Someone Who is totally unconflicted about this function, and unconflicted about wanting to guide us back into it.

> 3. The Will of the Father and of the Son are one [Ur: together], by Their extension. Their extension is the result of Their oneness, holding Their unity together by extending Their joint Will. This is perfect creation by the perfectly created, in union with the Perfect Creator. The Father must give fatherhood to His Son [Ur: Sons], because His Own Fatherhood must be extended outward. You who belong in God have the holy function of extending His Fatherhood by placing no limits upon it. Let the Holy Spirit teach you how to do this, for you can [Ur: will] know what it means only of God Himself.

We love the feeling of joining wills with another, so that rather than the two wills contending with each other, we are both pulling in the same direction. We love this even more when we deeply believe in the purpose we are jointly trying to accomplish, and when we also believe in ourselves and the other person.

Given these considerations, it couldn't get any better than the picture described in the above paragraph. There, we share a "joint Will" with all our brothers and with God. We are all pulling, all willing, in the exact same direction. We love all the parties involved, because they are in fact "perfect." And the purpose we are accomplishing together is the most glorious one conceivable—indeed, it is glorious *beyond* conception. We are extending God's Fatherhood outward. We are increasing the limitless Kingdom of God. This line captures the entire picture: "This is perfect creation by the perfectly created, in union with the Perfect Creator."

Would it not be worth eons of effort on the spiritual path if, at the end, we returned to a function like this?

> 4. When you meet anyone, remember it is a holy encounter. As you see him you will see yourself. As you treat him you will treat yourself. As you think of him you will think of yourself. Never forget this, for in him you will find yourself or lose [Ur: sight of] yourself. Whenever two Sons of God meet, they are given another chance at salvation. Do not leave anyone without giving salvation <u>to</u> him and receiving it yourself. For I am always there <u>with</u> you, in remembrance of *you.*

This is one of my favorite paragraphs in the Course. It is an extremely important one. Based on comments from the end of the paragraph, and from elsewhere in the Course, we could say every encounter is a *potential* holy encounter, "another chance at salvation." This potential is so important that Jesus is always present, supporting you in actualizing it. You actualize the potential by realizing that you and the other person share the same interests. If he gains, you gain. If he loses, you lose. Thus, you cannot see him as degraded in order to build yourself up. Rather, "As you see him you will see yourself." You cannot attack him in order to get your needs met. Rather, "As you treat him you will treat yourself." You cannot think of him as a worm so that you will feel like an eagle. Instead, "As you think of him you will think of yourself." Out of this sense of shared interests, you then give salvation to him. What else would you do if his gain is your gain? What else would you do if blessing him is the way to find yourself?

Thus, a holy encounter is a meeting in which one person's perception of shared interests leads that person to give. This then draws the other person into that same perception of shared interests, and thus into returning the gift in gratitude. Both are then lifted into an experience of the mutual sharing of salvation.

Application: Think of someone you will soon be encountering and silently say these powerful words to that person:

> *As I see you I will see myself.*
> *As I treat you I will treat myself.*
> *As I think of you I will think of myself.*
> *In you I will find myself or lose myself.*

Do your best to carry these words into your encounter with that person. See if they don't spark something different to happen.

5. The goal of the curriculum, regardless of the teacher you choose, is "<u>Know thyself</u>." There is nothing else to seek [Ur: learn]. Everyone is looking for himself and for the power and glory he thinks he has lost. Whenever you are with anyone [Ur: *else*], you have another opportunity to find them. Your power and glory are in <u>him</u> <u>because</u> they are yours. The ego tries to find them in <u>yourself</u> alone, because it does not know where to look. The Holy Spirit teaches you that if you look only at yourself you <u>cannot</u> find yourself, because that is <u>not</u> what you are. Whenever you are with a brother, you are learning what you are because you are <u>teaching</u> what you are. He will respond either with pain or with joy, depending on which teacher <u>you</u> are following. <u>He</u> will be imprisoned or released according to your decision, <u>and so</u> <u>will you</u>. Never forget your responsibility to him, because it is your responsibility to <u>yourself</u>. Give him <u>his</u> place in the Kingdom and you will have <u>yours</u>.

We are all trying to find ourselves. We are all looking for the power and glory we think we lost. Those of us on the spiritual path already recognize we are doing that. Yet we make the mistake of looking for our power and glory in ourselves alone. What could be more natural than to seek the inner light *within*? Yet that search implies a wrong view of ourselves. It implies that we are ourselves alone. Listen to this correction: "If you look only at yourself you cannot find yourself, because that is not what you are."

Instead, we need to look for our power and glory in our brothers. We need to focus on releasing them, on teaching them who they are, on giving them back their place in the Kingdom. This is so crucial that we have this line, which surely surprises many self-focused spiritual seekers: "Never forget your responsibility to him, because it is your responsibility to yourself." We are *responsible* to our brothers.

Yet all this implies that we can only find ourselves if we give to our brothers *and* they respond by joining us in a holy encounter. Doesn't that make us dependent on how they respond? Doesn't that mean our salvation waits on them doing the right thing? Yes, in a sense it does. But their response is really in our hands. "He will respond either with pain or with joy, depending on which teacher *you* are following. He will be imprisoned or released according to your decision, *and so will you*" (emphasis from Urtext). Could it be that if we truly gave love, our gift would unclench our brothers' fists and open their hearts?

> 6. The Kingdom cannot be found alone, and you who are the Kingdom cannot find yourself [Ur: *yourselves*] alone. To achieve the goal of the curriculum, then, you cannot listen to the ego, whose purpose is to defeat its own goal. The ego does not know this, because it does not know anything. But you can know it, and you will know it if you are willing to look at what the ego would make [Ur: has made] of you. This is your responsibility, because once you have really looked at it you *will* accept the Atonement for yourself [which was earlier billed as "your sole responsibility"]. What other choice could you make? Having made this choice you will [Ur: begin to learn and] understand why you once believed that, when you met someone else, you thought he *was* someone else. And every holy encounter in which you enter fully will teach you this is not so.

Application: Carry out what this paragraph says is your responsibility. Ask yourself, "What has the ego made of me?" To answer this honestly, you have to appreciate the original past tense ("has made" rather than "would make"). That is a subtle reference to the fact that you started out as a pure spirit of boundless being and limitless love, like an angel, except that Jesus told Helen that God created you "above the angels." So compare how you started out—"above the angels"—to what your ego has (apparently) turned you into now. What descriptive terms come to mind to describe "what the ego has made of you"?

After coming up with a suitable list of terms, say to yourself,

> **No**. *I do not accept that I am this.*
> *I choose to know myself as God created me, not as what my ego has made of me.*
> *I choose to accept the Atonement for myself.*

You need to decide, in other words, that you will not listen to the ego's version of you, because the ego has no idea what you are. And then you need to find what you really are—by entering fully into one holy encounter after another.

7. You can encounter <u>only</u> part of yourself because you are part of God, <u>Who is everything</u>. His power and glory are everywhere, and you <u>cannot</u> be excluded from them. The ego teaches that your strength is in you <u>alone</u>. The Holy Spirit teaches that <u>all</u> strength is in God and *therefore* in you. God wills <u>no one</u> suffer. He does not will <u>anyone</u> to suffer for a wrong decision [Ur: you have made], including you [Ur: *yourself*]. That is why He has given you the means for <u>undoing</u> it. Through His power and glory all your wrong decisions are undone <u>completely</u>, releasing you <u>and</u> your brother [Ur: *brothers*] from <u>every</u> <u>imprisoning thought any</u> part of the Sonship holds. Wrong decisions <u>have</u> no power, <u>because</u> they are not true. The imprisonment they <u>seem</u> to produce is no more true than <u>they</u> are.

The ego starts with you. In its view, you clearly have independent existence, and so your strength, if you have any, must be in yourself alone. The Holy Spirit starts from a whole different place. He starts with God. His premise is that God shares all of Himself, including all His power and glory, with everyone, making everyone fully part of Him. That means that "all strength is in God and *therefore* in you," *and* in everyone you see and everywhere you turn.

The latter part of the paragraph is an interesting discussion. The

Course makes clear that each of our decisions ripples through the entire Sonship, affecting everyone else, since all minds are one. How can my decision affect me but not affect others who are part of me? Yet this can be a frightening idea. As the Workbook says, "It seems to carry with it an enormous sense of responsibility" (W-pI.19.2:2). It makes you wonder just how much imprisonment your wrong decisions, unbeknownst to you, have actually caused.

Yet this worry leaves out the key fact: "God wills no one suffer." This means that even though He grants power to decisions, He also grants no power to what is wrong, what is untrue. Therefore, wrong decisions are a combination of illusion and power, which means they only carry *power* in the *illusion*. Further, God has provided the means for undoing even this illusory power. You can get in touch with His power and glory, and thereby actually undo your wrong decisions and release everyone from their effects. This release then spreads outward, releasing all "brothers from *every imprisoning thought any* part of the Sonship holds" (Urtext version). What a relief! This reminds me of a wonderful line at the end of Chapter 5: "*I do not feel guilty, because the Holy Spirit will undo all the consequences of my wrong decision if I will let Him*" (T-5.VII.6:10).

> 8. Power and glory belong to God alone. So do you. God gives whatever belongs to Him because He gives of Himself, and everything belongs to Him. Giving of yourself [Ur: *your* self] is the function He gave you. Fulfilling it perfectly will let you remember [Ur: will teach you] what you *have* [Ur: *you* have] of Him, and by this you will remember also what you *are* in Him [Ur: and this will teach you what you are *in* Him]. You cannot be powerless to do this, because this is your power. Glory is God's gift to you, because that is what He is. See this glory everywhere to remember [Ur: learn] what you are.

This is such a beautiful vision of God. He gives all of Himself to everything, placing His attributes at the root of everyone's being. As a result, His power and glory belong to you *just as much* as they belong to Him. And just as His function is giving of Himself, so your function is "giving of *your* self" (Urtext version).

Application: Say to yourself,

*My function is to give of **my** self just as fully as God gives of Himself.*

What we give to our brothers comes from the hidden power and glory that are our forgotten inheritance from God. Thus, as we give of ourselves, that power and glory come out, and we learn of them again. Through giving, our true nature pours out of us, allowing us to finally see it and remember it. We probably feel powerless to give this fully, but Jesus reminds us, "You *cannot* be powerless to do this, because this *is* your power."

This brings us back to the central point of this section. How do we know ourselves again? How do we rediscover the power and glory we forgot so long ago? We see that power and glory in the brother who is in front of us now, and seeing it there, we give of ourselves to this brother, lifting both of us into a holy encounter. And by fully encountering this brother, we at last encounter ourselves.

IV. The Gift of Freedom
Commentary by Robert Perry

1. If God's Will for you is complete peace and joy, unless you experience <u>only</u> this you <u>must</u> be refusing to acknowledge His Will. His Will does not vacillate, being changeless forever. When you are not at peace it can only be because you do not believe you are <u>in Him</u>. Yet He is All in all. His peace <u>is</u> complete, and you <u>must</u> be included in it. His laws govern you because they govern <u>everything</u>. You cannot exempt yourself from His laws, although you <u>can</u> disobey them. Yet if you do, and <u>only</u> if you do, you <u>will</u> feel lonely and helpless, because you are denying yourself everything.

We generally associate God's Will with obeisance and sacrifice. Yet what God really wills is that we have "complete peace and joy." Obeying His Will, therefore, means accepting complete peace and joy. Conversely, if we aren't experiencing peace and joy, it's not because something took them away from us. Rather, it's because *we* refused His Will. Yet this refusal isn't as powerful as we think. We are still part of God's peace, for we are still part of God. How can we be outside of God when "He is All in all"? His laws still govern us "because they govern everything." We still have total peace and joy; we just refuse to look at them.

2. I am come as a light into a world that <u>does</u> deny itself everything. It does this simply by dissociating itself <u>from</u> everything. It is therefore an illusion of isolation, <u>maintained</u> by fear of the same loneliness that *is* its illusion. I said that I am with you always, even unto the end of the world. That is <u>why</u> I am the light of the world. If I am with you in the loneliness of the world, <u>the loneliness is gone</u>. You <u>cannot</u> maintain the illusion of loneliness if you are <u>not</u> alone. My purpose, then, <u>is</u> still to overcome the world. I do not attack it, but my light must dispel it because of <u>what it is</u>. Light does not <u>attack</u> darkness, but it <u>does</u> shine it away. If my light goes with you everywhere, <u>you</u> shine it away <u>with me</u>. The light becomes <u>ours</u>, and you <u>cannot</u> abide in darkness any more than darkness can abide wherever you go. The remembrance of me <u>is</u> the remembrance of yourself, and of Him Who sent me to you

236

Jesus has come to a world that is denying itself everything. Yet this denial—in the sense of *refusal*—is really just denial in the sense of *dissociation*. Everything is still ours, we have just erected a partition in our mind that blocks our awareness of it. "It is therefore an illusion of isolation." We only *seem* to be alone and walled off from everything. Jesus has come to dispel this illusion with his light—not the light of his specialness, but the light of his *companionship* ("I am with you always"). If he is with us in spite of our wall, then the wall hasn't worked; in fact, the wall must not be really there. Thus, if you have ever felt his presence or had some definite experience that showed you he was there, you need to see that as evidence of so much more. It is the evidence that your rejection of infinity didn't work, that your denial (refusal) was just denial (dissociation).

Imagine being in Jesus' role, where your simple presence was the proof that the separation never occurred. Yet that is what he promises us. For if his light goes with us, then *we* become the living proof that the separation never occurred. We do this presumably the same way that Jesus does—through our ability to be so fully present to others that they feel they are no longer alone. Imagine seeing that as your life purpose!

> 3.   You <u>were</u> in darkness until God's Will was done completely by <u>any</u> part of the Sonship. When this was done, it was perfectly accomplished by <u>all</u>. How else could it <u>be</u> perfectly accomplished? My mission was simply to <u>unite</u> the will of the Sonship <u>with</u> the Will of the Father by being aware of the Father's Will myself. This is the awareness I came to give <u>you</u>, and <u>your</u> problem in accepting it <u>is</u> the problem of this world. Dispelling it is salvation, and in this sense I *am* the salvation of the world. The world <u>must</u> therefore despise and reject me, because the world *is* the belief that love is impossible. [Ur: *Your* reactions to me *are* the reactions of the world to God.] If you will accept the fact that I am with you, you are <u>denying</u> the world and <u>accepting God</u>. My will <u>is</u> His, and <u>your</u> decision to hear me <u>is</u> the decision to hear His Voice and abide in His Will. As God sent me to you so will I send you to others. And [Ur: But] I will go to them <u>with</u> you, so we can teach them peace and union.

The first part of this paragraph refers to the Course's idea that when Jesus awoke, he took all of us with him. With his awakening, some part of our mind awoke that had been asleep, and this awakening produced reverberations that reached all the way to our conscious mind, which now experienced God as more experientially accessible. How did Jesus accomplish this? Simply by being fully aware of God's Will Himself. That is the exact awareness he is trying to give us now.

This means that we are not *really* aware of God's Will now, and when Jesus tries to make us aware—when he tells us to forgive, for instance— we tend to resist. We figure he doesn't know what it's like to be down here. We doubt that he is really with us. We in some way marginalize his counsel. We don't see him as standing right in front of us and being the perfect guide for every step along our way. We have the same problem with him that the rest of the world does. And as we reject him, we reject God. Yet on the other hand, if we accept him—that he is with us and that he knows what we should do—we are "denying the world and accepting God." And when we do that, we become his arms and legs in the world, allowing him to travel in disguise to those in need and serve them in the guise of us.

> 4.   Do you not think the world needs peace as much as you do? Do you not want to give it to the world as much as you want to receive it? For unless you do, you will <u>not</u> receive it. If you want to have it of me, you <u>must</u> give it. Healing [Ur: Rehabilitation] does not come from anyone else. [Ur: You can have *guidance* from without, but you must *accept* it from within.] You must accept guidance from within. The guidance must be [Ur: become] what <u>you</u> want, or it will be meaningless to you. That is why healing [Ur: rehabilitation] is a collaborative venture. I can tell you what to <u>do,</u> but you must [Ur: but this will not really help unless you] collaborate by believing that I <u>know</u> what you should do. Only then will your <u>mind</u> choose to follow me. [Ur: Only then will your *mind* will to follow me. Without *your* will, you cannot be rehabilitated. *Motivation to be healed* is the crucial factor in rehabilitation. Without this, you are deciding *against* healing,] Without this choice you could not be healed because you would have decided against healing, and this rejection [Ur: and your veto] of my decision <u>for</u> you <u>makes healing impossible.</u>

This paragraph speaks of how we reject Jesus: We assume that he doesn't really know what we should do. Let's be honest: We *do* assume this. A great example of this is in our reaction to the very first lines of this paragraph. He says, in essence, "If you want peace, you have to give peace to the world. And this giving must be totally genuine. You need to want to *give* peace to the world as much as you want to *receive* it for yourself." When we hear that, do we instantly go out and follow that advice? Probably not. And if we don't, doesn't that mean that we don't really *believe* the advice? If advice promises to give you peace, and you believe the advice, you follow it.

Jesus can give us guidance all day long, but we have to accept that guidance with our own will. We need to embrace it ourselves. We need to put the power of our motivation behind it. When we don't do that, when we think "that sounds wonderful but I'm not going to actually do it," we are actually vetoing his decision for us. We are refusing to collaborate with him. And we are thus deciding against our own healing.

> 5.   [Ur: If healing *is* our joint will, unless our wills *are* joined you *cannot* be healed.] Healing reflects our joint will. This is obvious when you consider what healing is <u>for</u>. Healing is the way in which the separation is overcome. Separation is overcome by <u>union</u>. It <u>cannot</u> be overcome by separating. The decision [Ur: *will*] to unite must be unequivocal, or the mind [Ur: the will] <u>itself</u> is divided and [Ur: itself is separated or] <u>not whole</u>. Your mind [Ur: Your will] is the means by which you determine your own condition, because mind [Ur: because will] is the <u>mechanism of decision</u>. It is the power by which you separate or join, and experience pain or joy accordingly. My decision [Ur: will] cannot <u>overcome</u> yours, because <u>yours is as powerful as mine</u>. If it were not so the Sons of God would be unequal. All things are possible through our <u>joint</u> decision [Ur: will], but mine alone cannot help you. Your will is as free as mine, and God Himself would not go against it. I cannot will what God does <u>not</u> will. I <u>can</u> offer my strength [Ur: will] to make <u>yours</u> invincible [Ur: by this sharing], but I <u>cannot</u> oppose your decision [Ur: oppose yours {your will}] without competing with it and thereby violating God's Will for you.

The first part of this paragraph presents a simple but compelling train of reasoning: Healing is the way out of separation. Therefore, healing must come from joining, not separating. Specifically, healing is joining with Jesus. We join with Jesus by joining with his will for us, by fully uniting with his guidance for us. His guidance for us (in this case) is to funnel just as much motivation into giving peace to the world as into receiving peace for ourselves. Therefore, to be healed, we have to unite with *this* guidance, or we are separating from Jesus and rejecting our own healing.

I will bet, however, we are still doing exactly that. For instance, in the time you've been reading this, how seriously have you considered pouring as much motivation into giving peace as you normally pour into receiving it? Have you thought about how you're going to do that? Or is something in your mind more or less writing off the idea? *That* is how it happens. We listen, we get inspired, but we don't really join our will with Jesus' guidance.

You might think that Jesus could do that for us, but the last part of the paragraph introduces perhaps the best discussion in the Course of why he cannot. This part says, in essence, that God gave all of His Sons an equally free will, and having given that to them, He would not take it away—He would not oppose their decisions. Jesus, as one of those Sons, has a will that is equal with ours and thus *cannot* overpower ours. And as one who wills with God, he would never *want* to overpower ours, since that is not God's Will.

The conclusion: We have to decide ourselves to unite our will with his guidance.

> 6. Nothing God created can oppose your decision, as nothing God created can oppose His Will. God <u>gave</u> your will its power, which I can only acknowledge in honor of <u>His</u>. If you want to be <u>like</u> me I will help you, knowing that we <u>are</u> alike. If you want to be <u>different</u>, I will wait until you change your mind. I can <u>teach</u> you, but only you can choose to <u>listen</u> to my teaching. How else can it be, if God's Kingdom <u>is</u> freedom? Freedom cannot be learned by tyranny of <u>any</u> kind, and the perfect equality of <u>all</u> God's Sons cannot be recognized through the dominion of one mind [Ur: one will] over another. God's Sons are equal in will, all being the Will of their Father. This is the <u>only</u> lesson I came to teach [Ur: *only* lesson I can teach, knowing that it is true].

Since God gave our will its power, then for something to go against our will would be to literally overpower God, and Jesus neither wants to do that nor can do that. Therefore, the ball is still in our court. We still have to give our will to what he's telling us. We still have to give our assent. If we say "no" to him, then all he can do is wait until we ourselves elect to change that "no" to a "yes."

We may wish Jesus would just zap us and make us want it. Yet that would amount to his overpowering us. It would amount to "tyranny." It would be "the dominion of one will over another." And this is totally antithetical to the very nature of the Kingdom. We have to get there through total freedom because the Kingdom *is* freedom.

Application: Say to Jesus,

> *Jesus, I want to be like you.*
> *Teach me how to be like you.*
> *Teach me that in truth we **are** alike.*
> *I will follow you, trusting that you know the way, for I do not.*

7.   If [Ur: When] your will were [Ur: is] <u>not</u> mine it would not be [Ur: it is not] our Father's. This would mean [Ur: This means] you have imprisoned <u>yours,</u> and have not <u>let</u> it be free. Of yourself you can do nothing, because of yourself you *are* nothing. I am nothing without the Father and <u>you</u> are nothing without me, because by <u>denying</u> the Father [through denying Jesus] you deny <u>yourself.</u> I will <u>always</u> remember you, and in <u>my</u> remembrance <u>of</u> you lies your remembrance of <u>yourself.</u> In our remembrance of <u>each other</u> lies our remembrance of God. And in this remembrance lies your freedom because your freedom is in Him. Join, then, with me in praise of Him <u>and</u> you whom He created. This [praise for His creation of us] is our gift of gratitude to Him, which He will share with <u>all</u> His creations, to whom He gives equally whatever is acceptable to Him. <u>Because</u> it is acceptable to Him it is the gift of freedom, which is His Will for all His Sons. By <u>offering</u> freedom you will be free [Ur: because freedom is the only gift which you can offer to God's Sons,].

Our true will *is* God's Will. Our natural, relaxed, unbridled impulses are exactly the same as God's eternal Will. Yet we are not aware of *that* will. We have imprisoned it. That is why we need Jesus' help. We can't free it with our solitary will, for our solitary will and our solitary self are nothing ("of yourself you *are* nothing"). We need Jesus' remembrance of us to awaken our will. He will always remember us (an amazing thought, isn't it?). And if we can return his remembrance and remember him, then together we can remember God. That is how we find our true will, our true freedom, for our freedom lies *in* God.

Application: The final sentences of this paragraph seem to tell us how to join with Jesus in order to free our will. I have tried to translate their counsel into the following lines, which are meant for us to say to Jesus:

Jesus, I join with you in praise of our Father,
And in praise of the perfection he created in me.
I join with you in gratitude for God and His creation of me.
I feel that gratitude with you.
And I know that God will take our gratitude and share it with all
  of His Sons.
He will present it to them as the gift of freedom.
And He will return it to me by setting me free.
He will free my true will, which is to be with Him.

8.   Freedom is the only gift you can offer to God's Sons, being an acknowledgment of what they are and what He is. Freedom is creation, because it is love. Whom you seek to imprison you do not love. Therefore, when you seek to imprison anyone, including yourself, you do not love him and you cannot identify with him. When you imprison yourself you are losing sight of your true identification with me and with the Father. Your identification is with the Father *and* with the Son. It cannot be with one and not the other. If you are part of one you must be part of the other, because they are one. The Holy Trinity is holy *because* It is One. If you exclude yourself from this union, you are perceiving the Holy Trinity as separated. You must be included in It, because It is everything. Unless you take your place in It and fulfill your function as part of It, the Holy Trinity is as bereft as you are. No part of It can be imprisoned if Its truth is to be known.

Freedom is the only gift you can offer others, for that is how you acknowledge what they are. When you try to imprison someone, you do not love him. If we only carried out this one injunction, imagine what it would do to our relationships!
Freedom is also the only gift that we can offer to ourselves. How do we imprison ourselves? Based on the context in this paragraph and the

preceding one, I would say that we imprison ourselves by not letting our *true* will, our holy will, come out, by suppressing our true impulses to love and to join. In other words, when we deny our union with everything (paragraphs 1 and 2) or when we refuse to join with Jesus' guidance for us (paragraphs 4 and 5), *we are not exercising our true freedom.* We are chaining our will, rather than freeing it. This reminds me of Helen's vision of the ancient priestess, who began in a kneeling posture, all wrapped in chains. Yet as Helen chose to pursue Jesus' "better way," she saw the chains slowly fall off and the priestess slowly rise, unbound. That priestess symbolized Helen's true will. Are we removing the chains from the ancient priestess in us, or further binding her?

When we imprison our holy will, we deny our union with God and Jesus and the entire Sonship. We deny that we ourselves are part of the Holy Trinity. And when we do that, we see the Holy Trinity in pieces, as if our part had been torn out. Our part hasn't been torn out, but it has been imprisoned. And when we do that, we affect the Trinity as a whole ("the Holy Trinity is as bereft as you are"). We aren't the only one who loses from this proposition.

V. The Undivided Will of the Sonship
Commentary by Robert Perry

1.   Can you be separated from your identification and be at peace? Dissociation is <u>not</u> a solution; it is a <u>delusion</u>. The delusional believe that truth will <u>assail</u> them, and they do not recognize it [Ur: *do not see it*] because they prefer the delusion. Judging truth as something they do <u>not</u> want, they perceive their illusions which [Ur: they perceive deception and] block knowledge. Help them by offering them <u>your</u> unified mind [Ur: will] on their behalf, as I am offering you mine on [Ur: *yours.*] behalf of yours. Alone we can do nothing, but <u>together</u> our minds [Ur: wills] fuse into something whose power is far beyond the power of its separate parts. By [us] <u>not being separate,</u> the Mind [Ur: Will] of God is established <u>in</u> ours and <u>as</u> ours. This Mind [Ur: Will] is invincible <u>because</u> it is undivided.

The previous section said that we have all dissociated from our true identification with everything. Someone who has dissociated from his real identity is delusional. How can such a person truly be at peace? In his delusions, he may think he is Alexander the Great, but will he really experience true rest within himself? Will he really "be at peace"? That is the position we are in. We fear the truth (our identification with everything) and so prefer our delusion (the false identity we have made). But we are not at peace.

Our job is to unify our will, to unify it behind overcoming our dissociation (by uniting with Jesus; see IV.5:6-8), and then to offer this unified will to our brothers as a way of healing their dissociation. In this task, we will be joining with Jesus, and "together our wills fuse into something whose power is far beyond the power of its separate parts." How wonderful it would be to be part of such a power! Faced with the power of these united minds, each of which is united within itself, how can our brothers' dissociation stand?

2.   The <u>undivided</u> will of the Sonship is the perfect creator, being wholly in the likeness of God, Whose Will it <u>is</u>. <u>You</u> cannot be exempt from it if you are to understand what it is and what <u>you</u> are. By the belief

that your will is separate [Ur: By separating your will] from mine, you <u>are</u> exempting yourself from the Will of God which *is* yourself. Yet to heal is still to make whole. Therefore, to heal is to <u>unite</u> with those who are <u>like</u> you, because perceiving this likeness <u>is</u> to recognize the Father. If <u>your</u> perfection is in Him and <u>only</u> in Him, how can you <u>know</u> it <u>without</u> recognizing Him? The recognition of God is the recognition of yourself. There <u>is</u> no separation of God and His creation. You will realize this when you understand that there is no separation between <u>your</u> will and mine. Let the Love of God shine upon you by your acceptance of me. <u>My</u> reality is yours and His. By joining <u>your</u> mind [Ur: will] with mine you are signifying your awareness that the Will of God is one.

The Will of God is not a separate will, but rather a will that encompasses all true wills, including the joint will of the Sonship. Our goal is to realize that our will is part of this larger totality, part of this vast constellation of will. Recognizing that we are part of this is how we recognize ourselves and know our perfection.

All of this sounds wonderful, but then we are told the specific way in which we do this: We have to join our will with Jesus' will. We have to unite our will with his guidance, so that what he *tells* us to do becomes what we genuinely *want* to do (as the last section said). That is how we learn that our will is united with God's Will and with "the undivided will of the Sonship."

> 3. God's Oneness and ours are not separate, because His Oneness <u>encompasses</u> ours. To join <u>with</u> me is to restore His power <u>to</u> you <u>because</u> we are sharing it. I offer you only the recognition of His power in you, but in that lies <u>all</u> truth. As <u>we</u> unite, we unite with Him. Glory be to the union of God and His holy Sons [Ur: because all glory lies *in* them…]! All glory lies in them *because* they <u>are</u> united. The miracles <u>we</u> do bear witness to the Will of the Father for His Son, and to our joy in uniting <u>with</u> His Will <u>for</u> us.

This paragraph contains a similar message to the previous one. Let me summarize it: By joining our will with what Jesus tells us to do, we unite with Jesus. By uniting with Jesus, we unite with God. And then we recognize His power in us. And then we discover His glory in us. And then we do miracles. They are the proof that we understand that His Will and our will are one.

4.   When you unite with me you are uniting <u>without</u> the ego, because I have renounced the ego in myself and therefore <u>cannot</u> unite with yours. <u>Our</u> union is therefore the way to renounce the ego in you. The truth in both of us is <u>beyond</u> the ego. [Ur: By willing that, you *have* gone beyond it toward truth.] Our success in transcending the ego is guaranteed by God, and I share this confidence for both of us and all of us [Ur: and I can share my perfect confidence *in* His Promise because I know He gave me this confidence for both of us and *all* of us.]. I bring God's peace back to all His children because I received it of Him for us all. Nothing can prevail against our united wills because nothing can prevail against God's.

Perhaps we fear uniting with Jesus, especially since we do so by uniting with his counsel for us. This has overtones of surrendering to the overblown ego of some authority figure—a scary proposition. Yet joining with Jesus is not a joining of egos—our subservient ego joining his authoritative ego—for the simple reason that he *has* no ego. Thus, when we join with him, our ego must be left at the door. Rather than a joining of egos, joining with Jesus is the way to *renounce* our ego. It is an egoless joining. As such, it is the epitome of innocence and purity, as well as safety.

Somewhere inside, we all long to be free of the ego, that monkey on our back with its fingers around our throat. Yet, unless we are engaged in a rather common form of denial, it can easily seem like the ego is here to stay. However, God has promised that we will one day transcend the ego We *will* be ego-free. God has guaranteed it. Think about that. Jesus has perfect confidence in that promise, and he shares that confidence with us. And as we join with him, our ego hasn't a ghost of a chance of prevailing "against our united wills."

5.   Would you know the Will of God for <u>you</u>? Ask it of me who know it for you and you will find it. I will deny <u>you</u> nothing, as God denies <u>me</u> nothing. Ours is simply the journey back to God Who is our home. Whenever fear intrudes anywhere along the road to peace, it is [Ur: *always*] because the ego has attempted to <u>join</u> the journey with us <u>and cannot do so</u>. Sensing defeat and angered by it, the ego regards itself as rejected and becomes retaliative. You are invulnerable to its retaliation <u>because I am with you</u>. On this journey you have chosen me as your companion *instead* of the ego. Do not attempt to hold on to both, or you will try to go in different directions and will lose the way.

246

I love these paragraphs where Jesus speaks to us in the first person. Here he says, "I will deny you nothing, as God denies me nothing." Just as God pours out His gifts onto Jesus, so Jesus will pour out his gifts onto us. If there is anything we want, all we need do is ask. If we want to know God's Will for us, all we need do is ask Jesus.

On our journey through time, we can choose either Jesus or the ego as our traveling companion. It is an either/or choice, for one companion only walks to God while the other always wanders off in the opposite direction. The fact that we have decided to journey to God means that we have chosen Jesus as our companion instead of the ego. Yet the ego won't take this lying down. It has been rejected, so it decides to retaliate—against *you*. It badgers you: "Don't you realize what you're doing? You're sacrificing your rights, your image, and your pleasure all for the sake of some ethereal truth, all so that you can tell yourself that you're being good. How pathetic!" If we listen, we start to get afraid about this path we're on. We think, "Do I really know what I'm doing?" And with these thoughts, we begin to walk the other way, to follow the ego back where we started. Instead of listening, we need to call on Jesus. With him by our side, we are invulnerable to the rantings of the ego.

Application: How has your ego told you that the spiritual path (or some aspect of it like forgiveness or defenselessness or giving) compromises your self-interest and is therefore foolish?

Once you have an answer, ask Jesus what his response to this is, and listen for his answer.

> 6.   The ego's way [the way or direction it travels] is not mine, but it is also <u>not yours</u>. The Holy Spirit has one direction for <u>all</u> minds, and the one He taught me <u>is</u> yours. Let us not lose sight of His direction through illusions, for <u>only</u> illusions of another direction can obscure the one for which God's Voice speaks in all of us. Never accord the ego the power to interfere with the journey [Ur: because it *has* none, and the journey is the way to what is *true*]. It has none, because the journey is the way to what is true. Leave <u>all</u> illusions [Ur: deception] behind, and reach beyond all attempts of the ego to hold you back. I [Ur: *do*] go before you because I am [Ur: *am*] beyond the ego. Reach, therefore, for my hand because you <u>want</u> to transcend the ego. My strength [Ur:

My will,] will <u>never</u> be wanting, and if you choose to share it you will do so [Ur: *you will*]. I give it willingly and gladly, because I need you as much as you need me.

This paragraph continues the discussion from the previous one. The situation is this: The ego is trying to seduce you into abandoning Jesus as your traveling companion. It is trying to sow doubts about how good Jesus' journey will really be for you, so that you will instead head off with it, the ego, the other way. That is what it means to accord the ego the power to interfere with the journey. That is what it means to let fear intrude on the road to peace (paragraph 5).

This happens, all the time, right? Our ego is constantly trying to seduce us away from the journey that Jesus is taking us on. I suspect that 90% of the time, the ego is so successful at this that we don't even notice. When we do notice, the solution is to reach for Jesus' hand as a way of transcending the ego. If we reach for his hand, he will gladly share with us his will.

Application: The following is a visualization, which is best done with someone else reading it to you (or you reading it to yourself on tape).

> See Jesus and yourself on a journey, walking along a smooth, straight path.
> The road is great, the sun is shining, you are happy to be traveling with your companion.
> But then you detect a note of fear in you.
> Will this path be able to satisfy everything you want?
> Sure, it is great for some things, but for everything?
>
> Suddenly, you see a side path branching off, but still heading in basically the same direction.
> Just down this side path is something that often attracts your ego.
> Maybe it is a grievance you cherish against someone.
> Maybe it is money.
> Maybe it is a body.
> Look at what that thing is.

There doesn't seem any harm in taking this little side trip.

Then you see something else. Just in front of you, beckoning you to take this path, is a little dark cloud: your ego.

Out of this cloud a hand extends, a skeleton hand, silently beckoning you to take it and follow it as your guide along this side path.

Now you remember; you know what lies down this path.

You've been down this way before.

It only seems to go roughly in the same direction as the path you're on with Jesus.

In fact, it slowly loops back and heads in the opposite direction.

And once you lay your hands on that attractive image that is enticing you down this path,

it always changes into something else, something less desirable.

Further, the path eventually disappears and leaves you alone in the trackless forest.

Now turn your eyes back to Jesus. Hear him speak to you:

"Never accord the ego the power to interfere with the journey.

It has none, because the journey is the way to what is true.

Leave all illusions behind, and reach beyond all attempts of the ego to hold you back.

I go before you, [hear him speak your name], because I am beyond the ego.

Reach, therefore, for my hand because you want to transcend the ego." (paragraph 6)

See him reach out his hand, waiting for yours.

Now reach your hand out to take his, knowing that he is beyond the ego, that he has no ego, and that reaching for him signifies reaching beyond the ego.

"My will will never be wanting, and if you choose to share it *you will.*

I give it willingly and gladly, because I need you as much as you need me, [name]." (paragraph 6)

Feel your hand in his. Feel his will pouring from his hand to yours, from him to you.

Now his will has become yours, and all temptation to head off down the ego's path leaves you.

You look up into Jesus' eyes and then look on ahead down the path.

And the two of you continue walking.

VI. The Treasure of God
Commentary by Robert Perry

> 1.   We are the joint will of the Sonship, whose wholeness is for all. We begin the journey back by setting out together, and gather in our brothers as we continue together. Every gain in our strength is offered for all, so they too can lay aside their weakness and add their strength to us. God's welcome waits for us all, and He will welcome us as I am welcoming you. Forget not the Kingdom of God for anything the world has to offer.

It is important to see the "we" in this paragraph in light of the previous section's discussion. (Remember, the section breaks were put in by the editors.) "We" therefore refers to you and Jesus. In other words, you begin the journey with Jesus as your companion (instead of the ego). Then you and he gather in your brothers as further companions. Walking with Jesus, you gain in strength, and this strengthens your brothers who walk with you, while their renewed strength turns around and strengthens you. All the while your growing throng draws closer and closer to your goal, God, Who welcomes all of you just as warmly and fully as Jesus originally consented to walk with you.

> 2.   The world can add nothing to the power and the glory of God and His holy Sons, but it can blind the Sons to the Father if they behold it. You cannot behold the world and know God. Only one is true. I am come to tell you that the choice of which is true is not yours to make. If it were, you would have destroyed yourself. Yet God did not will the destruction of His creations, having created them for eternity. His Will has saved you, not from yourself but from your illusion of yourself. He has saved you *for* yourself.

We are vainly hoping that the world can increase our power level and our glory level, yet while we seek these things from it, all we achieve is the loss of our awareness of God. Either God is true or the world is true. One is false, the other is eternally true. We therefore cannot see both because which we see is our affirmation of which is real. We see

251

the world before us right now because we have decided that *it* is what's real; God, at best, is a footnote. Yet having such a decision in our hands is like putting a child behind the steering wheel of a car. If we actually had this power, the power to wipe God out of the picture, we would have wiped out our own being, which is *in* God. Not a good idea. Thank God the decision is not in our hands. The world will never be true; God will always be true. Our role is to simply acknowledge *what is*.

> 3.   Let us glorify Him Whom the world denies, for over His Kingdom the world has no power. No one created by God can find joy in anything except the eternal; not because he is <u>deprived</u> of anything else, but because nothing else is <u>worthy</u> of him. What God <u>and</u> His Sons create <u>is</u> eternal, and in this and this only is their joy.

God remains the only reality. However real the world may seem, it has no power over God and His Kingdom whatsoever. It also has no power over us. We may think the world has the power to make us feel all sorts of pleasurable and even joyful things, but it has no such power. In reality, we can only find true joy in the eternal; specifically, in our joyous function of *creating* the eternal. Quite frankly, nothing else is good enough for us.

> 4.   Listen to the story of the prodigal son, and learn what God's treasure is and <u>yours</u>: This son of a loving father left his home and thought he had squandered everything for nothing of any value, although he had not understood its worthlessness at the time. He was ashamed to return to his father, because he thought he had hurt him. Yet when he came home the father welcomed him with joy, because [Ur: only] the son himself *was* his father's treasure. <u>He</u> [the father] <u>wanted nothing else</u>.

This is the only biblical parable that Jesus retells in the Course. I've thought a great deal about this retelling over the years, and one thing stands out to me. Whereas the Bible tells the outer story, the Course tells the inner story. It tells what the father and the son were really thinking and feeling. It thereby brings out a point implicit in the original telling but not openly stated: The son thought he had thrown away his father's treasure, but in fact *he* was his father's treasure.

5.   God wants only His Son because His Son is His only treasure. You want your creations as He wants His. Your creations are your gift to the Holy Trinity, created in gratitude for your creation. They do not leave you any more than you left your Creator, but they extend your creation as God extended Himself to you. Can the creations of God Himself take joy in what is not real? And what is real except the creations of God and those that are created like His? Your creations love you as you love [Ur: as your Soul loves] your Father for the gift of creation. There is no other gift that is eternal, and therefore there is no other gift that is true. How, then, can you accept anything else or give anything else, and expect joy in return? And what else but joy would you want? You made neither yourself nor your function. You made only the decision to be unworthy of both. Yet you cannot make yourself unworthy because you are the treasure of God, and what He values is valuable. There can be no question of its [the treasure's] worth, because its value lies in God's sharing Himself with it and establishing its value forever.

"You are the treasure of God." This is a line we should never forget. Remember how the father of the prodigal reacted to his son's homecoming? That is how God will react to ours. We are "His only treasure." We are not a burden. We are not mistakes that He regrets. We are not sinners to be punished. We are not details to be forgotten about. We are His only treasure. All He wants is us.

Application: Repeat these words with deep conviction:

I am the treasure of God.
And what He treasures is valuable forever.

The rest of the paragraph speaks of our creations. Just as God extended His Being and brought us into being, so we extend our being and bring our creations into being. These creations are simply our spirit extended outward, just as we are God's Spirit extended outward.

The paragraph, then, sketches a chain of creation, going from God to us, and from us to our creations. Virtually all of its sentences add up to a single crucial idea: All the joy that is known in Heaven is about this chain of creation. The creator (whether God or us) takes endless joy in giving the gift of creation. Once that gift is given, the creator infinitely treasures the children he has brought into being. And the created take endless joy in receiving the gift of creation, and forever love their creator in deep gratitude for having been granted the gift of life. Each side in the creator/created relationship completely treasures the other side. This treasuring is the joy of Heaven.

> 6.   Your function is to add to God's treasure by creating yours. His Will *to* you [in creating you] is His Will *for* you [for you to create]. He would not withhold [the function of] creation from you because His joy is in it. You cannot find joy except as God does. His joy lay in creating you, and He extends His Fatherhood to you so that you can extend yourself as He did. You do not understand this because you do not understand Him. No one who does not accept his function can understand what it is, and no one can accept his function unless he knows what [Ur: who] he is. Creation is the Will of God. His Will created you to create. Your will was not created separate from His, and so you must will [Ur: and so it wills] as He wills.

Have you ever wondered what God finds joy in? According to this paragraph, He finds joy in creating. "His joy lay in creating you." And like any father, He wants to pass on to His Son that which gives Him joy. He therefore gave you the joy of being able to create. In doing so, you increase His joy. You "add to God's treasure." You extend His line. This is the only thing that really gives you joy, which is why nothing in this world ever quite does it.

All of this sounds rather foreign, and Jesus understands that. He says that if you only understood God, if you only understood yourself, if you only really accepted your function, all of this would make perfect sense. God's act of creating you stamped itself on your nature, and that means that it is your nature to create.

> 7.   An "unwilling will" does not mean anything, being a contradiction in terms that actually means [Ur: leaves] nothing. [Ur: You can make yourself powerless only in a way that has *no meaning at all*.] When you think you are unwilling to will with God, you are not thinking. God's Will *is* thought. It cannot be contradicted *by* thought. God does not contradict Himself, and His Sons, who are like Him, cannot contradict themselves or Him. Yet their thought is so powerful that they can even imprison the mind of God's Son, if they so choose. This choice does

make the Son's function unknown <u>to him</u>, but never to his Creator. And <u>because</u> it is not unknown to his Creator, it is forever knowable to him.

Your will by its very nature wills with God. It wills to create. If you are unwilling to create (and you wouldn't be here unless you were), that means you have an "unwilling will," which of course is an oxymoron. It doesn't make any sense. Having an unwilling will not only makes you powerless; it puts you in a state of nonsense. You become (or seem to become) something like "unwet water" or "powerless power." Quite simply, you cease to make sense. If you really think you are such a strange creature, then you're just not thinking.

In this state, your thought (about yourself and your will) seems to run directly counter to God's. You seem to contradict His Thought. Yet you can't really do that. Nothing can contradict God. Instead of having real thoughts that contradict His, then, you actually pass into a state of non-thought. Your mind is really just a blank. In this blankness, your true power remains hidden. Your function remains unknown. But God still knows it, and one day you too will know it.

> 8.   There is no question but one you should ever ask of yourself;—"Do I want to know my Father's Will for me?" <u>He</u> will not hide it. He has revealed it to me because I asked it of Him, and learned of what He had already given. Our function is to work [Ur: function] together, because apart from each other we cannot function at all. The whole power of God's Son lies in all of us, but not in any of us alone. God would not have us be alone because *He* does not will to be alone. That is why He created His Son, and gave him the power to create with Him. Our creations are as holy as we are, and we are the Sons of God Himself, as holy as He is. Through our creations we extend our love, and thus increase the joy of the Holy Trinity. You do not understand this [Ur: for a very simple reason.], because you who are God's Own treasure do not regard yourself as valuable. Given this belief, <u>you cannot understand anything</u>.

In our mental state of pure nonsense and blank unknowing, there should be only one question on our minds: What is the function God gave me when He created me? What was I made to do? Surely my Creator fashioned me to do something. *What was it?* Jesus asked this question, and he received the answer ("He has revealed it to me because I asked it of Him"). Now he comes to give it to us. Here is the answer: We were created to join with all of our brothers in a single universal will, and with this will *to create*. To create something as pure and holy as God Himself, to extend our love and "increase the joy of the Holy Trinity" Itself.

Notice how Jesus keeps bringing up that we don't understand this function ("You do not understand this"). All of this talk sounds so abstract, doesn't it? It seems so far from what feels relevant. It's as if he is trying to stir a memory in us of something that meant everything to us, yet that we have totally forgotten. Here, as in paragraph 5, he explains why this function seems so distant. Quite simply, it is because we don't feel worthy of it. We don't regard ourselves as valuable enough to do what he's talking about here. If we only understood that we are God's Own treasure, then the role of creating the eternal would seem like a perfect fit.

> 9.   I share with God the knowledge of the value <u>He</u> puts upon you. My devotion to you is of Him, being born of my knowledge of myself <u>and</u> Him. We cannot <u>be</u> separated. Whom God has joined <u>cannot</u> be separated, and God has joined all His Sons <u>with Himself</u>. Can you be separated from your life and your being? The journey to God is merely the reawakening of the knowledge of where you are always, and what you are forever. It is a journey without distance to a goal that has never changed. Truth can only be <u>experienced</u>. It cannot be described and it cannot be explained. I can make you aware of the <u>conditions</u> of truth, but the experience is of God. Together we can meet its conditions, but truth will dawn upon you of itself.

We have no idea how valuable we are. We don't know that we are valuable enough to create the eternally valuable. Yet Jesus knows. He knows our value because he knows it with God's Own knowing. And God has joined us with Jesus forever. We can no more be separate from him than we can be separated from our own being. He will guide us along the way to the knowledge that we have forgotten. He will help us meet its conditions.

The beautiful lines about the "journey without distance" add up to a single idea to me. Truth is not of our making. Truth is not decided by us. Truth is not assembled by us in our mind. Truth is not constructed by our words. We do not make truth. Truth *is*. It always has been exactly as it is now. That is why our journey to truth is a journey without distance, because truth is already there, within us and all around us, eternally as it has always been. When it finally dawns on our sight, it will seem like the most obvious thing in the universe. But it will only dawn on us when we stop trying to make it, when we are utterly *passive* in the face of it, when we acknowledge it as a pure given and receive it as a pure gift.

> 10. What God has willed for you *is* yours. He has given His Will to His treasure, whose treasure it is. Your heart lies where your treasure is, as His does. You who are beloved of God are wholly blessed. Learn this of me, and free the holy will of all those who are as blessed as you are.

This paragraph turns on a masterful application of the biblical saying, "Where your treasure is, there will your heart be also." Jesus applies the saying both to us and to God. Our treasure is the will to create that was placed in us by God. We don't know it, but that is where our heart truly is. And God? God's treasure is us. That is where God's Heart is. His Heart lies forever with us. What could this mean but that we are wholly blessed? And isn't this the truth that Jesus is guiding us toward (paragraph 9)? Isn't this the truth that, at the end of the journey, will finally dawn on us of itself?

VII. The Body as a Means of Communication
Commentary by Robert Perry

Today's reading is the first part of a major discussion on the body, perhaps the most important discussion on the body in the Course.

> 1.   Attack is <u>always</u> physical. When attack in <u>any</u> form enters your mind you are <u>equating yourself with a body</u> [Ur: *body. This is the ego's interpretation*], since this is the ego's <u>interpretation</u> of the body. You do not have to <u>attack</u> physically to accept this interpretation. You <u>are</u> accepting it simply by the belief that attack can <u>get you something</u> <u>you want</u>. If you did <u>not</u> believe this, the <u>idea</u> of attack would have no appeal for you. When you equate yourself with a body you will <u>always</u> experience depression. When a child of God thinks of himself in this way he is belittling himself, and seeing his brothers as similarly belittled. Since he can find himself <u>only</u> in them, he has cut himself off from salvation.

The whole idea of attack requires separate forms which can collide, leaving one form damaged and allowing something of value to transfer to the other. Attack, then, is always about forms, it is always about bodies. Thus, whenever you are even contemplating attack, you are equating yourself with the body.

Yet the chain doesn't stop there. Here is the full version: Attack = equating yourself with the body = belittling yourself = depression. When you are depressed, consider the possibility that it's because you have belittled yourself by equating yourself with the body, and that you've done that by thinking you can attack. You are depressed, in other words, not because you've *been* attacked but because you *have* attacked.

Here is another version of the chain. Attack = equating yourself with the body = equating your brothers with their bodies = belittling your brothers = cutting yourself off from salvation.

2.   Remember that the Holy Spirit interprets the body <u>only</u> as a means of communication. Being the communication link between God and His separated Sons, the Holy Spirit interprets everything <u>you</u> have made in the light of what <u>He</u> is. The ego <u>separates</u> through the body. The Holy Spirit reaches <u>through</u> it to others. You do not perceive your brothers as the Holy Spirit does, because you do not regard bodies [Ur: their bodies *and yours*] solely as a means of joining minds and uniting them with yours and mine. This interpretation of the body will change your mind entirely about its value. Of itself it has <u>none</u>.

The Holy Spirit uses the body only as a means of communicating with other minds and joining with them (first reference was 6.V(A).5:5). The word "communication" is being used in a special sense here, as joining. Yet that sense is really inherent in the word. The root of the word is *communis*, or common. It means to transmit information, thought, or feeling so that what is transmitted is held *in common* by both minds. Given this definition, most communication is really only partial communication. Somewhere along the way, the real heart of what we communicate drops out, leaving only the outer shell to be received and held in common, and leaving us feeling alone.

Imagine using the body only to reach your brothers and join their minds with yours. You don't use the body to get your way in the world. You don't use it to find pleasure. You don't use it to make yourself look special. You see it as nothing in itself, only a tool to reach and join with those radiant minds. What would your life be like?

3.   If you use the body for attack, it is harmful to you. If you use it <u>only</u> to reach the minds of those who believe they <u>are</u> bodies, and teach them *through* the body that <u>this is not so</u>, you will understand the power of the mind that is in [Ur: both of] you. If you use the body for this and <u>only</u> for this, you <u>cannot</u> use it for attack. In the service of uniting it becomes a beautiful lesson in communion, which has value until communion *is*. This is God's way of making unlimited what <u>you</u> have limited [the mind]. The Holy Spirit [Ur: His Voice] does not see the body as <u>you</u> do, because He knows the <u>only</u> reality of <u>anything</u> is the service it renders [Ur: can render] God on behalf of the function He gives it.

Many Course students feel that behavior is not part of the Course's picture. Yet when Jesus talks here about *using the body*, what else is he talking about but behavior? The picture he paints is very beautiful. He asks us to use our behavior only to reach the minds that seem to be locked away inside their fleshy prisons, and to take away their bars by teaching them that they are something much greater than a body. If we do this, we will learn that we ourselves are much greater than a body. If this is all that we do, then there is no room for attacking behavior on our part. As a result, we will cease to look on the body as an impure thing that drags us down to earth. We will instead see it as a beautiful instrument for serving God and freeing His minds from their isolation ("making unlimited what you have limited").

> 4. Communication <u>ends</u> separation. Attack <u>promotes</u> it. The body is beautiful or ugly, peaceful or savage [Ur: savage or holy], helpful or harmful, according to the use to which it is put. And in the body of another you will see the use to which you have put <u>yours</u>. If the body becomes [Ur: for you] a means you give to the Holy Spirit to use on behalf of union of the Sonship, you will not see <u>anything</u> physical except as <u>what it is</u>. Use it for truth and you will see it truly. <u>Misuse</u> it and you <u>will</u> misunderstand it, because you have already done so *by* misusing it. Interpret <u>anything</u> apart from the Holy Spirit and you will mistrust it. This will lead you to hatred and attack and <u>loss of peace</u>.

Our attitudes toward the body seem to be determined by its condition—its health, its looks, its age. Yet they are secretly determined by what we use it for. If we use our body to attack our brothers, we will see it as savage, harmful, and ugly. If we use it to join minds, we will see it as helpful, holy, and even beautiful. A photograph of Mother Teresa does not call to mind aesthetic beauty, but it does immediately call to mind another, more important, kind of beauty.

How can we tell what we are using our body for? By how we see the bodies of others. If we want to get something from those bodies or if we want to punish those bodies, then we know that we are using our body for the ego's uses.

If we use the body simply to join minds, then we will see it "as what it is": a mere tool for communication. If we don't, we will invest it with all kinds of made-up significance and grandiose goals. And then when it can't deliver on those goals, we will stop trusting it ("you will mistrust it"), leading us to ultimately hate it and attack it.

> 5.   Yet all loss comes only from your own misunderstanding. Loss of any kind is impossible. But when you look upon a brother as a physical entity, his power and glory are "lost" to you and so are yours. You have attacked him, but [Ur: and] you must have attacked yourself first. Do not see him this way for your own salvation, which must bring him his. Do not allow him to belittle himself in your mind, but give him freedom from his belief in littleness, and thus escape from yours. As part of you, he is holy. As part of me, you are. To communicate with [Ur: a] part of God Himself is to reach beyond the Kingdom to its Creator, through His Voice Which He has established as part of you.

Your loss doesn't come from the body not delivering what you decided it should. Rather, it "comes only from your own misunderstanding," from your own decision to look on your brother as a body. This seemingly natural decision is actually an attack on your brother, in which you exclude his true power and glory from your picture of him. Instead, free him from his belief in being a tiny body ("give him freedom from his belief in littleness"), and you will free yourself. Treat him as part of God Himself, and you will "reach beyond the Kingdom to its Creator."

Application: Think of someone whose body figures large in your perception of him or her, and say:

> *I refuse to see you as a body.*
> *I refuse to belittle you in my mind.*
> *I restore to you the power and glory that are yours*
> *And thus restore them to myself.*

> 6.   Rejoice, then, that of yourself you can do nothing. You are not *of* yourself. [Ur: And] He of Whom you are has willed your power and glory for you, with which you can perfectly accomplish His holy Will for you when you accept it for [Ur: when you so will it] yourself. He has not withdrawn His gifts from you, but you believe you have [Ur: but *you* have] withdrawn them from Him. Let no Son of God remain hidden for His Name's sake, because His Name is yours.

Thank God we can do nothing of ourselves—which means, we don't have the power to throw our power and glory away. It seems like we have done so by seeing ourselves and others as bodies. Yet we are not of ourselves—which means, what we are is not up to us. God *willed* us power and glory. They are therefore ours forever. Rather than hiding these gifts, let us use them to draw aside the heavy curtain of the body that veils the true glory of our brothers ("Let no Son of God remain hidden"), for thus we will unveil our own true glory.

> 7.   The Bible says, "The Word (or thought) was made flesh." Strictly speaking this is impossible, since it seems to involve the translation of one order of reality into another. Different orders of reality merely appear to exist, just as different orders of miracles do. Thought cannot be <u>made</u> into flesh except by belief, since thought is <u>not</u> physical. Yet thought <u>is</u> communication, for which the body can be used. This is the only <u>natural</u> use to which it can be put. To use the body <u>unnaturally</u> is to lose sight of the Holy Spirit's purpose, and thus to confuse the goal of His curriculum.

The biblical reference to the Word being made flesh is a reference, of course, to the Divine incarnating as Jesus. Yet Jesus deals with this verse in a surprisingly impersonal way. He says first of all that Word also means "thought." "Word" is actually a translation of the Greek *Logos*, which means speech, word, or reason. In Christianity it has been seen as the divine wisdom. All in all, "thought" seems close enough. Then he says that thought cannot be made flesh, because they are two different orders of reality—one being real and the other being unreal. What does the verse really mean, then? It means that thought can be communicated *through* the flesh, through the body.

It isn't said, but we could see this as Jesus' interpretation of the Incarnation. What did it mean to say that divinity was incarnate in him? It meant that he used his body *only* to reach his brothers and join with their minds.

> 8.   There is nothing so frustrating to a learner as [Ur: to place him in] a curriculum he cannot learn. His sense of adequacy suffers, and he <u>must</u> become depressed. Being faced with an impossible learning situation [Ur: *regardless* of why it is impossible] is the most depressing thing in

the world. In fact, it is ultimately <u>why</u> the world itself is depressing. The Holy Spirit's curriculum is <u>never</u> depressing, because it is a curriculum of joy. Whenever the reaction to learning is depression, it is because the true goal of the curriculum has been lost sight of.

When we use the body unnaturally, it becomes an end, rather than purely a means. This causes us to lose sight of the real end, which is the overcoming of separation. Now, having forgotten the real goal of the curriculum, we become really bad at learning the curriculum. Our progress along the path becomes incredibly slow. We start feeling inadequate as learners, as seekers. And then we become depressed.

Application: Do you feel inadequate as a learner of the Course's way? If so, consider that it's because you've seen your body as an end, rather than purely a means of reaching your brothers.

Many students believe that to focus on reaching out and helping and joining with others is to "make the error real"—to make the illusion of separation real. The following paragraphs, however, say exactly the opposite. They say that to *refrain* from using the body to reach out to your brothers is to make separation real. Here we have a case of Course lore colliding head-on with what the Course actually teaches. Let's allow the Course to overturn our ideas about it so that we can fully adopt its ideas and give up our own.

> 9.   In this [Ur: the] world, not even the body is perceived as whole. Its purpose is seen as fragmented into many functions with little or no relationship to each other, so that it appears to be ruled by chaos. Guided by the ego, it *is*. Guided by the Holy Spirit, it is <u>not</u>. It becomes [Ur: *only*] a means by which the part of the mind you tried to separate *from* spirit [Ur: which you have separated from your Soul] can reach beyond its distortions and <u>return</u> *to* spirit [Ur: *return* to the Soul]. The ego's temple thus becomes the temple of the Holy Spirit, where devotion to Him replaces devotion to the ego. In this sense the body <u>does</u> become a temple to God; [Ur: because] His Voice abides in it by directing the use to which it is put [Ur: *to which you put it*].

We see the body as ruled by a long list of different purposes and therefore serving a long list of different functions. Think of various body parts and with each one ask yourself, "What do I see my_____ as being for?" We see the body like a Swiss army knife—each part has a different purpose. And this means we don't see it as whole. And since we see the body as having a fragmented *purpose*, we see it as having a fragmented *meaning*. We see it as a bundle of chaos.

Under the Holy Spirit's guidance, things are different. We see one purpose for the body: to allow the mind to reach beyond its isolated cell and reconnect with other parts of itself. The body is not inherently the temple of the Holy Spirit. What makes it His temple is letting Him direct its use, its *behavior*. In this way, everything we do becomes an act of "devotion to Him."

> 10. Healing is the result of using the body solely for communication. Since this is natural it heals by making whole, which is also natural. All mind is whole, and the belief that part of it is physical, or not mind, is a fragmented or sick interpretation. Mind cannot be made physical, but it can be made manifest *through* the physical if it uses the body to go beyond itself. By reaching out, the mind extends itself. It does not stop at the body, for if it does it is blocked in its purpose. A mind that has been blocked has allowed itself to be vulnerable to attack, because it has turned against itself.

The natural state of the mind is wholeness. The natural purpose of the mind is communication, joining. If the mind expresses its natural purpose (communication), it will be in touch with its natural state (wholeness). In relation to the body, then, the mind can do one of two things. First, it can use the body as an instrument for the mind's purpose of communication. This will put the mind in touch with its own wholeness, and this wholeness will then get projected onto the body, making its healthy and whole. Or second, the mind can see the body as a foreign substance that imposes its own purposes onto the mind, purposes that are not about the mind's need to join, but about the body's needs.

Now, the mind's impulse to extend reaches the body and says, "Hey body, I want to use you to reach out to my brothers and join with them." But the body says, "Sorry, I'm too busy painting my toenails." Now the body becomes a *barrier* to extension, rather than a *means* of extension. The body's purposes have seemed to overrule the mind's purpose. Yet only mind is real. It is the only real player here. So what has really happened is that the mind "has turned against itself."

> 11. The removal of blocks, then, is the only way to guarantee help and healing. Help and healing are the normal expressions of a mind that is working through the body, but not *in* it. If the mind believes the body is its goal it will distort its perception of the body, and by blocking its own extension beyond it, will induce illness by fostering separation. Perceiving the body as a separate entity [an independent entity that exerts power over the mind] cannot but foster illness, because it is not true. A medium of communication loses its usefulness if it is used for anything else. To use a medium of communication as a medium of attack is an obvious confusion in purpose.

"The removal of blocks" refers to removing the *body* as a block to *communication*. It becomes a block to communication when you see it as an end in itself, rather than a means, when you see its needs and urges as ruling the mind, when you think with its parts rather than with your mind. When the mind devotes its energies to the body, it pulls those energies away from its brothers. The mind withdraws in on itself. It separates. It spends all its time painting and buffing and tinkering with its vehicle, rather than actually going somewhere in it. This can't help but foster illness, since separation is the mother of all illness.

And while we spend all our time tinkering with our vehicle, aren't we losing sight of its real purpose? Aren't we misunderstanding what it is? A vehicle is supposed to take you places. This vehicle is supposed to carry your mind into your brother's mind, so that the two become one. To use it as an end in itself neglects its real use, thus making it useless. It actually "loses its usefulness."

> 12. To communicate is to join and to attack is to separate. How can you do both simultaneously with the same thing and not suffer? Perception of the body can be unified only by one purpose. This releases the mind from the temptation to see the body in many lights, and gives it over entirely to the One Light in Which it can be really understood. To confuse a learning device with a curriculum goal is a fundamental confusion that blocks the understanding of both ["that blocks the understanding of both" was apparently added by the editors]. [Ur: Learning can hardly be meaningfully arrested at its own aids, and hope to understand them

or its real purpose]. Learning must lead <u>beyond</u> the body to the re-establishment of the power of the mind <u>in</u> it. This can be accomplished <u>only</u> if the mind <u>extends</u> to other minds, and does not <u>arrest itself</u> in its extension. This arrest [Ur: The arrest of the mind's extension] is the cause of all illness, because <u>only extension is the mind's function</u>. [Ur: Block this, and you have blocked health because you have *blocked the mind's joy*.]

Right now, the mind experiences itself as cooped up in a body. It wants to get out, to join with other minds. This is its joy. But this natural impulse is thwarted by the prison within which it's enclosed. Or is it? Why not use the body to *express* that impulse? It's as if you were trapped inside a telephone. You can either lament your isolation and spend your time redecorating the phone, or you can make phone calls. You can see the phone as the cause of isolation or as a means of transcending isolation. It's up to you.

In the same way, you have a choice with how you use your body. If you use it only to extend to other minds, then you will rediscover its power. Right now, the mind is like a powerful bear that has been trained to wear an apron and serve tea to its weak little master. In its state of servitude, its true power is hidden. Just so, while the mind serves the body, its true power of joining with other minds remains hidden.

Instead, the mind has been placed under house arrest. Notice the word "arrest" occurring three times in this paragraph. It refers to a sudden stopping of the movement or operation of something. That's what happens when the mind's impulses to join hit the body's impulse to paint its toenails—those impulses stop cold. They get arrested. By letting those impulses get blocked, we block our joy, and thus we block our health—including our *physical* health. Making the body an end in itself makes it sick.

13. The opposite of joy is depression. When your learning promotes depression <u>instead</u> of joy, you <u>cannot</u> be listening to God's joyous Teacher and [Ur: you *must* be learning amiss.] learning His lessons ["learning His lessons" was apparently added by the editors]. To see a body as anything <u>except</u> a means of communication [Ur: means of pure extension] is to limit your mind and to <u>hurt yourself</u>. Health is therefore nothing more than united purpose. If the body is brought under the

purpose of the mind, it becomes whole because the mind's purpose <u>is</u> one. Attack can only be an assumed purpose of the body, because <u>apart</u> from the mind the body <u>has no purpose at all</u>.

He is really presenting one idea here in many different forms. If you let the mind's natural impulse to join express through the body, then you are releasing (and thereby rediscovering) the mind's wholeness, joy, power, glory, and unified purpose. You are letting the mind reassume its true expanded state. If you let the body arrest this natural impulse, however, then you are blocking the mind's whole nature and making it appear limited and belittled and separate. It therefore becomes depressed.

These two choices in turn determine the body's health. If a body is used to express the mind's wholeness and joy, its condition will become an expression of the mind's wholeness and joy. It will become healthy.

Application: Go through various body parts and repeat the following line for each one:

My [name of body part] is nothing but a means of pure extension. To see it as anything else is to limit my mind and hurt myself.

14. You are <u>not</u> limited by the body, and thought <u>cannot</u> be made flesh. Yet mind can be manifested through the body if it goes beyond it and <u>does not interpret it as limitation</u>. Whenever you see another as limited <u>to</u> or <u>by</u> the body, you are imposing this limit <u>on yourself</u>. Are you willing to <u>accept</u> this, when your whole purpose for learning should be to escape <u>from</u> limitations? To conceive of the body as a means of attack [Ur: of any kind] and to believe [Ur: and to entertain even the possibility] that joy could <u>possibly</u> result, is a clear-cut indication of a poor learner. He has accepted a learning goal in obvious contradiction to the unified purpose of the curriculum, and one that is interfering with his ability to accept its purpose <u>as his own</u>.

How do you learn that you are not limited by the body? You don't allow the body to contain your mind's natural impulse to join. To do this, though, you cannot see your brothers as bodies that are there for your body to strip-mine, but as minds that your mind can commune with. If you see your brothers as limited to the body, you will see yourself that way, too. And isn't the whole point of the spiritual path "to escape from limitations"?

If we're not using the body to extend and join, we are using it to attack, and thinking that joy can come from attack. This means that we are "a poor learner." We can't quite bring ourselves to embrace the Holy Spirit's goal because we have embraced a competing goal.

> 15. Joy is unified purpose, and unified purpose is <u>only</u> God's. When yours is unified it <u>is</u> His. Believe you can interfere with His purpose [Ur: Interfere with His purpose], and <u>you need salvation</u>. You have condemned yourself, but condemnation is not of God. Therefore it is not true. No more are any of its seeming results. When you see a brother as a body, you are condemning him <u>because</u> you have condemned yourself. Yet if <u>all</u> condemnation is unreal, and it <u>must</u> be unreal since it is a form of attack, then it can *have* no results.

"Joy is unified purpose." What? Doesn't having only one purpose seem like imprisonment to us? Yet anyone can see that having conflicting purposes puts you at war within yourself. You can only feel joy when all your horses are pulling in the same direction. And that can only happen when they are all pulling in God's direction. ("Unified purpose is only God's.") Right now, a lot of our mind's horses are pulling away from God. We condemn ourselves for this, and then we condemn our brothers by seeing them as bodies. Yet what we don't realize is that "condemnation is not of God" and is therefore "unreal." It doesn't have any actual results. We'll see the practical implications of this in the next paragraph.

> 16. Do not allow yourself to suffer from imagined ["imagined" was added by the editors] results of what is not true. Free your mind from the belief that this is possible. In its complete impossibility [Ur: and your full awareness *of* its complete impossibility,] lies your only hope for release. But what other hope would you want? Freedom from illusions lies only in not <u>believing</u> them. There is no attack [Ur: *There is not attack*], but there *is* unlimited communication and therefore unlimited power and wholeness. The power of wholeness is <u>extension</u>. Do not arrest your thought in this world, and you will open your mind to creation in God.

We attack and then we suffer for it. Yet we are suffering needlessly. We attacked someone in a dream, and thus our guilt is unnecessary. Dream attacks don't warrant guilt. Yet realizing that the attack didn't happen is not just the way out of guilt. It's also the way out of addiction to attack. When you stop believing in the reality of attack, you stop attacking.

Thus, we only seem to be faced with two options for how to use our body. The first option is just a heap of illusions. It's not actually there. This leaves only one option: "unlimited communication." Seeing that there's only one option, let us be realistic and take it. Let us allow our mind's true impulse to join to flow freely through our behavior. By taking the limits off of our extension, we will rediscover our mind's true power and wholeness. Eventually, the final limit—the body itself—will fall away, and our extension will flow forth unimpeded in the joyous act of creation. Using our body to communicate love in this world, therefore, is preparation for creating in Heaven. "Do not arrest your thought in this world, and you will open your mind to creation in God."

VIII. The Body as Means or End
Commentary by Greg Mackie

1.   Attitudes toward the body are attitudes toward <u>attack</u>. The ego's definitions of <u>anything</u> are childish, and are <u>always</u> based on what it believes the thing is *for*. This is because it is incapable of true generalizations, and equates what it sees with the function <u>it</u> ascribes to it. It does <u>not</u> equate it with what it *is*. To the ego the body <u>is to attack</u> *with*. Equating <u>you</u> with the body, it teaches that *you* are to attack with [Ur: because *this is what it believes*]. The body, then, is not the source of its own health. The body's condition lies solely in your interpretation of its function. [Ur: The reasons {sic} why definitions by function are inferior is merely because they may well be inaccurate.] Functions are part of being since they arise <u>from</u> it, but the relationship is <u>not</u> reciprocal. The whole does define the part, but the part does <u>not</u> define the whole. [Ur: This is as true of knowledge as it is of perception.]

Being determines function, but function does not determine being. In other words, what something is determines what it does; using it to do something it wasn't designed to do doesn't change what it is. A saw's function is sawing. If I choose to hammer nails with it, I can't conclude that it's a hammer. It is still a saw, no matter how I choose to use it.

Our being, too, determines our function. God created us as beings of love, so the extension of love through creation is our function. Because this is so, anything our minds make must have the extension of love as its *true* function, whatever we may think it is for. Therefore, the true function of our bodies, as we saw in the last section, must be to communicate—to extend love to our brothers through our words and behavior. But the ego has everything backwards. In its view, the function *it* ascribes to our body determines our being. It capriciously decides that the function of the body is to attack, and since it believes that we are bodies, it concludes that our being is attack—we are attackers by nature.

Which will we choose to use the body for: love or attack? Our choice will determine the body's condition.

Yet [Ur: The reason why] to <u>know</u> in part is to know entirely [Ur: is merely] because of the fundamental difference between knowledge

270

and perception. In perception the whole is built up of parts that can separate and reassemble in different constellations. But knowledge never changes, so its constellation is permanent. The idea of part-whole relationships has meaning only at the level of perception, where change is possible. Otherwise, there is no difference between the part and whole. [Ur: The only areas in which part-whole relationships have any meaning are those in which change is possible. There *is* no difference between the whole and the part where change is impossible.]

This passage highlights the crucial distinction the Course makes between part-whole relationships on earth and in Heaven. On earth, a bunch of separate parts are assembled to form a whole, like a set of Legos assembled to build a model car. The Legos can easily be disassembled and reassembled to make a model plane instead, thus changing their "constellation." But in Heaven, separate parts aren't assembled to form the whole; the parts aren't separate, and in some inscrutable way, each part *is* the whole. A rough earthly analogy is a hologram, in which each part contains the whole image. Thus in Heaven, the parts only go together one way; the constellation of knowledge is permanent. It is because part and whole are the same in Heaven that part-whole relationships as conventionally understood are only meaningful on the level of perception, and to *know* in part is to know the whole.

2. The body exists in a world that seems to contain two voices fighting for its possession. In this perceived constellation the body is seen as capable of shifting its allegiance [Ur: control] from one to the other, making the concepts of both health and sickness meaningful. The ego makes a fundamental confusion between means and end as it always does. Regarding the body as an end, the ego has no real use for it [Ur: at all] because it is *not* an end. You must have noticed an outstanding characteristic of every end that the ego has accepted as its own. When you have achieved it, *it has not satisfied you.* This is why the ego is forced to shift ceaselessly from one goal to another [Ur: shift from one end to another without ceasing], so that you will continue to hope it can yet offer you something.

In this world, we seem to have the devil of the ego on one shoulder and the angel of the Holy Spirit on the other. Listening to the ego literally makes us sick, while listening to the Holy Spirit brings us health. But we don't see this, because the ego has bamboozled us into seeing the body as an end in itself, obscuring the Holy Spirit's interpretation of it as a means of communication to serve the end of salvation. The body is not an end in itself, and the proof of this is that when we have achieved some body-oriented goal the ego held out to us, *it has not satisfied us*. If the body were truly an end, achieving such a goal *would* satisfy us.

The ego doesn't want us to figure this out, so it keeps shifting the goal, saying, "Well, maybe that Ferrari didn't satisfy you, but the Porsche in the window surely will." When we listen to the ego, we are like a compulsive gambler. We've lost our house, the wife and kids have left, our car has been repossessed, and the collection agencies are at our door, but surely this *next* bet will bring us the jackpot that will make it all worthwhile.

Application: Bring to mind ego-oriented goals you have achieved. Now, ask yourself, with as much honesty as you can muster: "*Did it satisfy me?* Even if it was temporarily pleasing, did it give me true and lasting happiness? If not, then can I reasonably expect the ego-oriented things I'm pursuing *now* to give me happiness?"

> 3.   It has been particularly difficult to overcome the ego's belief in the body as an end, because it is synonymous with the belief in <u>attack as an end</u>. The ego has a profound [Ur: *real*] <u>investment in sickness</u>. If you are sick, how can you object to the ego's firm belief that you are <u>not</u> invulnerable? This is an [Ur: a particularly] appealing argument from the ego's point of view, because it obscures the obvious attack that underlies the sickness. If you recognized [Ur: accepted] <u>this</u> and also decided <u>against</u> attack, you could not give this false witness to the ego's stand.

Let's face it: We all see the body as an end. Whatever we may profess, the way we actually live day to day demonstrates that we think getting things of the world to satisfy ourselves as separate entities is the way to happiness. Why do we have such a hard time giving up this belief? Here, the answer is *sickness*. Sickness is manna from hell for the ego, because sickness seems to provide unimpeachable testimony that we really are frail, vulnerable bodies, and if this is the case, it makes perfect sense to see the body as an end. This witness, however, is a liar. The truth is that sickness is not evidence of vulnerability, but the illusory result of our *attack*. If we figured this out, we would stop attacking and discover that we are not bodies, but absolutely invulnerable Sons of God.

> 4.   It is hard to perceive sickness as a false witness, because you do not realize that it is entirely out of keeping with what you want. This witness, then, appears to be innocent and trustworthy because you have not seriously cross-examined him. If you had, you would not consider sickness such a strong witness on behalf of the ego's views. A more honest statement would be that those who want the ego are predisposed to defend it. Therefore, their choice of witnesses should be suspect from the beginning. The ego does not call upon witnesses who would [Ur: might] disagree with its case, nor does the Holy Spirit. I have said that judgment is the function of the Holy Spirit, and one He is perfectly equipped to fulfill. The ego as a judge gives anything but an impartial judgment [Ur: trial (judgment)]. When the ego calls on a witness, it has already made the witness [Ur: it] an ally.

The ego has set up a kangaroo court, a mock trial in which the verdict is predetermined. How could the trial be fair when the ego is both the defendant and the judge? Identifying with the ego, we play along. To reword the first sentence: the reason we don't see sickness as a lying witness is because we *want* sickness. And we want sickness because we want the ego, and therefore defend it. Like any good defense attorney, we pick witnesses that support our defendant's case, and we coach them carefully so they sound trustworthy even when they are lying through their teeth. We present this "evidence" to the ego to judge and—surprise!—it gives a verdict in its favor.

If we want a fair trial of the ego, we need to turn the whole courtroom over to the Holy Spirit. With His counsel, we will give sickness the rigorous cross-examining it deserves, which will expose its lies. We will call upon witnesses that support *His* case, witnesses that will speak the truth because His case is true. And we will let Him be the judge as well, a judge whose verdict is true because He *knows* the truth.

> 5.   It is still true that the body has no function of itself, because it is not an end. The ego, however, establishes it as an end because, as such, its true function is obscured [Ur: as such, *it will lose its true function*].

This is the purpose of everything the ego does. Its sole aim is to lose sight of the function of <u>everything</u>. A sick body does not make any sense. It <u>could</u> not make sense because sickness is not what the body is <u>for</u>. Sickness is meaningful only if the two basic premises on which the ego's interpretation of the body rests are true; that the body is for attack, and that you <u>are</u> a body. Without these premises sickness is [Ur: completely] inconceivable.

The true function of the body, as we've seen, is to be a means of communication, a device for extending the Love of God to our brothers. Obviously, as long as we see the body as an end in itself, this function will be lost to us. We can't simultaneously scavenge from our brothers to feed our bodily identity and communicate selfless love to them. Blinding us to the true function of the body (and everything else) is the ego's entire goal, because it keeps the ego in business.

Sickness serves this goal extremely well. Why? Because sickness is rooted in the premises we saw in the first paragraph—the body is to attack with, and you are a body—and attack is the exact opposite of communication. As long as we play the ego's game, we will think that attack and sickness are what the body is for. But they are actually totally out of accord with the body's true function, which means they make no real sense at all. If we really saw the situation clearly, we would not only never get sick, but we would find sickness utterly "inconceivable." Can you imagine what that would feel like?

6.   Sickness is a way of demonstrating that <u>you can be hurt</u>. It is a witness to your frailty, your vulnerability, and your extreme need to depend on external guidance. The ego uses this as its best argument for your need for *its* guidance. It dictates endless prescriptions for <u>avoiding</u> catastrophic outcomes [Ur: this catastrophic outcome {sickness}]. The Holy Spirit, perfectly aware of the same situation [Ur: data], does not bother to analyze it at all. If data are meaningless there is no point in analyzing [Ur: treating] them [Ur: at all]. The function of truth is to collect information that is [Ur: data which are] <u>true</u>. [Ur: There is no point in trying to make sense out of meaningless data.] *Any* way you handle error [Ur: *Any* way they are handled] results in nothing. The more complicated the results become the harder it may be to recognize their nothingness, but it is not necessary to examine <u>all</u> possible outcomes to which premises give rise in order to judge them truly.

The first two sentences here echo the idea in the third paragraph—sickness seems to demonstrate that you are not invulnerable. This is what sickness witnesses to in the ego's kangaroo court. If you are vulnerable, the ego's logic continues, you must need the ego's guidance to protect you. It then "dictates endless prescriptions"—both literal medical prescriptions and prescriptions in a more general sense—for avoiding the "catastrophic outcome" of sickness.

The Holy Spirit, Who knows the truth and recognizes that sickness is a false witness, throws this logic out completely. The "evidence" of vulnerability provided by sickness is utterly meaningless data, like the meaningless number you would get if you tried to measure the length of something by putting it on a bathroom scale. You don't have take multiple readings with different objects to test your theory that a bathroom scale can measure length—sane thinking would see at once that the very idea is pure nonsense. This is how the Holy Spirit regards sickness.

> 7.   A learning <u>device</u> [the body] is <u>not</u> a teacher. <u>It</u> cannot tell you how you feel. <u>You</u> do not <u>know</u> how you feel because <u>you have accepted</u> <u>the ego's confusion</u>, and <u>you</u> therefore believe that <u>a learning device</u> *can* <u>tell you how you feel</u>. Sickness is merely another example of your insistence on asking guidance of a teacher who <u>does not know the</u> <u>answer</u>. The ego is <u>incapable</u> of knowing how you feel. When I said that the ego <u>does not know anything</u>, I said the one thing about the ego that is wholly true. But there is a corollary; if only knowledge has being and the ego has no knowledge, then the ego <u>has no being</u>.

The body cannot tell you how you feel—what an amazing idea! We all think that the body can and does tell us how we feel all the time. If our body feels sick, we say, "*I* feel sick." But the body cannot dictate to us how we feel. Since it is only a learning device, thinking it can tell us how we feel is like thinking that the overhead projector in a classroom can teach the class. If the body feels sick, it simply means we've asked the ego to teach us how we feel, and the ego doesn't have a clue. We *really* feel joyous, since our true being resides in Heaven. To recognize this, we need to admit that we don't know how we really feel and be willing to be led from the nothingness of the ego to the truth of who we really are.

Application: Take a moment to notice how your body feels right now. Notice especially feelings of discomfort. When your body feels discomfort, it seems that *you* feel discomfort, but this isn't so. Now, let go of how you think you feel by saying, *"My body cannot tell me how I feel. I do not know how I feel because I have accepted the ego's confusion, and therefore believe that a learning device—my body—**can** tell me how I feel. I'm letting my ego teach me how I feel, but my ego is incapable of knowing how I **really** feel."*

8.   You might well ask how the voice of something that does not exist can be so insistent. Have you thought about [Ur: seriously considered] the distorting power of something you <u>want</u>, even if it is not real [Ur: true]? There are many instances of how what you want distorts perception [Ur: can distort what you see and hear]. No one can doubt the ego's skill in building up false cases. Nor can anyone doubt your willingness to listen until <u>you</u> choose not to accept [Ur: will not to tolerate] anything <u>except</u> truth. When <u>you</u> lay the ego aside, it will be gone. The Holy Spirit's Voice is as loud as your willingness to listen. It cannot be louder without violating your freedom of choice [Ur: your will], which the Holy Spirit seeks to restore, never to undermine [Ur: seeks to free but never to command].

Probably every Course student has asked at some point: If the ego is an illusion, why is it so dang tough to get rid of? The blunt answer: Because we *want* it. A person who wants something bad enough will find a way to get it, even if it is pure fantasy. In the extreme, an insane person yearning to live in ancient Egypt can convince herself that she's Cleopatra, Queen of the Nile. But we all do this in milder forms. The crude Lothario convinces himself he's God's gift to women. The politician who wants a war sees enemies lurking everywhere. The woman on a diet tells herself the diet soda will cancel out the hot fudge sundae. Can you think of times when you've done something like this?

So it is with the ego. It is so persistent because we want it, and therefore have convinced ourselves that it is real. This is why we have such a hard time hearing the Holy Spirit: we want the ego more than we want Him, and He won't force Himself upon us against our will. Only when we finally decide that we won't tolerate anything but truth will the ego leave us in peace.

9.   The Holy Spirit teaches you to use your body <u>only</u> to reach your brothers, so He can teach His message through you. This will heal them and <u>therefore</u> heal you. Everything used in accordance with its function as the Holy Spirit sees it <u>cannot</u> be sick. Everything used otherwise <u>is</u>. Do not allow the body to be a mirror of a split mind. Do not let it be an image of your own perception of littleness. Do not let it reflect your decision [Ur: will] to attack. Health is seen as ["seen as" was apparently added by the editors] the natural state of everything when interpretation is left to the Holy Spirit, Who perceives no attack on anything. Health is the result of relinquishing <u>all</u> attempts to use the body lovelessly. Health is the beginning of the proper perspective on life under the guidance of the one Teacher Who knows what life <u>is</u>, being the Voice for Life Itself.

I have always loved this line: "Health is the result of relinquishing all attempts to use the body lovelessly." When we listen to the ego, we think the body is an end in itself and health comes from attack in the name of "defending" the body: attack on germs, attack on people who "threaten" our body, etc. Ironically, the end result of all this attack is not health but sickness. Health comes only from giving up the "will to attack," and seeing the body as the Holy Spirit sees it: as a means of communicating His message of love to our brothers. Real health comes not from the proper diet and exercise and pills, but through extending miracles of healed perception to our brothers everywhere.

Application: Think of a person you've recently attacked with your body, be it through actual physical assault, harsh words, an icy stare, or any other form. Imagine you are with this person now, and say, *"Health is the result of relinquishing all attempts to use my body lovelessly. Holy Spirit, teach me to use my body only to reach [name], so You can teach Your message through me. This will heal [name] and therefore heal me."* See yourself physically communicating love to this person however He directs. (If you will have an encounter with this person later, try saying these words silently during that encounter.)

IX. Healing as Corrected Perception
Commentary by Greg Mackie

1.   I said before that the Holy Spirit is the Answer. He is the Answer to <u>everything</u>, because He knows what the answer to everything <u>is</u>. The ego does not know what a <u>real</u> question is, although it asks an endless number. Yet <u>you</u> can learn this [what a real question is] as you learn to question the value of the ego, and thus establish your ability to <u>evaluate</u> its questions. When the ego tempts you to sickness do not ask the Holy Spirit to heal the body, for this would merely be to accept the ego's belief that the body is the proper aim of healing. Ask, rather, that the Holy Spirit teach you the right *perception* of the body, for perception alone can be distorted. <u>Only perception can be sick</u>, because only perception can be <u>wrong</u>.

Like the private detective Guy Noir on Garrison Keillor's *Prairie Home Companion*, we're all trying to "find the answers to life's persistent questions." We have two teachers to consult in this endeavor. One, the Holy Spirit, *is* the Answer and knows the answer to everything. The other, the ego, not only doesn't know any answers, but doesn't even know any real questions. The choice between them is a real no-brainer. But to make the right choice and receive the Answer, we need to ask one of those real questions: What value does the ego really have? This will enable us to evaluate its questions truly, and see that they and the ego that asks them have no real value.

One of the "endless number" of false, ego-based questions is: Holy Spirit, would You heal my body? This is not a real question but rather a statement of the ego's belief that we *are* bodies, so sickness and healing must be of the body. The real question to ask is: Holy Spirit, would You heal my *perception* of my body? This affirms the truth that we are minds, so sickness and healing are of the mind. Only through changing our perception of the body can true healing occur.

2.   Wrong perception is the wish that things [Ur: is *distorted willing*, which *wants* things to] be as they are not. The reality of <u>everything</u> is totally harmless, because total harmlessness is the <u>condition</u> of its

278

reality. It is also the condition of your <u>awareness</u> of its reality. You do not have to <u>seek</u> reality. It will seek you and <u>find</u> you <u>when you meet its conditions</u>. Its conditions are part of <u>what it is</u>. And this part only is up to you. The rest is of itself. You need do so little because your little part is so powerful that it <u>will</u> bring the whole to you. Accept, then, your little part, and <u>let</u> the whole be yours.

Wrong perception, the cause of sickness, is the desire to push reality away. As such, it is an attack on reality, a desire to harm it. If we want to see reality, then, we need to give up the desire to harm and replace it with *total harmlessness*. I love the play on two definitions of "condition" here: Harmlessness is the condition (state) of reality, and also the condition (prerequisite) of our *awareness* of reality. In other words, by being totally harmless in our daily lives—living in a way that reflects the totally harmless state of reality—we will awaken to reality. We will not need to go on a quest for reality; if we do our little part of living harmlessly, *it* will come to *us*.

Application: Think of a situation in which you believe a particular person has harmed you, so that you are tempted to attack in retaliation. Say, *"The reality of everything is totally harmless, including both [name] and me. If I just do my little part of being totally harmless to [name], total awareness of the reality of everything will be mine."*

3.   Wholeness heals <u>because</u> it is of the mind. All forms of sickness, even unto death, are physical expressions of the <u>fear of awakening</u>. They are attempts to reinforce sleeping [Ur: *Unconsciousness*] out of fear of waking [Ur: *Consciousness*]. This is a pathetic way of <u>trying not to</u> see [Ur: *know*] by rendering the faculties for seeing [Ur: knowing] ineffectual. "Rest in peace" is a blessing for the living, not the dead, because rest comes from waking, not from sleeping. Sleep is withdrawing; waking is <u>joining</u>. Dreams are <u>illusions</u> of joining, because they reflect the ego's distorted notions [Ur: *illusions* of joining, taking on the ego's distortions] about what joining is [Ur: what joining means, if you are sleeping under its guidance]. Yet the Holy Spirit, too, has use for sleep, and can use dreams on <u>behalf</u> of waking if you will let Him.

Why don't we just choose harmlessness and awaken to reality? Because, identifying with the ego, we are *afraid* of awakening. We don't want to become conscious of reality, so we devise various ways of withdrawing into unconsciousness. One is *sickness*, which generally involves withdrawing from others and slipping into a less than fully conscious state; as the Course says elsewhere, "Sickness is isolation" (W-pI.137.2:1). Another is *sleep*, which is literally a nightly withdrawal into unconsciousness. Finally, there is *death*, the big sleep from which we never wake up.

We think these things will bring us rest: we get to slow down and rest when we're sick, we rest nightly when we sleep, and we say "Rest in peace" when our loved ones go into the grave. But in Jesus' eyes, all of this is "pathetic." True rest comes not from knocking ourselves out cold, but from waking to reality.

> 4. How you wake is the sign of how you have used sleep. To whom did you give it? Under which teacher did you place it? Whenever you wake dispiritedly, it was <u>not</u> given to the Holy Spirit [Ur: it was *not* of the Spirit]. <u>Only</u> when you awaken joyously have you utilized sleep <u>according to</u> His [Ur: *the Holy Spirit's*] <u>purpose</u>. You can indeed be "drugged" by sleep, if [Ur: but this is *always* because] you have <u>misused it on behalf of sickness</u>. Sleep is no more a form of death than death is a form of unconsciousness. Complete <u>unconsciousness is impossible</u> ["Complete" was apparently added by the editors]. You can rest in peace only <u>because you are awake</u>.

The discussion now shifts from spiritual to physical sleep. When we wake groggy and dispirited, we may blame it on anything from the mayhem on the Eleven O'clock News to the husband's snoring to that spicy burrito we ate at midnight. But here we are told it is for one reason alone: we didn't give our sleep to the Holy Spirit. If we had done that, we would have awakened with joy. As someone who is not at all a morning person, I need to remember that.

What is the Holy Spirit's purpose for sleep? Since He is a "teacher" under whom we place our sleep, the implication is that He uses that time to teach us. Other Course passages suggest that Jesus teaches us while we're asleep (see T-4.IV.11:2) and even that we teach others while we're asleep (see M-In.1:6). If it is impossible to be totally unconscious as it says here (see also T-2.VI.9:5-6), it makes perfect sense that this can occur. In truth we are already awake—we *are* resting in peace, and we can extend that peace to others as we sleep, with the Holy Spirit's help.

Application: This week, make a conscious effort to turn your sleep over to the Holy Spirit. Use whatever words you like to do this. I like these words from the prayer in Lesson 232, which is addressed to God: "And let me sleep sure of my safety, certain of Your care, and happily aware I am Your Son" (W-pII.232.1:5).

> 5.   Healing is release from the fear of waking and the substitution of the decision [Ur: will] to wake. The decision [Ur: will] to wake is the reflection of the will to love ["the reflection of" was apparently added by the editors], since all healing involves replacing fear with love. The Holy Spirit cannot distinguish among degrees of error, for if He taught that one form of sickness is more serious than another, He would be teaching that one error can be more real than another. His function is to distinguish only between the false and the true, replacing the false with the true.

If all forms of sickness stem from the fear of awakening, then healing comes from replacing that fear with the will to awaken. What an amazing idea! We think there are many different forms of sickness, each with its own particular cure. We think some are more difficult to cure than others—indeed, there are some that seem to have no cure at all, especially the terminal disease that gets us all in the end: death. But all of this is just one big mistake. In the Holy Spirit's eyes, the only sickness is the illusion of fear, and the only cure is the reality of love. Do we want to be free of sickness? Do we want to wake up? Do we want to extend love to our brothers? These are all different forms of the same question.

> 6.   The ego, which always wants to weaken the mind, tries to separate it from the body in an attempt to destroy it. [Ur: The ego, which always *weakens* the will, wants to *separate* the body from the mind. This *is* an attempt to *destroy* it {the body}.] Yet the ego actually believes that it [the ego] is protecting it [the body]. This is because the ego believes that mind is dangerous, and that to make mindless is to heal. But to

make mindless is impossible, since it would mean to make nothing out of what God created. The ego <u>despises</u> weakness, even though it makes every effort to <u>induce</u> it. The ego [Ur: *It*] <u>wants only what it hates</u>. To the ego this is perfectly sensible. Believing in the power of attack, the ego <u>wants</u> attack.

This is a difficult paragraph. I'll sort it out as best I can here:

The ego wants to survive, and it survives through attack, since attack was the "power" that made it. So, it attacks by separating the body from the mind—essentially, by getting us to identify with the body instead of the mind. Because the mind has the power to undo the ego and the body, the ego fears the mind and sees body-identification as a way of protecting the body that is its chosen home. But separating the body from the mind has the actual effect of *weakening* both the body and the mind, because it is an attack. This attack weakens the body by making it sick and ultimately destroying it through death. It weakens the mind by apparently making us mindless, apparently rendering the mind powerless and thus "destroying" it as well.

The ego is ambivalent about all this weakness. On the one hand, it isn't fond of weakness—who is? But on the other hand, it strives to induce this weakness because this ensures that the *ego* will remain strong. The body's weakness strengthens the ego because "the body's vulnerability is [the ego's] own best argument that you cannot be of God" (T-4.V.4:2). The mind's weakness strengthens the ego because a weak mind is much less of a threat to undo the ego. In short, this bizarre process is the ego's best shot at survival.

> [Ur: You have begun to realize that this is a very practical course, because it means *exactly* what it says. So does the Bible, if it is properly understood. There has been a marked tendency on the part of many of the Bible's followers, and also its translators, to be entirely literal about fear and *its* effects, but *not* about love and *its* results. Thus, "hellfire" means burning, but raising the dead becomes allegorical. Actually, it is *particularly* the references to the outcomes of love that should be taken literally because the Bible is *about* love, being about *God*.]

This Urtext passage is a great lead-in to the final paragraphs, where Jesus assures us that we can quite literally do everything he asks us to do. Here, he begins by assuring us that the Course means *exactly* what it says. When he says this is a course in miracles, he means it literally. He underscores the point by saying that those biblical accounts of miracles like his raising of Lazarus from the dead should also be taken literally. (I think he has mainly the miracle stories in mind here—I doubt that he wants us to take stories like Noah's Ark literally.) Fear has led many to preach literal fire and brimstone, but what's really literal in the Bible are the "outcomes of love" that testify to the limitless Love of God.

> 7. The Bible enjoins you to be perfect, to heal <u>all</u> errors, to take no thought of the body <u>as separate</u> and to accomplish all things <u>in my name</u>. This is not my name alone, for ours is a shared identification. The Name of God's Son is one, and you are enjoined to do the works of love <u>because</u> we share this oneness. Our minds are whole <u>because</u> they are one. If you are sick you are withdrawing from me. Yet you <u>cannot withdraw from me alone</u>. You can only withdraw from yourself *and* me.

Having just spoken about taking the outcomes of love in the Bible literally, Jesus continues by reiterating biblical injunctions given to his followers. Here is my best guess at the biblical passages referred to in the first sentence:

- "Be ye therefore perfect, even as your Father which is in heaven is perfect." (Matthew 5:48)
- "He gave [his twelve disciples] power against unclean spirits, to cast them out, and to heal all manner of sickness and all manner of disease." (Matthew 10:1)
- "Therefore I say unto you, Take no thought for your life, what ye shall eat; neither for the body, what ye shall put on." (Luke 12:22; cf. Matthew 6:31)
- "And whatsoever ye do in word or deed, do all in the name of the Lord Jesus, giving thanks to God and the Father by him." (Colossians 3:17)

You really get the sense that Jesus is calling us to continue the legacy, to follow him now just as his disciples and others like Paul (the author of the last quote) followed him then. Yet there is an important clarification: While his past followers came to worship him as the only begotten Son of God, the "Lord Jesus," we are to recognize our equality with him.

When we withdraw into sickness we lose sight of the name we share with him and the calling it brings with it, but when we recognize our oneness with him and the wholeness of the entire Sonship, we will join him and do the same "works of love" he did.

> 8.   You have surely begun to realize that this is a very practical course, and one that means exactly what it says. I would not ask you to do things you <u>cannot</u> do, and it is impossible that I could do things <u>you</u> cannot do. Given this, and given this <u>quite literally</u>, nothing can prevent you from doing <u>exactly</u> what I ask, and <u>everything</u> argues *for* your doing it. I give you <u>no</u> limits because God lays none upon you. When you limit <u>yourself</u> we are <u>not</u> of one mind, and that <u>is</u> sickness. Yet sickness is not of the body, but <u>of the mind</u>. <u>All</u> forms of sickness [Ur: *dis*function] are [Ur: merely] signs that the mind is split, and does not accept a <u>unified purpose</u>.

Jesus' appeal to join him as miracle workers continues. Who among us hasn't felt that the Course asks too much of us? Surely he doesn't *really* want us to be perfect and heal *all* sickness and raise the dead; it must be metaphorical. But he really means it. We seem so limited now because our minds are torn between his calling and the call of our egos—the "dis-ease" that makes us sick. All we must do to find healing and work miracles as he did is make up our minds to unify our purpose with his.

Application: Read the first four sentences of this paragraph as a personal message to you from Jesus. To make it more personal, insert your name at appropriate points.

> 9.   The unification of purpose, then, is the Holy Spirit's <u>only</u> way of healing. This is because it is the only level [the level of the mind] at which healing <u>means</u> anything. The re-establishing of meaning in a chaotic thought system *is* the [Ur: only] way to heal it. Your task is only to meet the conditions <u>for</u> meaning, since meaning itself is of God. Yet your <u>return</u> to meaning is essential <u>to His</u>, because <u>your</u> meaning is <u>part</u> of His. Your healing, then, is part of <u>His</u> health, since it is part of His Wholeness. He cannot lose this, but you *can* [Ur: *you* can] not know it. Yet it is still His Will for you, and His Will <u>must</u> stand forever and in all things.

IX. Healing as Corrected Perception

If sickness comes from not accepting a unified purpose, then healing comes from unifying our purpose with the Holy Spirit's: the purpose of joining Jesus in working miracles. I'm a little unclear about the discussion of "meaning" here, but here's what I think Jesus is saying. Earlier, he said the meaning we share with God in Heaven is consistency (T-7.V.6) and extension (T-7.II.7). Therefore, we meet the conditions of heavenly meaning here on earth by acting in a way that *reflects* our heavenly meaning: consistently extending healing to our brothers. Healing consistently restores meaning to our chaotic thought system, and this ultimately restores our awareness of the meaning we share with God.

.

Commentaries on Chapter 9

THE ACCEPTANCE
OF THE ATONEMENT

I. The Acceptance of Reality
Commentary by Greg Mackie

1. Fear of the Will of God is one of the strangest beliefs the human mind has ever made. It could not possibly have occurred unless the mind were already profoundly split, making it possible for <u>it</u> to be afraid of what it really is. [Ur: It is apparent that] Reality <u>cannot</u> "threaten" anything except illusions, since reality can only <u>uphold truth</u>. The very fact that the Will of God, which <u>is</u> what you are, is perceived as fearful [Ur: *to* you], demonstrates that you *are* afraid of what you are. It is not, then, the Will of God of which you are afraid, but <u>yours</u>.

Fear of the Will of God is virtually universal. It rears its ugly head in many ways—for instance, in how quick we are to blame God when a disaster like the tsunami or Hurricane Katrina hits. Yet when you think about it, isn't it strange that we are so terrified of a God Who is supposed to be Love? What's going on here?

According to this paragraph, what's really going on is that we're afraid of *what we really are*. The logic is simple:

* We fear the Will of God.
* The Will of God is what we really are.
* Therefore, we fear what we really are.

Why do we fear what we really are? When we separated, we split our minds into a part that is invested in ego illusions and a part that knows what we really are. The ego-invested part is afraid of reality, because reality "threatens" illusions. Since we now *identify* with the ego, we now fear what we really are. So, we may think we fear the Will of an external God poised to strike us dead with His thunderbolts, but we are really afraid of the will of our real Self poised to strike our illusory self-image "dead" with the light of truth.

2. Your will is <u>not</u> the ego's, and that is why the ego is against you. What seems to be the fear of God is really [Ur: only] the fear of <u>your</u>

own reality. It is impossible to learn anything consistently in a state of panic. If the purpose of this course is to help you remember [Ur: learn] what you are, and if you believe [Ur: if you have *already decided*] that what you are is <u>fearful</u>, then it <u>must</u> follow that you will <u>not learn this course</u>. Yet [Ur: But you might remember that] the reason <u>for</u> the course is that you do <u>not</u> know what [Ur: who] you are.

Why do we find the Course so difficult? Why do we avoid studying it? Why do we make convenient excuses for missing our assigned practice periods? Why do we have such strong resistance to forgiving and healing as the Course instructs us to do? We could probably come up with all sorts of reasons, but the real reason is our fear of what we really are. Again, the logic is simple:

- We fear what we really are.
- The purpose of the Course is to teach us what we really are.
- Therefore, we fear the Course, and while this fear persists, we won't learn the Course.

How can we overcome this fear? The last sentence suggests an answer: We should remember we don't *know* what we are. Why this helps is discussed in the next paragraph.

3. If you do not know what your reality is [Ur: do not know your reality], why would you be so sure that it is fearful [Ur: how would you know whether it is fearful or not]? The association of truth and fear, which would be highly artificial at most [Ur: best], is particularly inappropriate in the minds of those who do not know what truth is. All this could mean [Ur: All that this kind of association means] is that you are arbitrarily associating [Ur: endowing] something [Ur: quite] beyond your awareness with something <u>you do not want</u>. It is evident, then, that you are judging something of which you are totally unaware. You have set up this strange situation so that it is impossible [Ur: *completely impossible*] to escape from it <u>without</u> a Guide Who *does* know what your reality is. The purpose of this Guide is merely to remind you of what <u>you</u> want. He is not attempting to force an alien will <u>upon</u> you. He is merely making every possible effort, within the limits <u>you</u> impose on Him, to <u>re-establish</u> your <u>own</u> will in your awareness [Ur: consciousness].

I. The Acceptance of Reality

Here we see why our ignorance of what we are helps us overcome our fear. If we don't know what we are, how can we be so sure it's fearful? It makes no sense to assume that the unknown must be fearful and undesirable; it's like assuming that the neighbor with the Arabic name, whom we've never met, must be a member of al-Qaeda.

This admission of ignorance can give us the little willingness we need to get a second opinion from a Guide Who *does* know what we are: the Holy Spirit. He will assure us that our reality is not fearful or undesirable at all. On the contrary, it is what we really want. It is not some alien thing out to destroy us, but our *true will*. This recognition will undo our fear of our reality, and this in turn will enable us to learn the Course.

Application: Think about some of the ways you resist the Course— not reading it, "forgetting" to practice, withholding forgiveness, etc. Then say, *"My resistance shows me that I am afraid of learning the Course, because I am afraid of what I am. But I don't know what I am, so how can I be so sure it is fearful? Holy Spirit, I open my mind to You. Please tell me what I really am."* You may want to write down what you receive.

4. You have <u>imprisoned</u> your will beyond your own awareness [Ur: in your *un*conscious], where it remains [Ur: available], but cannot help you. When I said that the Holy Spirit's function is to sort out the true from the false in your mind [Ur: unconscious], I meant that He has the power to look into what <u>you</u> have hidden and recognize [Ur: perceive] the Will of God there. His recognition [Ur: perception] of this Will can make it real to <u>you</u> because <u>He</u> is in your mind, and therefore He <u>is</u> your reality. If, then, His perception <u>of</u> your mind brings its reality <u>to</u> you, He *is* helping you to remember what you are [Ur: He *is* teaching you what you are]. The only source of fear in this [Ur: whole] process is [Ur: can *only* be] <u>what you think you will lose</u>. Yet it is only what the Holy Spirit sees that you can possibly <u>have</u>.

Our fear of losing the illusory self we made has buried our true will in our unconscious, so now we can't access it without help. The Holy Spirit is that help. He is in our mind *and* He has the ability to look past our defenses to the reality we've hidden: the Will of God, the Will we share with Him, the Will we are. His recognition of the Will of God, our reality, makes it real to us; it brings our reality to us. This is how He teaches us what we are.

> 5.   I have emphasized many times that the Holy Spirit will never call upon you to sacrifice anything. But if you ask the sacrifice of reality of yourself [Ur: *of yourselves*], the Holy Spirit <u>must</u> remind you that this is not God's Will <u>because</u> it is not yours. There is <u>no difference</u> between your will and God's. If you did not have a split mind [Ur: divided wills], you would recognize that willing is salvation because it <u>is</u> communication.

One of the classic reasons for fearing God's Will is the fear that it will demand sacrifice from us. After all, look at the lives of people who *did* do God's Will, like Jesus, Saint Francis, Gandhi, and Martin Luther King, Jr. Such people typically gave up riches, family life, leisure time, creature comforts, and sometimes their very lives for God's sake. Yet Gandhi, who did use the word "sacrifice" frequently, nonetheless said that giving one's life to God truly "lightens the mind of the doer and gives him a sense of peace and joy. The Buddha gave up the pleasures of life because they had become painful to him." The Holy Spirit reminds us that throwing away God's Will for the "pleasures" of the world is the actual sacrifice, because it is a rejection of *our own* will, our very reality. Accepting the will we share with God is salvation itself, because it restores the communication with Him that the separation seemed to sever.

> 6.   It is impossible to communicate in alien tongues. You and your Creator can communicate through creation, because that, and only that, <u>is</u> your joint Will. A divided mind cannot communicate, because it speaks [Ur: Divided wills do not communicate because they speak] for different things <u>to the same mind</u>. This loses the ability to communicate simply because confused communication <u>does not mean anything</u>. A message cannot be [Ur: said to be] communicated <u>unless</u> it makes sense. How sensible can your messages be, when you ask for <u>what you do not want</u>? Yet as long as you are afraid of your will, that is precisely what you are asking for [Ur: what you *will* ask for].

We continue with the theme of communication with God. In Heaven, we communicate with God through creation, our joint Will. This is our native language. But now that our minds are split, most of the time we speak "ego," a language alien to God. Moreover, the part of our split mind that remains on God's side is still speaking *His* language, so we're trying to use two languages at once.

This language barrier expresses itself in our ambivalence when we pray to God. Part of our split mind truly prays for God's Will, recognizing that it is our true will as well. But the other part is afraid of God's Will, and thus desires to avoid it at all costs. Our prayers, then, are sending God mixed messages: "God, come reveal your Will to me; God, get the hell away from me!" This obviously makes no sense at all. How can we get through to God or hear His response when we're spouting gibberish like this?

> 7.   You may insist that the Holy Spirit does not answer you, but it might be wiser to consider the kind of questioner [Ur: asker] you are. <u>You do not ask only for what you want</u>. This is [Ur: *solely*] because you are afraid you might receive it, <u>and you would</u>. That is [Ur: *This is really*] why you persist in asking the teacher who could not possibly give you what you want [Ur: teach you your will]. Of him you can never learn what it is, and this gives you the illusion of safety. Yet you cannot be safe *from* truth, but only *in* truth. Reality is the <u>only</u> safety. Your will is your salvation <u>because it is the same as God's</u>. The separation is nothing more than the belief that it is <u>different</u>.

Virtually everyone who prays asks at one point or another: Why doesn't God answer me? Many answers have been offered over the ages: the rituals weren't performed properly, we haven't done enough penance, God works in strange and mysterious ways, etc. But the real reason we don't hear God's Voice, the Holy Spirit, is that we do not wholly *want* to hear Him. Again, the problem is our split mind. One part really wants what the Holy Spirit offers, but the other part hears the ego whispering in our ear: "Careful what you ask for. You just might get it." Precisely because we *would* get it if we asked wholeheartedly, we ask the ego to give us what *it* wants, in order to keep us "safe" from the ego-dispelling "threat" of getting what we *really* want.

But of course, this is absurd. Real safety resides in our true will, not in fighting against it. Reality is the only safety. Truth is the only safety. God is the only safety. Salvation lies not in avoiding God's Will, but in recognizing that God's Will and ours are the same.

8.   <u>No</u> right mind can believe that its will is <u>stronger</u> than God's. If, then, a mind believes that <u>its</u> will is different <u>from</u> His, it can only decide either that there <u>is</u> no God or that <u>God's Will is fearful</u>. The former accounts for the atheist and the latter for the martyr, who believes that God demands sacrifices [Ur: Martyrdom takes many forms, the category including *all* doctrines which hold that God demands sacrifices of *any* kind]. Either of these insane decisions [Ur: Either basic type of insane decision] will induce panic, because the atheist believes he is alone, and the martyr believes that God is crucifying him. [Ur: Both really fear both abandonment *and* retaliation, but the former is more reactive against abandonment and the latter against retaliation. The atheist maintains that God has left him, but he {the atheist} does not care. He will, however, become very fearful, and hence very *angry*, if anyone suggests that God has *not* left him. The martyr, on the other hand, is more aware of guilt, and believing that punishment is inevitable, attempts to teach himself to *like* it.] Yet no one really wants either abandonment or retaliation [Ur: The truth is, very simply, that *no-one wants either abandonment or retaliation*], even though many may seek both [Ur: Many people *seek* both, but it is still true that they do *not* want it].

This is a fascinating paragraph, especially with the added Urtext material. It discusses two options open to us if we believe that our will is different from God's.

First, we have the atheist. On the surface, she says there is no God— her own will is the only game in town. Beneath the surface, though, the atheist *does* believe in God, but believes that God has abandoned her. She claims not to care about this—she may even exultantly proclaim that "God is dead"—but she is really terrified of being all alone. Beneath this terror, though, lies yet another terror: the fear that God has *not* abandoned her and is poised to retaliate against her for her "sins." This is why the militant atheist gets angry at anyone who suggests that God actually exists. Methinks she doth protest too much.

Second, we have the martyr. On the surface, he says he loves God and gladly sacrifices himself for the sake of doing God's Will. Beneath the surface, though (or perhaps on the surface, next to his joyful sacrifice), the martyr is terrified of God's retaliation for the sins he's sure he has committed. Beneath this terror, though, lies yet another terror: the fear that God will abandon him. He doesn't like punishment, but he'd rather have a punishing God than no God at all. This is why he convinces himself to *like* God's punishment. He says with Job, "Though [God] slay me, yet will I trust in him" (Job 13:15). Like an abused spouse, he fears being left all alone and clings to the abuser. Like the fraternity pledges being paddled in *Animal House*, he says, "Thank you, sir, may I have another?"

All of this is totally nuts. No one *really* wants retaliation or abandonment; both are against the will we share with God. The only reason we seem to want these things is, again, the split mind. The ego side of the split wants to assert an independent will and avoid the true God of Love, no matter how many mental hoops we have to jump through to do this.

> Can you ask the Holy Spirit for "gifts" such as these, and actually expect to <u>receive</u> them? He cannot give you something you do not want. [Ur: The Holy Spirit is totally incapable of giving *you* anything that does *not* come from God. His task is *not* to make anything *for* you. He *cannot* make you want something you *don't* want.] When you ask the Universal Giver for what you do not want, <u>you</u> are asking for what <u>cannot</u> be given <u>because it was never created</u>. It was never created, because it was never your will for *you*.

Back to the question of why the Holy Spirit doesn't seem to answer us. When our mind is split and we think God's Will is different than ours, we are essentially asking for retaliation and abandonment, things we don't truly want. The Holy Spirit, though, is incapable of giving us what we don't truly want—thank God! We're asking for what can't be given because it doesn't exist; that's why we don't get it.

> 9.   Ultimately everyone must remember [Ur: learn] the Will of God, because ultimately everyone must recognize <u>himself</u>. This recognition <u>is</u> the recognition that <u>his will and God's are one</u>. In the presence of truth, there are no unbelievers and no sacrifices. In the security of reality, fear is totally meaningless. To deny what <u>is</u> can only *seem* to be fearful. Fear cannot be real without a cause, and <u>God</u> is the only Cause. God is Love and you <u>do</u> want Him. This *is* your will. Ask for <u>this</u> and you <u>will</u> be answered, because you will be asking only for what <u>belongs</u> to you.

After all that depressing stuff about our futile asking for what we don't really want, a paragraph of reassurance. Ultimately, we *will* learn the Will of God, which brings with it the saving recognition that our will and God's are the same. Reality is reality. We can't deny what *is* forever. In the light of truth, atheism ("unbelievers") and martyrdom ("sacrifices") are unthinkable. In the perfect safety of reality, fear is utterly absurd. What we really want is God's Love, and when we ask for this, we cannot fail to receive it.

Application: Think of some of your "unanswered" prayers. The reason this happened is that you didn't ask for what you truly want, at least not wholeheartedly. Now, use these words to ask for what you truly want—God's Love: *"God is Love and I do want Him. This **is** my will. I ask for this and I will be answered, because I will be asking only for what belongs to me."*

> 10. When you ask the Holy Spirit for what would hurt you He <u>cannot</u> answer because <u>nothing</u> can hurt you, and <u>so you are asking for nothing</u>. <u>Any</u> wish [Ur: desire] that stems from the ego <u>is</u> a wish [Ur: desire] for nothing, and to ask for it <u>is not a request</u>. It is merely a denial in the <u>form</u> of a request. The Holy Spirit is not concerned with form [Ur: at all], being aware only of <u>meaning</u>. The ego cannot ask the Holy Spirit for <u>anything</u>, because there is <u>complete communication failure</u> between them. Yet *you* can ask for <u>everything</u> of the Holy Spirit, because <u>your</u> requests to Him are real, being of your right mind [Ur: being of your will]. Would the Holy Spirit deny the Will of God? And could He fail to recognize it in His Son [Ur: God's Sons]?

When we ask the Holy Spirit for what would hurt us (like abandonment or retaliation), He can't give it to us because there *is* nothing that can hurt us. It's like asking the local pet shop for one of those cute little "tribbles" you saw on *Star Trek*—there's just no such animal. Remember that earlier paragraph (T-8.IX.1) that said the ego is incapable of asking a real question? This is another example of that. When we listen to the ego and ask for what would hurt us, we are not asking a real question. We are merely declaring, "I don't want the Will of God" in a way that *looks* like a question.

The good news, though, is that while the ego can't make a real request of the Holy Spirit, *we* can. We can say, "Holy Spirit, I ask for gifts that are in accord with the will I share with God. I ask for love, peace, joy, and everything I can share with my brothers." Our non-egoic requests of the Holy Spirit *are* real questions, because they are affirmations that God's Will and ours are the same. How could the Holy Spirit, the Voice that speaks for God's Will and ours, possibly turn us down? He will happily answer our real requests by giving us the glorious gift of everything that is real.

> 11. [Ur: The energy which you withdraw from Creation you expend on fear. This is not because your *energy* is limited, but because *you have limited it*.] You do not recognize the <u>enormous</u> waste of energy you expend in denying truth. What would <u>you</u> say of someone who persists in attempting the impossible, believing that to <u>achieve</u> it is to succeed? The belief that you <u>must have the impossible</u> in order to be happy is totally at variance with the principle of creation. God <u>could</u> not will that happiness <u>depended</u> on what you could never have. The fact that God is Love does not require belief, but it <u>does</u> require <u>acceptance</u>. It is indeed possible for you to <u>deny</u> facts, although it is <u>impossible</u> for you to <u>change</u> them. If you hold your hands over your eyes, you will <u>not</u> see because you are interfering with the laws of seeing. If you deny love, you will <u>not know it</u> because your cooperation is the <u>law of its being</u>. You cannot change laws you did not make, and the laws of happiness were created <u>for</u> you, <u>not by</u> you.

When my ex-wife and I saw someone intensely devoted to a purpose that seemed trivial to us (like a guy who had a museum full of stuffed gophers dressed up in various costumes), we'd sometimes say jokingly, "Some people just have too much spare time." Well, that describes all of us. We waste an incredible amount of time and energy in a pursuit that is not only trivial but impossible: denying the truth. What would you call a person who truly believed that her happiness depended on achieving something impossible—say, stopping the sun from rising? You would call that person insane. We are equally insane when we think we can deny truth itself.

We are told that believing we must have the impossible to be happy violates the "principle of creation." What is that principle? I think it is the idea at the end of the eighth paragraph, which I would express this way: Because God's Will and your will are one, whatever you want has been created; whatever you don't want has not. When we want the impossible, we are violating this principle by saying we want what hasn't been created. We need to get our heads out of the sand and stop denying the facts. It's pointless to deny them; as John Adams once said, "Facts are stubborn things." We need to accept the happy fact that God is Love, and as Love, He created everything we need to be happy. The laws of happiness were created *for* us, not *by* us, and all we must do to recognize them is to cooperate with them by accepting the fact that, as Workbook Lesson 102 says, "I share God's Will for happiness for me" (W-pI.102. Heading).

> 12. Any attempt to deny what *is* must be fearful, and if the attempt is strong it <u>will</u> induce panic [Ur: Attempts of any kind to deny what *is* are fearful, and if they are strong they *will* induce panic]. <u>Willing against</u> reality, though impossible, can be <u>made</u> into a very persistent goal <u>even though you do not want it</u>. But consider the result of this strange decision. You are <u>devoting</u> your mind to what you <u>do not want</u>. How real can this devotion be? If you do not want it, it was never created. If it were [Ur: was] never created, it is nothing. Can you <u>really</u> devote yourself to nothing?

The inevitable result of trying to deny reality is *fear*. Fear has cropped up repeatedly in this section: fear of sacrifice, getting what we really want, God's abandonment and/or retaliation, learning the Course, God's Will, and ultimately our own reality. If you think about it, denial of reality inevitably leads to fear of that reality, because deep down we *know* it's reality so we can't keep it at bay forever. Like the alcoholic in denial who finds himself in the gutter, when we deny reality it has a way of rising up and biting us in the posterior. As they say, "You can run, but you can't hide."

But we don't *really* want to run or hide from our reality—it is the only thing that can make us happy. We can stubbornly tell ourselves otherwise, but deep down we know we're kidding ourselves. We know we don't want the fear that denial brings, and as the principle of creation says, "If you do not want it, it was never created." We are therefore devoted to nothing, like the emperor who had no clothes but nevertheless had the "very persistent goal" of showing them off. How long can we keep this charade up?

> 13. God in His devotion to <u>you</u> created you devoted to <u>everything</u>, and <u>gave</u> you what you are devoted *to*. Otherwise you would not have been created perfect. Reality <u>is</u> everything, and you [Ur: therefore] have everything <u>because</u> you are real. You cannot make the <u>un</u>real because the <u>absence</u> of reality is fearful, and fear cannot <u>be</u> created. As long as you believe that fear is possible, <u>you will not create</u>. Opposing orders of reality <u>make reality meaningless</u>, and reality *is* <u>meaning</u>.

The last paragraph said that trying to deny reality leads to fear, but the good news is that this fear is unreal, because fear cannot be created. It is simply an illusory effect of our futile attempt to make illusions. All the while, our reality in Heaven shines on undisturbed. Anything less than total devotion to everything would be a lack, a limit, an imperfection. This is impossible, because we were created perfect, and perfect we remain.

I love the third sentence here. There is a beautiful logic in this line that goes like this:

- Reality is everything.
- You are real.
- Therefore, you are everything.
- What you are is what you have (in Heaven, *having* and *being* are the same).
- Therefore, you have everything as well.

Can we really devote ourselves to nothing when we have everything?

> 14. Remember, then, that God's Will is <u>already</u> possible, and nothing else will <u>ever</u> be. This is the simple acceptance of reality, because only that is real. You cannot <u>distort</u> reality and <u>know what it is</u>. And if you <u>do</u> distort reality you will experience anxiety, depression and ultimately panic, because you are trying to <u>make yourself unreal</u>. When you feel these things, do not try to look <u>beyond</u> yourself for truth, for truth can only be <u>within</u> you. Say, therefore:

Christ is in me, and where He is God <u>must</u> be,
for Christ is <u>part</u> of Him.

This section began by saying that the fear of God's Will is one of the strangest beliefs we've ever come up with. It went on to say that we fear God's Will because we've convinced ourselves that our will is different from His. This is a distortion of reality. We are trying to make ourselves unreal, like the character in *The Matrix* who talked himself into being satisfied with virtual steak. But we can never be satisfied with unreality; on the contrary, trying to make ourselves into ephemeral illusions brings us nothing but "anxiety, depression, and ultimately panic." The antidote? *Accept reality.* Remember that God's Will is all there is, and therefore our will is one with His.

The section concludes with a practice to help us remember this when we are experiencing those negative emotions that come from trying to make ourselves unreal. I think the assumption behind the practice is that Christ is our reality, and He shares God's Will because He is part of God. When we believe our will is different, we're essentially saying the opposite: "Only my ego is in me, and where it is God is totally absent, for my ego and God are forever opposed." The words of the practice are meant to replace this view with the reality of our intimate union with God and His Will.

Application: Bring to mind any feelings of anxiety or depression. They show that you are denying the will you share with God and therefore trying to make yourself unreal. Dispel them by affirming your reality as Christ, using the words of the concluding practice.

II. The Answer to Prayer
Commentary by Greg Mackie

1. Everyone who ever tried to use prayer to ask for something has experienced what appears to be failure. This is not only true in connection with specific things that might be harmful, but also in connection with requests that are strictly in line with this course. The latter in particular might be incorrectly interpreted as "proof" that the course does not mean what it says. You must remember, however, that the course states, and <u>repeatedly</u>, that its purpose is the <u>escape from fear</u>.

Virtually every spiritual seeker has wrestled with the question addressed here: Why don't I always get answers to my prayers? This is an important question for those of us who walk the Course's path, because our trust in the Course is at stake. It is constantly telling us that prayers are *always* answered. (For instance, see T-6.V.4:2.) When we don't hear an answer, especially when our request is "strictly in line with this course," this seems to suggest that the author of the Course isn't being straight with us. What's going on here?

2. Let us suppose, then, that what you ask of the Holy Spirit <u>is</u> what you really want, but <u>you are still afraid of it</u>. Should this be the case, your <u>attainment</u> of it would no longer *be* what you want [Ur: even if *it* is]. This is why <u>certain specific forms</u> of healing are not achieved, even when [Ur: even though] the <u>state</u> of healing <u>is</u>. [Ur: It frequently happens that] An individual may ask [Ur: asks] for physical healing because he is fearful <u>of bodily harm</u>. [Ur: However,] At the same time, if he <u>were</u> healed physically, the threat to his thought system might be considerably <u>more</u> fearful to him than its physical <u>expression</u>. In this case he is not really asking for <u>release</u> from fear, but for the removal of a symptom that he himself selected [Ur: *which he has selected*]. This request is, therefore, <u>not</u> for healing at all.

Why do some prayers seem to fail? The short answer: because we're *afraid* of what we're asking for.

301

The example given here is asking the Holy Spirit for a miraculous healing of the body. On the surface, we think we want this with all our heart. But deeper down, we're not so sure. We're identified with the ego, so we have a huge investment in preserving its thought system—indeed, we chose our physical symptoms for this very purpose. If we experienced a miraculous spiritual healing of those symptoms, that thought system would be gravely threatened, and this threat is far more fearful to us in our ego-invested state than the physical symptoms that hold the ego in place.

Our prayers to the Holy Spirit, then, do not ask for healing wholeheartedly. They say, in essence, "Please make my physical symptoms go away, but without touching my thought system in any way." Since real healing stems from *changing* our thought system, this request isn't for healing at all. This is why our prayers for healing seem to fail.

> 3.   The Bible emphasizes that all prayer is answered [Ur: *all* prayers are answered], and this is indeed true [Ur: if no effort is wasted]. The very fact that the Holy Spirit has been asked for anything will ensure a response. Yet it is equally certain that no response given by Him will ever be one that would increase fear. It is [Ur: even] possible that His answer will not be heard [Ur: at all]. It is impossible, however, that it will be lost. There are many answers you have already received but have not yet heard. I assure you that they are waiting for you. [Ur: It is indeed true that no effort is wasted.]

The last paragraph said that our prayers can bring about the *state* of healing even if we don't experience certain specific forms of healing. How can this be? What happens is this: When we pray to the Holy Spirit for healing, that prayer is answered, since *all* prayer is answered. Deep in our minds, we are healed. But since the Course's purpose is the escape from fear, if a physical healing would threaten our thought system so much that it would terrify us, He will withhold physical healing until we are ready to receive it without fear. (This idea also appears in a Manual section that discusses the attitude the spiritual healer should take if it seems his attempt to heal another didn't work—see M-6.1-2.)

All prayers are answered. What an amazing and reassuring thought! We all have thousands of healing messages from the Holy Spirit waiting for the moment when we're no longer afraid to check our answering machine. Have you ever had a miracle that seemed to come out of nowhere, without you asking for anything? Perhaps that was one of those answers you prayed for long ago and were finally ready to receive.

4.   If you would know your prayers are answered, never doubt a Son of God. Do not question him and do not confound him, for your faith in him is your faith in <u>yourself</u>. If you would know God and His Answer, believe in me whose faith in <u>you</u> cannot be shaken. Can you ask of the Holy Spirit truly, and doubt your brother? Believe his words are true because of the truth that is in him. You will unite with the truth in him, and his words will *be* true. As you hear him you will hear me. <u>Listening</u> to truth is the only way you can hear it now, and finally <u>know</u> it.

5.   The message your brother gives you is <u>up to you</u>. What does he say to you? What would <u>you</u> have him say? Your decision <u>about</u> him determines the message <u>you</u> receive. Remember that the Holy Spirit is in him, and His Voice speaks to <u>you</u> through him. What can so holy a brother tell you <u>except</u> truth? But are you <u>listening</u> to it? Your brother may not know who he is, but there is a light in his mind that <u>does</u> know. This light can shine into yours, giving truth to <u>his</u> words and making you <u>able to hear them</u> [Ur: making *his* words true, and you *able to hear them*]. His words <u>are</u> the Holy Spirit's answer to <u>you</u>. Is your faith in him strong enough to <u>let</u> you [Ur: listen and] hear?

How do we recognize the Holy Spirit's answer to our prayers? Surprisingly, the way to hear His answer is to not doubt our brothers, to believe their words are true. Now, it's easy to believe our brothers when they're actually saying something that's true. But does this instruction mean we should regard everything that comes out of their mouths, no matter how crazy or deceitful, as literally true? When Hitler said that all the Jews should be exterminated, should our response have been, "Yes, you're absolutely right"?

I don't think so. Jesus recognizes that what someone says may be pure nonsense on the surface: "[Your brother] may be making no sense at the time, and it is certain that, if he is speaking from the ego, he will not be making sense" (T-9.III.2:5). Rather, the idea here is that even when a brother is saying senseless things that reveal his ignorance about his true nature, "there is a light in his mind that does know." He is a holy being who has the Holy Spirit in him. If we believe this, we can "unite with the truth in him, and his words will *be* true." We will hear the Holy Spirit (and Jesus) in him, and They will reveal a hidden element in his words that is true, even if on the surface the words are false. The Holy Spirit will communicate to us through him, and this is the answer to our prayers.

What does this look like in daily life? Robert recently wrote an excellent article on this topic, in which he gives examples of Jesus seeing more holy meaning in people's words than they consciously intended to convey. (I'll be sending that article to everyone.) We also see this in Jesus' reinterpretation of Bible passages, such as in T-5.VI.5-9. The original biblical writer probably intended "Vengeance is mine, saith the Lord" to mean that we should let God take revenge for us, but Jesus saw past that to the Holy Spirit's interpretation that vengeance should be given to Him to be undone. What holy truth could you hear from your brothers right now, if only you had ears to hear?

Application: Think of a brother whose words you don't always trust, someone whom you have a tendency to doubt. Say to him in your mind, *"Because I want to know my prayers are answered, I will not doubt you. I will believe your words are true because of the truth that is in you. Let me remember that the Holy Spirit is in you, and His Voice speaks to me through you. Let me hear in your words the Holy Spirit's answer to me."*

6.   You can no more pray for yourself alone than you can find joy for yourself alone. Prayer is the restatement of inclusion, directed by the Holy Spirit under the laws of God. [I don't know where these last two sentences originally came from.] Salvation is of your brother. The Holy Spirit extends from your mind to his, and answers *you*. You cannot hear the Voice for God in yourself alone, because you are <u>not</u> alone. And His answer is only for what you <u>are</u>. You will not know the trust I have in you unless you <u>extend</u> it. You will not trust the guidance of the Holy Spirit, or believe that it is for <u>you</u> unless you hear it in others. It <u>must</u> be for your brother *because* it is for you. Would God have created a Voice for you alone? Could you hear His answer <u>except</u> as He answers <u>all</u> of God's Sons? Hear of your brother what you would have me hear of <u>you</u>, for you would not want <u>me</u> to be deceived.

We all want our prayers answered, yet at the same time we see our brothers as untrustworthy. The implication is that we deserve answers to our prayers, but our devious brothers don't. We therefore seek the Holy Spirit in ourselves alone. But this will never work, because we are not alone. If our very asking assumes the ego's view of us as separate, solitary beings, how will we ever hear the Holy Spirit?

This is why we must trust our brothers—believe their words are true—if we want to hear the Holy Spirit's answer to our prayers. We will not know the trust Jesus has in us unless we extend trust to our brothers. We will not trust the Holy Spirit's guidance or feel we deserve it unless we hear Him in others. The Holy Spirit is in everyone, and His answers are thus intended for everyone. The way to hear His answer, then, is summed up in these beautiful words: "Salvation is of your brother. The Holy Spirit extends from your mind to his, and answers *you*."

The last line is great food for thought. What would you want Jesus to hear about you? Wouldn't you want him to hear the best about you, those things that reflect your goodness instead of your faults? If so, then listen only for the best in your brothers.

> 7. I love you for the truth in you, as <u>God</u> does. Your deceptions may deceive <u>you</u>, but they <u>cannot</u> deceive <u>me</u>. Knowing what you <u>are</u>, I <u>cannot</u> doubt you. I hear only the Holy Spirit in you, Who speaks to me through <u>you</u>. If you would hear <u>me</u>, hear my brothers in whom God's Voice speaks. The answer to <u>all</u> prayers lies in them. You will be answered as you <u>hear the answer in everyone</u>. Do not listen to anything else or you will not hear truly [Ur: not hear truth].
>
> 8. Believe in your brothers <u>because</u> I believe in you, and you will learn that my belief in you is justified. Believe in me *by* believing in them, for the sake of what God gave them. <u>They will answer you</u> if you learn to ask only truth of them. Do not ask for blessings without blessing <u>them</u>, for only in this way can <u>you</u> learn how blessed <u>you</u> are. By following this way you <u>are</u> seeking the truth in <u>you</u>. This is not going <u>beyond</u> yourself but <u>toward</u> yourself. Hear only God's Answer in His Sons, and <u>you</u> are answered.

Jesus is really hammering home this idea of believing in our brothers, isn't he? I find his personal call to us very moving: "Believe in your brothers because I believe in you." Jesus believes in us so completely. He loves us for the truth in us. He knows what we are. He doesn't doubt us. He hears only the Holy Spirit in us. All he asks of us is to believe in our brothers the same way. This will enable us to believe in *him*—to hear his (and the Holy Spirit's) answer to our prayers, to believe in the reality of his love and guidance, to trust him when he says his belief in us is justified. The bottom line, once again, is that we receive the gifts of the Holy Spirit by extending them to our brothers: "Do not ask for blessings without blessing them, for only in this way can you learn how blessed you are."

"This is not going beyond yourself but toward yourself." To me, this is a very important line. The Course often says that truth lies within ourselves, and many Course students take this to mean that we shouldn't look to others for salvation or guidance. After all, isn't this seeking outside ourselves? No, it isn't, because others are not outside ourselves. Hearing God's Answer in our brothers is going toward ourselves.

Application: These are beautiful paragraphs to read as Jesus' personal message to you. Read them in that way now, inserting your name at appropriate points.

> 9.   To disbelieve is to side <u>against,</u> or to <u>attack</u>. To believe is to accept, and to <u>side with</u>. To believe is not to be credulous, but to accept and <u>appreciate</u>. What you do <u>not</u> believe you do <u>not appreciate,</u> and you <u>cannot</u> be grateful for what you do not value. There is a price you will pay for judgment, because judgment <u>is</u> the setting of a price. And as you set it you <u>will</u> pay it.

To me, this paragraph offers further clarification on what it means to believe our brothers. It doesn't mean we should be "credulous," naïvely accepting everything they say as gospel truth. Rather, believing our brothers is accepting and appreciating them, recognizing their infinite worth and being grateful for it. Anything else is an attack, a judgment of them for which we will pay a price. The next few paragraphs will say more about this.

> 10.   If paying is equated with <u>getting,</u> you will set the <u>price</u> low but demand a high <u>return</u>. You will have forgotten, however, that to price is to <u>value</u>, so that <u>your</u> return is <u>in proportion to your judgment of worth</u>. If paying is associated with giving <u>it cannot be perceived as loss,</u> and the <u>reciprocal</u> relationship of giving and <u>receiving</u> will be recognized.

The price will then be set high, because of the value of the <u>return</u>. The price for <u>getting</u> is to <u>lose sight of value</u>, making it inevitable that you will <u>not</u> value what you receive. Valuing it little, you will not appreciate it and you will not <u>want</u> it.

11. Never forget, then, that <u>you</u> [Ur: have] set the value on what you receive, and price [Ur: have priced] it [set the value on it] <u>by</u> what you give. To believe that it is possible to get much <u>for</u> little is to believe that you can bargain with God. God's laws are <u>always</u> fair and <u>perfectly</u> consistent. <u>By</u> giving you receive. But to receive is to <u>accept,</u> <u>not</u> to get.

Jesus now seems to launch into a discussion of economics that has little to do with believing in our brothers, but really has everything to do with it.

Two options are contrasted here. The first option is "paying…equated with getting." This assumes we are lacking and must therefore pay in order to get something from others to fill our lack. Yet precisely because we are lacking, we will try to pay as little as we can. This is what we all do with money, isn't it? We clip coupons, shop around, and try to get the best deal, which means to "get much for little."

The second option is "paying…associated with giving." This assumes we are not lacking, but are flush with the gifts of God. We "pay" these gifts to others not to *get* something to fill our lacks, but because we recognize that giving is receiving, and therefore giving to others will enable us to *accept* what we already have.

Now let's apply this to the current context. When we disbelieve a brother, we're judging him. We're essentially saying he is worthless. We "set the price" on this brother low by giving very little and very grudgingly to him, and demanding a high return on our investment— he'd better be good to us! However, because we're giving so little and giving is receiving, we will receive little and not value what we get. This is the price we pay for judgment: we lose sight of the infinite value of our brothers and therefore feel deprived ourselves. When we trust a brother, though, we're seeing his great worth. We "set the price" on him high by giving the gifts of God lavishly to him. Now we actually will get a high return on our investment. Because we're giving so much and giving is receiving, we will receive gifts of infinite value from him, gifts we will appreciate just as we appreciate him.

It is impossible not to <u>have,</u> but it <u>is</u> possible <u>not to know you have</u>. The recognition of <u>having</u> is the willingness for <u>giving</u>, and <u>only</u> by this willingness can you <u>recognize</u> what you have. What you give is therefore the value you put on what you have, being the exact measure of the value you <u>put</u> upon it. And this, in turn, is the measure of <u>how much you want it</u>.

The punch line of this discussion is the first sentence of the eleventh paragraph, which I would paraphrase this way: We set the value on what we receive from our brothers by what we give to them. The more we give to them, the more we will value what we receive from them and the more we will recognize what we have. These concluding lines continue in the same vein: The way to recognize what we have is to give. Therefore, if we don't give, it must mean that we don't want to recognize what we have, because we don't value it. Conversely, our giving is the sign that we value the gifts God has given us and thus want to experience them in full awareness.

12. You can <u>ask</u> of the Holy Spirit, then, <u>only</u> by giving <u>to</u> Him, and you can <u>give</u> to Him only <u>where you</u> recognize [Ur: *see*] <u>Him.</u> If you recognize [Ur: *see*] Him in everyone, consider how much you will be <u>asking of</u> Him, and <u>how much you will receive</u>. He will deny you nothing because you have denied Him nothing, and so you can <u>share everything</u>. This is the way, and the <u>only</u> way to have His answer, because His answer is all you can ask for and <u>want</u>. Say, then, to everyone:

> *Because I will to know myself, I see you as God's*
> *Son and my brother.*

We conclude with some final counsel on the topic of this section: the answer to prayer. How can we recognize the Holy Spirit's answer to our prayers? By giving to Him. How do we give to Him? By giving to our brothers in whom He abides. How do we give to our brothers? By recognizing Him in them, recognizing that they are God's Sons along with us. When we see them as they truly are, we will come to know who we truly are.

Application: Think of someone you are seeing as untrustworthy and worthless, and say the words of the closing practice to him, recognizing that by so doing you will receive the answer to your prayers and come to know who you truly are: *"Because I will to know myself, I see you, [name], as God's Son and my brother."*

III. The Correction of Error
Commentary by Greg Mackie

1.   The alertness of the ego to the errors of other egos is <u>not</u> the kind of vigilance the Holy Spirit would have you maintain. Egos are critical in terms of the kind of "sense" they <u>stand for</u>. <u>They</u> understand this kind of sense, because it <u>is</u> sensible to them. To the Holy Spirit it makes no sense at all.

The Holy Spirit wants us to be vigilant only for God and His Kingdom (T-6.V(C).2:8)—vigilant for the truth and holiness in everyone and everything. Unfortunately, we're too busy being vigilant for other people's screwups. Our egos love to judge how well others measure up to our standards, standards which make such perfect sense to us that we think they're patently obvious. "Everybody knows that you should call before coming over." "How could you have voted for that guy?" "You idiot, use your turn signal!" We place so much importance on getting people to behave the way we want. But to the Holy Spirit, Who doesn't evaluate people on the basis of behavior at all, this is complete nonsense.

2.   To the ego it is kind and right and good to point out errors and "correct" them. This makes <u>perfect</u> sense to the ego, which is [Ur: *totally*] unaware of what errors <u>are</u> and what correction <u>is</u>. Errors <u>are</u> of the ego, and <u>correction</u> of errors [Ur: of *any* kind] lies [Ur: solely] in the <u>relinquishment</u> of the ego. When you <u>correct</u> a brother, you are telling him that he is <u>wrong</u>. He may be making no sense at the time, and it is certain that, if he is speaking from the ego, he <u>will</u> not be making sense. But your task is still to tell him <u>he is right</u>. You do not tell him this verbally, if he is <u>speaking</u> foolishly [Ur: because] He needs correction <u>at another level</u>, because [Ur: since] his error <u>is</u> at another level. <u>He</u> is still right, because he is a Son of God. His ego is <u>always</u> wrong, no matter <u>what</u> it says or does.

To the ego, errors are specific words and behaviors that don't measure up to its standards, so correction is putting a stop to those words and behaviors. But to the Holy Spirit, the only error that matters is the very

belief we are egos, so correction is the total relinquishment of the ego—
the recognition that everyone is a holy Son of God.

These definitions lead to very different ways of dealing with error.
The ego's way is to tell our brothers that they're wrong. The Holy
Spirit's way is to tell them that while their *egos* are wrong, *they* are right.
This doesn't mean we verbally tell them this when they're spouting
nonsense. As I said in a previous commentary, when Hitler said the Jews
should be exterminated, the Course wouldn't have had us say, "Yes,
you're absolutely right." The real error isn't on the level of particular
words or behaviors, but in their source: the ego. Therefore, our job is to
communicate to our brothers in some way that they are *not* egos, that
they are right in the way that really matters: they are Sons of God.

> 3.   If you point out the errors of your brother's ego you <u>must</u> be seeing
> through yours, because the Holy Spirit <u>does not perceive his errors</u>.
> This *must* be true, since [Ur: if] there is no communication [Ur: *at all*]
> between the ego and the Holy Spirit. The ego makes <u>no</u> sense, and the
> Holy Spirit does not attempt to understand <u>anything</u> that arises from
> it. Since He does not understand it, He <u>does not judge it,</u> <u>knowing</u> that
> nothing the ego makes [Ur: nothing it engenders] <u>means anything</u>.

The main point of this paragraph is clearly expressed in the first
sentence. Yet how does the idea that "the Holy Spirit does not perceive
his errors" square with other Course passages like the following: "In
time, the Holy Spirit clearly sees the Son of God can make mistakes.
On this you share His vision" (T-19.III.5:1-2)? I think when this section
says the Holy Spirit doesn't see error and neither should we, it means the
Holy Spirit doesn't see error *as real* and neither should we. A passage
from *The Song of Prayer* says this very thing: "*Do not see error.* Do not
make it real. Select the loving and forgive the sin by choosing in its place
the face of Christ" (S-2.I.3:3-5). Not seeing error means not seeing it as
a real "sin" that must be understood, judged, and pointed out. Instead, we
should look past the senseless errors of the ego to the face of Christ in
our brothers, the reality within them that is always right.

> 4.   When you react <u>at all</u> to errors, you are <u>not listening to the Holy</u>
> <u>Spirit</u>. He has merely disregarded them, and if you <u>attend to</u> them you
> are <u>not hearing Him</u>. If you do not hear <u>Him</u>, you are listening to <u>your</u>

ego and making as little sense as the brother whose errors you perceive. This <u>cannot</u> be correction. Yet it is more than merely a lack of correction for him. It is the <u>giving up</u> of correction in <u>yourself</u>.

Have you ever noticed how easy it is to get angry at others for getting angry? That kind of fighting ego *with* ego is the focus here. We think our brothers are listening to their egos and therefore making no sense at all. This may well be true. The irony, though, is that our typical judgmental reaction to their errors comes from our egos, so our "correction" is just our version of the same error. It's as if someone said "Three plus two is six," and you responded with "No, that's wrong, you idiot! Actually, two plus three is six." The bad news is that this response ensures that neither our brothers' errors nor ours will be truly corrected.

> 5.   When a brother behaves insanely, you can heal him <u>only</u> by perceiving the <u>sanity</u> in him. If you perceive his errors and <u>accept</u> them, you are accepting <u>yours</u>. If you want to give <u>yours</u> over to the Holy Spirit, you must do this with <u>his</u>. Unless this becomes the <u>one</u> way in which you handle <u>all</u> errors, you cannot understand <u>how all errors are undone</u>. How is this different from telling you that what you teach you <u>learn</u>? Your brother is as right as you are, and if you think he is <u>wrong</u> you are condemning <u>yourself</u>.

We see here why our false correction of our brothers leads to giving up of correction in ourselves. Whatever we *teach* our brothers about their nature, we will *learn* about our nature. If we accept that their errors are real, we will accept that our errors are real. If we condemn our brothers by seeing them as error-prone egos, we will condemn ourselves for the same thing. But if we give their errors over to the Holy Spirit, we will do the same with ours. If we see our brothers as right because they are Sons of God, we will see that the same thing is true about us.

Application: The first sentence is one worth memorizing and practicing frequently. Think of someone you know who has been behaving inappropriately. Notice how much you want to point it out and get this person in line. Now silently repeat these words to this person: *"When you, [name], behave insanely, I can heal you only by perceiving the sanity in you."*

6.   *You* cannot correct <u>yourself</u>. Is it possible, then, for you to correct another? Yet you <u>can</u> see him truly, because it <u>is</u> possible for you to see <u>yourself</u> truly. It is not up to you to <u>change</u> your brother, but merely to accept him <u>as he is</u>. His errors do not come from the truth that is in him, and <u>only</u> this truth is yours. His errors cannot change this, and can have no effect at all on the truth in <u>you</u>. To perceive errors in anyone, and to <u>react</u> to them <u>as if they were real,</u> is to <u>make</u> them real to you. You will not escape paying the price for this, <u>not</u> because you are being <u>punished</u> for it, but because you are following the wrong guide and will therefore lose your way.

"To perceive errors in anyone, and to react to them as if they were real, is to make them real to you." As I mentioned in the paragraph 3 commentary, the problem is not so much noticing that errors occur— people do speak foolishly and behave insanely—but rather *making them real*, seeing them as sins that corrupt our brothers' very nature. The price we pay for this is that we will see ourselves as equally corrupt. The antidote is to see our brothers as they truly are: holy Sons of God whose nature is completely unaffected by any errors they may make. This will enable us to see ourselves the same way.

Application: Think of the same person that you used earlier (or a different one if you like). Then say these words to him or her: *"It is not up to me to change you, [name], but merely to accept you as you are. Your errors are not part of who you are. They cannot change the truth in you, and have no effect at all on the truth in me."*

7.   Your brother's errors are not of him, any more than yours are <u>of</u> <u>you</u>. Accept his errors as real, and you have attacked <u>yourself</u>. If you would find <u>your</u> way <u>and keep it,</u> see only truth beside you for you walk together. The Holy Spirit in you forgives all things in you <u>and</u> in your brother. <u>His</u> errors are forgiven <u>with</u> yours. Atonement is no more separate than love. Atonement <u>cannot</u> be separate because it <u>comes</u> from love. <u>Any</u> attempt you make to correct a brother means that you believe correction by <u>you</u> is possible, and this can <u>only</u> be the arrogance of the ego. Correction is of God, Who does not know of arrogance.
8.   The Holy Spirit forgives everything <u>because God created</u> <u>everything</u>. Do not undertake <u>His</u> function, or you will forget <u>yours</u>.

Accept <u>only</u> the function of healing in time, because that is what time is <u>for</u>. <u>God</u> gave you the function to create in eternity. You do not need to learn that, but you <u>do</u> need to learn to <u>want</u> it. For that all learning was made. This is the Holy Spirit's use of an ability [learning] that you do not need, but that you made. Give it to Him! You do <u>not</u> understand [Ur: know] how to use it. He will teach you how to see <u>yourself</u> without condemnation, by learning how to look on <u>everything</u> without it. Condemnation will then not be real to you, and all <u>your</u> errors <u>will</u> be forgiven.

As the section concludes, Jesus summarizes his counsel to us about the correction of error. Don't accept your brothers' errors as real, because to do so is to attack yourself. Don't take on the function of correcting your brothers, because to do so is arrogant and will cause you to forget your true function. Instead, give over the function of correction to the One Whose function it is: the Holy Spirit. He will correct both you and your brothers through *forgiving* errors. He will enable you to fulfill your true function on earth: healing through perceiving your brothers truly. "He will teach you how to see yourself without condemnation, by learning how to look on everything without it." When you forgive all your brothers' errors, all your own errors will be forgiven, and you will be restored to your function of creation in eternity.

How do we really live this section? Its teaching sounds very simple and direct, but I think actually living it requires careful discernment. It can easily be abused. Some Course students take the section's counsel as an absolute behavioral injunction against correcting our brothers. Ironically, this view often leads people to silence anyone who disagrees with them with the statement: "The Course says you shouldn't correct your brother." Of course, this statement in itself is a correction of a brother, a violation of the injunction.

The section certainly confronts our addiction to fault-finding, but does it really mean that it is *never* appropriate to correct a brother? I don't think so. Jesus corrected Helen and Bill, and he corrects us on virtually every page of the Course. There are many ordinary situations where correction is warranted and desired, such as when a person is about to step into the path of an oncoming truck. Correction is often appropriate and even vital when one is in a legitimate mentoring role such as parent, therapist, or teacher. Indeed, the Course itself says (in the context of spiritual teaching and psychotherapy) that "It may help someone to point out where he is heading" (T-9.V.7:2), and it speaks approvingly of correcting a child's misperception of the objects in his room as terrifying monsters (see T-11. VIII.13). And discussing disagreements in a non-attacking spirit, rooted in the mutual quest for truth, can be totally appropriate. Jesus spoke approvingly of an intellectual debate Helen had with her colleague Jack, saying that "The virtue lay in the complete respect each of your offered to the other's intellect." I think discussing disagreements in this way is actually far healthier than silencing them with misused teachings from the Course.

How, then, do we really live this section? I think we do two things. First, with the Holy Spirit's help, we practice to truly attain the mindset the section advocates. We must truly see past our brothers' errors to their inherent rightness, their sanity, the Son of God in them. Second, we ask the Holy Spirit for specific guidance about how to behaviorally address our brothers' errors. I'm sure that if we're really listening to Him, we'll point out errors far less frequently than we do now, yet He will also let us know when it is appropriate. I think there is a real art of discernment to this: we could err both by claiming our egoic finger-pointing is "guided" and by being so afraid to correct that we don't do it when we actually *are* guided. But if we try our best to see our brothers truly and let the Holy Spirit guide our behavior, we can learn a whole new way to respond to our brothers' errors.

Note: I have written another article on this section entitled "Never Correct a Brother's Error?" It can be accessed on the Circle's website at www.circleofa.org/articles/NeverCorrect.php.

IV. The Holy Spirit's Plan of Forgiveness
Commentary by Robert Perry

This section follows on the previous, which said that we shouldn't see ourselves as the heroic corrector of our brother's errors. This one says that, instead, we must overlook those errors. This section is the beginning of the Course's real teaching on forgiveness. Up until this point, forgiveness has been mentioned only 22 times (four of those in the last two paragraphs of the preceding section). This section, then, begins the recurring exposition of the central teaching of the Course.

> 1.   Atonement is for all, because it is the way to <u>undo</u> the belief that <u>anything</u> is for you <u>alone</u>. To forgive is to <u>overlook</u>. Look, then, <u>beyond</u> error and do not let your perception rest <u>upon</u> it, for you will believe what your perception <u>holds</u>. Accept as true only what your brother <u>is,</u> if you would know yourself. Perceive what he is <u>not</u> and you <u>cannot</u> know what you are, <u>because</u> you see <u>him</u> falsely. Remember always that your Identity is shared, and that Its sharing <u>is</u> Its reality.

The goal is to remember our Identity, yet this Identity is shared, and therefore we remember It by seeing It in our brother. How do we do that? We forgive him. Yet this is not the conventional meaning of "forgive." We forgive him by not letting our perception rest on his error, by not dwelling on his error, but by instead seeing beyond it to the truth in him. The rest of this section will elaborate on this key notion.

> 2.   You have a <u>part</u> to play in the Atonement, but the plan of the Atonement <u>is</u> beyond you. You do not understand how to <u>overlook</u> errors, or you would not make them. It would merely be further error to believe either that you do <u>not</u> make them, or that you can <u>correct</u> them without a <u>Guide to correction</u>. And if you do not <u>follow</u> this Guide, your errors will <u>not</u> be corrected. The plan is not yours <u>because</u> of your limited ideas about <u>what you are</u>. This sense of [Ur: But this] limitation <u>is</u> where <u>all errors arise</u>. The way to <u>undo</u> them, therefore, is not *of* you but *for* you.

We each have our own part to play in the Atonement, but the essence of that part is the overlooking of our brothers' errors, and we frankly don't know how to do that. Surely we've learned that much by now. It's as if Jesus said, "You have an important role to play in my plan. The essence of it is this: Whatever you do, don't look at or even think about that 8-foot, 500 lb. naked person walking across the street right now." We would quite naturally respond, "I don't think I can do that." And that is why we need help, why we need to constantly rely on a Guide Who *does* know how to overlook error.Reliance on this Guide can only take place out of a profound respect for just how error-bound we are. Notice all the things Jesus says we need to admit in this paragraph: that we make errors, that we can't correct them without a Guide, that we don't know how to overlook them in others. Are we willing to admit all this? All of these errors are simply the natural product of believing we are separate and limited. Thus, as long as we have that belief, errors will be inevitable, and we'll need to just accept that and turn to our Guide.

Application: Say to the Holy Spirit,

I admit that I make errors.
I acknowledge that I don't know how to correct them.
I concede that I don't know how to overlook my brothers' errors.
Holy Spirit, I turn to You as my Guide.

3.   The Atonement is a lesson in sharing, which is given you because *you have forgotten how to do it.* The Holy Spirit merely reminds you of the natural use of your abilities [Ur: of what is your *natural* ability]. By reinterpreting the ability to attack [Ur: which you *did* make,] into the ability to share, He translates what you have made into what God created. [Ur: But] If you would accomplish this through Him you cannot look on your abilities through the eyes of the ego, or you will judge them as *it* does. All their harmfulness lies in the ego's judgment. All their helpfulness lies in the judgment of the Holy Spirit.

Attack is the opposite of sharing. Yet there is an underlying commonality. In attack, you take an idea in your mind and try to get this idea (forcibly) into your brother's mind. If you think he is a jerk, you try to force him to share this demeaning conviction. If you look closely enough, however, this scenario contains the essence of sharing, for sharing is taking an idea that is in your mind and giving it to your brother, so that both of you now share it. For this reason, an aggressive salesman who is only bent on pushing the idea "buy this!" into his brother's mind actually has great potential for sharing. Under the Holy Spirit's training, he could become a real expert in sharing, if only he would grow up.

That is the position we are in. Like preschoolers, we have forgotten how to share. But in our ability to attack lies the actual potential to share, a potential the Holy Spirit can draw out. What are we supposed to share? Our Identity.

> 4.   The ego, too, has a plan of forgiveness because you are <u>asking</u> for one, though not of the right teacher. The <u>ego's</u> plan, of course, <u>makes no sense</u> and <u>will not work</u>. By following its plan you will merely place yourself in an impossible situation, to which the ego <u>always</u> leads you. The ego's plan is to have you <u>see error clearly first</u>, and <u>then</u> overlook it. Yet how <u>can</u> you overlook what you have made real? By seeing it clearly, you <u>have</u> made it real and *cannot* overlook it. This is where the ego is forced to appeal to "mysteries," insisting [Ur: and begins to insist] that you must accept the meaningless to save yourself. Many have tried to do this in my name, forgetting that my words make <u>perfect</u> sense because they come from <u>God</u>. They are as sensible now as they ever were, because they speak of ideas that are eternal.

I had an exchange some years ago with one of the leaders of the current forgiveness movement in the psychological community. I began our dialogue by saying that a fruitful direction for forgiveness work might be to have people focus on changing their perception of the person they were trying to forgive. I said that being free of resentment toward this person was inconsistent with seeing him or her as a sinner who had actually wounded them and deserved punishment. Thinking these two things would go together (*freedom* from resentment and seeing the other person as *deserving* resentment) didn't make sense. He dismissed the idea and said that I was engaging in brittle either/or thinking. I needed to broaden my mind enough to make room for paradox.

This exchange reflects the essence of this paragraph. How can you first dwell on someone's error as real (which leads to resentment) and then free yourself of this resentment by acting as if it's not there (which is what is normally called forgiveness)? Proponents of this view may say, "Aah, it's a paradox, a mystery. It's like the unity of the yin and the yang." But the plain fact is that the mind rebels when trying to carry out this mystery. It thinks, "If this guy really deserves my resentment, how can I not feel it?"

> 5.   Forgiveness that is learned of <u>me</u> does not use fear to <u>undo</u> fear. Nor does it make real the <u>un</u>real and then destroy it. Forgiveness through the Holy Spirit lies simply in looking beyond error from the beginning, and thus <u>keeping</u> it unreal for you. Do not let any belief in its realness enter your mind [Ur: *at all*], or you will also believe that you must <u>undo</u> what you have made in order to <u>be</u> forgiven. What has no effect does not exist, and to the Holy Spirit the effects of error are [Ur: *totally*] nonexistent. By steadily and consistently cancelling out <u>all</u> its effects, <u>everywhere and in all respects,</u> He teaches that the ego does not exist and <u>proves</u> it.

"Looking beyond error from the beginning" does not mean that you don't notice that your husband is drinking himself to death. It means that you constantly remind yourself that that's not who he is. You don't dwell on the error as the definer of his identity. If you do, you will see your errors as the definers of *your* identity.

This doesn't mean you don't observe error or deal with it. Therefore, what you need is to maintain a dual state of mind. You have to be observing and dealing with a world of effects while constantly reminding yourself that none of it is real, none of it defines the identity of those involved. You have to remind yourself that even while the effects are being produced, the Holy Spirit is cancelling out their reality, leaving them hollow images with no actual core.

Application: Think of someone whose errors you've been dwelling on lately, and say,

> *I will not let my perception rest on [name's] errors.*
> *I will not let any belief in their realness enter my mind.*
> *I look past them to who [name] really is.*
> *I want to see our shared Identity.*

> 6.   Follow the Holy Spirit's teaching in forgiveness, then, because forgiveness is His function and He knows how to fulfill it perfectly. That is what I meant when I said that miracles are natural, and when they do not occur something has gone wrong. Miracles are merely the sign of your willingness to follow the Holy Spirit's plan of salvation, recognizing [Ur: in recognition of the *fact*] that you do not understand [Ur: know] what it is. His work is not your function, and unless you accept this you cannot learn what your function is.

Miracles are the result of forgiveness. When Jesus said that miracles are natural, and when they do not occur something has gone wrong (miracle principle #6), he didn't mean that we would *experience* them as a natural expression of our separate will. Rather, he meant that something already *has* gone wrong, making miracles seem deeply *unnatural* to us. However, they are perfectly natural to the Holy Spirit, and we can follow Him. That is how miracles become natural to us, and how forgiveness does, too. Yet unless we admit that we need Him, we will not learn how to forgive and will therefore not fulfill our function of being miracle workers.

> 7.   The confusion of functions is so typical of the ego that you should be quite familiar with it by now. The ego believes that all functions belong to it, even though it has no idea what they are. This is more than mere confusion. It is a particularly dangerous combination of grandiosity and confusion that makes the ego likely to attack anyone and anything for no reason at all. This is exactly what the ego does. It is unpredictable in its responses, because it has no idea of what it perceives [Ur: *what* it heard].

When we think, "I (by myself, without the Holy Spirit's help) know how to overlook error and perform miracles," we are listening to the grandiose voice of our ego. In making this claim, our ego is like a tyrant who is utterly confused about how to actually run a country, but who, in his arrogance, thinks that no function is too big for him. He doesn't at all understand the cues he gets from his country, and so has no real idea how to respond. He responds, therefore, purely from his grandiosity. He acts boldly and blindly, not caring what gets in his way. He is like a rampaging elephant, trampling people right and left, all in the name of saving his country.

This familiar image is actually an image of us when we think we can heal our brothers and save the world without being a follower of the Holy Spirit.

> 8.   If you have [Ur: If one has] no idea what is happening, how appropriately can you expect [Ur: *expect* him] to react? You [Ur: But you still] might ask yourself, regardless of how you may <u>account</u> for the reaction, whether its unpredictability places [Ur: *account* for the reactions, whether they place] the ego in a sound position as your guide [Ur: as a guide for *yours*]. Let me repeat [Ur: It seems absurd to have to emphasize repeatedly] that the ego's qualifications as a guide are singularly unfortunate, and that it is a remarkably poor choice as a teacher of salvation. [Ur: Yet this question, ridiculous as it seems, is *really* the crucial issue in the whole separation fantasy.] Anyone who elects a totally insane guide <u>must</u> be totally insane himself. Nor is it true that you do not realize [Ur: know] the guide is insane. You realize it because I realize it [Ur: *You* know it because I know it], and you <u>have</u> judged it by the same standard I have.

In our day-to-day lives, we are following that tyrant I described above, the tyrant within. And he *is* blind, and unpredictable, and completely insane. And deep down inside—or perhaps not so deep down—we *know* he's insane. We see the results of following him. We see the ruin he has brought to the country of our mind. We have decided repeatedly to impeach him and throw him out of office. Yet we haven't followed through. Why are we still following this guy? Why don't we act?

> 9.   The ego literally lives on borrowed time, and <u>its</u> days <u>are</u> numbered. Do not fear the Last Judgment, but welcome it and do not wait, for the ego's time is "borrowed" from <u>your</u> eternity. This <u>is</u> the Second Coming that was made <u>for</u> you as the First was created. The Second Coming is merely the return of <u>sense</u>. Can this <u>possibly</u> be fearful?

As with all tyrants, this tyrant's days are numbered. There *will* be a day of reckoning. At some point we will, with ruthless dispassion, evaluate his time in office, and kick the bum out. This, as we saw at the end of Chapter 2, is the Course's notion of the Last Judgment—a judgment we ourselves carry out on our own beliefs. And this will lead to the Second Coming, not the second coming of Jesus in the sky, but of

Christ in our mind. This Second Coming is analogous to the liberation of a country from a tyrant. It is the return of sense to a mind formerly ruled by an insane ego. It is our own personal independence day. We, therefore, should ask ourselves, just as Jesus asks us here: "Can this possibly be fearful?"

> 10.   What can be fearful but fantasy, and who turns to fantasy unless he despairs of finding satisfaction in reality? Yet it is <u>certain</u> that you will <u>never</u> find satisfaction in fantasy, so that your <u>only</u> hope is to change your mind about <u>reality</u>. Only if the decision that reality is fearful is <u>wrong</u> can <u>God</u> be right. And I <u>assure</u> you that God *is* right. Be glad, then, that you <u>have</u> been wrong, but this was only because you did not know who you <u>were</u>. Had you known [Ur: *remembered*], you could no more have been wrong than God can.

Strangely, we fear the day of losing our ego, the day that sanity returns. Sanity seems fearful because we think reality (true reality) can never satisfy us. Thus, we have retreated into fantasies, hoping to find satisfaction there. Yet, as we all know, fantasies never satisfy, for the simple reason that *they are fantasies*. Our only hope is to decide that we've been wrong, that reality is infinitely satisfying. Being wrong need not humiliate us, though, because the only reason we were wrong is that we did not know who we are. If we had known, we could only have been right. It is our nature to be as right as God.

> 11.   The impossible can happen <u>only</u> in fantasy. When you search for reality in fantasies you will not find it. The symbols of fantasy are of the ego, and of <u>these</u> you will find many. But do not look for meaning in them. They have no more meaning than the fantasies into which they are woven. Fairy tales can be pleasant or fearful, [Ur: pretty or ugly,] but <u>no one</u> calls them <u>true</u>. Children may believe them, and so, for a while, the tales <u>are</u> true for them. Yet when reality dawns, the fantasies are gone. <u>Reality</u> has <u>not</u> gone in the meanwhile. The Second Coming is the awareness of reality, not its <u>return</u>.
> 12.   Behold, my child, reality is here. It belongs to you and me and God, and is perfectly satisfying to all of us. Only <u>this</u> awareness heals, because it is the awareness of truth.

Read in context, I believe paragraph 11 is specifically about trying to find the reality of our *brothers* in their *errors*. Since those errors are not true, this amounts to trying to find reality in fantasies. In other words, when you look at your brothers' errors, realize you are looking at the symbols of the ego. You are looking at fairy tales. Thinking that you are seeing the reality of your brothers in their errors amounts to believing in a fairy tale.

Application: Think of someone you have had trouble forgiving. If this person was in a fairy tale, what character would he or she be? An ogre? A wicked king? A thief? A witch? Then repeat the following lines, filling in the blanks:

> *Once upon a time, there was a [name the character—ogre, thief, etc.] named [give the person's name].*
> *But I do not believe in fairy tales.*
> *I want only [name's] reality.*
> *Reality belongs to me and is perfectly satisfying.*

Note: The notion of making our brothers' errors real by dwelling on them is what the Course actually means by the phrase "making error real." The oft-quoted idea of "making *the* error real"—meaning, making the *separation* real by focusing on outwardly joining with others, helping others, or fixing the world—is not found in the Course. So if anyone says to you, "Hey, that's making the error real," be confident that that idea is not in the Course. It is part of what we call Course lore. You might want to see Greg Mackie's article on this at: http://www.circleofa.org/articles/error_real.htm.

V. The Unhealed Healer
Commentary by Robert Perry

I have always felt that this is a very important section. It shows the ego's plan for forgiveness at work in the therapist and in the theologian, and it tells us something of the Course's philosophy of how to be a true healer.

> 1.   The ego's plan for forgiveness is far more widely used than God's. This is because it is undertaken by unhealed healers, and <u>is</u> therefore of the ego. Let us consider the unhealed healer more carefully now. By definition, he is trying to <u>give</u> what he has <u>not</u> received. If an unhealed healer is a theologian, for example, he may begin with the premise, "I am a miserable sinner, and so are you." If he is a psychotherapist, he is more likely to start with the equally incredible belief that attack is real for both himself and the patient, but that it does not matter for either of them [Ur: the equally incredible idea that *he* really believes in attack [in attacking], and so does the patient, but it does not matter in *either* case].

This section is obviously following on the previous section's discussion of the ego's plan of forgiveness vs. the Holy Spirit's. The ego's plan (which, as one would expect, is "far more widely used"), is to make someone's errors real, but then find some way to "forgive" them. Both the theologian and the therapist follow this plan in different forms. They don't really give forgiveness, and they can't, because they haven't really received it. Indeed, as unhealed healers, by definition they are trying to give what they don't have (healing).

The therapist's error as stated in the final sentence (Urtext version—the published version obscures the meaning) is crucial to understand. Based on earlier, related discussions, we can understand the therapist's stance as this: "So your mind is full of attack thoughts? Mine is too, but that's OK. After all, they're just thoughts. They don't really matter." This is meant to make the patient feel forgiven. Yet, as we'll see, it doesn't work.

2.   I have repeatedly said that beliefs of the ego <u>cannot</u> be shared, and <u>this is why they are</u> unreal [Ur: *not real*]. How, then, can "<u>uncovering</u>" them <u>make</u> them real? Every healer who searches fantasies for truth <u>must</u> be unhealed, because he <u>does not know where to look for truth</u>, and therefore does not have the answer to the problem of healing.

3.   There <u>is</u> an advantage to bringing nightmares into awareness, but <u>only</u> to teach that they are <u>not</u> real, and that <u>anything</u> they contain is meaningless. The unhealed healer cannot <u>do</u> this because he does not <u>believe</u> it.

What does this talk about nightmares and fantasies mean? In the previous section, trying to find the truth in fantasies meant trying to find the truth of who your brother is within his errors, which are part of "the whole separation fantasy." Here, it is the same basic idea, but is specifically about the therapist (who is clearly Freudian). He searches the patient's nightmares and fantasies to try to "uncover" the ego beliefs that are really driving him. The problem with this is that once the therapist finds those ego beliefs, he says, "Now we know who you really are." This, of course, implies that who you are is an ego. Just as in the previous section, the therapist has looked for his brother's reality within his errors. The Course, in contrast, also tries to uncover our ego beliefs, but only in order to teach us that they are *not* who we are.

All unhealed healers follow the ego's plan for forgiveness in one form or another. If they are theologians they are likely to condemn <u>themselves,</u> <u>teach</u> condemnation and advocate a fearful solution. Projecting condemnation onto God, they make Him appear retaliative, and <u>fear His retribution</u>. What they have done is merely to <u>identify</u> with the ego, and by perceiving what <u>it</u> does, condemn <u>themselves</u> because of this [Ur: profound] confusion. It is understandable that there have been revolts [Ur: has been a revolt] against this concept, but to revolt <u>against</u> it is still to <u>believe</u> in it. [Ur: The *form* of the revolt, then, is different, but *not* the content.]

Now Jesus discusses the theologian. As he looks at what his ego does, the theologian concludes that he is clearly "a miserable sinner," because he thinks he *is* his ego. He also concludes the same thing about those he is trying to help. He then says, "The only way that we can be forgiven is by some magical procedure that will save us from God's wrath"—a magical procedure that is fearful because it involves making sacrifices to God.

Modern therapy is, according to Jesus, a revolt against this approach. It wants to cure the soul in a whole different way, or does it? For we wouldn't need to revolt against it unless we felt it still had power, and we only believe that ideas have power when we still believe *them*. Thus, even though the new form has effectively overthrown the old, it carries within it a *belief* in the old. It therefore carries the same content; only the form is different. This, of course, is true of political revolts as well as intellectual revolts. As Pete Townsend said, "Meet the new boss, same as the old boss."

> 4. Some newer forms [Ur: The new form] of the ego's plan are [Ur: is] as unhelpful as the older ones [Ur: one], because form does not matter [Ur: to the Holy Spirit, and therefore *does not matter at all.*] and the content has not changed [this final phrase was apparently added by the editors]. In one of [Ur: According to] the newer forms, for example ["for example" was added by the editors], a psychotherapist may interpret the ego's symbols <u>in</u> a nightmare, and then use them to <u>prove</u> that <u>the nightmare is real</u>. Having <u>made</u> it real, he then attempts to dispel its <u>effects</u> by <u>depreciating the importance of the dreamer</u>. This <u>would</u> be a healing approach if the <u>dreamer</u> were also [Ur: were properly] identified <u>as unreal</u>. Yet if the dreamer is equated <u>with</u> the mind, the mind's corrective power through the Holy Spirit is <u>denied</u>. [Ur: It is noteworthy that] This is a contradiction even in the ego's terms, and one which it usually notes [Ur: *does* note] even in its confusion.

Now we get a description of the new form: psychotherapy (specifically, Freudian analysis). Here, the therapist interprets the ego's symbols in a nightmare as the way to unlock who the patient is. This effectively makes the nightmare real. But then the therapist says, "It's OK. Don't worry about that ugly thing in your mind that produced that dream. It doesn't matter. As long as you don't act it out, then it's unimportant. Therefore, you don't need to feel guilty about it." This would be fine if the ugly thing that produced the dream—the ego—were also said to be unreal. But otherwise, the therapist has just disempowered the mind, the only thing that can bring correction.

Early in the Urtext, Jesus spoke of this exact same thing:

Therapists try to help people who are afraid of their own death wishes by depreciating the power of the wish. They even attempt to "free" the patient by persuading him that he can think whatever he wants, without *any* real effect at all…. This is the usual psychoanalytic approach. This *does* allay guilt, but at the cost of rendering thinking impotent.

5. If the way to counteract fear is to reduce the importance of the mind [Ur: of the *fearer*], how can this build ego <u>strength</u>? Such [Ur: These perfectly] evident inconsistencies account for why [Ur: except for certain stylized verbal accounts,] no one has really explained what happens in psychotherapy. Nothing really <u>does</u>. Nothing real has happened to the unhealed healer, and he must learn [Ur: *he learns*] <u>from his own teaching</u>. His ego [Ur: *Because* his ego is involved, it] will <u>always</u> seek to get something [Ur: to gain some support] from the situation. The unhealed healer therefore [Ur: Seeking to *get* something for *himself*, the healer] does <u>not</u> know how to give, and consequently <u>cannot share</u>. He <u>cannot</u> correct because he is not working <u>correctively</u>. He believes that it is up to him to teach the patient what is <u>real</u>, although [Ur: but] he does not know it <u>himself</u>.

How can you help the patient feel stronger and more secure if you tell him that his mind is impotent? These kinds of contradictions are evidence of a sobering fact: nothing real happens in psychotherapy. This is because nothing real has happened to the unhealed therapist. Instead of making real movement beyond his ego, his ego is running the show. He therefore uses the situation to get something for himself, which obviously leaves him unable to give something to the patient. Further, his ego, in its grandiosity, tells him that he is in the god-like position of telling the patient what is real, even though he doesn't actually know what's real. As the previous section said, "The ego believes that all functions belong to it, even though it has no idea what they are" (IV.7:2)

6. What, then, <u>should</u> happen? When God said, "Let there be light," there *was* light. Can you find light by <u>analyzing</u> darkness, as the psychotherapist does, or like the theologian, by <u>acknowledging</u> darkness in yourself and looking for a distant light to remove it, while emphasizing the distance? Healing is <u>not</u> mysterious. Nothing will change unless it is understood [Ur: Nothing occurs {a reference to nothing happening in therapy} *unless* you understand it], since light *is*

understanding. A "miserable sinner" cannot be healed without magic, nor can an "unimportant mind" esteem itself without magic.

Now we are perhaps in our fullest position to understand both the therapist and the theologian. The (Freudian) therapist tries to find the light of understanding by analyzing the darkness of the patient's psyche, by poking through his fantasies and nightmares. What he finds there, lurking in the dark, is the prince of darkness, the ego. The patient feels understandably guilty over this, and so, as a gesture of forgiveness, the therapist says, "That darkness in you is not important. Thoughts by themselves are too weak to be important. Just don't act them out and you're fine." Of course, the patient doesn't feel fine. He's just been told his mind is unimportant and powerless. How can he esteem himself now?

The theologian looks within himself and his audience and sees the same darkness the therapist sees—the darkness of the ego. Unlike the therapist, however, he interprets this religiously, as sin. He then tells everyone, "But it's OK. You see, if we believe in Jesus, and go to church, and give alms, and pray every day, and make lots of other sacrifices, then this really, really distant God will come and forgive our sin. The sin in us will probably still be there, but God will *consider* it gone, which is what counts."

Notice how in both cases, the sin, the ego, isn't actually removed. Due to some magical act, the sin is just pronounced ineffectual and forgiven, either by the therapist or by God. Light hasn't *really* entered and so nothing has really changed.

> 7.   Both forms of the ego's approach, then, <u>must</u> arrive at an impasse; the characteristic "impossible situation" to which the ego <u>always</u> leads. It may help someone to point out [Ur: It *can* be helpful to point out to a patient] <u>where he is heading</u>, but the point is <u>lost</u> unless he is also helped to change his direction. The unhealed healer [Ur: The therapist] cannot do this for him, since he [Ur: but he also] <u>cannot do</u> it [Ur: *this*] <u>for himself</u>. The only <u>meaningful</u> contribution the healer can make is to present an example of one whose direction has been changed *for* him, and who <u>no longer believes in nightmares of any kind</u>. The light in <u>his</u> mind will therefore <u>answer</u> the questioner, who <u>must</u> decide with God that there <u>is</u> light *because* <u>he sees it</u>. And by <u>his</u> acknowledgment <u>the</u> healer [Ur: *therapist*] <u>knows it is there</u>. That is how perception

ultimately is translated into knowledge. The miracle worker begins by <u>perceiving</u> light, and translates <u>his</u> perception into sureness by continually extending it [to others] and <u>accepting its acknowledgment</u> [from others]. Its <u>effects</u> assure him <u>it is there</u>.

To make someone aware of his ego and where it is taking him can be useful, but only if you can actually help him change his direction. How do you do this? As God said, you let there be light. *You show him the light in you.* You show up as an example of someone who has been changed by the light. The light in you then becomes his answer. It shows him what direction he is to take in life.

But this does more than heal the patient. It heals you. As he acknowledges the light he sees in you, you become convinced that the light really is there. You *thought* it was there, but now that you see the effect it has on him, you are *sure* it is there.

Application: Can you think of someone in your life that has so acknowledged the light in you, because that light has shone on and blessed this person, that his or her acknowledgment has convinced you that the light really is in you?

8. A therapist does not heal; *he lets healing be.* <u>He</u> can point to darkness but he <u>cannot</u> bring light <u>of himself</u>, for light is <u>not</u> of him. Yet, being *for* him, it <u>must</u> also be for his patient. The Holy Spirit is the <u>only</u> Therapist. He makes healing [Ur: *perfectly*] clear in <u>any</u> situation in which He is the Guide. You [Ur: The human therapist] can only <u>let Him fulfill His function</u>. He needs no help for this. He <u>will</u> tell you <u>exactly</u> what to do to help <u>anyone</u> He sends to you <u>for</u> help, and will speak to him through you <u>if you do not interfere</u>. Remember that you choose the [Ur: that you *are* choosing a] guide for helping, and the wrong choice will <u>not</u> help. But remember also that <u>the right one will</u>. Trust Him, for help is His function, and He is of God. As you awaken other minds <u>to</u> the Holy Spirit through <u>Him</u>, and not yourself, you will understand that you are not obeying the laws of this world. But the laws you <u>are</u> obeying <u>work</u>. "The good is what works" is a sound though insufficient statement. <u>Only</u> the good *can* work. Nothing else works at all.

Your role as a healer is simply to be a receptacle and a channel for the Holy Spirit. You are there to let His light visibly shine in you, so that the patient can see it. And you are there to let Him speak through you, so that the patient can hear it. You are not the healer; the Holy Spirit is. But He needs to work through you. So let His light shine through everything about you—your thoughts, your words, your deeds, your life. If you choose Him as your Guide, you will find that His ways work, and nothing else works.

> 9.   This course offers [Ur: This course is a guide to behavior. Being] a very direct and a very simple learning situation, and [Ur: it] provides the Guide Who tells you what to do. If you do it, you will <u>see</u> that it works. Its <u>results</u> are more convincing than its words. <u>They</u> will convince you that the words are true. By following the right Guide, you will learn the simplest of all lessons:

> *By their fruits ye shall know them, and **they** shall know **themselves**.*

The original version of that first line is a doozy: "This course is a guide to behavior." Wow! Despite the fact that it got edited out, it fits perfectly in this discussion. Jesus is telling us that we heal others through our example (7:4). How exactly do you "present an example" to someone without behavior? Jesus is saying that the Holy Spirit will tell us what to do and what to say (8:8, 9:1), and the results of this will be our proof that the Course really works. How do you say and do things without behavior?

Our behavior, then, is crucial in our role of healing others. However, it also plays a critical role in our own awakening. For by the fruits we produce in the lives of others, we come to know ourselves. By extending the light to them (which happens largely through our behavior), we become convinced that the light is in us, and finally realize that we *are* the light.

Application: Think of your fruits in the lives of several people around you. In relation to each one say,

> *By my fruits [name] shall know me,*
> *And I shall know myself.*

With those cases where doing this makes you feel worse, imagine being in that relationship in such a way that light shone through your thoughts, your words, your deeds, your life. Then, within that scenario, say the above lines again.

VI. The Acceptance of Your Brother
Commentary by Robert Perry

This section continues the previous section's discussion of the idea that we only discover the light in us by giving that light to our brothers.

> 1.   How can you become increasingly aware of the Holy Spirit in you <u>except</u> by His <u>effects</u>? You cannot see Him with your eyes nor hear Him with your ears. How, then, can you perceive Him at all? If you <u>inspire</u> joy and others react to you <u>with</u> joy, even though you are not experiencing joy yourself there must be <u>something in you</u> that is <u>capable of producing it</u>. If it is in <u>you</u> and <u>can</u> produce joy, and if you see that it <u>does</u> produce joy in others, you <u>must</u> be dissociating it in yourself.

I cannot emphasize enough how important this paragraph is. Its main idea is central to the Course's whole path. Yet this concept is not at all part of conventional Course wisdom, and even tends to be ruled out by it.

Yet the idea is very clearly (and repeatedly) presented: You become aware of the Holy Spirit in you by observing His effects *through* you on other people. The final two sentences track the thought process that we go through as we see ourselves inspire joy in others. We think, "Hmmm. I seem to be inspiring joy in others and they agree that it's coming from me [they "react to you with joy"]. Therefore, I must have within myself the source of joy. I haven't been particularly aware of it in myself, but it simply *must* be in there. Holiness must be inside me!" The logical conviction that "it must be in there" reinforces your *awareness* of it in there. And that is how you become increasingly aware of the Holy Spirit in you. That is how you go from guilt to redemption. That is how you are saved.

Application: Go through a list of people in your life, applying the following line to each one of them in turn. Note how it makes you want to be in your relationship with this person.

332

VI. The Acceptance of Your Brother

How can I become increasingly aware of the Holy Spirit in me except by His effects on [name]?

2. It seems to you that the Holy Spirit does not produce joy consistently in you <u>only</u> because <u>you do not consistently arouse joy in others</u>. Their reactions to you <u>are</u> your evaluations of His consistency. When you are inconsistent you will not always <u>give rise</u> to joy, and so you will not always recognize <u>His</u> consistency. What you offer to your brother you offer to Him, because He cannot <u>go beyond</u> your offering in <u>His</u> giving. This is <u>not</u> because <u>He</u> limits His giving, but simply because <u>you</u> have limited your <u>receiving</u>. The decision [Ur: will] to receive is the decision [Ur: will] to accept.

This seemingly jumbled paragraph presents a couple of simple ideas:

- What I offer to my brothers is what I am willing to accept from the Holy Spirit.
- Therefore, if I offer inconsistent joy to my brothers, I will accept only inconsistent joy from the Holy Spirit and then judge *Him* to be inconsistent.

Application: Ask yourself, "On a practical level, have I judged the Holy Spirit to be inconsistent? If so, could it be not because of His inconsistency but *mine*?"

Please read those ideas over again a couple of times. Do your best to suspend disbelief and let them in. Then ask yourself, "How would my life be different if I took to heart the idea that if I want consistent joy from the Holy Spirit then I must inspire consistent joy in my brothers?"

Finally, repeat, *"I must arouse joy consistently in [name] for Him to arouse joy consistently in me."*

3. If your brothers <u>are</u> part of you, will you <u>accept</u> them? Only they can teach you what you are, for [Ur: and] your learning [what you learn from them about yourself] is the result of what you taught <u>them</u>. What you call upon in them you call upon in <u>yourself</u>. And as you call upon it <u>in them</u> it becomes real to <u>you</u>.

Whatever we teach our brothers about what they are, they will turn around and teach us about what *we* are. This will happen through how they actively respond to us (as we saw in the first two paragraphs), and it will happen in a purely internal way. By the simple act of us calling on something in them, we will reinforce the reality of that same thing in us.

This makes the opening question all the more poignant. Won't we accept them? Do we really want to teach them rejection when doing so will teach ourselves that *we* are rejected?

> God has but one Son, knowing them all as one. Only God Himself is more than they but they are not less than He is. Would you know what this means? If what you do to my brother you do to me, and if you do everything for yourself because we are <u>part</u> of you, everything <u>we</u> do belongs to you as well. Everyone [Ur: Every Soul] God created is part of you and shares His Glory <u>with</u> you. His Glory belongs to Him, but it is equally <u>yours</u>. You cannot, then, <u>be</u> less glorious than He is.

The first sentence above is a very clear affirmation that the Son is not either one *or* many, but rather both one ("one Son") *and* many ("them all"). Then comes a real puzzle: God is more than His Sons, but they are not less than He is. Huh? The explanation amounts to this: In Heaven, something that one member has or does belongs to everyone else. This has stunning implications. It means that in Heaven, everything that anyone has belongs to *me*. Example: what God did in creating my brothers belongs to me, which means that *they* belong to me. Further, His glory belongs to them, which means that His glory in each of them belongs to me. Thus, all of God's glory belongs to me, and so (conclusion) I cannot be less (glorious) than He.

> 4.   God is more than you <u>only</u> because He <u>created</u> you, but not even this would He keep from you. Therefore you <u>can</u> create as He did, and <u>your</u> dissociation <u>will not alter this</u>. Neither God's Light nor <u>yours</u> is dimmed because you do not see.

Now we get the other side of the equation: "God is more than you *only* because He created you." Unlike God's glory, God's creation of me can't belong to me in the same way it belongs to Him, for that would mean *I* created me, a logical impossibility. What does belong to me, however, is the power He used in creating me, the power of creation. This is a power

I am exercising in Heaven even now, though I don't know it.

> Because the Sonship <u>must</u> create as one, you remember creation [the activity of creating] whenever you recognize part of creation [recognize a brother]. Each part you remember adds to <u>your</u> wholeness because each part *is* whole. Wholeness is indivisible [each part is not a separate whole but part of the one Wholeness], but you cannot learn of <u>your</u> [Ur: learn *your*] wholeness <u>until you see it everywhere</u>. You can know yourself only as God knows His Son, for <u>knowledge</u> is shared <u>with</u> God. When you awake in Him you will know your magnitude by accepting <u>His</u> limitlessness as <u>yours</u>. But meanwhile you will judge it as you judge your brother's, and will accept it as you accept his.

The logic here is easy to miss, but profound when followed. We remember the function of creating when we recognize one of our fellow creators. It's as if you used to play baseball but a severe case of amnesia has blocked this memory. Then you meet and recognize one of your former teammates. Wouldn't that bring the memory of baseball closer to the surface?

I love the process sketched by the last several sentences. Each brother you really recognize adds to your wholeness, because each brother "*is* whole." He's not a separate whole, but part of the one "indivisible" Wholeness. This makes it seem that by knowing just one brother, you could remember your wholeness completely. But it is not so. "You can know yourself only as God knows His Son," and He knows us all as one. To really know yourself, then, you must know *everyone*. To really remember your wholeness, you must see wholeness everywhere, in *all* your brothers. As long as you are in time, you will judge your wholeness as you judge the wholeness of each and every brother.

> 5.   You are not yet awake, but you can learn <u>how</u> to awaken. Very simply the Holy Spirit teaches you to awaken others. As you see them waken you will learn <u>what waking means,</u> and because you have chosen [Ur: willed] to wake them, their gratitude and their appreciation of what you have given them will <u>teach you its value</u>. <u>They</u> will become the witnesses to your reality, as <u>you</u> were created witnesses to God's. Yet when the Sonship <u>comes together</u> and accepts its oneness it will be known by <u>its</u> creations, who witness to its reality as the Son does to the Father.

Imagine reading an article in a spiritual magazine entitled "Do You Want to Learn How to Awaken?" What are the odds that its answer would be: Let the Holy Spirit teach you how to awaken others? Probably next to nil, yet that is the answer given here. Now imagine the author of that article offering the following testimony: "I never knew how valuable waking up was until I saw someone close to me experience a genuine taste of it, a taste that I had given her. What I saw pass across her face, and what I saw happen in her life afterwards, showed me what an incalculable gift awakening really is. And her overwhelming gratitude to me showed me what an incalculable gift I had given her. I had read for years that my reality was divine, I had even had experiences of that, but here was something new. Here was concrete, objective evidence of it in the world. She became the living proof that there is something awake in me, for what else could spark that awakening in her? She became the witness to my divinity."

> 6. Miracles have no place in eternity, because they are reparative. Yet while you still need healing, your miracles are the only witnesses to your reality <u>that you can recognize</u>. You cannot perform a miracle <u>for yourself</u>, because miracles are a way of <u>giving acceptance and</u> receiving it. In <u>time</u> the giving comes <u>first</u>, though they are simultaneous in eternity, where they cannot <u>be</u> separated. When you have learned they <u>are</u> the same, the need for time is over.

When we talk about inspiring joy in others, teaching them what they are, and waking them up, we are talking, of course, about giving miracles—not to ourselves; to *others*. This giving is the way we prove to ourselves that our reality is Christ, for the most powerful way that we learn of our reality is by the effects we cause in the world. If we cause unholy effects, we conclude our reality is sinful. If we cause holy effects, we conclude our reality is holy. And the people in whom these effects are caused become the witnesses to our holiness, the walking testimony to the divinity in us—not testimony to the world but to *us*.

Thus, we can only have the realization of our holiness by giving it to others. While we are in time, this giving must precede the receiving. Yet the day will come when we realize that giving and receiving are the same and simultaneous, and then we will be done with time.

7.   Eternity is <u>one</u> time, its <u>only</u> dimension being "always." [Ur: But] This cannot mean anything to you until you remember God's open Arms, and finally know His open Mind. Like Him, *you* are "<u>always</u>"; in His Mind and with a mind like His. In your open mind are <u>your</u> creations, in perfect communication born of perfect understanding. Could you but accept one of them you would not want <u>anything</u> the world has to offer. Everything else would be totally meaningless. God's meaning is incomplete without you, and you are incomplete without your creations. Accept your brother in this world and accept <u>nothing else</u>, for in him you will find your creations because he created them <u>with</u> you. You will never know that you are co-creator with God until you learn that your brother is co-creator with <u>you</u>.

When the opening sentences says eternity has one dimension, it means in contrast to the three dimensions of past, present, and future. In eternity, in place of the past, there is "always." In place of the present, there is "always." In place of the future, there is "always." In eternity, then, it is always *always*.

But this can't really mean anything to us until we are back. There, we will discover what means *everything* to us, what makes us feel complete: our creations. If we could only accept one of them, we would throw away the whole world, saying, "Who needs this?" How do we accept them back into our awareness? We accept those who created them with us. We accept our brothers.

VII. The Two Evaluations
Commentary by Robert Perry

1.   God's Will is your salvation. Would He not have given you the means to find it? If He wills you to <u>have</u> it, He <u>must</u> have made it possible and [Ur: very] easy to obtain it. Your brothers are everywhere. You do not have to seek far for salvation. Every minute and every second gives you a chance to save <u>yourself</u>. Do not lose these chances, <u>not</u> because they will not return, but because delay of joy is needless. God wills you perfect happiness <u>now</u>. Is it possible that this is not also <u>your</u> will? And is it possible that this is not <u>also</u> the will of your brothers?

If God wills that we be saved, surely He would have made the means for our salvation accessible. And He did. The means are our brothers, and they are all around us. As Jesus told us in the previous chapter, "Whenever two Sons of God meet, they are given another chance at salvation" (8.III.4:6). This is how we must approach encounters with our brothers, as priceless opportunities to find our own salvation, opportunities we must not allow to pass us by. Yes, there will always be more, but why miss the one in front of us now? Why delay our happiness? After all, God's Will is for us to be happy now. And *our* will is to be happy now. Our brothers, too, want to be happy now. Thus, the true will of everyone involved is for us to enter fully and joyfully into the holy encounter that stands in front of us right now.

2.   Consider, then, that in this joint will you <u>are</u> all united, and <u>in this only</u>. There may [Ur: *will*] be disagreement on anything <u>else</u>, but <u>not</u> on this. This, then, is where peace <u>abides</u>. And <u>you</u> abide in peace when you so decide. Yet you cannot abide in peace unless you accept the Atonement, because the Atonement *is* the way to peace. The reason is very simple, and so obvious that it is often overlooked. [Ur: That is because] The ego is <u>afraid</u> of the obvious, since obviousness is the essential characteristic of reality. Yet *you* cannot [Ur: You *cannot*] overlook it unless you are <u>not looking</u>.

338

VII. The Two Evaluations

Application: The initial sentences give us the mindset with which to enter a holy encounter. We can apply them in this way: Think of someone you plan to meet today and silently repeat to him or her the following

> *Whatever our differences, we are both united in the will for perfect happiness.*
> *Abiding together in this joint will, we are at peace.*

Yet we cannot really abide in peace unless we accept the Atonement. The reason (which the rest of the section will explain) is obvious. We don't see this reason only because our ego is afraid of the obvious. Reality itself is obvious. It's plain to see, but we prefer not to look. It makes you wonder what we would see if we were willing to truly observe the obvious.

> 3.   It is <u>perfectly</u> obvious that if the Holy Spirit looks with love on all He perceives, He looks with love on <u>you</u>. His <u>evaluation</u> of you is based on His knowledge of what you <u>are,</u> and so He evaluates you truly. And this evaluation <u>must</u> be in your mind, because <u>He</u> is. The ego is also in your mind, because you have <u>accepted</u> it there. <u>Its</u> evaluation of you, however, is the exact opposite of the Holy Spirit's, because the ego does <u>not</u> love you. It is unaware of what you are, and wholly mistrustful of <u>everything</u> it perceives because its [Ur: own] perceptions are so shifting. The ego is therefore capable of suspiciousness at best and viciousness at worst. That is its range. It cannot exceed it because of its uncertainty. And it can never go <u>beyond</u> it because it can never *be* certain.

The reason we can be at peace only by accepting the Atonement is that that means accepting the Holy Spirit's evaluation of us, and only His evaluation can bring us peace.

Application: Reflect on the following syllogism:

> *The Holy Spirit looks with love on everything He perceives.*
> *He perceives me.*
> *Therefore, the Holy Spirit looks with love on me.*

This paragraph introduces the main theme of the section: We have two evaluations of us that are both in our mind yet are completely opposite. The Holy Spirit's evaluation of us is contained in His love for us. This is based on the certain knowledge of who we really are. The ego, in contrast, is not sure of what we are, but it *is* sure that it doesn't love us. It is unsure of everything and as a result is constantly changing its mind about things. This makes things themselves appear to be constantly changing and therefore untrustworthy. The ego is therefore in a constant state of mistrust, in which it is suspicious at best and vicious at worst.

> 4.   You, then, have two conflicting evaluations of yourself in your mind, and they <u>cannot both be true</u>. You do not yet realize how <u>completely</u> different these evaluations are, because you do not understand how lofty the Holy Spirit's perception of you really is. He is not deceived by <u>anything</u> you do, because He <u>never</u> forgets what you are. The ego is deceived by <u>everything</u> you do, especially [Ur: even] when you respond to the Holy Spirit, because at such times <u>its confusion increases</u>. The ego is, therefore, particularly likely to attack you when you react lovingly, because it has evaluated you <u>as unloving</u> and you are going <u>against its judgment</u>. The ego will [Ur: begin to] <u>attack</u> your motives as soon as they become clearly out of accord with its perception of you. This is when it will shift abruptly from suspiciousness to viciousness, since its uncertainty is <u>increased</u>. Yet it is surely pointless to attack in return. What can this mean except that you are <u>agreeing</u> with the ego's evaluation of what you are?

When we think about the Holy Spirit's evaluation of us, we probably imagine it to be higher than the ego's, but how much higher? What if it is *immeasurably* higher? That would mean we have radically opposite evaluations within us and we have to choose between them.

The Holy Spirit has such certainty of who we are that even when we do crazy or cruel things, He is not deceived by them. He sees them in light of our true nature. The ego, on the other hand, doesn't understand the real reasons behind anything we do. This is especially true when we follow the Holy Spirit, which means when we react lovingly. This doesn't fit its view of us as unloving, which makes it even more unsure of who we are. In this state of heightened insecurity, it turns vicious. Specifically, it attacks our motives. It tries to convince us that our motives weren't as loving as we thought, that they really did fit its demeaning view of us.

Application: Think of the most egoless thing you've thought or done recently. Can you think of any uncharitable things you told yourself about why you *really* did that?

> 5.   If you choose [Ur: If you are willing] to see yourself as unloving <u>you will not be happy</u>. You are condemning yourself and <u>must</u> therefore regard yourself as inadequate. Would you look to the ego to help you escape from a sense of inadequacy it has <u>produced,</u> and must <u>maintain</u> for its existence? Can you <u>escape</u> from its evaluation of you by using its methods for keeping this picture <u>intact</u>?

This egoless thing you have thought or done has power to change your whole view of yourself. The ego wants to make sure that doesn't happen. By attacking your motives, it is trying to talk you back into its view of you as unloving. Don't go there. It will not help you climb out of feeling inadequate, but will rather reinforce your feelings of inadequacy. It will simply reinforce your belief in being unloving, which is not a happy feeling.

Application: Go back to the example from the previous application. Realize that, whatever other motives may have been present, the pure motive that was there contains the seeds of a radically new view of yourself. Try not to let your ego obscure this fact.

> 6.   You cannot evaluate an insane belief system from <u>within</u> it. Its [Ur: own] range precludes this. You can only <u>go beyond</u> it, look back from a point where sanity exists and *see the contrast*. Only <u>by</u> this contrast can insanity be judged as insane. With the grandeur of God in you, you have chosen to be little and to lament your littleness. Within the system that <u>dictated</u> this choice the lament <u>is</u> inevitable. Your littleness is <u>taken for granted</u> there and you do <u>not</u> ask, "Who granted it?" The question is meaningless <u>within</u> the ego's thought system, because it would open [Ur: it *opens*] <u>the whole thought system to question</u>.

Our ego's system is insane. Its basic premise is that we who share the grandeur of God are actually little, inadequate, and mean. How insane is *that*? Yet we cannot see the insanity of this system while we are inside it, where our littleness is a given. We don't ask, "Who gave it?" Yet asking that is a major step in getting out of it.

The way out of the ego's insanity is the way out of all insanity: Momentarily step outside the insane system, get in touch with real sanity, and then from that standpoint, look back on the insanity. That's what we need to do here, which raises the question: What is sanity in this case?

Application: Go ahead and ask yourself, "Who granted me this littleness I believe I have? Who gave it to me?" If you assume it was God, ask yourself if God would do that. Try to let your questioning undo your sense that your littleness is a genuine given, an unalterable fact.

> 7.   I have said that the ego does not know what a real question is [8.IX.1:3]. Lack of knowledge of <u>any</u> kind is <u>always</u> associated with <u>unwillingness</u> to know, and this produces a <u>total</u> lack of knowledge simply because <u>knowledge</u> is total. <u>Not</u> to question your littleness therefore is to deny <u>all</u> knowledge, and keep the ego's <u>whole</u> thought system intact. You cannot retain <u>part</u> of a thought system, because it can <u>be</u> questioned only at its foundation. And this <u>must</u> be questioned from beyond it, because <u>within</u> it its foundation <u>does</u> stand. The Holy Spirit judges against the reality of the ego's thought system merely because He knows its <u>foundation</u> is not true. Therefore, nothing that arises from it <u>means</u> anything. He judges every belief you hold in terms of where it comes from. If it comes from God, He knows it to be true. If it does not, He knows that it is meaningless.

The ego is never going to ask "Who granted your littleness?" The ego can't ask real questions for the simple reason that it doesn't want to know. It is quite rightly afraid that if it asks this question, its whole system might fall apart. For this question puts your littleness up for question, and your littleness is foundational for the ego. Therefore, if *you* are unwilling to ask this question, this means that *you* don't want to know, and that you want to "keep the ego's whole thought system intact."

Perhaps it seems easier to start out by questioning some minor aspect of the ego's system, rather than the very foundation. Yet Jesus tells us that the ego's thought system "can be questioned only at its foundation." Otherwise, the whole thing stands. Yet to really question it, we need to get outside it and get in touch with the Holy Spirit. He's the One Who knows that the ego's system—foundation and all—is utterly meaningless.

8. Whenever you question your value, say:

God Himself is incomplete without me.

Remember this when the ego speaks, and you will not hear it. The truth about <u>you</u> is so lofty that nothing unworthy of God is worthy of you. Choose, then, what you want in these terms, and accept nothing that you would not offer to God as wholly fitting for <u>Him</u>. <u>You</u> do not want anything else. Return your part to Him, and He will give you all of Himself in exchange for the return of what belongs to Him and renders Him complete.

Application: To appreciate the practice given in this paragraph, we need to see it in the context of the whole section. The following application is my attempt to do that.

First, call to mind the earlier application where you thought of some loving thing you recently thought or did. You may want to write it down here on the page.

Now remember those things you told yourself about why your motives really weren't so noble and pure. Write those down, too.

Look at those accusations and notice how inadequate they make you feel, how little. Notice, too, how readily your mind takes in that littleness, simply because you take your littleness for granted. Realize you are listening to the voice of the ego.

It is time to question your littleness. Ask yourself, "Who granted it?" If you answer "God," then ask, "Would God do that to me?" If you answer "me," then doesn't this mean your littleness is not a given, a fact, but can be undone? Use this line of questioning to sincerely and deeply question your littleness.

Finally, to answer the question of your littleness and where it came from (or, rather, didn't come from), repeat:

God Himself is incomplete without me.

Repeat it over and over. See it as God acknowledging your grandeur. Let this practice overturn your sense of littleness.

As you let in this new view of yourself, see if it passes the following test. Ask yourself, "Is this a grandeur that is worthy of God? Would I offer it to Him as wholly fitting for Him?" If the answer is no, then reject it as unworthy of you, His Son. If the answer is yes, then accept it as fully worthy of you, and try to let it all the way in.

Now you have stepped outside the ego's system and looked back on it from a point where sanity exists. Now you have questioned its very foundation. And now its voice cannot be heard.

VIII. Grandeur versus Grandiosity
Commentary by Robert Perry

The previous section asked us to respond to the ego's accusations of littleness by accepting the grandeur of God. This section describes the ego's countermove: to lure us back with phony grandeur, or grandiosity. Grandiosity is a synonym for what the Text will later call specialness.

> 1. Grandeur is of God, and <u>only</u> of Him. Therefore it is in you. Whenever you become aware of it, however dimly, you abandon the ego automatically, because in the presence of the grandeur of God the meaninglessness of the ego becomes perfectly apparent. When this occurs, even though it does not understand it, [Ur: Though it does not understand this] the ego believes that its "enemy" has struck, and attempts to offer gifts to induce you to return to its "protection." <u>Self</u>-inflation is the only offering it can make. The grandiosity of the ego is its alternative to the grandeur of God. Which will you choose?

In the last section, we saw that when the ego tells us of our littleness, we need to respond by getting in touch with our true grandeur. Yet when we really touch that grandeur, the ego feels deeply threatened. Like someone trying to sell us a cheap imitation of an expensive watch, it says, "If you liked that grandeur, I've got something nearly identical for you, every bit as good." Its counterfeit version is grandiosity. This is not the limitlessness of our true Self. Rather, it is our limited self all puffed up and inflated like a balloon. The ego will even base this grandiosity on our grandeur. Have you ever met people whose whole claim to superiority was that they had had experiences of their true Self?

> 2. Grandiosity is <u>always</u> a cover for despair. It is without hope because it is not real. It is an attempt to <u>counteract</u> your littleness, based on the belief <u>that the littleness is real</u>. <u>Without</u> this belief grandiosity is meaningless, and you could not possibly <u>want</u> it. The essence of grandiosity is competitiveness, because it <u>always</u> involves <u>attack</u>. It is a delusional attempt to <u>outdo</u>, but <u>not</u> to <u>undo</u>. We said before that the ego vacillates between suspiciousness and viciousness. It remains

suspicious as long as you <u>despair</u> of yourself. It shifts to viciousness when you decide not to tolerate self-abasement and seek relief. Then it offers you the illusion [Ur: delusion] of <u>attack</u> as a "solution."

Being a little self is depressing. When you despair of ever being anything else, you think, "I know—I'll be a bigger little self. I'll be bigger than all the other little selves around me." This familiar idea is captured well in Aesop's fable about the toad that wanted to be as big as an ox and so puffed itself up (until it exploded).

We all know that being the biggest ego on the block is an implicit attack on everyone else, for it implies that they are all smaller than you. Jesus says that for the ego to recommend this course of action is actually vicious. Imagine, for instance, that you purposefully tricked someone into committing a crime, a crime he would feel guilty for and that was likely to ruin him. Wouldn't doing this be a vicious act on your part? That is how the ego is treating you when it urges you to attack in order to puff yourself up.

> 3.   The ego does <u>not</u> understand [Ur: know] the difference between grandeur and grandiosity, because it sees no [Ur: it does not know the] difference between miracle impulses and ego-alien beliefs of its own. I told you [4.V.2-3] that the ego <u>is</u> aware of threat to its existence, but makes no distinctions between these two very [Ur: between two *entirely*] different kinds of threat. Its <u>profound</u> sense of vulnerability renders it incapable of judgment <u>except</u> in terms of attack. When the ego experiences threat, its <u>only</u> decision is whether to attack <u>now</u> or to withdraw to attack later. If you <u>accept</u> its offer of grandiosity it will attack immediately. If you do not, it will wait.

I am not sure how well this paragraph fits with the rest of the section, but here is my best attempt to make sense of it: The ego really believes that you are little. The idea that you are actually a *bigger* little self is therefore alien to it and somewhat threatening to it. And the only way it knows how to respond to threat is with attack. Thus, if you accept the ego's offer of self-inflation, it will attack you. It will tell you how stupid and little you are for presuming to be superior to your brothers. It will try to drag you back down to littleness. If, on the other hand, you refuse grandiosity and stick with grandeur, the ego will withdraw and plan to attack later.

4.   The ego is immobilized in the presence of God's grandeur, because His grandeur establishes your freedom. Even the faintest hint of your reality literally drives the ego from your mind, because you will give up all [Ur: because of the complete lack of] investment in it. Grandeur is totally without illusions, and because it is real it is compellingly convincing. Yet the conviction of reality will not remain with you unless you do not allow the ego to attack it. The ego will make every effort to recover and mobilize its energies against your release. It will tell you that you are insane, and argue that grandeur cannot be a real part of you because of the littleness in which it believes. Yet your grandeur is not delusional because you did not make it. You made grandiosity and are afraid of it because it is a form of attack, but your grandeur is of God, Who created it out of His Love.

Let's say you are a kid playing a computer game in which your character is a shriveled, deformed lizard. And let's say that your mind's own energy is what actually propels this character. (It's a very high-tech game.) The more you forget who you are and identify with the lizard, the more life and vitality it acquires; the more freely it moves about. Now imagine that for a moment you fully remember who you are. You think, "This is who I really am. I'm sixteen years-old. I have a life. I have a family. This lizard is completely unreal and totally worthless. This is bogus!" And with that thought, the lizard stops moving. It has lost the energy from your mind that animated it. It can't attack you because it's paralyzed.

But now the experience of your reality begins to fade. The lizard then begins to stir to life again and gathers every last bit of strength for a clever tongue-lashing: "Who do you think you are?" it says. "How arrogant of you to think you are more than a tiny lizard. What delusions of grandeur! You really are losing your grip on reality."

It is hard to imagine listening to the lizard at this point, yet isn't that what we do? After the experience of grandeur, the ego's voice starts to work away at us. It doesn't just say a few lines. It whispers constantly. It wears us down. Eventually we start to listen.

5.   From your grandeur you can only bless, because your grandeur is your abundance. By blessing you hold it in your mind, protecting it from illusions and keeping yourself in the Mind of God. Remember always that you cannot be anywhere except in the Mind of God. When you forget this, you *will* despair and you *will* attack.

While your grandiosity is an attack on others, your grandeur is so full that it can only bless them. Yet this blessing is more than a byproduct. It has power to actually hold your grandeur in your mind, keeping you aware that you are in God's Mind. Thinking you are anywhere else (such as in this world) will make you feel little, and then you will attack, seeking to be a bigger little self.

> 6.   The ego depends <u>solely</u> on your willingness to tolerate it. [Ur: But] If you are willing to look upon your grandeur you <u>cannot</u> despair, and therefore you <u>cannot</u> want the ego. Your grandeur is God's <u>answer</u> to the ego, because it is true. Littleness and grandeur cannot coexist, nor is it possible for them to alternate. Littleness and grandiosity can and <u>must</u> alternate, since both are untrue and are therefore on the same level. Being the level of shift, it is experienced as shifting and extremes are its essential characteristic.

If you are willing to look on your grandeur, you will be unable to tolerate the notion of being a tiny ego. The real answer, then, to all the ego's assertions that you are little is the simple willingness to look on your grandeur. Your grandeur will chase littleness from your mind. Yet your grandiosity will not. It and littleness will constantly flip-flop. In response to the pain of littleness, you will seek to puff yourself up, while in response to your self-inflation, your ego will seek to drag you back down to littleness. And back and forth you will go. It does not take much reflection to see that you have been going back and forth in just this way.

> 7.   [Ur: But] Truth and littleness are <u>denials</u> of each other because grandeur <u>is</u> truth. Truth does not vacillate; it is <u>always</u> true. When grandeur slips away from you, <u>you have replaced it with something you have made</u>. Perhaps it is the belief in littleness; perhaps it is the belief in grandiosity. Yet it <u>must</u> be insane because it is <u>not true</u>. Your grandeur will <u>never</u> deceive you, but your illusions <u>always</u> will. Illusions <u>are</u> deceptions.

Grandeur is truth and truth does not vacillate. Therefore, grandeur does not vacillate (unlike grandiosity and littleness). If your grandeur slips away, you have pushed it away. You have replaced it with something you made, something insane.

VIII. Grandeur versus Grandiosity

You <u>cannot</u> triumph, but you *are* exalted. And in your exalted state you seek others like you and rejoice with them.

8.　It is easy to distinguish grandeur from grandiosity, [Ur: simply] because love is returned and pride is not. Pride will not produce miracles, and will therefore deprive you of the true witnesses to your reality. Truth is not obscure nor hidden, but its obviousness to <u>you</u> lies in the joy you bring to its witnesses, <u>who show it to you</u>. They attest to your grandeur, but they cannot attest to pride because pride is not shared. God <u>wants</u> you to behold what He created because it is <u>His</u> joy.

Here is how to tell the difference between grandeur and grandiosity: "Love is returned [by others] and pride is not." Grandiosity is an attack. It says, "I am so much grander than you are." Who is going to experience that as love? Who is going to be healed by that thought? And who is going to return that thought to you in gratitude?

Grandeur, on the other hand, blesses others (paragraph 5). Grandeur sees others as like you and wants to "rejoice with them" in your shared splendor. Grandeur, then, is love, and this love will perform miracles. It will heal others, and they will return the gift in gratitude. Their gratitude will be their acknowledgment of the grandeur in you. These people will therefore become the witnesses to your grandeur. Only through them will your reality become truly obvious to you. And God wants it to be obvious to you.

9.　Can your grandeur be arrogant when God <u>Himself</u> witnesses to it? And what can be real that has <u>no</u> witnesses [referring to your pride]? What good can come of it? And if no good can come of it the Holy Spirit cannot use it. What He cannot <u>transform</u> to the Will of God does not exist at all. Grandiosity is delusional, because it is used to <u>replace</u> your grandeur. Yet what God has created cannot <u>be</u> replaced. God is incomplete without you because His grandeur is total, and you cannot be missing from it.

Application: Imagine reporting to someone an experience of your true reality and saying in hushed tones, "I realized that I have the grandeur of God." You can probably imagine your ego telling you that you are arrogant for saying this or even thinking it. With that in mind, repeat these lines:

God Himself witnesses to my grandeur.
How can it be arrogant?

What we call delusions of grandeur are really delusions of *grandiosity*. Grandeur is not delusional, but grandiosity *is*, for (as we saw in the previous paragraph) it has no witnesses. No one is going to take your thought "I am so much grander than you" and joyously share it and gratefully return it. No one will get up on the stand and testify for your grandiosity, and so it is not real. Further, it would replace your grandeur, which, having been created by God, cannot be replaced. It is thus *doubly* unreal.

> 10. You are altogether irreplaceable in the Mind of God. No one else can fill your part in it, and while you leave your part of it empty your eternal place merely waits for your return. God, through His Voice, reminds you of it, and God Himself keeps your extensions safe within it. Yet <u>you</u> do not know them until you return <u>to</u> them. You <u>cannot</u> replace the Kingdom, and you cannot replace yourself. God, Who <u>knows</u> your value, would not have it so, and so it is <u>not</u> so. Your value is in <u>God's</u> Mind, and therefore <u>not</u> in yours alone. To accept yourself as God created you <u>cannot</u> be arrogance, because it is the <u>denial</u> of arrogance. To accept your littleness *is* arrogant, because it means that you believe <u>your</u> evaluation of yourself is <u>truer than God's</u>.

Application: Say the following lines to yourself, with as much conviction as you can:

> *I am altogether irreplaceable in the Mind of God.*
> *No one else can fill my part in it.*
> *While I leave my part empty, my eternal place merely waits for*
>   *my return.*
> *And God Himself keeps my creations safe within it.*
> *I cannot be replaced because I am too valuable to God.*
> *I cannot replace the Kingdom because it is too valuable to me.*

The end of the paragraph introduces what will become the Course's typical teaching on arrogance and humility: It is actually arrogant to believe you are little, because it means you think you know better than God. And it is humble to accept your grandeur, because you are accepting a higher Authority's evaluation of who you are. In doing this, however, you are not giving in to an outside authority, for God's evaluation of you and your true evaluation of yourself are one (as the opening line of the next paragraph will tell us).

11. Yet if truth is indivisible, your evaluation of yourself must *be* God's. You did not establish your value and it needs no defense. Nothing can attack it nor prevail over it. It does not vary. It merely *is*. Ask the Holy Spirit what it is and He will tell you, but do not be afraid of His answer, because it comes from God. It is an exalted answer because of its Source, but the Source is true and so is Its answer. Listen and do not question what you hear, for God does not deceive. He would have you replace the ego's belief in littleness with His Own exalted Answer to what you are, so that you can cease to question it and know it for what it is.

Application: Repeat the following lines as a way of seeking the revelation of your true value:

I did not establish my value and it needs no defense.
Nothing can attack my value nor prevail against it.
*My value does not vary. It merely **is**.*
Holy Spirit, tell me what it is.
I am not afraid of Your answer.
I trust that You will tell me the truth.
Holy Spirit, what is my true value in God's Eyes?

Ask with a genuine desire to know—not because someone told you to ask, but because you sincerely want to know. Once you ask, listen with confidence and patience, holding your mind in quiet expectation of hearing the answer. And whenever your confidence wanes or your mind wanders, repeat your question again with all the sincerity you can.

About the Circle's
TEXT READING PROGRAM

An Unforgettable Journey through the Text in One Year

The Text is the foundation of *A Course in Miracles*, yet many students find it hard going. This program is designed to guide you through the Text, paragraph by paragraph, in one year.

Each weekday, you will receive an e-mail containing that day's Text section, along with commentary on each paragraph, written by Robert Perry or Greg Mackie. The readings contain material edited out of the published Course as well as exercises for practical application. This is the material that has been presented now in book format in our series *The Illuminated Text*.

By signing up for our online program, you will also receive:

- Weekly one-hour class recordings led by Robert Perry and Greg Mackie that summarize that week's sections and answer students' questions
- An online forum for sharing with others in the program
- Related articles on key Text sections e-mailed directly to you
- Your personal web archive, with access to all your commentaries and class recordings
- An unlimited "pause feature" for pausing your program while you're away

Want to learn more? Call us today on 1-888-357-7520, or go to www.circleofa.org, the largest online resource for *A Course in Miracles*!

We hope that you will join us for this truly enlightening program!

ABOUT THE AUTHORS

Robert Perry has been a student of *A Course in Miracles* (ACIM) since 1981. He taught at Miracle Distribution Center in California from 1986 to 1989, and in 1993 founded the Circle of Atonement in Sedona, Arizona. The Circle is an organization composed of several teachers dedicated to helping establish the Course as an authentic spiritual tradition.

One of the most respected voices on ACIM, Robert has traveled extensively, speaking throughout the U.S. and internationally. In addition to contributing scores of articles to various Course publications, he is the author or co-author of nineteen books and booklets, including the hugely popular *An Introduction to A Course in Miracles*. Robert's goal has always been to provide a complete picture of what the Course is—as a thought system and as a path meant to be lived in the world on a daily basis—and to support students in walking along that path.

Robert has recently authored his first non-ACIM book, *Signs: A New Approach to Coincidence, Synchronicity, Guidance, Life Purpose, and God's Plan*, available on Amazon sites internationally.

Greg Mackie has been a student of *A Course in Miracles* since 1991. He has been teaching and writing for the Circle of Atonement since 1999, and has written scores of articles for A Better Way, the newsletter of the Circle of Atonement, as well as other ACIM publications. He is the author of *How Can We Forgive Murderers?* and co-taught, along with Robert Perry, the Text Reading Program and the Daily Workbook Program, which consisted of 365 recordings.

CPSIA information can be obtained at www.ICGtesting.com
Printed in the USA
BVOW07s0205111113

335968BV00002B/13/P